Mastering ServiceN

Second Edition

Unleash the full potential of ServiceNow from foundations to advanced functions, with this hands-on expert guide fully revised for the Helsinki version

Martin Wood

BIRMINGHAM - MUMBAI

Mastering ServiceNow

Second Edition

Copyright © 2016 Packt Publishing

First published: May 2015

Second edition: October 2016

Production reference: 1141016

Published by Packt Publishing Ltd.
Livery Place
35 Livery Street
Birmingham
B3 2PB, UK.
ISBN 978-1-78646-595-5

www.packtpub.com

Credits

Author

Martin Wood

Reviewer

Andy Venables

Commissioning Editor

Kartikey Pandey

Acquisition Editor

Prachi Bisht

Content Development Editor

Rashmi Suvarna

Technical Editor

Mohit Hassija

Copy Editor

Madhusudan Uchil

Project Coordinator

Judie Jose

Proofreader

Safis Editing

Indexer

Pratik Shirodkar

Graphics

Kirk D'Penha

Production Coordinator

Shantanu N. Zagade

Notice

Martin wrote this book in his personal capacity. The views expressed are his own, and do not necessarily reflect that of ServiceNow.

About the Author

Martin Wood has spent almost 10 years spreading the word about ServiceNow. He has been lucky enough to see the company and platform grow from the very start, beginning as one of the earliest customers in 2008, when he built one of the first custom applications. He enjoyed the experience so much that he joined the company in 2009. There onwards, he worked with a variety of clients, from blue-chip enterprises to SMEs, helping them harness the power that the platform brings. More recently, he has taken that experience and used it to shape the latest services and products that ServiceNow creates. Martin has always been passionate about helping people make informed decisions, whether that is at the ServiceNow user conference, or over a pint in a pub.

Martin lives in the beautiful Berkshire countryside in the UK with his wife Sarah. They both love exploring the world and enjoying good food—and great wine!

His personal website is at www.dasos.com. He can be contacted at martin@dasos.com.

I must thank my wife, who has put up with my endless late-night writing sessions. Her patience, love, and understanding has, quite frankly, made this book possible.

About the Reviewer

Andy Venables joined ServiceNow in early 2013, and he works with a wide range of ServiceNow customers, helping them implement effectively and efficiently. Andy sees himself as a "full stack" technical architect and enjoys working with all aspects of technology, from design through development to testing. He has over 10 years of experience working with JavaScript on both client and server.

Since joining ServiceNow, Andy says that working with the platform has been highly motivating, sometimes challenging, but always exciting, and he thoroughly enjoys seeing new capabilities introduced to the platform and what customers do with them.

He lives in Surrey with his wife, Celia, and their Maltese puppy, Freddie. He enjoys running, rugby, scuba diving, and undertaking (smallish) DIY projects.

Andy is working on authoring a video series with Packt, also titled Mastering ServiceNow.

You can find him on LinkedIn at https://www.linkedin.com/in/andyvenables.

Thank you to Martin for mentoring me through my early ServiceNow days.

www.PacktPub.com

For support files and downloads related to your book, please visit www.PacktPub.com.

Did you know that Packt offers eBook versions of every book published, with PDF and ePub files available? You can upgrade to the eBook version at www.PacktPub.com and as a print book customer, you are entitled to a discount on the eBook copy. Get in touch with us at service@packtpub.com for more details.

At www.PacktPub.com, you can also read a collection of free technical articles, sign up for a range of free newsletters and receive exclusive discounts and offers on Packt books and eBooks.

https://www.packtpub.com/mapt

Get the most in-demand software skills with Mapt. Mapt gives you full access to all Packt books and video courses, as well as industry-leading tools to help you plan your personal development and advance your career.

Why subscribe?

- Fully searchable across every book published by Packt
- Copy and paste, print, and bookmark content
- On demand and accessible via a web browser

Table of Contents

Preface

Congratulations! You have just become the ServiceNow system administrator for Gardiner Hotels, one of the most successful chains in the region. The CIO realized that ServiceNow fits his needs exactly: it gives him a suite of feature-rich applications built to manage an array of service-management domains, including IT, HR, and facilities.

But what really caught his eye was what the platform brings. All the applications rely on a core set of capabilities, providing powerful logic, data manipulation, integration, and security features. Understanding all these elements not only helps you build your own applications quickly and easily, but it also allows you to understand how every other application works.

This book guides you through creating a custom application in the Helsinki version of ServiceNow. By building an application from the ground up, you will master the core foundational concepts that you can then apply to any other application. Each chapter builds on the last, with plenty of examples providing you hands-on experience in building out each feature.

Because the majority of the examples are built inside a scoped application, you can easily follow along by connecting your instance to a GitHub account. By switching branches, you can jump between chapters without needing to complete all the prerequisites. To do so, fork the repo at `https://github.com/gardinerhotels/hotel`. Further instructions are given at `https://www.gardiner-hotels.com/` and in the first chapter.

What this book covers

`Chapter 1`, *ServiceNow Foundations*, looks at how ServiceNow is structured from an architectural perspective. We explore how the platform is hosted and then dive into the building blocks of tables, fields, and building interfaces.

`Chapter 2`, *Developing Custom Applications*, explains the controls and capabilities around applications in ServiceNow. Application scopes bring significant changes to the API and bring much better protection to manage the flow of data.

Chapter 3, *Server-Side Control,* shows you how you can implement your business logic and then start to automate, validate, and verify data and processes.

Chapter 4, *Client-Side Interaction,* explores how you can make the life of the people using your application a little bit better by providing validation, feedback, and quick interaction techniques.

Chapter 5, *Getting Things Done with Tasks,* looks at some of the base application functionalities in ServiceNow. Understand how a task-driven process system is kick-started by the Task table and take advantage of Graphical Workflow and the Service Catalog.

Chapter 6, *Events, Notifications, and Reporting,* introduces another level of interaction with your users, by generating reports and scheduling jobs and handling incoming and outgoing e-mail. Keep everyone informed about what's happening.

Chapter 7, *Exchanging Data – Import Sets, Web Services, and other Integrations,* is about importing and exporting data from other systems, integrating ServiceNow in your application landscape. No instance is an island!

Chapter 8, *Securing Applications and Data,* focuses on the challenges of protecting your most important asset: your information. We make sure the right people have the right data.

Chapter 9, *Diagnosing ServiceNow – Knowing What Is Going On,* helps you when things go wrong. Troubleshooting and investigation hints and tips are explored so that you can get back to full power quickly.

Chapter 10, *Packaging with Applications, Update Sets, and Upgrades,* builds on the previous chapters to explore how you can get your hard work to the right place. Understand how upgrades work and how teams can work together to get stuff done.

Chapter 11, *Making ServiceNow Beautiful with Service Portal and Custom Interfaces,* focuses on the service portal and advanced UI techniques. Having a good-looking, well-designed self-service system really enhances adoption. One of the fundamental components of ServiceNow, Jelly, is used to supercharge the interface.

What you need for this book

ServiceNow is an enterprise SaaS platform. In order to work with the application, you will need access to a ServiceNow instance, with system administrator access. The examples in this book are about a custom application, but it is strongly recommended that any work be performed in a sub-production instance.

The best way to work through the book is with a developer instance. By signing up to the free program, you can get a fully capable instance that lets you work through all the examples. You can sign up at `https://developer.servicenow.com/`. Alternatively, contact your ServiceNow representative and request a temporary sandbox instance.

To make use of the source control integration and quickly download the code for each chapter, you will need a free GitHub account. Sign up at `https://www.github.com`.

The examples have all been built with the Helsinki version of ServiceNow, released in mid-2016. The concepts of ServiceNow are relevant for every version, but it is strongly recommended that you follow along with a Helsinki instance.

Who this book is for

This book will be most useful to those who have a good grounding in web technologies and computer science but don't know too much about ServiceNow. We discuss how ServiceNow implements common design patterns and technologies, enabling you to get a better understanding of how your instance works.

There is a great deal of functionality in ServiceNow, and it simply isn't possible to cram everything into a single book. ServiceNow has a comprehensive wiki and a popular community forum. The ServiceNow training department has a series of mixed-media courses to get you up to speed quickly. We aren't going to replicate those, especially the application-specific ones, but there will be some overlap.

There are several sources of documentation, which are frequently referred to throughout the book. The most common sources are the following:

- The product documentation covers the key features and capabilities of the ServiceNow platform and the available applications. It works on a how-to basis, giving you focused help to accomplish specific tasks. Access it at https://docs.servicenow.com/.
- The developer portal focuses on the needs of those using the platform building blocks. It importantly hosts the server and client APIs. Access it at https://developer.servicenow.com/.

Every ServiceNow system administrator needs to have at least a basic understanding of JavaScript. JavaScript underpins the ServiceNow foundations and hence is essential to fully master ServiceNow. An in-depth knowledge of all the intricacies of JavaScript is not needed, since many of the idioms and objects used are ServiceNow specific. Nonetheless, scripting is part of the product. A review of a good JavaScript manual may be helpful!

The book also assumes a working knowledge of basic web technologies, such as HTML and CSS, and standard concepts, such as databases and SQL.

Conventions

In this book, you will find a number of text styles that distinguish between different kinds of information. Here are some examples of these styles and an explanation of their meaning.

Code words in text, database table names, folder names, filenames, file extensions, pathnames, dummy URLs, user input, and Twitter handles are shown as follows: "Let's run the standard `Hello, World!` program as our first script"

A block of code is set as follows:

```
gs.info('Hello, world!');
```

Any command-line input or output is written as follows:

```
curl --user <username>
https://<instance>.service-now.com/u_maintenance_list.do?EXCEL --output
MaintenanceList.xls
```

New terms and **important words** are shown in bold. Words that you see on the screen, for example, in menus or dialog boxes, appear in the text like this: "To explore the roles provided in the ServiceNow platform, navigate to **System Security** > **Users and Groups** > **Roles.**"

Warnings or important notes appear in a box like this.

Tips and tricks appear like this.

Reader feedback

Feedback from our readers is always welcome. Let us know what you think about this book-what you liked or disliked. Reader feedback is important for us as it helps us develop titles that you will really get the most out of. To send us general feedback, simply e-mail feedback@packtpub.com, and mention the book's title in the subject of your message. If there is a topic that you have expertise in and you are interested in either writing or contributing to a book, see our author guide at www.packtpub.com/authors.

Customer support

Now that you are the proud owner of a Packt book, we have a number of things to help you to get the most from your purchase.

Downloading the example code

You can download the example code files for this book from your account at http://www.packtpub.com. If you purchased this book elsewhere, you can visit http://www.packtpub.com/support and register to have the files e-mailed directly to you.

You can download the code files by following these steps:

1. Log in or register to our website using your e-mail address and password.
2. Hover the mouse pointer on the **SUPPORT** tab at the top.
3. Click on **Code Downloads & Errata**.
4. Enter the name of the book in the **Search** box.
5. Select the book for which you're looking to download the code files.
6. Choose from the drop-down menu where you purchased this book from.
7. Click on **Code Download**.

Once the file is downloaded, please make sure that you unzip or extract the folder using the latest version of:

- WinRAR / 7-Zip for Windows
- Zipeg / iZip / UnRarX for Mac
- 7-Zip / PeaZip for Linux

The code bundle for the book is also hosted on GitHub at `https://github.com/PacktPubl ishing/Mastering-ServiceNow-Second-Edition`. We also have other code bundles from our rich catalog of books and videos available at `https://github.com/PacktPublishing/`. Check them out!

Downloading the color images of this book

We also provide you with a PDF file that has color images of the screenshots/diagrams used in this book. The color images will help you better understand the changes in the output. You can download this file from `http://www.packtpub.com/sites/default/files/downl oads/MasteringServiceNowSecondEdition_ColorImages.pdf`.

Errata

Although we have taken every care to ensure the accuracy of our content, mistakes do happen. If you find a mistake in one of our books-maybe a mistake in the text or the code- we would be grateful if you could report this to us. By doing so, you can save other readers from frustration and help us improve subsequent versions of this book. If you find any errata, please report them by visiting `http://www.packtpub.com/submit-errata`, selecting your book, clicking on the **Errata Submission Form** link, and entering the details of your errata. Once your errata are verified, your submission will be accepted and the errata will be uploaded to our website or added to any list of existing errata under the Errata section of that title.

To view the previously submitted errata, go to `https://www.packtpub.com/books/conten t/support` and enter the name of the book in the search field. The required information will appear under the **Errata** section.

Piracy

Piracy of copyrighted material on the Internet is an ongoing problem across all media. At Packt, we take the protection of our copyright and licenses very seriously. If you come across any illegal copies of our works in any form on the Internet, please provide us with the location address or website name immediately so that we can pursue a remedy.

Please contact us at `copyright@packtpub.com` with a link to the suspected pirated material.

We appreciate your help in protecting our authors and our ability to bring you valuable content.

Questions

If you have a problem with any aspect of this book, you can contact us at questions@packtpub.com, and we will do our best to address the problem.

1
ServiceNow Foundations

This opening chapter lays out the foundational aspects of ServiceNow, from the bottom up. Understanding the fundamentals of the ServiceNow platform is important. It provides insight into the concepts that determine how all the applications built on top work.

 Although long, the chapter is not exhaustive and expects basic familiarity with the ServiceNow interface. Remember to refer to the ServiceNow documentation and any training material you may have.

Perhaps you've decided to build a new hotel, and you want to ensure it won't fall down. The architect's drawings need to be understood and the right building materials ordered. It's costly (and career limiting!) if it collapses in the opening week!

In this chapter, we review the blueprints. We will understand the important design aspects of ServiceNow so that we can build on them later. The data structure available to us is critical, since it enables us to model information and processes in the right way.

In this chapter, we will cover:

- The physical components of the ServiceNow architecture
- How everything you see and do is in the database
- A review of the most important field types
- The magic of reference fields
- Using and building a good interface

Diving into the infrastructure

An **instance** is several things. It could be part of a URL (something like `https://<instance>.service-now.com/`), software running in the cloud, or your copy of the ServiceNow platform.

ServiceNow provides a platform and suite of applications as a service. They worry about the hardware, Internet connectivity, and operating system security, and provide you with the URL. All you need to get going is a modern web browser.

To follow the examples in this book, you need admin access to an instance. It'll be better if you have your own, dedicated instance rather than one being used by many people. It allows you to make system-wide configuration changes, and you won't affect anyone else.

 It is especially important not to use the production instance assigned to your company. This book uses the examples to teach you about ServiceNow, and you will not want all of these experiments being used by your whole company.

ServiceNow runs a developer program, through which you can obtain your own instance. It is lower powered and restricted in capabilities compared to normal instances, but it is an excellent resource to test out ideas. Be sure to read the FAQ to understand the limitations.

You can access the developer program at `https://developer.servicenow.com`.

Keeping up with the examples

All the examples in the book have been recorded as Update Sets, which we discuss in detail in `Chapter 10`, *Packaging with Applications, Update Sets, and Upgrades*. The hotels application is also in a public Git repository. You can apply them to short-cut the examples. Even if you you wish to work through all the examples, I recommend applying the first one, so your scope identifier is the same as the book. It'll make copying and pasting code much easier!

You can download the Update Sets at `http://www.gardiner-hotels.com`. Alternatively, you can fork the Git repository available at `https://github.com/gardinerhotels/hotel`. More instructions are at the website.

Being in charge

An instance is an independent implementation of ServiceNow. It is isolated and autonomous, meaning your code and data is not shared with other customers. ServiceNow uses a single-tenancy architecture, which means your instance is yours: you can do what you want with it, such as changing logic, updating the UI, and adding fields.

 ServiceNow's greatest advantage is also its biggest disadvantage. The power and flexibility can be intoxicating! Just because you can do what you want, doesn't mean you *should* it! This is discussed in detail throughout the book.

Every customer has several instances-again, each isolated and independent. One instance is usually marked out for developing on, another for testing, and yet another for production. And because each instance is independent, each one can be running a different release of ServiceNow. The production instance differs by having more powerful hardware.

 Chapter 9, *Diagnosing ServiceNow – Knowing What is Going On*, discusses how you can use your instances for tasks such as building functionality, testing it, and then making it live.

Changing your instance

A new instance starts with a few ServiceNow applications, some demo configuration, and example data. This is often called the out-of-the-box state. One of the example data elements is the **System Administrator** user. You are able to log in and get going, getting full control immediately.

Everyone makes changes to their instance. Unless the people who will be using the system are called **Beth Anglin** or **David Dan** (some of the default example users), you'll need to load some users at the very least. Some ServiceNow customers configure a lot, and some do the bare minimum. You can choose how much you wish to do. Because it is single-tenant, you can alter the configuration and data in almost any way you see fit-now, it might not always be smart to do that, but you can!

My favorite analogy, if you haven't guessed it yet, is a building. ServiceNow gives you an office that is yours. It starts off identical, built to the standard plans, but you can redecorate or remodel as you see fit-perhaps even knock down a wall! (Let's hope it's not load bearing.) This is the benefit of single tenancy.

Multitenancy is like an apartment in a block. It is generally more efficient to pack lots of people together in a single building, and you can build it pretty high. However, you don't have the flexibility that being in control gives you. The landlords of the block won't let you knock down a wall!

The vast majority of customers have their instance hosted by ServiceNow. This means that the people who built the house will also look after it, on their land. You get great economies of scale and the benefit of tools and automation design to perform maintenance and give support fast. All the gardeners and janitors are on site, ready to work-they don't need to travel to help out.

Knowing the platform

The heart of ServiceNow is the platform. This is a series of data, logic, and user interface layers, combined to provide a high-level environment that makes it really easy to build workflow and forms-based business applications. If you like, the platform takes raw materials and develops them into building blocks. You then plug them together to create what you need.

ServiceNow has already done a lot of building work. Prebuilt applications are available to perform service management, such as IT, HR, and facilities. Managing IT infrastructure is made easier with the ServiceWatch suite, while the needs of the business are helped with demand, project, and vendor management.

When you know how the platform works, you can more quickly use and support the applications built upon it. And, of course, you can build your own. Understanding the platform will help you in all respects-which is the focus of this book.

Choosing functionalities with plugins

All ServiceNow functionalities are delivered as **plugins**. When an instance is turned on, one of its first tasks is to load all the plugins that are turned on out of the box. There are quite a few of those: over 200 in the Helsinki version of ServiceNow. And there are several hundred more that you can turn on if you want. A plugin may provide an app, such as HR Service Management, or provide new platform functionality, such as domain separation.

 Chapter 9, *Diagnosing ServiceNow – Knowing What is Going On*, talks about plugins and upgrading ServiceNow in more detail.

When a plugin is turned on, all the data and configuration that the application needs is loaded into the database, meaning that it is ready for work in just a few moments. Many also contain demo data, giving you examples of how it could work.

Running the latest version

Each new version of ServiceNow brings new and improved applications and enhancements to the platform. These are packaged as updates to plugins.

ServiceNow tends to release twice a year, meaning it can be quite a task to keep up with the latest version! This book is written for the Helsinki version of ServiceNow, though most of the information is relevant for newer and older versions.

Aside from improved functionality and bug fixes, ServiceNow often creates improvements to the user interface. An instance provisioned with the Helsinki version of ServiceNow uses UI16 by default. The screenshots in this book show UI16, so if you use a different interface (perhaps for browser compatibility reasons or because of a different version), things may look slightly different, and all of the features may not work the same.

The product documentation lists the different interfaces available: `https:/` `/docs.servicenow.com/administer/navigation_and_ui/concept/c_Na` `vigationAndTheUserInterface.html`.

Digging into the hosting

A typical ServiceNow-hosted instance is split over two physical datacenters, forming a high-availability pair. Each location runs independently of the other, creating a semi-clustered environment. In the event of a catastrophic disaster with one location being completely unavailable, the other nodes will just pick up the load, with almost no downtime. In fact, the process of switching between locations is used for maintenance procedures, enabling your instance to be well protected against hardware and other failures.

The free developer instances are not replicated, and run only on a single node. A customer's production instance has many more resources!

When you visit your instance, you are directed through several layers:

1. By looking up DNS records, you are directed to the currently active datacenter for your instance.
2. The load balancer, by reading a cookie, directs you to the application server you have your session with.
3. If you aren't logged in, you get directed to the least busy application server.
4. Your application server then uses the database currently determined as active.

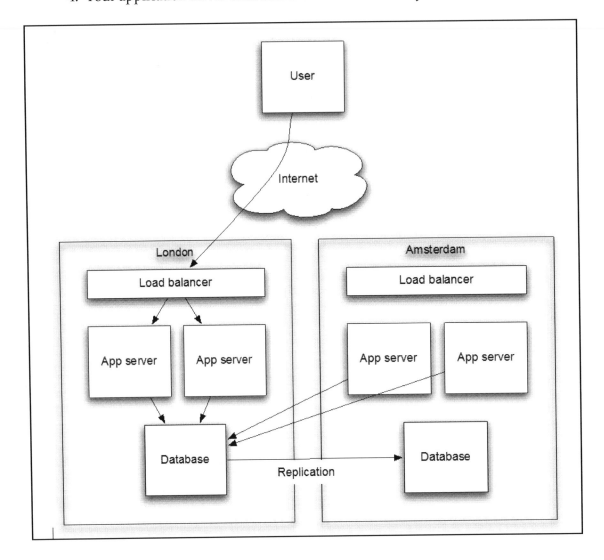

Knowing the nodes

From an architectural perspective, a ServiceNow instance is made up of several application and database servers or nodes. These generally run on shared hardware, meaning although your instance is logically separate and independent, it is physically hosted alongside another customer. At each location, there are generally at least two application nodes, each running a copy of the ServiceNow platform and working together to share load. Additionally, there may be worker nodes installed to process the noninteractive jobs, such as sending out e-mails or dealing with integrations. Even though you'll never directly log in to these worker nodes, they perform some background processing, allowing the interactive application servers to respond more quickly to user requests. While there are generally lots of application nodes, there is only one active database server, running on a separate physical server. It does have a redundant pair hosted in the remote datacenter.

Chapter 5, *Getting Things Done with Tasks*, explores the concept of event queues in more detail.

Exploring the database

So you've got an instance and have logged in. Great! What can we see? The answer: database records.

Almost everything in ServiceNow is an entry in a database. When you look at the user interface, virtually everything you see-from the data typed in by a user to log files and how the views are structured-is stored in the instance's relational database. The scripts you write are kept in a string field, and the files you attach to records are stored in chunks, all in the database.

All this data is organized into many **tables**. A table is a collection of records, with each record being a row. A **field** is a column in that table.

Everything is built on top of this structure. You don't need to reboot the server to apply new functionality; you just update data records. You don't need to reload configuration files-any properties you set will be read on the next operation. Even the database metadata-information about the fields themselves-is stored in another table.

This gives you a great deal of control. You organize, configure, and manage almost everything the same way, searching for a script like you search for users: by simply querying the right table. This means you can focus on designing and building great business applications, since the platform just works.

ServiceNow may be considered a high-level platform based on the **Model-view-controller** (**MVC**) concept. When building a ServiceNow application, you can first think of the data structure. You determine what information you need to store and how it all links together, creating tables and fields. This is the **model** aspect.

Automatically, you get a simple view of this data, with forms and lists showing your information.

You can then build simple ways to manipulate and change the data, through automation and simple manual updates, giving you the **controller**.

Introducing the Gardiner Hotel data structure

One of the first things that many people learn how to do in ServiceNow is to add a field. This is a straightforward operation: you add the new field to a form or list using the UI. Under the hood, the ServiceNow platform performs, among other operations, a simple SQL command to add a column to the table you are manipulating. When you add a field, you add a column to the table. When you remove a field, you drop it. There is no magic-the platform interface just makes it easy to do.

ServiceNow allows you to add fields to every table in the system. If you decide that adding another is a good idea, you have the power to do so!

In order to work through the ServiceNow functionality, we will build a hotel management application for your new employer, Gardiner Hotels. It will involve building a simple data structure, but one that is highly interlinked.

Here is a representation of the tables we will create in this and the following chapters:

- **Guests**: The reason Gardiner Hotels exists! Our guests' details are the most important information we have. We definitely need their names and, optionally, their e-mail addresses and phone numbers.
- **Room**: This details where our guests will sleep. We store the room number and the floor it is on.
- **Check-in**: When guests want their room key, they check in. We record who checked in to a room and when and who made the entry.

  We will create a link to the Room table so we can easily see information about the room, such as which floor it is on.

- **Reservation**: Our guests like staying with us, and they often book months in advance. One reservation might be for many guests, especially if an entire family is coming. A big family might need a big room. We need to record where exactly they might stay.

Over the course of the book, we will expand and further develop the application. Its primary use is to show you as much of the capability of ServiceNow as possible, so some of the examples may be better done in other ways.

Creating tables

Firstly, let's create an app to hold our configuration in. Applications are a container for custom configuration in ServiceNow. It's a great place to capture our work and keep everything we do logically separate. Depending on what configuration you do with it, there may be licensing implications to deploying it in production. But this application will stay safely on our sandbox developer system. Applications are discussed in more detail in the next chapter, and in Chapter 10, *Packaging with Applications, Update sets, and Upgrades.*

Throughout this book there will be examples to show off features of ServiceNow. To make them as easy to follow as possible, it's best to use the same application scope as me. To make this possible, you should import the very starting point of my Hotel application. At the moment, it's an empty shell.

The easiest way to import the application is through an Update Set. Follow these steps:

1. Download the Update Set from https://www.gardiner-hotels.com/sets/-Hot elApp.xml Save it to disk.
2. Navigate to **System Update Sets** > **Retrieved Update Sets**. Click **Import Update Set from XML**.

The convention for navigating through ServiceNow uses the following structure: **Application Menu** > **Module**. For modules with separators, it will be **Application Menu** > **Section** > **Module**. The easiest way to find a particular link is to type it in the **Application Filter** field at the top-left corner of the menu. Make sure you are choosing the right one, though, because some modules are identically named.

3. Click the **Browse** button, and choose the XML file you downloaded. Click **Upload**.
4. Click on the Hotel Bootstrap record, then click on the **Preview Update Set** button.
5. Once analyzed, click on **Commit Update Set**. Click **Close** once done.
6. If you navigate to **System Applications** > **Applications**, you should see the Hotel entry in the list.

An alternative is to fork my GitHub repository available at https://githu b.com/gardinerhotels/hotel.

7. Now, let's create our first table. Navigate to **System Definition** > **Tables,** and click **New.**

8. Fill in the following values, and click on **Create**, then **OK** to confirm. Some fields (like **Name**) will automatically populate.
   - **Label:** Check-in
   - **New menu name:** Hotel

Notice the auto-generated table name. If you imported the Update Set, the name should be x_hotel_check_in. It's made up of several parts: the vendor prefix, the application name, and the table name itself. More about this in Chapter 2, *Developing Custom Applications.*

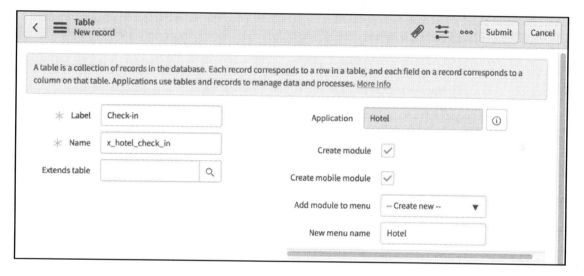

9. Click on **Submit** to create the table.

Many technical items in ServiceNow have a label and name that are used in the database and in scripts. In this case, the database table is called x_hotel_check_in, while an entry in the **Field Labels** (sys_documentation) table contains the mapping between the name and the label. I'll use the Label (database_name) format throughout the book.

Adding fields

Let's inspect the table that was just created. Navigate again to **System Definition** > **Tables**. Helsinki comes with over 2,000 different data tables, and all of them can be seen here. But we are only after one of them. Find **Check-in** (sort by **Updated** or filter the list) to see what has been made.

		Label	Name	Extends table	Extensible	Updated ▼
☐	ⓘ	Check-in	x_hotel_check_in		false	2016-08-08 23:49:44

When you create a new table, you get some system fields. You may need to scroll down the **Table** form to see them. They include two dates (when a record was created and when it was last updated), two string fields (containing the user ID of who created it and who updated it), a unique GUID called `sys_id`, and a field that counts the number of updates to the record. They are all updated automatically, and it is generally good practice to leave them alone. They are useful just as they are!

The following screenshot shows how the system fields are represented within the tables:

		Column label	Type	Reference	Max length	Default value	Display
	ⓘ	Created by	String		40		false
	ⓘ	Created	Date/Time		40		false
	ⓘ	Sys ID	Sys ID (GUID)		32		false
	ⓘ	Updates	Integer		40		false
	ⓘ	Updated by	String		40		false
	ⓘ	Updated	Date/Time		40		false
		Insert a new row...					

The autogenerated fields are very helpful to the system administrator for finding records quickly. I always add the **Updated on** field to my lists, since it makes finding the records I've been working on (such as scripts) much faster.

In addition to these automatic fields, we need to create some of our own. We will need several, but right now, let's create something to store any requests that the guest may have. Perhaps they may have specifically requested a high floor. Scroll down the table form, and create a new field called `Comments` by double-clicking on **Insert a new row...**. Fill out the row, and save the record by clicking on the **Update** button. Either use the Tab key or double-click to enter the following data:

- **Column label**: `Comments`
- **Type**: `String`
- **Max length**: `500`

The following screenshot displays how the list of columns looks before saving the changes:

	Column label	Type	Reference	Max length	Default value	Display
(i)	Created by	String			40	false
(i)	Created	Date/Time			40	false
(i)	Sys ID	Sys ID (GUID)			32	false
(i)	Updates	Integer			40	false
(i)	Updated by	String			40	false
(i)	Updated	Date/Time			40	false
	Comments	String		500		false
	Insert a new row...					

Knowing what's happening

Once you've clicked the **Update** button, the instance gets busy. Behind the scenes, the application server is running SQL commands against the database. Specifically, at the time of creating the field, the following is executed:

```
ALTER TABLE x_hotel_check_in ADD `comments` MEDIUMTEXT
```

If you wish to see these commands, navigate to **System Diagnostics** > **Debug SQL**. This will place lots of information at the bottom of the page. Other diagnostic tools such as this are discussed in `Chapter 8`, *Securing Applications and Data*.

This demonstrates a key concept: whenever you perform an action in ServiceNow, it results in a string of database commands. The database is altered and the platform's internal state is updated. These actions are generally carried out quickly, with the whole process completed in about half a second. No downtime is necessary.

Introducing the dictionary

The **dictionary** is a metatable. It describes your table and fields-their names, how big they are, and any special attributes they may have, similar to information_schema views. For example, one field might be dependent upon another. A dictionary entry might also be referred to as an **element descriptor**, since it describes the how the field (or element) works.

The table is represented by an entry in the dictionary with a table value, type of `Collection`, and no column name. When the **Comments** field was added to the **Check-in** table, the platform also made a dictionary entry with the table and a column name. You can view it if you want by navigating to **System Definition > Dictionary**.

The options that are available in the dictionary depend on the type of field you are working with. Reference fields, which we will explore in a moment, have extra functionality that is controlled here, such as dynamic creation.

As we work through ServiceNow, we'll spot functionality that is enabled through the dictionary. However, much of it can be achieved in other ways, often in a better manner.

Older versions of ServiceNow have a read-only tick box available in the dictionary form by default. While it's included and can be used in later versions, it is a better idea to use security rules instead. They give you much more granularity and control than a binary checkbox. We will explore security rules in `Chapter 7`, *Exchanging Data*.

The easiest way to navigate to a dictionary entry is by right-clicking on the label of the field (not the text-entry box) and choosing **Configure Dictionary**. You can see some details about a field, such as which table it is in, by choosing the **Show** option from the menu that appears on right-clicking.

The globally unique identifier

The ServiceNow database is a relational database. This means that one data element can relate to another. To ensure that every record or row can be referenced easily, every record has a unique identifier: a **primary key**.

In ServiceNow, this primary key is something that isn't related to the data itself. It is a **globally unique identifier** or **GUID**. This GUID is stored as a 32-character string, made of hexadecimal characters (the numbers 0-9 plus the letters a-f). The number of unique GUID values is so large that the probability of two accidently being the same is negligible. This is an example GUID: 5137153cc611227c000bbd1bd8cd2005.

This type of identifier is sometimes known as an OID or object identifier. It has no special significance; it just uniquely identifies a data row. It can also be called a surrogate key.

Whenever you create a record in ServiceNow, the platform generates a new GUID. The characters generated are random-a mixture of several sources, including the date and time and details specific to the instance, meaning they're not sequential or predictable. The GUID is saved alongside the record, in a special field called sys_id. The sys_id field is heavily used in the ServiceNow platform-you will start seeing GUIDs everywhere!

As an example of how ServiceNow uses the sys_id field, conduct the following experiment: construct a URL similar to the one that follows, substituting <instance> with the name of your instance, and visit it with your browser:
https://<instance>.service-now.com/sys_user.do?sys_id=5137153cc611227c000bbd1bd8cd2005.

In the new instance, you should happen across the user record of **Fred Luddy** (if the demo data has been removed, you will get a **Record not found** message).

If the system sees -1 as a sys_id, it'll assume it is a new record, and will generate a new GUID.

It is useful to examine the structure of the URL. First, spot the sys_user table. Then, spot the GUID. With these two items, the instance knows exactly what data it needs to pull up and present to you.

Every record has a sys_id field. It is the only field that ServiceNow really cares about. It also looks after itself. You don't need to worry about it during day-to-day operations.

Reference fields, as we'll see, are very reliant upon the sys_id fields. When we get into scripting in Chapter 2, *Developing Custom Applications*, you'll be seeing more of them.

Every other field is optional and non-unique to the database platform. You can have two records that are otherwise identical but only have a differing `sys_id` field. (It is possible to enforce uniqueness in other fields too, as we'll see later.)

This means that, in general, you can change the value of fields to whatever you like and still maintain referential integrity; no system errors will occur. If you want to rename a user or a group, go ahead. Since everything related to that user will be associated to the user via the `sys_id` field, the user's name is not important.

Many other products do not use surrogate keys; data is linked together using user-provided data. If you change the name of a group, for example, this could remove all group memberships and task assignment. Not in ServiceNow, though!

An important exception to this behavior is with roles. Roles are referred to by name in scripts, so if you change the name, all scripts that use it will need to be altered (though security rules do refer to the role through the `sys_id` field). In general, it is a good idea to keep the names of roles the same.

It is a good idea not to interfere with this flexibility. When building functionality, don't refer to records using their names or `sys_id` values in scripts. Instead, use the properties or attributes of the record itself to identify it. So, rather than hardcoding the condition that a particular room in our hotel needs special treatment, create another field and use it as a flag. The VIP flag on the `User` table is a good example of this.

Storing data

There are various types of fields provided by the ServiceNow platform. We will explore some of the simpler ones before moving on to the fundamental backbone of the data structure with reference fields:

- **String**: These fields are simple text fields. The UI displays a string field as an editable text box. If the `Max length` attribute in the dictionary is more than `255`, then a multiline field is shown. Most fields in ServiceNow are enhanced versions of the string field.
- **Choice**: These fields are string fields, but rendered as `HTML select` fields. The value that is stored in the database is plain text. Another table, the `Choices` [`sys_choice`] table, stores the options and labels. This lets the platform convert `wip` in the database to present **Work in Progress** to the user. Any values that don't have a label are highlighted in blue in the dropdown.

- **Integer choice**: These fields use numbers instead of text to achieve the same result as normal choice fields. They are useful for representing states, since they allow you to use greater-than or less-than conditions, but they have proven difficult to work with since the numbers don't mean much!

 Use caution when dealing with the out-of-the-box integer choice fields, such as **State** on the **Task** table. If you reuse them (which is a good idea), you should always align your states to the existing ones. For example, 3 should represent Closed. If you do not align them, then users will be confused when reporting. This is discussed in detail in Chapter 4, *Client-Side Interaction*.

- **Date**: There are several date fields in ServiceNow. The time is stored as UTC in the database, and the appropriate display value is calculated by the user's profile.
- **Currency**: These are string fields that combine the currency and amount. USD;1000 represents $1,000. The platform uses this information to provide conversions between different currencies. For example, if I prefer to see amounts in GBP, the platform will, if it has the latest currency rates, display **£675**.
- **True/false**: These fields are simple boolean values in the database. They are rendered as tick boxes.
- **URL**: These fields provide space to enter a link, which can toggled to be clickable.
- **Email**: Similar to URL, the email field lets you type an e-mail address and provides a button to launch your e-mail client through a **mailto:** link.
- **HTML** and **Wikitext**: Other fields, such as these, provide different interfaces to manipulate strings. It is tempting to use HTML fields in lots of places, but they do come with overhead, and browsers have different capabilities. Test carefully if you want to use capabilities such as these.

Storing files as attachments

In addition to text, ServiceNow can also store binary data. This means that anything (images, music, or even a multitude of PowerPoint documents) can be saved in ServiceNow. Just like everything else, binary data is stored in the database. However, rather than using a BLOB field, binary data is split into 4-KB chunks and saved into the **Attachment Documents** (sys_attachment_doc) table. Each chunk of a file refers back to the **Attachments** (sys_attachment) table, where the filename, content type and size, and other metadata are stored.

A file is always related to another record (this is why they are referred to as attachments). Information on this other record is stored with the other metadata in the **Attachments** table. For example, if a record had a PDF of the booking form attached to it, the **Attachment** record would contain the filename of the document as well as the sys_id of the **Reservation** record.

We'll see in later chapters that there are often better ways than manually adding attachments containing booking information. Why not have the e-mail come directly into ServiceNow? (We'll see how in Chapter 5, *Getting Things Done with Tasks.*) Or, even better, why not have the guests perform the booking directly with ServiceNow? (Chapter 10,*Packaging with Applications, Update Sets, and Upgrades*, will show us how to do this.)

Setting properties

One of the simplest ways to control the platform is to set properties. There are lots of things you can change by just clicking on a box or changing a value. And just like everything else in ServiceNow, the configuration properties that you set are stored in a table-the **System Properties** [sys_properties] table to be precise.

To see how many options you can choose, type Properties in the filter-text box of the application navigator. Many matches will be shown, including **System Properties > UI Properties**. This collection contains some very useful options, including how forms look and feel, whether list editing is enabled, and whether **Insert and Stay** is always available. You may want to spend some time and find out what they do.

Some properties are not categorized, but all are accessible by typing sys_properties.list in the filter-text box of the application navigator. This will give you a large list-over 1000 in Helsinki.

This book will guide you to the more relevant properties, but many are documented in the product documentation:
https://docs.servicenow.com/administer/reference_pages/referen ce/r_AvailableSystemProperties.html

Reference fields

When designing the data structure for a hotel, you want to know which room a guest has checked in to. It won't be good for business if we don't know who is sleeping where! This is exactly what a reference field does: it creates a link between two records, one pointing to another.

When we examined the URLs earlier, we saw they contained two parts: the table and the sys_id value of the record. These are the two items needed to reference a record. So when you create a reference field, you need to select which table it should point to, which is stored in the dictionary. And the contents of the field will be a 32-character string. Sound familiar? Yep, you will be storing a sys_id in that field.

Reference fields are one of the most important items to understand in ServiceNow. The database sees a string field containing the sys_id value, a foreign key. However, this is meaningless to a person. Therefore, the platform allows you to pick a field that will be displayed. For a person, this might be their name. Other records might have a user-friendly reference number, like TSK0001. This is usually an incremental number-there are scripts that generate one automatically. You can choose which field to show by ticking the **Display** field in the **Dictionary** entry. But remember: only the sys_id value is important to the platform.

Reference fields are used throughout ServiceNow, just like a proper relational system should be. Scripting, lists, and forms all understand references fields, as we'll see while we work through the chapters.

Creating a reference field

Let's think about something that the hotel application needs-a room directory. Each room has several attributes that defines it: its room number, how many beds it has, and which floor it is on. We can represent this information as fields in a Room record, all stored in a dedicated table.

We also need to store guest information. When designing a data structure, it's a good idea to reuse functionality wherever possible. ServiceNow already has a table that stores information about people: the user table. Let's use that for now to store guest information.

It is sometimes a difficult decision to should reuse an existing table. The benefits are obvious: you save time from not duplicating work, both in configuration and maintenance. But sometimes, you need the table to work slightly differently for two different scenarios. We'll see one way to deal with this in Chapter 2, *Developing Custom Applications*.

Once we have these items in place, we can modify the Check-in table to record which room has been taken by which guest.

Building out the data structure

Let's create the tables and fields we need step by step. Let's start with the Room table first.

1. Return to **System Definition** > **Tables** to create another new table. Use the **New** button on the list. Fill out fields as follows, click on the menu button, and then click on **Save** (don't click on **Submit!**):

    - **Label**: Room

    - Add module to menu: Hotel

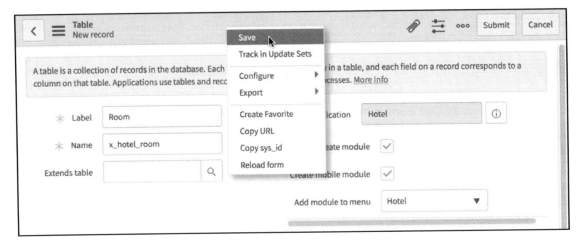

I suggest using the **Save** button, accessible via the three-line menu icon (or right clicking on the header) rather than using **Submit** to commit records to the database. This ensures that the updated record is shown on screen after saving rather than redirecting to the previous page, like **Submit** does.

2. Now create a field to store the room number by scrolling down the **Columns** tab to **Insert a new Row**. Double-click again to enter the information.
   - Column label: Number

 Don't use the auto-number option; create a new field using the related list.

We need another field to store the floor it is located on:

- **Column label**: Floor
- **Type**: Integer

The final result should look like this:

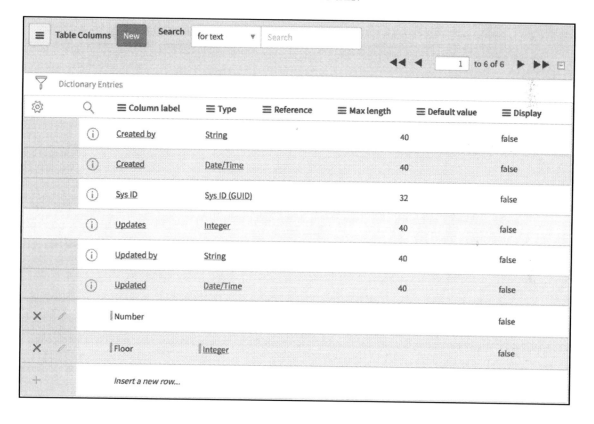

	Column label	Type	Reference	Max length	Default value	Display
ⓘ	Created by	String		40		false
ⓘ	Created	Date/Time		40		false
ⓘ	Sys ID	Sys ID (GUID)		32		false
ⓘ	Updates	Integer		40		false
ⓘ	Updated by	String		40		false
ⓘ	Updated	Date/Time		40		false
✕ ✎	Number					false
✕ ✎	Floor	Integer				false
+	Insert a new row...					

1. Use **Save** to make the changes in the database.

2. Let's see what we've created. When we created the table, ServiceNow also created a module in the Hotel application menu that will show us all the room data in the instance. Navigate to **Hotel** > **Rooms**. You shouldn't be surprised to see **No records to display**– we haven't created any yet!

3. Using the **New** button, create a few example records, giving each one a different number. Make several on the same floor. One of them could be Room **101** on the first floor. As you do so, try using the **Save** and **Submit** buttons, and notice the difference between them.

Note that the platform does not force you to choose different numbers for each record. Unless you mark a field as unique or create a rule to check, the platform will allow you to create them.

To mark a field as unique, you can edit the dictionary entry of that field (you will need to configure the dictionary form and add the **Unique** checkbox). By ticking that field, you are asking the database to enforce it. It does this by making that field a unique key. This has two impacts. It creates an index on that field, which is good. However, if a user attempts to save a duplicate value, they will get a message saying **Unique Key violation detected by database**. This can be a little jarring for a non-technical user. Try to catch the error with a Business Rule first.

Linking the data together

Now that we have a list of rooms, we need to create the link between the **Room** and **Check-in** records.

A reference field can be referred to as a one-to-many relationship. This is because a room may be checked in to multiple times (you might have one particular guest one day, and the next day, another might sleep in the same room after our fabulous cleaners have done their work), but for a single check-in, you can only select one room. You can only sleep in one bed at a time!

A classic example of a one-to-many relationship is between a mother and her children. A child can only have one biological mother, but a mother can have many children.

The following diagram shows the relationship needed between the **Room** and **Check-in** records:

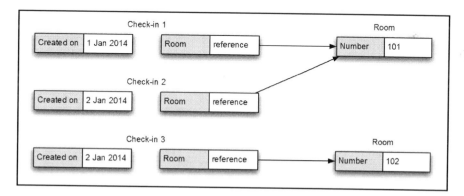

1. Go back to **System Definition** > **Tables** and find the **Check-in** table. Once there, create two new reference fields-one will be for the room, using the following data:
   - **Column label**: Room
   - **Type**: Reference
   - **Reference**: Room

   The other will be for the guest:

   - **Column label**: Guest
   - **Type**: Reference
   - **Reference**: User [sys_user]-be careful to select the right one here!

2. **Save** your changes.
3. Now is a good time to rearrange the new fields on the form so that they look good. To do this, click on **Design Form** in the **Related Links** section near the bottom of the form. It'll open a new tab or window.
4. Once in the form designer, drag the section containing the Room and Guest fields above Comments. Then, click on **Save**, and close the tab. If you have trouble, try using Form Layout, and move Comments to the bottom of the list, so it is under Guest and Room. The form should end up looking like the next screenshot.
5. Now, create a few example **Check-in** records. To simulate someone going into room 101, create a new entry in the **Check-in** table by navigating to **Hotel** > **Check-in**, and clicking **New**. Populate both the **Guest** and **Room** fields, and then click on **Submit**:

Looking from different perspectives

You can view the relationship between **Room** and **Check-in** entities from both directions. If you are on the **Check-in** form, you can see which room is in use through the reference field. The reference icon is very useful for viewing more details about the record-just hover over it.

If you hold down the Shift key while you move your cursor over the reference icon and then go into the pop-up window, the information will remain until you click on the **Close** button. This is quite useful when copying data from that record without losing position.

You can easily view the relationship from the other perspective, too. When you create a reference field, you can add a related list to the form, or a list of the referenced tables. This will let you see all the records that are pointing to it.

1. Navigate to **Hotel** > **Rooms,** and select a room that you have created a check-in record for. (I made one for room 101 for David Loo, as above.) On the **Room** form, click on the menu button (or right-click on the header bar), and then go to **Configure** > **Related Lists**. The one we want will be named in this format: `table->field`-in our case, it's **Check-in** > **Room**. Add that to **Selected** list, and click **Save**.

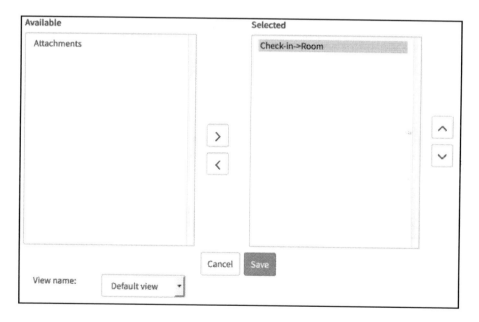

2. To make things look better, right-click on the list headings, go to **Configure** > **List Layout**, and remove **Comments**. Click **Save**.

The related list gives you a **New** button. When you click on it, you will see the **Check-in** form but with the reference field already filled in. So, if we know which room we want to check a guest in to, we can navigate to the **Room** record, click on the **New** button in the **Check-in** related list, and need not type in the room number again.

Using reference qualifiers

By default, a reference field can select from any record in the referenced table. However, often, you want to filter the results. For example, you may want to specify a guest as inactive, perhaps representing someone who won't be visiting Gardiner Hotels any longer. Therefore, let's filter out inactive users so they cannot be inadvertently checked in.

Reference qualifiers allow you to do this. When you edit the dictionary entry of a reference field, you can specify the filter you want to apply. These can be specified in three different ways:

- **Simple**: This lets you specify which records should be returned using a condition builder.

Simple is the default reference qualifier. Click on **Advanced view** in **Related Links** to see the other options.

- **Dynamic**: This lets you pick from prebuilt scripts. The choices they provide often differ depending on the context of the record or the session. A good example is **Me**, one of the dynamic filter options. This will return whoever is currently logged in, meaning that users who use the reference field will have personalized results. A dynamic filter option is the most reusable

You can build your own dynamic filter options by navigating to **System Definition** > **Dynamic Filter Options**. This will be covered in Chapter 2, *Developing Custom Applications*.

- **Advanced**: This is the original way of creating reference qualifiers. It accepts an encoded query. JavaScript can be embedded in these queries, by prefixing them with javascript.

An encoded query is a field-operator-value triplet, separated by the caret (^) symbol. This string represents part of the `where` clause of the resulting SQL query. For example, `active=true` specifies all records where the active field is true, while `active=true^last_name=Smith` represents `active` being ticked and the contents of the `last_name` field being `Smith`.

One easy way to obtain an encoded query is to build a filter in the list view, right-click on the result, and choose **Copy Query**.

For our Hotel application, let's use a simple reference qualifier. Navigate to **Hotel** > **Check-In**, and select a record. Right-click on the **Guest** field label, and choose **Configure Dictionary**.

Fill out the fields as below, and **Save**.

- **Reference qual condition**: `Active - is - true`.

Now, if you mark a user as inactive (by unchecking the **Active** checkbox and saving), they cannot be selected when checking in, neither through the magnifying-glass lookup window, nor using the type-ahead functionality.

Dot-walking through data

Dot-walking is a very important concept in ServiceNow. It means you can access information through reference fields quickly and easily. It can be leveraged throughout ServiceNow-both through the interface and through code.

You've already used dot-walking. When you hover over the reference icon, you can see information from that record. That's the whole concept! We are using the platform's capability to "see through" reference fields and pull out information from that record. And, as we'll see in `Chapter 3`, *Server-Side Control* the same is possible through code.

Using derived fields

Dot-walking can be used throughout the user interface. Another example is adding **derived fields** to lists, forms, and queries. A derived field is a field from another record that is found through a reference field.

For example, we could add the floor number of the room to the check-in form as a derived field. The floor number doesn't belong to the check-in record, and if we change the room on the form, the system will dynamically change the floor number displayed.

With scripting, you have the option to copy data through the reference field onto the record you are dealing with. That data then becomes part of the record. Derived fields will exist through the link only.
This concept is important to understand. If the referenced record gets deleted or changed, it will then affect our current record. For example, if we delete the room record, the check-in form won't be able to show which floor it is on. If we change the floor value on the room record, our check-in form will show the new value.

The simplest example of derived information is the display value, which was mentioned earlier. If the display value of the referenced record changes, you'll see it altered everywhere. Since `sys_id` is the primary key for a record, you can easily rename groups, alter the names of users, or update virtually any record without penalty.

1. Navigate to the Check-in form (**Hotel** > **Check-in**, then choose a record) . Use the menu icon and choose **Configure** > **Form Layout**.

Derived fields can only be added via **Form Layout** (rather than **Form Design**)

Even though the **Room** field has already been added to the form, it is still in the "available" list. It should have **[+]** as a suffix to the field name, showing it is a reference field that can be dot-walked to, for example, **Room [+]**.

2. On selecting it and clicking on the **Expand selected reference field** icon, you get to see the fields in the **Room** table. Choose the **Floor** field, and add it to the form. It should be labeled **Room.Floor**, showing that you are dot-walking. Click on **Save**.

The **Check-in** form should now have several fields in it: the **Room** reference field, the **Floor** derived field, and a simple **Comments** field. Here they are:

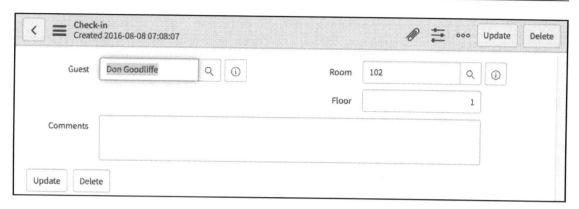

Notice how the **Floor** field is editable. If the value is changed and the **Submit** button is clicked on, it is actually the **Room** record that will be altered.

Building the interface

We've already spent some time with the ServiceNow interface. But some of the fundamentals of how the platform is used and what it provides deserve repeating.

If we rewind to our opening consideration that everything is in a database, ServiceNow provides two basic interfaces that we spend the majority of our time with: **forms** and **lists**. The form and the list are the two major views of data within ServiceNow. You can, of course, create custom user interfaces, and we'll cover those in Chapter 11, *Making ServiceNow Beautiful with Service Portal and Custom Interfaces*.

Lists

Lists show several records in a table, line by line. Pretty obvious, but let's break out of the frames and examine some URLs again. Remember how we navigated to a specific record in a field? Let's instead show a list of **User** records. The table name is suffixed with _list, with the usual .do. Here's an example:

```
http://<instance>.service-now.com/sys_user_list.do.
```

You might be wondering what the `.do` extension is all about. This is the typical suffix that is used by Apache Struts, which has become the go-to framework for developing Java web applications such as ServiceNow. This provides a hint to the technologies used within the ServiceNow platform.

We've already seen that the `sys_id` value can be used as a parameter to immediately jump to a record. There are other parameters that are useful, too. Here's an example that shows how you can specify a database query through a URL:

```
http://<instance>.service-
now.com/sys_user_list.do?sysparm_query=user_name=fred.luddy.
```

If you navigate to this URL, you will be presented with a list of the records that match this query. If you remove the `_list` part from the URL, you will be presented with the first record that matches.

These URLs do not open up the familiar navigation interface, but simply show the content. You may want to have multiple browser tabs open, without the clutter to get in your way. Edit the URL directly, and get to where you want to go quickly. If you must have the Application Navigator and it's friends, try

```
http://<instance>.service-now.com/nav_to.do?uri=sys_user_list.do.
```

Choosing the fields to show

A list in ServiceNow can include any of the fields that are on the table. But a list works best when you show only the most relevant information. Adding in lots of columns makes it take longer to load (more data to get from the instance, to be sent across the Internet, and parsed by your browser) and often only adds to clutter and complexity.

Typically, a good list includes something that identifies the individual record (usually a name and number and maybe a short description) and when it was last updated. If there is a categorization field, that should be included too. It is very helpful to sort or group records by these values. The **Go to** quick search option also allows you to search these fields.

The number of records shown on a list is configurable by the user. The system administrator sets the choices they have in **UI Properties**. Keep the maximum number low, again to minimize the amount of data that needs to be worked with. Setting it to 1,000 is useful to be able to perform mass deletion, but if everyone has it selected, it will impact performance.

Having reference fields on lists

Reference fields are treated slightly differently in a list view. The majority of fields are shown as simple text, but a reference field is always shown as a link to the referenced record. The first column in the list is also converted into a link, this time linking to the record itself.

Never put a reference field as the first column on a list. While the system will understand this and consequently make the *second* column the link to the record, it is incredibly confusing to the user. People become very used to clicking on the first column, and they expect to see that record in the list.

You can always get to the record by clicking on the icon to the left of a particular column.

The varied capabilities of lists

Users of ServiceNow often forget about the extra functionality lists provide. Functionality such as list editing and the powerful context menus (such as **Show Matching** when you right-click on a list) should be thought about carefully and explained to users of the system to ensure they use the interface in an efficient manner.

A hierarchical list is not used that often, but it is very powerful. It allows you to display the related lists of records in the list view. So, even while looking at the **Reservations** list, the guests can be inspected. You can turn on this functionality in **List Control** when you right-click on the headers and choose **Configure**.

Here are some tips to keep in mind when creating lists:

- Try not to include journal, HTML, or other multiline fields in the list. They grow big and the interface truncates their display.
- Think carefully about **List Control**. Do you want **New** or **Edit** buttons? This matters especially for related lists.
- When running a query on a list, if you click on the **New** button, the values you searched for will be copied into the form.

Forms

In contrast to the simple concept of lists, a **form** generally contains more detailed information. It is where users usually interact with the data.

Try not to break away from the convention of having two columns of fields, with the labels to the left. Although it might be considered plain, it also means the forms are consistent, easy to read, and relatively uncluttered. The emphasis should therefore be on creating logic and a process to control the data while keeping the interface simple.

> If you want to make things more exciting, CSS can be applied to the main interface using themes. Chapter 11, *Making ServiceNow Beautiful with Service Portal and Custom Interfaces*, explores how completely custom interfaces can be made. Check out the product documentation for more information:
> https://docs.servicenow.com/bundle/helsinki-servicenow-platform/
> page/administer/navigation-and-
> ui/task/t_CreateOrCustomizeATheme.html.

Annotations allow you to add text and even HTML to forms. They are especially useful for adding simple work instructions, but be careful to ensure that the forms don't get cluttered.

Finally, formatters allow you to include Jelly in your form. Rather than being a sugary treat, Jelly is a scriptable language used to build the ServiceNow interface. Chapter 11, *Making ServiceNow Beautiful with Service Portal and Custom Interfaces*, discusses custom interfaces in more detail.

Creating useful forms

By following some best practices, you can make the ServiceNow interface a more pleasant place to be:

- Every table needs a form, even if it is basic.
- Forms should read from top to bottom, with important fields at the top left.
- The reference name or number of the record is normally at the top left.
- Lay out the fields in the order you'd fill them in. Users can tab between fields.
- Mandatory fields should be obvious-again, usually towards the top.
- Keep to the standard layout for consistency-two columns at the top and full width at the bottom.

- Keep forms as short as possible. Don't include unnecessary fields. Views can be very useful for providing targeted designs.

- Use annotations to create section separators (not form sections) to partition content on the page and provide a logical hierarchy or workflow of the data.

- For larger forms, use form sections. These are useful for creating tabs.

- Fields with multiple lines (such as descriptions or comments) should expand across the whole page, not half of it. This means they go at the bottom of the form.

Adding related and embedded lists

We've already covered related lists when discussing reference fields, but they come with a few disadvantages. Embedded lists remove some of those constraints:

- Embedded lists can be placed anywhere on the form, rather than just at the bottom.

- Since related lists show related records, they will only be displayed on a saved record. If it is unsaved, no records can be linked. Embedded lists will show at all times.

Embedded related lists are not always appropriate, though. They are designed to have an interface where you often create new related records with minimum information. There is no way to disable the creation of new records, for instance. Chapter 2,*Developing Custom Applications* has an example of embedded related lists.

Defining your own related lists

Defined related lists provide a list of any records you want at the bottom of the form. For example, a simple defined related list that lists other rooms on the same floor may be placed on the **Room** form. This helps you quickly navigate between them.

 In order to create a defined related list, we'll need to use a little JavaScript. We'll work through this in more detail in Chapter 3,*Server-Side Control.*

1. Navigate to **System Definition** > **Relationships** and click on **New**. Use the following details, and Save.
   - **Name:** Rooms on the same floor
   - **Applies to table:** Room [x_hotel_room]
   - **Queries from table:** Room [x_hotel_room]
   - **Query with:**

```
(function refineQuery(current, parent) {
    current.addQuery('floor', parent.floor);
})(current, parent);
```

This code extracts records where the floor field is the same as the record we are viewing. Two JavaScript variables are being used here: current is the table you are extracting the records from and parent is the record that is being displayed in the form.

2. Navigate to the **Room** form (**Hotel** > **Rooms**, then choose a record) and add the new related list to the form (**Configure**, then **Related Lists**, then select Rooms on the same floor). You'll now see the other rooms listed as well-useful!

Enjoying views

If you find that you need to include lots of fields in a form or list, consider using views. They enable you to present a different set of elements specific to a situation. For example, in our hotel, a guest may be enrolled in our points program. In that case, we may want two views of user records: a simple uncluttered view for one-time guests (containing the minimum amount of information required to load quickly and without extraneous data) and a more detailed view for frequent visitors (containing extra information to help serve them better).

A system administrator (or a user with the `view_changer` role) can change views by clicking on the name of the table and choosing **View**. Otherwise, the view for the record is set through rules, through the view specified in the module link in the application menu to the left, or it is inherited.

The view of a record is inherited as you navigate through the interface. If you follow reference links, the system will attempt to be consistent and use the same view as before. If there isn't one with the same name, it will show the default one. Be aware of this behavior when you are naming and configuring forms.

Controlling views

View rules (available under **System UI > View Rules**) are a great way to force the display of a particular view. They work with a condition that uses information on the record itself. For example, you may decide to create a VIP view that shows extra fields. The VIP view is then only shown when the VIP field is ticked.

If you need more control, then create a script that can use other information to make the correct choice. A great use case for this is selecting a view based on the role of the logged-in user. Learn how to do this by going through the *Special function calls* section in Chapter 3, *Server-side Control*.

Learn more from the product documentation:
`https://docs.servicenow.com/bundle/helsinki-servicenow-platfor m/page/administer/navigation-and-ui/concept/c_ViewManagement.h tml`.

Views are often useful, but they can become frustrating. You end up managing several forms; for example, if you create a field and want it on all of them, you must repeat yourself several times and change each form separately. And since the view you are using is maintained as you navigate through the interface, be aware of which view you are editing: you may end up creating new views on forms unintentionally.

Menus and modules

To help you navigate applications in ServiceNow, the interface provides you with the **application navigator**-or, as I like to call it, "the menu to the left". At its heart, this is a series of links to either forms or lists of data. They can specify a view name directly, and lists can include a filter, enabling you to decide exactly what the user sees upon clicking on it. This gives you a great deal of control.

What is shown in the application navigator is only natively controlled by roles. However, modules, like all configurations, are stored in a database table-the `sys_app_module` table, to be exact. This gives rise to the possibility of restricting who sees modules in other ways. One example is creating a query business rule on this table to filter modules by group. `Chapter 8`, *Securing Applications and Data*, explores how that is accomplished.

Setting a filter

When providing links to lists, it is a good idea to include a filter. Not only does it let you find the data you are looking for more quickly, but it also reduces the need to immediately create a filter yourself. Often, you aren't interested in records that are 6 months old, for instance, so filter them out of the link. If you always filter the list (to find guests who have recently checked in, for example), why not create a new module so you can jump straight to them?

Speak to the users of the system and understand what they are looking for. Not only can you make their interaction slightly easier, but you can also reduce the load on the instance by only displaying appropriate information. Adding modules is really easy, and it can make a dramatic difference to usability.

Let's create a new module that shows check-ins that have been made today.

1. Navigate to **System Definition** > **Modules** and click on **New**. Use these details, then Save.
   - **Title**: `Check-ins created today`
   - **Application menu**: `Hotel`
   - **Table**: `Check-in [x_hotel_check_in]` (In the Link Type tab)
   - **Filter**: `Created - on - Today`
   - The menu on the left should refresh, and a new option should be available. Try out **Hotel** > **Check-ins created today**.

Building the right modules

Menus and modules should be appropriately named. The navigation filter at the top is incredibly useful for selecting from the enormous list available to you as an administrator. It is also helpful to power users. But the filter only matches on the **Name** parameter. For example, one of the module names that really frustrates me is the name of the link to view all the items in the system log: **All**. The text to find this precise entry will therefore be `all`. Using `log` or `all` or other strings will either produce a lot of completely irrelevant entries or nothing at all, which to me is quite unintuitive. Besides that, **All** is not very descriptive! Something like **All log entries** will help in every respect.

Making the most of the UI

ServiceNow is constantly improving the user interface to help you use the platform more effectively. The version used for fresh instances in Helsinki is UI16, and it takes advantage of modern browsers to provide a clean look while giving some really useful features, some of which are touched on here.

Old browsers (such as IE 7 and 8) can't use UI16 and default back to UI11. Instances that were upgraded from an older version must activate the plugin manually. The product documentation has much more information:

```
https://docs.servicenow.com/bundle/helsinki-servicenow-platform/page/adminis
ter/navigation-and-ui/concept/c_NavigationAndTheUserInterface.html.
```

Finding your way around the interface

Do you lose things? Me too. I lose my hotel key all the time. Perhaps you are writing several difficult scripts that you want just a couple of clicks away, or you need to quickly navigate to a **User** record. **Tags** are a way to collect arbitrary records together, making them easy to find, while **favorites** let you save links very easily. **History** follows you about, so you can easily go back to where you were.

Adding a favorite

The **All Applications** view of the application navigator is very busy, with lots of modules. Start building up some the items you use often so that you can access them quickly. Just click on the start icon next to module you use a lot in the **All Applications** view (**Tables** in **System Definition** is a good one!), and it gets placed in the favorites list. Then, view it by clicking on the star icon in the Application Navigator. You can edit your favorites and change colors and icons through a link at the bottom.

Even better is the ability to drag links (usually from a list) onto the favorites panel. This saves them for one-click access.

 Your favorites are displayed front and center when using your instance through the ServiceNow mobile app.

Since ServiceNow is a real web application, you can obviously add bookmarks through your browser. As you navigate through the platform, you might see the URL change in your browser change. However, you can right click both form headers and list breadcrumbs and choose **Copy URL** to get a cleaner, more precise link.

Seeing back in time

The history list tracks where you have been. Access it through the clock icon in the application navigator. A useful list of records and lists is shown, letting you jump backwards quickly and easily.

Defining a tag

Tags collect records together. To create one, go to a record form. Click on the "more options" button (three dots), and click on **Add Tag**. Type in a label, and hit enter.

Find your tags by navigating to **Self-Service** > **My Tagged Documents**. You may want to add this to your favorites!

Tag configuration is possible by going to **System Definition** > **Tags**. This includes global tags (which show for every user) and dynamic tags (which try to automate the selection of labels for you-for example, the most recently used records or records that meet a certain filter criterion).

Tags can be shared between multiple users and used for filters and in reports. There are also many ways other ways you can add tags, such as through the list context menu and inline editing. The product documentation provides more information:

`https://docs.servicenow.com/use/common_ui_elements/concept/c_Tags.html.`

Connecting with people

Connect is the way to be social with ServiceNow. It provides a real-time chat and messaging system that lets you send files, mention users, and get work done together. The idea of user presence extends even to the form, to encourage collaboration rather than conflict.

Connect uses the HTML5 notifications API to alert you about new messages, even when you aren't actively using your browser. The method depends on your browser and OS, but typically, a little message appears in the top-right corner of your screen. This means that even if you have switched tabs away from ServiceNow at that moment, you can still be alerted that your colleague has found a new cat video.

ServiceNow has released an app for Android and iOS, available in their respective stores. This is very useful for Connect, since chats will use native notifications. So the cats can follow you even up Everest. You can control the notifications you get per conversation:
`https://docs.servicenow.com/use/collaboration/task/t_EditNotif RecAConv.html`

Chatting over records

Opening the **Connect** sidebar is the first step. Click on the Connect icon near your name in the top right to see the sidebar. From here, you can add people from the user table and start a conversation, adding more people to make group chats. If you aren't around when someone starts chatting to you, ServiceNow can alert you through your browser or send an e-mail notification.

While Connect, and instant messaging, is freeform by nature, chatting about the recent political scandal won't help Gardiner Hotels serve guests better. To focus on the topic, you can use Connect in association with records that exist in the database. The staff at Gardiner Hotels love to discuss the peculiarities of the unique rooms, so let's enable conversation recording for the **Room** table. This is done by setting an attribute on the **Room** table's dictionary entry.

1. Navigate to **System Definition** > **Tables** (you set a favorite, right?), find the **Room** entry and open up the record.
2. Then, use the **Menu** button, and click on **Show Dictionary Record**.
3. Under Related Links, click on **Advanced view**.
4. Edit the **Attributes** field as follows, and Save.

    Attributes: `live_feed=true` (If `hasLabels=true` is already there, append with `live_feed=true`, separating the two with a comma.)

To see Connect in action, navigate to a **Room** record. There should now be a **Follow** button. Interested employees at Gardiner Hotel can now follow a room and chat about it.

Live record updates

The idea of working together extends to UI16's ability to show live record updates when two users change details at the same time. This incredibly powerful capability lets users identify whether they are working together and, if not, to start a chat conversation to work things out.

To see how this works, you need two sessions open. The easiest way for a single person to do this is to open a new browser window in private browsing mode(might be called Incognito) and log in again. If possible, and for maximum realism, use another user account, perhaps even another computer!

In both browsers, navigate to the same record-perhaps Room 101. When both of you are there, you should see the profile picture of the other user in the record header at the top of the form. Instantly, you'll know someone else is viewing the same record. In the screenshot below, David Loo is viewing the same record as me.

Next, in one of the browsers, make a change to a field in a record, such as altering the floor number, and click on **Save**. In the other browser window, a little blue circle will appear and the value of the field will be updated, giving them the latest data. Wow!

If the two users disagree on the update, a Connect chat session is the perfect way to resolve it!

Summary

This chapter explored the key design principles that ServiceNow is built on, ensuring the foundations of the platform are well understood. A ServiceNow instance is a single-tenancy design, giving you a great deal of control and independence over how the platform works for you. The architecture of the system relies upon its database to store all configuration and data, so the hosting of ServiceNow gives a redundant pair for maintenance, disaster recovery, and performance reasons.

Creating tables and fields is a fundamental part of administrating ServiceNow. There are many field types available, from strings to URLs and choice fields. The dictionary stores information about each field and can make the values of the field either unique or act as the record's display value.

In a relational system, linking records together is a key part of data design. Reference fields provide links between two records and provide a great deal of capability and configuration choice, such as the ever-useful dot-walking.

The ServiceNow interface is built on lists and forms. These relate to the database tables they display and provide a great deal of functionality, from hierarchical lists to tags and views to filtered modules. UI16 contains some great features to make it really easy to work in, such as favorites, history, Connect, and live form updates

The next chapter will build on the data structure we've started here. We will progress into some of the advanced features of ServiceNow and begin by exploring the developer studio, the one-stop shop for your application. Application scope will start coming into its own, and we will dive into some complex relationships, such as many-to-many.

2
Developing Custom Applications

The ServiceNow platform provides a rich functional interface for getting things done, whether you are building a new application or using it. Chapter 1, *ServiceNow Foundations*, looked at some basic elements, such as creating tables and fields to store your data, and how your data is displayed in tables and fields. This chapter builds on those fundamentals, looking at more ways to connect and model data, build applications faster, and prevent unintended consequences through conflicts. It's a little like having an architect providing that extra flourish to make our hotel not only sturdy, but also work well.

In this chapter, we will cover the following topics:

- How ServiceNow Studio provides a single, integrated IDE that collects everything in one place
- Seeing how applications control the flow of information with myriad of settings and options
- Use Delegated Development to let other users configure your application
- Using hierarchical tables to improve reuse through inheritance
- Connecting records using many-to-many relationships
- Handling the deletion and creation of records through reference fields

Developing applications in Studio

In the previous chapter, we started building the Hotel application. This included defining the data storage needed by building tables, exploring the dictionary, and creating relationships. All these items are in different menus, meaning you need to keep navigating to different places, without a consistent overview.

ServiceNow Studio is designed to help with this. It provides a single location where all the configuration for the app is collected together. This lets you jump among the things you are working on without the clutter of configuration from other areas. Here's how to use it:

1. Open up Studio by navigating to **System Applications > Studio**, click on the **Go** button under **Open Studio**, and then click on **Hotel** in the **Load Applications** dialog.
2. Studio collects all the configuration together, making it easy to find existing artifacts and create new ones. The **Application Explorer** sidebar contains a categorized list of Application Files, while the **Go To** and **Code Search** capabilities lets you jump right to what you want.
3. Using **Application Explorer**, click on **Check-In** Table under **Tables** in **Data Model**.

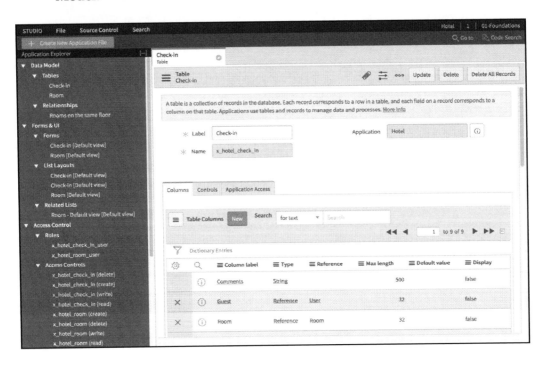

You should see a familiar interface-the same **Table** form we used in Chapter 1, *ServiceNow Foundations*-to add fields to.

4. The **Go-To** search bar is really useful for quickly switching to other artifacts. Click on the **Go-To** link in the top right, or use the Control + Shift + O (Cmd + Shift + O on Mac) keyboard shortcut, and search for Check-In. Several relevant options are available, essentially filtering the items available in **Application Explorer**. For now, click on the **Form** option.

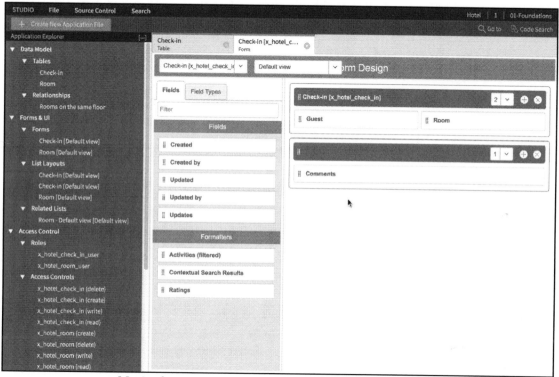

Notice how **Form Designer** has opened in a new tab, keeping the **Table** form accessible with a single click.

5. Click **File**, then **Settings** to open up the **Application Settings** form. This gives many options that control how the application works. Several will be discussed later in this chapter, others as we work through the book. For now, let's make our lives easier by associating the Hotel menu (that appears in the left menu) with our application. It sets the default whenever we create a table. Set the following field, then save.

   - **Menu**: Hotel

6. Another fantastic feature of Studio is **Code Search**. While we will be investigating scripting in the next two chapters, it would be remiss to not point this out. Click on the link in the top right, or press Control + Shift + F (Cmd + Shift + F on Mac) to bring up the dialog. Search for TableUtils and select the **Search in all applications** checkbox to see how it can scan over 20 scripting tables in one go. I can't tell you how much time this saves!

Ensure you try out all the features of Studio. Letting you easily and quickly find and switch between all the items you are creating will really help you accelerate your application development.

Recording files

Application Explorer shows all the application files associated with the application. Every time you make any configuration, an entry is made in the **Application Files** [sys_metadata] table. This associates the table, form, e-mail notification, or script that you made with your application. But which application is that? Let's find out:

- If you are using ServiceNow Studio, the configuration you make is always associated with the application you opened Studio against (this is listed in the top right of the Studio interface).
- In the standard interface, the application you are editing is the one you selected in **System Settings**. This can be changed by clicking on the cog icon next to your name, going to **Developer**, and then choosing it from the **Application Menus** selector. (It's much easier if you enable the **Show application picker in header** option.)

Consider the application file's application as metadata that provides the instance with information about the configuration.

Follow these steps:

1. To see what Application Files are created, click on the blue **Create New Application File** button in the Studio interface. The dialog that appears does a much better job of organizing the platform-configuration options into logical categories than the standard application navigator, providing help text and great filtering. Notice how there are almost 80 options-and that doesn't even cover them all! Close the dialog when done.

2. Normally, you don't need to worry about the application files and the data they store. The instance looks after it. However, let's open one up to see how it works. The Application File for a configuration artifact is always accessible through the menu of the record. Open up the **Check-In** table record (use the **Application Explorer** or **Go To** search, or just click on the tab if it's open), and then choose **Show File Properties** from the **Additional Actions** menu.

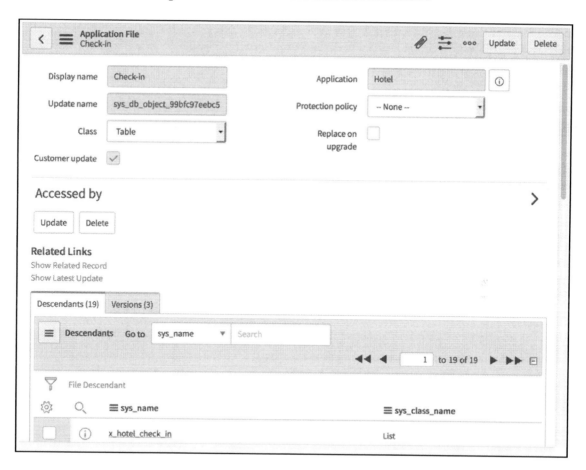

Several interesting options are available in the application file. The related lists at the bottom show any related items (the fields in the **Check-In** table are listed, for example), while **Versions** stores the changes that the record has gone through.

Versioning is incredibly useful for scripts. It can show you, using a line-by-line difference view, how your code has evolved over time. Chapter 10, *Packaging with Applications, Update Sets, and Upgrades* dives into this-and the **Protection policy** field-in more detail.

Scoping out limits

Running multiple applications on the ServiceNow platform brings benefits of scale. You may have IT using it to organize production issues, HR may perform case management, while the maintenance team use it to track leaky taps-each using separate, specialist applications that are built for their use. Since you are using a single platform, it makes it possible to share some data.

The **Users** table is a great example of this. While each department will want to control the privileges that each person has (someone from the facilities team probably shouldn't have access to all the payroll data), sharing the core data means there is one place to go and update. If you change your name, isn't it nice to do it on one system, without relying on complex integrations to simulate a cohesive system?

The diagram below represents how many applications all need to reply upon shared resources, like the user table.

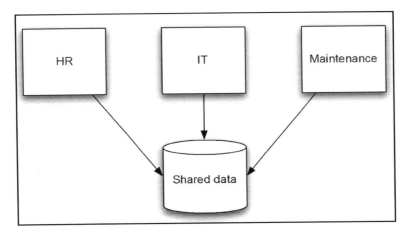

Also, you often want applications to talk to each other. Consider that a new employee is joining Gardiner Hotels. As part of HR's "onboarding" process, several activities need to take place: the employee needs to be given an ID badge, undergo some training, get issued a mobile phone, and more. Each of these activities may be handled by different teams: HR might ask IT to provide the new employee with the phone, while the Facilities Maintenance team could create ID badges. Having the HR application automatically interface with the IT app saves time and increases productivity by eliminating double typing and miscommunication.

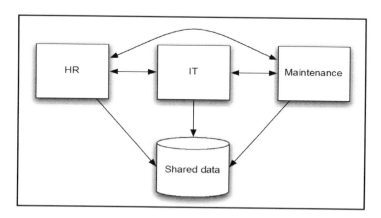

But this level of integration also causes challenges. The HR application can contain sensitive data-how do you ensure the IT app doesn't access it? The HR team needs to know that the rules and policies in place can't be circumvented, that another app doesn't have free access. And what exactly is in the HR app? Applications scope separate functionality, at both a naming level, and to provide extra security.

Separating by name

The previous chapter discussed how `sys_id` is the unique identifier for the majority of items you build. This lets you have multiple records that otherwise look identical-while people will get confused, the system will cope just fine with having 500 groups with the same name.

But some things are referred to by name, especially in code. A few notable examples are tables, roles and Script Includes (discussed in `Chapter 3`, Server-Side Control). It would be very cumbersome to refer to the **Check-in** table in a script as `84fc62b1eb111200e744e08a5206fee8` in order to ensure the right one is identified. And just by looking at the `sys_id`, you have no idea which application that table is part of.

So, for items that can be accessed across many applications, the platform uses a slightly more user-friendly system of scope names. This uniquely identifies your configuration, and makes ownership very obvious.

The scope name is made up of two parts-a vendor prefix and the application name:

- The vendor prefix is generated when the instance is created. It cannot be chosen. It is shared across all the instances of a customer. If you are using a developer instance, you will have a vendor prefix that looks like x_69373.

  It is called the vendor prefix because it shows who created the application. In Chapter 10, *Packaging with Applications, Update Sets, and Upgrades*, we see how applications can be downloaded from the ServiceNow App Store.

- The application name is specified when the application is created. We chose hotel in the previous chapter.

The two are joined with underscores (<vendor>_<app>), and every time an application is created, it is registered with a central ServiceNow repository to ensure uniqueness.

This scope name is then used as the prefix for many configuration elements, including the real table name (<vendor>_<app>_<table>), role (<vendor>_<app>.<role>), and Script Includes (<vendor>_<app>.<name>).

By including the scope in the name of these items, we ensure that there will never be two tables named the same, even if apps are shared over many different instances.

Seeing the scope

As you start exploring the platform, you will often see notices that you are editing configuration that belongs to another application, especially the global application. Unless you take ownership of that configuration and put it into your current application (often not a good idea, since it is global so everyone has access), you would need to switch scope to make the changes.

The global application is where most ServiceNow functionality lies. It means there are no scope controls, and all applications can use it.

To see this in action, follow these steps:

1. Close Studio (if open) and using the standard interface, and click on the settings menu (the cog icon, top right of the screen).
2. Switch to the Developer tab, and toggle on the **Show application picker in header** option. Once done, close the dialog. You should see that the application picker is now available in the interface.
3. Navigate to **System Properties** > **System**. You should receive a message saying you are in the wrong scope, and that all of the properties are read-only.

This record is in the Global application, but Hotel is the current application. To edit this record click here.

4. Using the application picker, switch to global. The properties page should refresh. The message should have gone, and the properties will be editable. If you wanted to switch temporarily, just for that just, you can click the link in the message. This would not change what application those elements belonged to however.
5. Once done, ensure you switch back into the Hotel application.

Note the consequences of this: by switching temporarily to global, you will be not be associating your work with the application you are building.

Moving between applications

Whilst you can move items between applications, it is typically not a good idea. It is a bad idea if you move items from global to an application, and a *really* bad idea if you move global platform functionality to an application.

If, nonetheless, you mistakenly create a record and it is associated with the wrong application, use the **Move to application**... option in the Additional actions menu.

Moving configuration into an application means it'll be treated as part of that application. Any protection mechanisms (as discussed in the next section) will start to apply. This means that other apps that were dependent upon it may break. For example, if a piece of shared data that was used by both HR and IT is moved into the HR app, the IT application may not be able to access it any longer. The protection mechanism available to applications are discussed in the next section.

 Additionally, as discussed in `Chapter 10`, *Packaging with Applications, Update Sets, and Upgrades* applications can be uninstalled. If you move platform functionality into an application, and then uninstall it, bad things could happen. Don't do it!

Enforcing the separation

Consider your ServiceNow applications as a room (or floor) within a building (what an original metaphor, right?). While open-plan living is sometimes an advantage, it doesn't afford much privacy. Sometimes you want a door (and lock) to stop people wandering in and out of your room.

The ServiceNow platform gives you control. It acts as the application's doorman, deciding what comes in and what can go out. We'll see that there are many ways to be specific about how apps can affect each other. This is especially important when you install apps you haven't developed yourself.

Whenever the platform performs an action, it checks to see if it crosses a scope boundary. If a script was run in an IT scope, it will have access to all the tables and data that belong to the IT app. But it may not have access to data in the HR scope. The scope acts as the containing bubble; if all the elements have the same scope, it's fine. But the doorman will intervene if it crosses the boundary.

 Much of the functionality delivered with the ServiceNow platform (for example, the ITSM applications) are not actually held within an application, but are associated with Global. This is not an application per se, but the absence of one. Functionality in Global is like being in the living room. It's fair game for everyone-no control.

Taking control of your application

ServiceNow provides three key features to control what and who comes in and out of the application bubble:

- **Delegated Development** can grant users special privileges to work with your application – but *only* with this app. You can, for example, give a user the ability to create reports for the Hotel application, but unless you grant other (perhaps global) privileges, the user won't be able to create reports for another.

- **Scoped Administration** (to be renamed Local Administration) restricts global administrators from accessing the application. Typically, if you have the System Administrator (admin) role, you have access to everything on the instance. With Scoped Administration, this may no longer be the case. Scoped Administration is discussed more in Chapter 8, *Securing Applications and Data*.

- **Application Access** controls how multiple applications work together. The two controls above work with users; Application Access lets you decide if the functionality of one application (in particular, the data structure) should be shared with others. Normally, a script running on the instance will have full access to the database, as we'll see in the next few chapters. Application Access controls that.

Delegating to developers

To build applications in ServiceNow, you've usually needed to give a user the admin role. As discussed in Chapter 8, *Securing Applications and Data*, the admin role gives System Administrative abilities; you get access to the whole instance, and all the global configuration available to it. That's a lot of power, if you only need to build a single app!

Delegated Development allows a user to get privileges to edit specific parts of a single application. This stops the need for granting powerful, system wide permissions to many users, giving much better separation of duties.

To see how it works, follow these steps.

1. Firstly, identify a test user who currently doesn't have any development permissions. Ross Spurger in the demo data is a great choice.

2. Let's use a feature we'll learn about more in Chapter 8, *Securing Applications and Data*, impersonation. Impersonation allows us to login in as that user, without knowing their password. In the standard interface, open the user menu (click your name, top left) and choose **Impersonate User**.

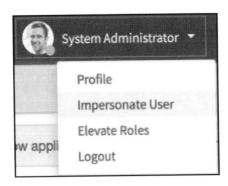

3. In the selection box, choose Ross Spurger. The interface will refresh, you can now interact with ServiceNow as this user. Note that the only options in the left menu are Self-Service and Collaborate.

4. Finish your impersonation by using the User menu and clicking **Impersonate User** again. Pick your admin user (likely to be System Administrator).

5. Let's give Ross the capability to edit the Hotel app. Open up Studio by navigating to **System Applications** > **Studio**, then click **Go** in the Open Studio section.
6. Select Hotel from the Applications list.
7. From the File menu, click **Manage Developers**.
8. In the Developers filter box, select Ross Spurger. The options you can grant to Ross are shown in the right pane.
9. Toggle on All File Types, and click Save.

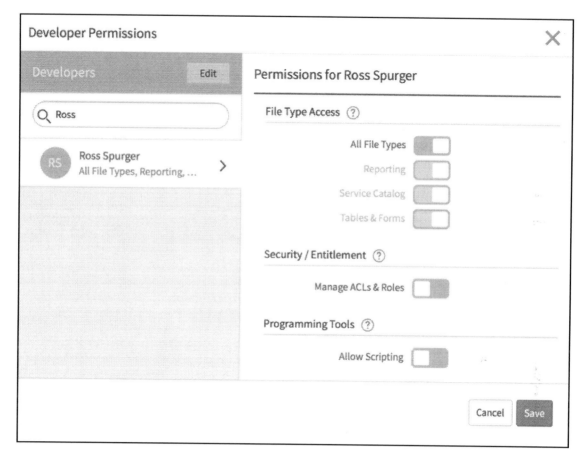

10. To see what this change has resulted in, close Studio, and impersonate Ross Spurger again by repeating steps 2 and 3.
11. Immediately, you can see that there are many more options available to Ross. Navigate to **System Definition** > **Tables**.

12. As a global administrator, you would see over 2000 tables. As Ross, you would see only two: **Check-in** and **Rooms**. Those are the only two tables that are associated with the Hotel application.

The product documentation explains the different developer permissions that are available: `https://docs.servicenow.com/bundle/helsinki-app lication-development/page/build/applications/task/t_AddADevelo per.html`.

13. End your impersonation by repeating step 4, so you are back as the normal System Administrator.

Allowing other applications access

Having two applications working together can be quite nonintuitive, so I'll use an extended example. Consider that HR has built a wonderful custom application for their use. It stores information about every employee at Gardiner Hotels, in an employee profile table. There are several fields containing information, such as whether they are a contractor, permanent employee, or intern. It's kept up to date by the HR team.

This type of data is really useful for other departments, too. So, the HR team has added lots of security rules (discussed in `Chapter 8`, *Securing Applications and Data*) to control sensitive information.

The facilities team wants to leverage this regularly updated data source and record what assets an employee has. The latest mobile technology is used at Gardiner Hotels, and some employees like it so much, they want to keep using it even when they leave the company. The facilities team doesn't really like this!

To help with this, the facilities team proposes to add a field to the employee profile table. It might store the serial number of the device, so the facilities teams knows which employee has which device. Even though this table is associated with the HR app, facilities wants its configuration as part of their own app so that they can control and update it.

This split control is key to the scenario. In this example, the facilities team is relying upon the HR employee profile table but also wants to add some functionality to their own app that they look after.

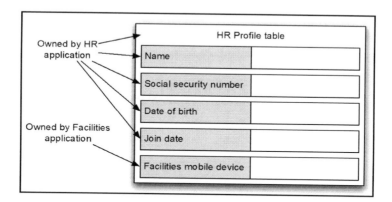

If the HR team wants to let this happen (and therefore have their data structure changed), they would tick the **Allow configuration** checkbox in the Table record. This lets other applications add to the table. (Navigate to **System Definition** > **Tables** to see the option,)

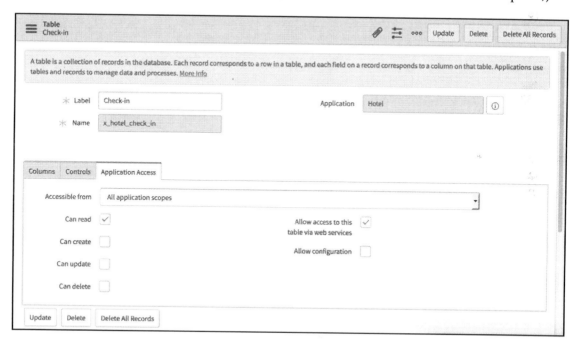

Note that although you can add fields to the table, you cannot change the default form. That belongs to HR. The facilities team could create a new view, or the HR team would still need to add the field to the default form. The facilities team, though, could control other items, like choice-list options.

Controlling application access

As you might have seen from the screenshot above, there are more ways to control what other apps can do. The starting point of **Application Access** is the **Accessible from** option:

- **This application scope** means that no other application can affect this table. Use this when you don't want to share any data at all.
- **All application scopes** lets you be more granular. This default option then lets you specify exactly what those applications can do.

The first four options (**Can read**, **Can create**, **Can update**, and **Can delete**) affect scripting. Every application can includes code that may attempt to interact with any tables in the database; these controls stop that. By default, **Can read** is checked, meaning scripts can look at data, but do nothing else. **Allow access to this table via web services** pretty much works as you think: if it's checked, outside systems can connect and work with the data, as long as they follow the right security rules (Chapter 7, *Exchanging Data – Import Sets, Web Services, and other Integrations*, and Chapter 8, *Securing Applications and Data* provide much more information on web services and security rules).

 These options work at runtime, or when the application is being used. The platform ensures that these rules are enforced, so a HR application can ensure that their data is secure, as they need to.

Restricting your choices during development

In addition to controlling the ability of other apps to interact, you can also decide what you (and your application) can see and do. One option is to reduce the selection of tables shown within the platform.

Whilst that may sound not very useful, it can help you from making mistakes. For example, it guides you away from building configuration that is dependent on others applications. To turn this option on, open up Studio, use the File menu and select Settings. The **Restrict Table Choices** option can be toggled on there.

The application settings record also stores about how your application interacts with others. By default, the instance notices what you are working with, and if it is using functionality outside of your application, it is recorded.

When you were making the Relationships in `Chapter 1`, *ServiceNow Foundations,* you may have noticed the following message:

> Access to API 'ScopedGlideRecord' from scope 'x_hotel' was granted and added to 'x_hotel' cross-scope privileges

And if you look at the bottom of the Hotel application settings, you will see this recorded:

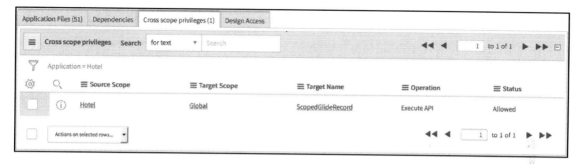

The cross scope privileges list tells you what functionality stored outside of your app that your application is using. In this case, ScopedGlideRecord (used in the code of the relationship, and explored in much more detail in the next chapter) is flagged, with a status of allowed. Of course, you can review this list and decide not to grant access privileges. By default, cross scope access is recorded and allowed; you can turn this around by changing the Runtime Access Tracking to Enforcing.

If you did decide to revoke the access of ScopedGlideRecord, the **Rooms on the same floor Related** List would not work properly any longer. Specifically, you would get an error message when you visited the Room form, and you would see all the rooms across all floors.

> Access to api 'ScopedGlideRecord' from scope 'x_hotel' has been refused due to insufficient privileges granted to scope 'x_hotel'

Building hierarchical tables

Chapter 1, *ServiceNow Foundations,* introduced the foundations of ServiceNow. One of the most fundamental parts of an application is how it stores its data, and we saw how virtually everything you see and do in the platform is stored in the database.

Specifically, ServiceNow is built on a relational database. Instances hosted by ServiceNow use MySQL, a popular open source database that is robust, well featured, and scalable. These kinds of relational databases are relatively simple to understand, which is one of the reasons they are most commonly used: data is held in tables and columns, and relationships may exist between rows.

The ServiceNow platform can run on almost any relational database, such as Oracle or SQL Server. But supporting different architectures is difficult, so it is not a standard offering.

Benefiting from an object-oriented design

The simplicity of a relational database means that, on its own, it does not easily represent the data structures used in modern object-oriented programming languages. One particularly useful function of an object-oriented approach is **inheritance**.

Inheritance allows one object to build on the functionality of another. Why duplicate effort when you can reuse existing capability?

In ServiceNow, a table can inherit another. The parent table defines the base functionality, while the child table, built on top, can continue to use it. That means that any fields you add to the base table are automatically available to the child as well. In fact, almost all functionality you add to the base table is available to the child.

Inheritance is another solution to allowing facilities to use HR's Employee Profile table, as mentioned previously. It means that there are two separate tables, but facilities would benefit from all the work that HR did.

In our hotel application, we want to store information about our guests. We need to know their names, their telephone numbers, and perhaps their addresses. ServiceNow has got a built-in table for storing people: the **User** table. But we want a special type of person: guest. Let's keep staff in the **User** table and guests in a new extension table.

> The **User** table in ServiceNow defines who can log in and use the platform's functionality. Sometimes, you need a contact database, which stores information about people: their names, phone numbers, location, and who their manager might be. It's tempting to build the contact database as a separate table and keep the two separate, but I recommend using the **User** table as the basis for both. It saves the duplication of data and allows reuse of the special functionality that is built specifically for the built-in table.

Extending the User table

Let's extend the ServiceNow **User** table in order to have a special class for guests. We'll try to us the Studio as much as possible to see how it works.

First, we have to mark the **User** table as extendable. This needs to be done in the main interface, since the **User** table is in **Global** (keep the Studio window open-it's useful having both accessible).

1. Go to **System Definition** > **Tables** and find the **User**[sys_user] table. (Ensure you find the right one – the name is sys_user. When you enter the form, you should get a message at the top of your screen saying this record is not part of the hotel app. Click on the link to edit the record.

> This means the change to the User table will not be recorded as part of the application. Alternatives to this (such as Update Sets) is Packaging applications is discussed in Chapter10, *Packaging with Applications, Update Sets, and Upgrades.*

2. Make the following change and save it once you're done:
   - **Extensible**: <ticked> (In the Controls tab)

3. Now, return to Studio, and choose **Create New Application File**. Choose **Table**, click **Create** and fill out the following data:
   - **Label**: Guest
   - **Extends table**: User

4. Click the Submit button to create the table.
5. If you look at the fields available in this new table, you'll see lots of fields already, besides the normal automatic five. These additional fields are those defined in the User table.

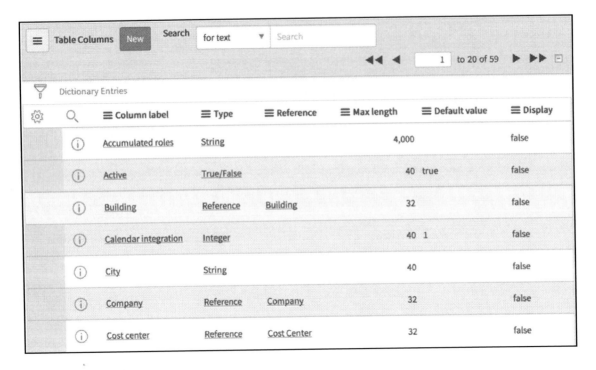

What does this mean? The Guest table has *inherited* the fields of the **User** table. I don't need to create new name, telephone, and e-mail fields-they are already available for use in the Guest table.

Indeed, when you create a table that inherits another, you gain all the functionality of the parent. Most of the scripts, rules, and policies of the parent automatically apply to the new table. But sometimes, you want to create the functionality only for the child table. To this end, ServiceNow lets you place it at the level you need.

 We'll cover how scripts are handled in ServiceNow in the next chapter.

Interacting with hierarchical tables

Our new table is the right place for storing information about our valued customers. While useful fields have been inherited from the **User** table, it doesn't contain everything. Let's make a new field to store the membership number of our guests..

1. Click on the Create New Application File button, choose **Table Column**, click **Create,** then fill out the following fields and **Save.:**
   - **Table:** Guest
   - **Type:** String
   - **Column label:** Membership number
   - **Max length:** 40

2. Next, add it to the form. Click on the **Create New Application File** button, choose **Forms & UI, Form** then click **Next.** Select Guest under My Tables, and click **Create.**

3. Find our new field called **Membership Number** from the list on the left, drag it underneath the **Last name** field in the layout, and click on **Save**.

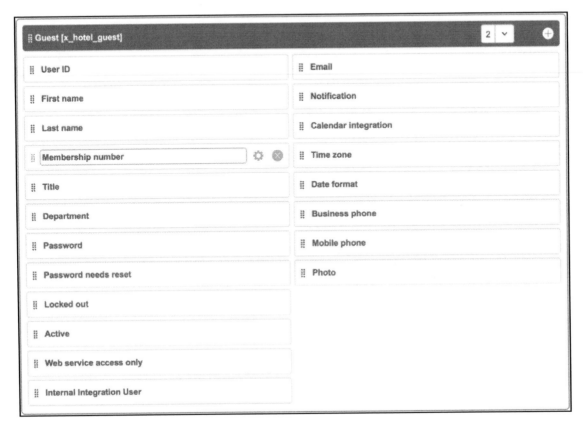

4. To test, let's create a new guest record. Switch to the standard interface, and navigate to **Hotel > Guests**. (You may need to refresh the page to see it.) Click **New**, use this data, and Save.
    - **First name**: Alice
    - **Last name**: Richards
    - **Membership number**: S2E1

Great! We can enter a membership number properly. And if we look at a standard **User** record, such as **Fred Luddy** (**User Administration > Users**), the **Membership number** field does not show up. That's because Fred is a user, not a guest.

Viewing hierarchical tables

You may have noticed that our new guest, Alice, showed up when you visit the **User** table. That's because Alice is both a user *and* a guest. A **Guest** record will be treated just like a **User** record, unless there is something specific that overrides that behavior. In our case, the only difference between a **User** and **Guest** record right now is that the latter has an extra field.

If you want to impress your friends, explain that this behavior is called **polymorphism**. I think it's pretty cool. It lets you use the base or extended functionality as you need it.

But this gives rise to something that confuses many. If I look at the **Guest** table, I can add, through **Personalize List**, the **Membership number** field.

However, if I try to add a **Membership number** field to the **User** table, I can't. Why?

This is because a **User** record doesn't have a membership number; only a **Guest** record does. Think carefully about where you position fields to ensure they can be seen at the right level.

Extended fields are not available while dot-walking. The **Membership number** field would not be available when dot-walking through a **User reference** field.

The **Allow base table lists to include extended table fields** property in UI **Properties** changes this for the UI. Scripts can use a special syntax when dot-walking. This is mentioned in Chapter 3, *Server-side Control,* and Chapter 5, *Getting Things Done with Tasks.*

Overriding field properties

Inherited fields allow you to easily reuse functionality. However, sometimes, you want the fields in the extended table to work differently from the base table. This is accomplished with dictionary overrides.

For example, let's change the default time zone for new guests so that it's different from the **User** table's. The current default for **Users** is the system time zone, and **Guests** inherits this setting.

1. Navigate to the dictionary entry for the **Time zone** field. Accomplish this in the Studio by clicking on the Guest table entry at the top of the Application Explorer list. In the Columns tab, find the Time zone field, and click on it.

2. Once there, look for the **Dictionary Overrides** Related List. Click on **New**, use the following data, and Save.
   - **Table**: Guest [x_hotel_guest]
   - **Override default value**: <ticked>
   - **Default value**: Europe/London (or your own choice!)

   Now, when you create a new **Guest** record, it sets the default time zone to Europe/London. Any new **User** records will be unaffected.

You can also change field labels so that they are different for the base and extended tables. Navigate to **System Definition** > **Language File** and create a new entry, populating **Table** with the extended table name (such as x_hotel_guest). The **Element** field should be the field name.

Understanding the background behavior

You might be wondering how this all works. Let's have a look.

A child table is a normal database table. However, it does not recreate all the fields of the parent. Instead, the only columns in that new table are the new fields. For example, if I were to run the DESCRIBE x_hotel_guest SQL command on the database, I'd only see two fields: u_membership_number and sys_id.

So, when I look at Alice's record in the **Guest** table, the ServiceNow platform is actually joining the parent table and child table behind the scenes. ServiceNow takes the independent tables and (invisibly) joins them, creating the illusion of a single, bigger table.

Our friend, the `sys_id` field, enables the platform to do this. If you remember, the `sys_id` field uniquely identifies a record. In the case of an extended table, the `sys_id` field is actually stored in two places: the parent and child tables. The platform joins both together whenever you query the **Guest** table. The following image shows how this works:

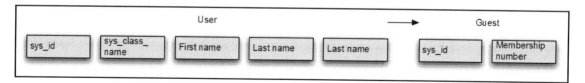

When you mark a table as extendable, you are also adding a second system field: **Class** (`sys_class_name`). It contains the name of the table that the record represents. For example, the User record representing Fred would have `sys_user` in the **Class** field, while the User record for Alice would be `u_guest`. With this information, ServiceNow can join tables if necessary and present you with the appropriate data.

There are actually two models for table extension: **hierarchical** and **flat**. The hierarchical method consists of multiple tables that are joined together as needed, as just described, while a flat structure consists of one very large table with all the columns of every table. When you make a new table and add a new field, in reality, it is simply adding another column to the base table. The platform again hides this from the user. The majority of the time this does not have an impact on how table extension works in ServiceNow and is purely undertaken for performance reasons. (The one occasion when this does matter is if you try to add more than 10 large string fields to a flattened table due to the MySQL row size limit. The Task table, discussed in `Chapter 5`, *Getting Things Done with Tasks*, suffers from this.)

The ServiceNow interface knows about this behavior. When you navigate to a record, ServiceNow will always show you its actual class. So, even if I am viewing a list of **Users**, when I click on **Alice**, I will see the **Guest** form, with all of the appropriate attributes.

Making it visual with the Schema Map

Sometimes it can be difficult to understand how this is structured. To help, use the schema map. It is really useful for visualizing what is going on.

1. In the standard interface, navigate to **System Definition** > **Tables**, and select the **User** [sys_user] table.
2. At the bottom of the form, in the Related Links section, click on **Show Schema Map**. For clarity, tick only the **Show extended tables** and **Show extending tables** checkboxes.
3. The following screenshot shows how the Guest table is related to the User table:

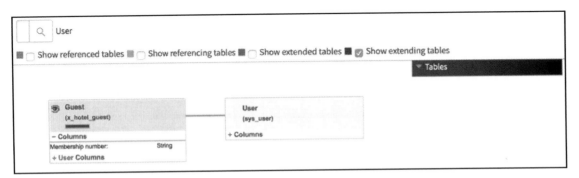

 The product documentation has more information on the schema map: ht
tps://docs.servicenow.com/bundle/helsinki-servicenow-platform/
page/administer/table-administration/concept/c_SchemaMapForTab
les.html.

Changing class

Once a record is stored in a particular table, a neat trick you can learn is moving it. If I decide that Alice is actually a user, I can alter the value of the **Class** field. The platform will drop any information specific to the **Guest** schema and start treating the record just like a **User** record. The **Class** field can be added to a form or list and is represented as a choice list. Often, you will want it to be read-only.

 The ability to change the class is a powerful feature, and you should be aware of the consequences. It is unusual to reclassify a record, and that may throw off reporting; for example, if you counted 10 users and nine guests, and suddenly one switched, you might have an overbooking. If there is data in a column that is not on the new table, it is lost. Be careful!

So far, we've discussed how you can add fields into a specific class and seen how they are inherited. But this will work with much more than fields! As we work through the chapters, we'll see how functionality such as business rules, access control rules, and import sets all benefit from hierarchical tables.

Repointing the reference field

At the moment, there is a field on the Check-in table called Guest that is actually pointing to the user table. Now we have a dedicated place for our valued customers, lets change that reference field.

1. In Studio, select the **Check-in** table from the Application Explorer.
2. In the Table Columns list, edit the Guest reference from User to be Guest. Do this by double-clicking on the cell, changing the value, then clicking the green tick, as per the screenshot below.

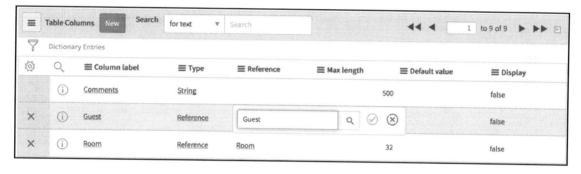

3. While we are improving the Check-in table, let's tidy up the Check-in related list. As mentioned in Chapter 1, *ServiceNow Foundations*, it's better to keep long string fields off lists.
4. Click on **Check-in** under List Layouts in the Application Explorer. Remove comments from the selected column and click Save.

Many-to-many relationships

Another type of relationship between records is many-to-many. The relationship between siblings is many-to-many. I can have many brothers and sisters, as can they. But how can I store this information? A reference field can only point to one record.

Adding a lot of reference fields into a form is one way. I could create as many reference fields as I have siblings. However, that's not great design. What if another brother or sister were born? Making new fields every time a new baby arrives is not cool.

Instead, we could create another table that sits in between two records, acting as the "glue" that sticks them together. This many-to-many table has two reference fields, each pointing to a different side of the relationship.

In the hotel application, we want to take reservations for our guests. Each reservation might be for more than one person, and each person might have more than one reservation. This sounds like the perfect use for a many-to-many table. Here's a representation:

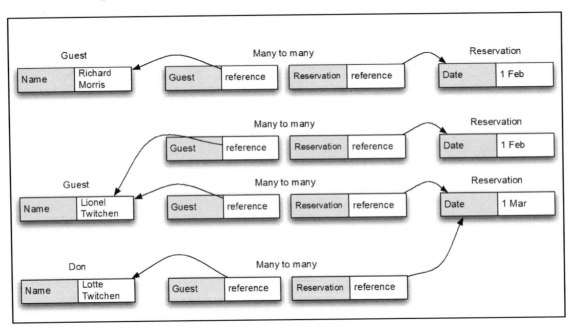

The diagram shows how it might work out. Richard is staying one night, on 1 Feb. That's easy enough. Lionel is staying two nights, on 1 Feb and 1 Mar. He liked our hotel so much that he came back, and encouraged his wife Lotte to stay with him.

The ServiceNow platform makes this a little easier to visualize, since it hides the complexities of the many-to-many table in most situations. It focuses on the records in the two target tables.

Building a many-to-many table

Let's begin building a many-to-many table. To do this, perform the following steps in Studio:

1. Click **Create New Application File**, select **Table**, then **Create**. Fill out the form, and Save.
   - **Label**: Reservation

2. Using the Table Columns related list, add the first date field to the table:
   - **Column label**: Arrival
   - **Type:**Date
   - Then add another, as below:
   - **Column label**: Departure
   - **Type:**Date

3. Finally, since we want to reserve a room, let's also create a reference field called **Room**:
   - **Column label**: Room
   - **Type:**Reference
   - **Reference:**Room [x_hotel_room]

4. Click **Submit** to save.

5. Then, click **Create New Application File**, select **Many to Many Definition**, then **Create**. Use the following data to fill out the form.
   - **From table**: Reservation [x_hotel_reservation]
   - **To table**: Guest [x_hotel_guest]

   The **From** and **To** tables are where we want to point our reference fields. It doesn't matter which way round you do it.

You'll see the other fields populate automatically. Make sure the table name makes sense – but leave the m2m part in, so you know what it is. The default (x_hotel_m2m_guests_reservations) makes sense in this case.

It should look like this:

 The way to do this in the standard interface is by entering sys_m2m.list in the filter text in the application navigator. It accepts a few shortcuts like this. For example, <table_name>.form will display the form of the table.

6. Click on **Create Many to Many**.
7. Finally, click **Create New Application File**, select **Related List**from **Forms & UI**, and click **Next**. Choose the **Guest** table, and click **Create**. Add in the new **Reservations** entry into the Selected column, remove all the others and click **Save**.
8. If you look at Alice Richard's Guest record in the standard interface, you should see the related list, as below:

Adding fields to a many-to-many table

Sometimes, just having the two reference fields in the many-to-many table is enough. However, since it is a real table, you can also add new fields to it. This technique is useful for identifying something particular about the relationship. Let's use this capability to store who the lead passenger in a reservation is:

1. In Studio, open the table record by finding **M2m Guests Reservations** at the top of the Application Explorer, and clicking it. Unfortunately, the default label is a little ugly, so change it as below.
   - **Label:** Guests Reservations

2. Then, add the following fields to the table, using the Table Columns.
   - **Column label:** Lead
   - **Type:** True/False

3. Once done, click **Update**.

   Once we added the Reservations list to the Guest form, we can see what reservations a guest has. Let's now add the Guests list to the Reservations form, and view the many-to-many table the other way round.

   Click **Create New Application File**, select **Related List** from **Forms & UI**, and click **Next**. Choose the **Reservation** table, and click **Create**. Add in the **Guests** entry into the Selected column, and click Save.

4. Let's check our reservations work. Jump into the normal interface, and navigate to Hotel > Reservations. Click New, and specify some sample Arrival, Departure and Room values. Once done, click Save.

5. Let's create a quick way to add a guest to the reservation. Right click on the field headers of the Guest Related list, and choose Configure, List Control, like the screenshot:

7. Fill out the following fields, and click Submit.
   - **List edit insert row**: `<ticked>`

8. You can then use list editing on the related list to record the information you want.

Comparing reference fields and many-to-many tables

Many-to-many tables are very flexible, but by using them, you lose some of the advantages of simple reference fields. The biggest disadvantage is that you can't dot-walk in the same way. This makes scripting more challenging.

Also, with a simple list view, you can't easily identify related records. One way round this is through hierarchical list views, which we will discuss later.

We'll look at further disadvantages of many-to-many tables as we progress.

Deleting a many-to-many table

Deleting a many-to-many table isn't straightforward. You need to do it in two parts: delete the table, and then delete the entry from the `sys_m2m` table. However, there are security rules that prevent you from deleting records in this table. You will need to disable or modify those rules to proceed. But beware of what you are doing!

Choosing lists

An alternative to many-to-many tables are list fields.

You may hear lists being referred to as **Glide lists**.

Lists store an array of `sys_id` values. That means that one field can reference multiple records. One field can work in a similar way to a many-to-many table. In our earlier example, a **List** field could be added to the **Reservations** form instead, pointing to the **Guest** table.

One disadvantage of lists is the interface. It is more difficult to interact with compared to other fields, both on the list and the forms, since there are more clicks and buttons. Also, since it contains multiple values, you can't dot-walk through it-which one would you walk to?

When you want to reference many records, compare the different advantages of the two approaches:

- Lists are represented as fields. They are more compact than many-to-many tables, and many built-in functions in ServiceNow accept comma-separated reference fields as input. For example, a comma-separated list of users can easily be sent an e-mail. Glide lists are usually simpler to deal with.
- Many-to-many relationships are represented as records in a table. This means there is no limit to the number of records stored, and you can easily extend the functionality. You can add extra fields (such as representation of the lead passenger). It also has better hooks for scripts and other functionalities. Many-to-many tables are generally more flexible.
- Reference fields deal with the deletion of the target data really well, as we'll see. Lists don't; they stay unaltered, meaning that sys_ids of records that don't exist anymore may hang around.

Cascading with reference fields

Reference fields are pretty special in ServiceNow. They let you link two records, letting you associate things such as which room you just checked in to. It represents a relationship that makes sense for your data.

Almost every reference field uses `sys_id` values to join records. But you do have the power to specify another field, by populating the **Reference** key in the advanced settings of the dictionary. This requires careful consideration for it to make sense, though.

Relationships change, though. Wouldn't it be great to create the other side if needed? And clear up broken links when one side goes? At least in ServiceNow, this is possible.

Dynamic creation

What happens if you try to associate with a record that doesn't exist, such as performing a check-in for a guest that has never been to the hotel before? If you type a name into the reference field that doesn't match an existing record, then the red background warns the user that the record won't be saved properly. Indeed, if you try, you will get a message saying **Invalid update**.

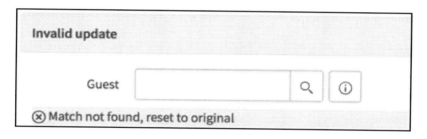

One way to create a record quickly is to use the reference icon and click on the **New** button in the list in the popup window. You then get a form that you can fill out, which comes with a **Save** button. But a faster way is to use **dynamic creation**, which allows you to type the name directly into the reference field. Here's how:

1. In Studio, click on the **Check-In** table in the Application Explorer, and in the Table Columns list, find **Guest** and click on it.
2. In the Guest Dictionary Entry form, click on **Advanced View** under **Related Link**. Make the following changes in the Reference Specification section and **Save.**
   - **Dynamic creation**: `<ticked>`

Note there is a Dynamic creation script field, but the default functionality works well enough.

3. Now, try going back to the **Check-In** table, and type in the name of a guest that hasn't been created. Instead of red, it will have a green background. This indicates that the record will be created.

By default, the new record will have the display value populated. For a **User** record, the display value is a field, called **Name**, that is actually dynamically created from the **First name** and **Last name** fields. The scripts for the **User** table will organize the data in the most appropriate place.

When you turn on dynamic creation, you'll see an area in the dictionary for scripting a more complex scenario. Sometimes, this is helpful, if only to flag that this record was dynamically created. Often, you want to track this happening, since it is very easy to create lots of duplicates with dynamic creation; for example, is it Tom, Thomas, or Tommy?

Deleting records

When you click on the **Delete** button in a form or a list, the platform removes the record from the database. But what if there is a reference-field value that points to that record? The **Check-in** table has a reference field that points to the **Room** table. If we delete a **Room** record, what happens to the **Check-in** records?

There are several ways in which ServiceNow can deal with the situation, and you can choose what happens with the dictionary entry of a reference field:

- By default (or when the choice is set to Clear), the platform will empty the reference fields that point to that record. When deleting a Room record, all of the Check-in records that point to it will have the Room field emptied.
- Delete or Cascade: Any record that pointed to the deleted record is also deleted. This means that deleting a room would also delete all the Check-in records that pointed to it! Delete no workflow is an extension of this; with this option, only directly related records will be deleted (it does not cascade).
- Restrict: This option will stop the transaction if there are related records. If there are any records pointing to the deleted record, then the deletion will be aborted. The platform will prevent you from deleting the room. This is the most conservative option, useful for preventing mistakes.

For instance, once a room has been checked in to, you may not want to delete it. You should first contact the customers staying there and let them know that a wrecking ball may come through their walls!

- **None**: This option will mean that the platform does not alter any related records. Reference fields will stay populated with a `sys_id` value that points to an invalid record.

The majority of the time, the default option of `Clear` is the right choice. It does mean, however, that you lose information when deletions occur. So, in general, the best idea is not to delete anything! Users should be deactivated in production systems, not deleted.

> If you accidentally delete something, it may be found by navigating to **System Definition** > **Deleted Records**. The platform will even allow you to restore data that has been removed through a cascade delete. This only works for audited tables however. Check out the product documentation for more information:
> `https://docs.servicenow.com/bundle/geneva-servicenow-platform/`
> `page/administer/system_logs/concept/c_RestDataRecordsDelAud.ht`
> `ml`.

This scenario also illustrates why the automatic fields are not reference fields, but instead copy information into the record. The **Created By** and **Updated By** fields store the text value of the user who performed the action, so they are not dependent upon the user record itself.

Summary

The ServiceNow platform has several more exotic features. This chapter explored some that help you create more complex applications faster.

ServiceNow Studio provides a place to add and edit your application. It collects application files and displays them in an organized manner to help you find what you need. It also provides a really useful code search feature, which will start to become useful over the next few chapters.

Applications can protect themselves by choosing whether data can be read or manipulated from outside their tables as well as choosing the level of cooperation between two apps being developed at the same time. The scope of an app provides a unique identifier, preventing two applications from being named the same.

Delegated Development lets you give other people control over the parts of the application that you choose, without giving them full system administrative rights.

Hierarchical tables provide the magic of inheritance. They allow the **Guest** table to take advantage of all the functionality provided by the out-of-the-box **User** table, reducing development time and improving maintenance.

Reference fields are incredibly powerful: create and delete records on the fly, as needed, to speed data entry and improve data quality. In addition, many-to-many tables and lists provide a great way to link multiple items together.

The next chapter will start adding some control. By adding logic to the ServiceNow platform, we go beyond just storing data, and instead start to manage it.

3
Server-Side Control

In the first few chapters, we've see how ServiceNow can hold your data. We've made a few tables, started to link it together, and collected it together in a new application. But simply storing data isn't going to make an award winning application.

So it's wonderful that ServiceNow also gives you great control over your data: you can check it, change it, or censor it using a variety of mechanisms. As we progress through this chapter, we'll see how information can be validated by a data policy, emailed out with notifications, or secured by an access control rule.

All of these are good options on their own, but ServiceNow also gives you complete control through code. You can write scripts to control almost any action you can think of. So the main focus of this chapter is to give you a good understanding of how server-side scripting in ServiceNow works. Here's how this chapter is structured:

- We will start by diving into server-side JavaScript, including how to access the database. Scripts using `GlideRecord` are probably the most common in ServiceNow.
- Business Rules are the starting point for logic in ServiceNow. We explore the different flavors by running through a variety of scenarios.
- Script Includes provide a place for your code libraries. We will look at how you can define classes, extend them, and run them.
- To really understand JavaScript in ServiceNow, we will explore the engine that powers the platform.
- Finally, data policies and advanced reference qualifiers show other ways of controlling data access and logic.

Deciding to write code

There are very often two way to do things in ServiceNow – point and click, or code. It's a good idea to use the point and click mechanism – it is often highly optimized, portable, maintainable, and upgradable. This book will look at many of these options, and guide you towards using them when possible. But sometimes you need total control. To be a ServiceNow master, you need to write scripts.

ServiceNow has hundreds of places where you can write code. Aside from a very few exceptions, JavaScript is used in all instances. JavaScript is a very flexible and powerful language and is most commonly known for its inclusion in almost every web browser. This has made it almost mandatory for web development these days, with its simple syntax allowing many people to quickly add simple logic to web pages with minimum effort. Taking advantage of this familiarity, ServiceNow uses JavaScript both on the server and client sides.

Using the developer community

Like most platforms, ServiceNow provides a variety of documentation sources. In addition to the product documentation (available at `http://docs.servicenow.com`), ServiceNow also runs the ServiceNow Developer Program, at `http://developer.servicenow.com`. This provides a wealth of useful documentation, including tutorials and self-paced training. You may have already used the Developer Program to get a free instance.

Especially useful is the API documentation. These next few chapters will explore the most important capabilities of the ServiceNow platform, but it isn't possible to be totally comprehensive. Dive into the API docs to obtain more examples and insight: `https://developer.servicenow.com/app.do#!/api_doc?v=helsinki`.

Running background scripts

The simplest place to experiment with server-side scripting is perhaps the *Background Scripts* section in ServiceNow. This provides you with a large text box in which you place your code and a button saying **Run Script**, without any fuss, formatting, or further complexity. Outputs from your session during execution (such as log statements) are captured and presented to the screen. This, therefore, provides an excellent place to run server-side code where you need to monitor the results, where you can experiment, or where you need to run one-off scripts.

Navigate to **Background Scripts** by going to **System Definition > Scripts (Background)**.

You will be presented with a large script box; however, before you get too enthusiastic, heed the warning shown. The reason that accessing background scripts requires elevated privileges is to remind you that some badly written code can, in fact, delete all your data. Never experiment in a live production instance!

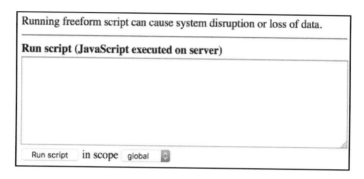

 Inefficient scripts get stuck in an infinite loop and can seriously impact performance or even cause outages or security breaches. Always test in a sandbox instance first. If you do get stuck, try going to `https://<instance>.service-now.com/cancel_my_transaction.do`, using the same browser session. The instance will attempt to halt execution of whatever it is doing in the other tab.

Let's run the standard `Hello, World!` as our first script:

```
gs.info('Hello, world!');
```

As the output, you should see the following:

```
*** Script: Hello, world!
```

The function used is in this code is not a standard JavaScript command, but is part of the ServiceNow platform. `gs` stands for `GlideSystem`, which is a collection of useful functions and utilities. The `info` function of `gs` writes a message to the system log, and **Background Scripts** echoes it back. In Chapter 8, *Securing Applications and Data*, we will explore logging in ServiceNow in much more detail.

The various functions of GlideSystem will be introduced throughout this book. For a detailed list of all its capabilities, refer to the product documentation:
`https://developer.servicenow.com/app.do#!/api_doc?v=genev a&type=server&scoped=true&to=class__scoped_glidesystem__g eneva`.

You must be wondering why it's called GlideSystem. Originally, the company now named ServiceNow was called **GlideSoft**, and they produced a platform called **Glide**. As the company and platform grew, they were both renamed to the more familiar monikers used today. You may see other references to Glide and GlideSoft, particularly in the less recent parts of the platform.

The gs object is one of several that are instantiated before the code is run. You will see many more as we journey through the ServiceNow platform. Which ones are available is dependent upon the context the code is running in.

Using GlideRecord (and its friends)

The previous two chapters demonstrated that ServiceNow is built around data. Background scripts, and scripts in general, can use the excellent database connectivity capabilities built into ServiceNow to easily access whatever information we want. GlideRecord is instrumental in doing this.

GlideRecord is a class that lets you work with a database table. With it, you can create, read, or update records in a database. In general, you work one record at a time, iterating through a result set.

It is easy to use, but I recommend reviewing the basics from the product documentation or a scripting course. In this chapter, we'll quickly run through the basics and start to explore the gotchas as well as some very interesting features that are misunderstood.

For full details, investigate the documentation at
`https://developer.servicenow.com/app.do#!/api_doc?v=helsi nki&type=server&scoped=true&to=class__scoped_gliderecord_ _helsinki`.

Let's run some code in **Background Scripts** to allow us to understand how GlideRecord works. This code is a little artificial, but the aim is to find out the last two times Alice checked in:

```
var results = [];
var gr = new GlideRecord('x_hotel_check_in');
gr.addQuery('guest.name', 'CONTAINS', 'Alice');
gr.setLimit(2);
gr.orderByDesc('sys_created_on');
gr.query();
while(gr.next()) {
  results.push(gr.sys_created_on + '');
}
gs.info(results.join(', '));
```

Now, let's look at the code in detail:

1. Perhaps it'd be useful to know when Alice is checking in to the hotel. The third line adds a filter that means the result set will only contain records where the guest's name contains Alice. You may recognize this as a SQL WHERE clause.

2. A GlideRecord object is always instantiated with the table you want to work with. The resulting object is a representation of that table. However, it isn't usable until a function is called to either make a new record (gr.newRecord()) or perform a query (gr.query()).

3. The very first line is a standard line of JavaScript. It creates a variable named results, making it an array. The output will be stored here.

Note that the condition can use dot-walking to navigate through reference fields. In the background, ServiceNow performs a join on the referenced table, allowing it to filter the results. This is invisible to the script writer since the resulting GlideRecord has exactly the same structure. This functionality is incredibly useful and can save significant development effort. However, because you are performing a join, the database does need to expend more effort, so be smart about how you do it.

Generally, you either pass two or three parameters to `addQuery`. The first and last are the fieldname and the value you are searching for, respectively. The optional middle value is which type of clause you want, from standard operations such as greater than and equal to. For example, using this on a Room `GlideRecord` query will return floors above 10:

```
gr.addQuery('floor', '>=', 10)
```

In this `CONTAINS` example, a pattern-matching text search is run (equivalent to the `LIKE '%<value>%'` SQL clause). It is looking for a name that contains `Alice` anywhere in it; `Alice Cooper` will match, as will `Steve Doralice`.

4. Next, the script instructs ServiceNow to only return a maximum of two records, no matter how many matching entries there might be in the database. When writing scripts, it is always a good idea to test them on a limited subset before unleashing your query on thousands of records.

Once the query has been returned, you can use `getRowCount` to return the number of rows that actually have been found. However, only use this function if you are actually going to deal with the records anyway, since it is rather inefficient.

For example, in a script that deletes records, use `getRowCount` to check how many you will be deleting. If you are expecting to delete five, but you see that there are instead 5,000, then make it stop!

`GlideAggregate`, discussed later in this chapter, is a more efficient way of counting if you are only interested in the number of results.

5. The next step is to order the results. Choose any column to order the result set.

6. Once the query has been set up, it's time to execute it and ask the database to get the information. From now on, the `GlideRecord` object is the result set.

7. A `while` loop is then executed to deal with all the data. The `next` function will iterate in the result set returning whether it was successful. This is a very common pattern for stepping through all the records.

Sometimes, you only want to get a single record in a table. On such an occasion, you can call the `get` function, which rolls several commands together-`setLimit(1)`, `query`, and `next`-skipping up to three lines. It returns a Boolean `true`/`false` value indicating if it found a record. If you pass a single parameter through, `get` will assume it is a `sys_id` value, allowing you to grab a record with little fuss. If you pass two parameters, the first allows you to specify the field, the second the value. This is a real timesaver. Consider the following code snippet:

var gr = new GlideRecord('u_check_in');
gr.get('guest.name', 'Alice Richards');
gs.info(gr.sys_created_on + ");

8. Some standard JavaScript functions are used for each result, appending the information we are interested in (the built-in **Created On** field) to the array. The script ensures that each value is converted to an string. The next section looks at the reason in much more detail.

9. After the loop is closed, the result set is joined together. Finally, it is written to the system log using the `gs` function we've already seen.

Understanding iterators

An iterator such as `GlideRecord` can be difficult to get your head around, but an analogy may help. Imagine that all our data is stored in a big filing cabinet, and in that cabinet is a file. Inside the file are sheets of paper, with each sheet of paper being a reservation for one of our fine rooms at Gardiner Hotels. When we want to know which room they are checked in to, we must consult the right bit of paper. But how to find it?

`GlideRecord` might be considered a remarkably efficient office administrator that does the searching for you. You provide the parameters of the search (such as the guest name being Alice, as seen previously), and they will come back with a stack of paper. Our office superstar shows you each sheet of paper, one by one. When you have that sheet, you can read or change the information on it as you wish, and when you are done, you hand it back and get the next one. Of course, while the paper is in your hand, you could also scrunch it up and toss it impressively into the bin.

This repetitive process of looking at a single sheet of paper in turn is like "iterating" over a result set. You are only working with the data from a single record at a time. If you want to compare two records together, you need save the information you want out in a separate variable. This is covered in the next section.

Accessing data from GlideRecord

As you iterate over a result set, you get access to all the fields in the table. But you don't just get the data itself-you also get information about the data. For example, you can protect data from changing or control who can see it. GlideRecord (using functions such as canRead and canWrite) lets you know what you are allowed to do.

To achieve this, GlideRecord uses an unusual ability of JavaScript to redefine objects on the fly. Every time the next function is called, the ServiceNow platform grabs the data in the table and attaches them as properties to the GlideRecord object. These properties are stored as GlideElement objects, which represent the field in the database.

Some of the most useful functions you can call on a GlideElement object are the changes and changesTo functions. These return true if the field value has been altered. As we'll see, this is invaluable for knowing what data is being altered, be it by the user or someone else.

The product documentation has more information on GlideElement objects: https://developer.servicenow.com/app.do#!/api_doc?v=helsi nki&type=server&scoped=true&to=class__scoped_glideelement __helsinki.

The field information (the GlideElement object) can be accessed in two ways: using the typical dot notation (gr.sys_created_on) or through a square-bracket notation (gr['sys_created_on']). This is very useful if you need to access fields programmatically:

```
var f = 'my_field';
gr[f] // is the same as:
gr.my_field
```

This allows you to quickly, for example, loop through several fields, clearing them in a fairly concise way:

```
var fields = ['u_field_1', 'u_field_2', 'u_field_3, u_field_4'];
for (var i = 0; i < fields.length; i++) {
  gr[fields[i]] = '';
}
```

Here, a for loop iterates through the array using the bracket notation to access the right property. The alternative, which just repeats code, is not as elegant.

Most of the time, you will just be interested in the value of the field. But it's important to understand what you are actually accessing, since it can lead to surprising results, as we'll soon see.

Walking through reference fields

Dot-walking lets you access information through reference fields using the dot notation. Accessing the name of a guest from a `GlideRecord` object of **Check-in** is as simple as using `gr.guest.name`.

The reference field has access to the fields of the table it's pointing to. A reference field pointing to the **User** table will have access to the user fields and not to any field in the **Guest** table, such as the **Membership number** field created in the previous chapter.

It is possible to access extended fields in a script using a special notation: `ref_<tablename>.<extended field>`. So, the **Membership number** field could be accessed through a **User** reference field such as `gr.ref_x_hotel_guest.membership_number`. Note you only need this syntax if the reference field points to the base table.

Converting data types

JavaScript is loosely typed. This means that it will convert values into the relevant types wherever it can. If you are performing arithmetic, it will convert it to a number according to the rules. `GlideElement` returns the value of the field when you access the object when you request a string. Most of the time, that's great. But the line where we got data from the database specifically converted the value into a string by adding the empty string (`+ ''`). This is important to do; if not done, weird stuff happens.

The surprising results of GlideElement

Line 8 of the previous script is this:

```
results.push(gr.sys_created_on + '');
```

Try changing it to this:

```
results.push(gr.sys_created_on);
```

Only a single tiny difference has been made, but it makes a big difference to the output. If you run it with the adjusted code (and you have two matching records), you will get two identical outputs. I now get this:

```
*** Script: 2016-08-16 21:06:23, 2016-08-11 22:12:41
```

With the original code, I would've got this:

```
*** Script: 2016-08-11 22:12:41, 2016-08-11 22:12:41
```

Why?

The key to understanding this is knowing what is being pushed into the `results` array. When an object (the `GlideElement` representing the `sys_created_on` field) is pushed into the array, it actually puts an object pointer into the array. This means that the two elements of the array populated are actually pointing to the *same object*. Therefore, when the contents of the array are output, the same value is printed twice.

To reiterate, when you get the repeated value, you are not storing the *value* of the field in the array, but the `GlideElement` object. And this matters, because when `gr.next()` is called, the value of `sys_created_on` changes.

Sometimes, this is exactly what you want. However, when you are manipulating a `GlideRecord` value, this is often not the case. The way to avoid this is to get the value of the field. An easy way to do that is to ensure that the data put into the array is converted into something you want to work with, such as a string.

Strings are primitive types. They don't use pointers, and so they don't exhibit this behavior. This is why you should convert `GlideElement` into strings unless you are careful. Check out the information on pointers at ht tp://cslibrary.stanford.edu/.

Getting the value another way

Of course, there are alternatives. There are some functions in `GlideRecord` and `GlideElement` that can help-specifically, `getValue` and `toString`– that perform the conversions for you. You may want to always do this so you don't forget. Both these lines are drop-in replacements for line 8:

```
results.push(gr.getValue('sys_created_on'));
results.push(gr.sys_created_on.toString());
```

But programmers generally avoid keystrokes whenever necessary (and so may prefer +
' '), and I certainly prefer manipulating GlideElement directly. Whatever you choose, it is
always important to know why you follow certain conventions.

Dealing with dates

Dates and times are generally tricky to work with, since while the idea of 60 minutes, 24
hours, 7 days, and 12 months is very normal to a person, the almost arbitrary nature of the
amounts causes some consternation through code. Therefore, ServiceNow provides access
to GlideSystem and GlideDateTime, both of which contain many functions to generate
and deal with time.

> For more information, check out the ServiceNow developer site:
> https://developer.servicenow.com/app.do#!/api_doc?v=helsi
> nki&type=server&scoped=true&to=class_scoped_glidedatetime
> _helsinki.

The developer site provides many examples of how to perform date arithmetic. This is
notoriously tricky to do manually, so I suggest using them if possible. The most useful
functions are available through GlideDateTime. For a date/time field, you can extract the
GlideDateTime object through a GlideElement object. For example, to increment a date
by a day, (and change the value of the sys_created_on field) you can use the following
code:

```
gr.sys_created_on.getGlideObject().addDays(1);
```

> Of course, you can also create your own GlideDateTime object, and make
> it do what you want, as the documentation shows.

If you go beyond simple situations (such as "How many weeks in a month?"), it can be
advantageous to extract information in Unix time and work from there. (Unix time is the
number of seconds since midnight, 1 Jan, 1970 UTC, which may be described as when time
began for computers!) This can then be manipulated like any other number. The following
line of code will give you the time in Unix time:

```
gr.sys_created_on.getGlideObject().getNumericValue();
```

Counting records with GlideAggregate

Earlier in this chapter, the `getRowCount` function of `GlideRecord` was introduced. It returns the number of results found. However, this is only determined by getting all the information from the database and then counting it. Wouldn't it be more efficient if we could get just the total number? We can, with `GlideAggregate`!

The developer site has more information available: https://developer.servicenow.com/app.do#!/api_doc?v=helsinki&type=server&scoped=true&to=class__scoped_glideaggregate__helsink.

Run the following lines of code to get the total number of records that were created yesterday:

```
var today = new GlideDate();

var yesterdayTime = new GlideDateTime();
yesterdayTime.addDaysUTC(-1);

var yesterday = new GlideDate();
yesterday.setValue(yesterdayTime);


var count = new GlideAggregate('x_hotel_check_in');
count.addQuery('sys_created_on', '<', today);
count.addQuery('sys_created_on', '>=', yesterday);

count.addAggregate('count');
count.query();
count.next();
var result = count.getAggregate('COUNT');
gs.info('Result: ' + result);
```

With `GlideRecord`, you should check that the next function is successful. But in this scenario `GlideAggregate` will always return something.

The style of working with `GlideAggregate` is very similar to that for `GlideRecord`. You can add filters, for example, in just the same way. Here, one of the functions of `GlideSystem` is used to return all the records created after the beginning of yesterday (that is, yesterday midnight). The main difference is that the `addAggregate` function is used to ask for the desired information, and the query call then returns that instead of a list of fields.

The `addAggregate` function accepts two parameters: the calculation (such as `min`, `max`, `count`, `sum`, or `avg` for average) and the field to perform it on. The `groupBy` function is used to divide the result set up and return multiple entries, which are then looped over.

To obtain the last time every guest checked in, the following code could be used:

```
var gr = new GlideAggregate('x_hotel_check_in');
gr.addAggregate('max', 'sys_created_on');
gr.groupBy('guest');
gr.query();
while(gr.next()) {
  gs.log(gr.guest.name + ' ' + gr.getAggregate('max', 'sys_created_on'));
}
```

Be aware that `GlideAggregate` only populates attributes in the object that are relevant. So you can only access the fields that you group by or have an aggregate of. In the preceding example, `guest` is available since it is grouped by field. Other fields are not available.

Scripting in scoped apps

Scoped applications represent a fresh start for ServiceNow. Application scope, introduced in the previous chapter, provides a bubble around each app, very carefully controlling what it can do.

 Almost all the code in this book is for our Hotel application. All the scripting functionality discussed, unless indicated otherwise, uses the scoped API.

Without scoping, when you run a server-side script, you have access to the whole database. Remember the warning when you ran a background script? You can easily delete every record in the user table. Your boss probably won't be happy if he can't log in to run some reports.

In many regards, scripting outside of a scoped application is like the Wild West: there is an "anything goes" attitude, where your clever moves might result in a gold mine-or the sheriff may take offence to your attitude. There are numerous clever tricks letting you access deep, dark parts of the platform, but this often results in relying on functionality that the ServiceNow developers wish you'd never found.

A good example is the use of Java packages, discussed later in this chapter, which in older versions provides access to the core platform.

To provide a clean, wholesome scripting environment, scoped applications have access only to the scoped API. Think of it like a newly designed and constructed town. The roads are straight, the grass trimmed, and the buildings neat. But it also means that many of the facilities of an older town are absent.

Being in scope

The scoped API gives a fresh start, but does mean that any fewer ServiceNow classes are available. Several have had methods renamed. But those that can be used are deemed to be 'safe', and much more documentation is available.

 For example, the old way of writing to the system log was `gs.log(<message>)`. One simple impact of the scoped API is that this has now changed to `gs.info(<message>)` (or `gr.error` and so on). The immediate impact of this means that copying and pasting old code might not work! The new method does work in non-scoped apps, though.

The Fuji release of ServiceNow introduced the scoped API, and it quickly became apparent that developers building apps on the platform wanted to do many more things than were initially allowed. Later versions of ServiceNow have dramatically expanded what is available.

 To see what has changed, navigate to the API on the developers portal, and toggle between the different API versions. Fuji has 35 classes available, Geneva has 49, and Helsinki has 50.

Improving scripting with ECMAScript 5

But what's most exciting about scripting in Helsinki-based scoped applications is the use of **ECMAScript 5**. JavaScript aficionados may roll their eyes since ECMAScript 5 is pretty old hat; being published in 2011. But considering that all server-side scripts historically used ECMAScript 3, this is a big change.

TIP ECMAScript is the standard that JavaScript is based on. The history of ECMAScript is outlined in this Wikipedia article: `https://en.wikipedia.org/wiki/ECMAScript#History`

ECMAScript 5 brings many improvements, including several new array functions. Previously, to work through an array, you would typically use a `for` loop. For example, if you wanted to log all the elements of an array, you could run this code:

```
var x = [1, 3, 5];
for (var i = 0; i < x.length; i++) {
  gs.info(x[i]);
}
```

But ECMAScript 5 gives you a `forEach` function, which accepts a callback function. Both these scripts give exactly the same output, but ECMAScript 5 is shorter and more descriptive.

```
[1, 3, 5].forEach(function (x) { gs.info(x) });
```

Direct JSON encoding and decoding is also available (with `JSON.stringify` and `JSON.parse`), as is support for getters and setters. Also rather exciting is the availability of trim – so `" test ".trim()` will remove the spaces.

Perhaps most importantly, ECMAScript 5 introduces strict mode. This removes some of quirks of JavaScript, making the execution of your code less forgiving. JavaScript was designed to be forgiving and easy, but this sometimes stores up errors for the future. For example, accidently making global variables is much harder.

Strict mode is invoked by starting the script or a function with `"use strict";`. For more information on strict mode, take a look at MDN: `https://developer.mozilla.org/en-US/docs/Web/JavaScript/Reference/Strict_mode`.

Whilst the majority of the code you write may not change, many libraries take advantage of these benefits. This lets you bring in outside code much more easily. Lodash is one of those libraries that can now be available in ServiceNow. Check out `https://lodash.com/` if you wish to take advantage of its many features.

There are many articles exploring what ECMAScript 5 can do. Try this one to start with: `http://speakingjs.com/es5/ch25.html`.

Activating ECMAScript 5

ServiceNow has a quite a few customers, who have written quite a lot of code. In order to protect it, and ensure it doesn't break when upgrading, the introduction of ECMAScript 5 in Helsinki is done using a compatibility mode. This mimics some of the idiosyncrasies of ServiceNow's version of ECMAScript 3, including ignoring references to properties of undefined objects and ignoring calls to non-existent functions. Strict mode is also not supported in compatibility mode.

ECMAScript 5 is only officially supported in scoped applications. To ensure it is turned on, open **Studio,** then go to the **Application Settings**, and verify that **ES5 Standards Mode** is selected in **JavaScript Mode**. Compatibility mode is always used for script in in the global scope.

However, there is only one JavaScript engine in ServiceNow. So while scripts in compatibility mode can access some of the great new features of ECMAScript 5 (such as `array.forEach`), it isn't fully compliant. So beware!

Protecting data from scripts

As we are seeing, scoped applications have many advantages, including being able to control and protect data from scripts. To see how this works, we need multiple interacting applications. Let's create another application that wants to interact with the information in our hotel application in order to alter the list of guests and look at their rooms. Consider that Gardiner Hotels is branching out into amusement parks and wants to build an application to manage the hair-raising rollercoasters and other attractions that will inevitably feature.

1. To create an application, navigate to **System Applications** > **Applications** and click on **New**.

2. Since we only want the container for this experiment, click on **Create** next to **Start from scratch**. Fill in the following values, and note the value that is automatically populated in the **Scope** field.

- **Name:** Theme Park

If you are using a developer instance, the scope field should be unique, and look something like `x_69373_theme_park`. Depending on your situation, you may need to adjust this to be unique.

3. Click on **Create**, then **OK** to create the application. Close the dialog box when you are told the application has been created.

4. Once done, ensure you are in the standard interface, and navigate to **System Definition** > **Scripts – Background**.

5. Paste in this code, but *before pressing* **Run script**, change the scope to `<prefix>_theme_park`, the application scope you just created:

```
var results = [];
var gr = new GlideRecord('x_hotel_room');
gr.setLimit(1);
gr.query();
while(gr.next()) {
  gr.update();
}
```

Run script (JavaScript executed on server)

```
var results = [];
var gr = new GlideRecord('x_hotel_room');
gr.setLimit(1);
gr.query();
while(gr.next()) {
    gr.update();
}
```

Run script   in scope   x_69373_theme_park

global
x_69373_theme_park
x_hotel

customer
     No scripts

This code creates a new `GlideRecord` object to query the **Room** table and attempts to save the record to the database. (Since no fields in the table were altered, nothing will actually change, but it is still a good test.)

6. You should get three messages:

> **Security restricted: Read operation against 'x_hotel_room' from scope 'x_69373_theme_park' was granted and added to 'x_69373_theme_park' cross-scope privileges Security restricted: Access to API 'ScopedGlideRecord' from scope 'x_69373_theme_park' was granted and added to 'x_69373_theme_park' cross-scope privileges Security restricted: Write operation against 'x_hotel_room' from scope 'x_69373_theme_park' has been refused due to the table's cross-scope access policy**

These three messages tell you what is happening:

- Firstly, the script attempts to query the **Room** [x_hotel_room] table. By default, read access from outside the scope is allowed. So this was granted, and recorded.
- Additionally, this was the first time that the Theme Park application used GlideRecord. You may remember this message from `Chapter 2`, *Developing Custom Applications.*
- It essentially says that you are using one of the ServiceNow APIs, which are also allowed by default. (You could stop the Theme Park application from querying the database through scripts by revoking this cross-site privilege.)

 Note that the message refers to ScropedGlideRecord rather than just GlideRecord. Global and scoped code actually use different ServiceNow APIs; the ones that are allowed are documented as noted above.

- Finally, your attempt to update the record is thwarted. By default, scripts running from a different application cannot update database tables. If you want to change this behavior, you can use the Application Access fields in the Table record, as described in the Controlling application access section in `Chapter 2`, Developing Custom Applications.

Running scripts in global

Helsinki brought a pretty fundamental change. Previously, scripts running in the global scope had access to everything – even tables of another application. But this has now changed. Now scripts running in the global scope are subject to the same access requirements as those running in application scopes.

To see this, try running the script again, but change the scope selection to `global`. You will notice that access to updating the table will again be denied. The diagram below shows how scripts from different scopes are handled.

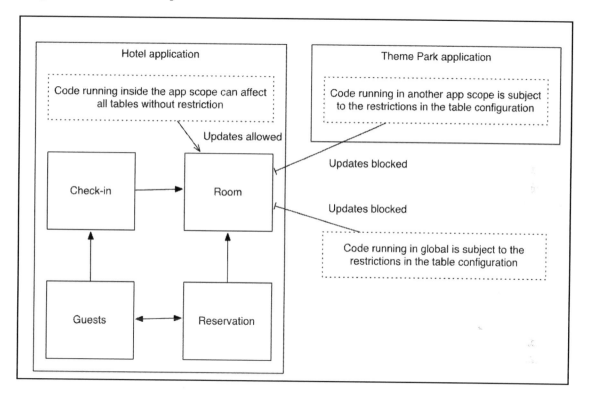

Building the restrictions

The behavior of restricting table access is designed to prevent applications from interfering with each other. It moves towards having sandbox-style protection, ensuring that two applications are separate and independent. It prevents malicious-or buggy!-apps from causing havoc by deleting or changing data they should not. As you build your applications, consider what data you want to expose. In general, keeping it restricted is a good idea. To let other applications control your data, consider building an API-explored later in the chapter.

 Table application access is a key protection mechanism to allow for applications that have been developed by third-party developers. As discussed in Chapter 10, *Packaging with Applications, Update Sets, and Upgrades*, the app store lets you download and use code that could potentially interact with your data.

Business rules

The home of server-side scripting in ServiceNow is **business rules**. They are so called because they allow you to apply business or process logic to applications hosted on ServiceNow. Do you want to update a remote system through an integration? Perhaps check a date? Or populate some fields automatically? Business Rules are a great way to accomplish this.

Some like to think of business rules as database triggers since they perform a very similar function. business rules run whenever a record is inserted, updated, or deleted or when a query is run against the table. Since ServiceNow is a data-driven platform, this enables great flexibility in manipulating and working with the information in the system.

To create a Business Rule, navigate to **System Definition** > **Business Rules**, and click **New**.

Setting the table

One of the thoughts to have when creating a business rule is to set which table it will run on. Most of the time, it is obvious: if you want to affect the **Check-in** records, you need to place it on the **Check-in** table.

However, what makes business rules pretty special is that you can run them on any level of the table hierarchy.

In the previous chapter the **Guest** table was created, extending the **User** table. This means it inherits the fields that **User** provides. Business rules are inherited too. So, if a business rule is created for the **Guest** table, it will run just for **Guest** records, but if it is placed against the **User** table, it will run for all **User** records, including **Guests**.

Being advanced

There are two sides to business rules. Some common actions can be performed without any code. You can use the options to display a message, set fields, or stop execution when a certain condition is met. So this means that whenever a room is created or a **Guest** record updated, you can easily inform the user. This is an example of the point and click or code option that ServiceNow gives you. It's a good idea to use this if possible.

However, ticking the **Advanced** checkbox enables the script and many other fields. Since we are Mastering ServiceNow, we'll concentrate on this side!

 For information on the simpler functions, check out the product documentation:
https://docs.servicenow.com/bundle/helsinki-servicenow-platfor m/page/script/business-rules/concept/c_BusinessRules.html.

Knowing the predefined variables

Whenever a Business Rule runs (and the **Advanced** checkbox is ticked!) the code in the script field is run. The script has access to several global variables provided by the platform:

- `current`: This is a `GlideRecord` object that represents the record in question. Any changes that the user (or a script) has performed on it are available for inspection.
- `previous`: This represents the record before any changes have been made.
- `g_scratchpad`: This is used as a temporary storage area for data; however, it's also available to client-side scripts. We'll explore this in more detail in the next chapter.
- `gs`: We've already met this; it contains several helpful functions for use in our scripts.

Even though these variables are global, the platform provides a pre-defined function that passes in `current` and `previous`. You should use this as your starting point.

Displaying the right table

For a very simple example of what a Business Rule can do, follow these steps:

1. Navigate to **System Definition** > **Business Rules**. Click on **New**.
2. Use the following information:
   - **Name:** `Display table on record creation`
   - **Table:** `User[sys_user]`
   - **Insert:** `<ticked>`
   - **Advanced:** `<ticked>`
   - **Script:**

```
gs.addInfoMessage ('You have created a ' + current.getTableName() + '
record');
```

Add the script inside the function that was created for you so that the script field looks like this:

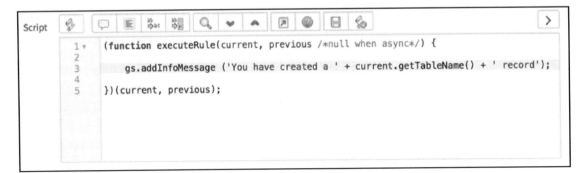

```
Script

1   (function executeRule(current, previous /*null when async*/) {
2
3       gs.addInfoMessage ('You have created a ' + current.getTableName() + ' record');
4
5   })(current, previous);
```

Always insert the code inside the executeRule script. This stop Business Rules from colliding and affecting each other. If you did not, there is the increased possibility that one Business Rule could affect the variables of another.

This code uses another of the `GlideSystem` functions to output a message. Instead of it being visible in the logfile, it is presented to the user who carried out the action. In the message, the table name of the current record is shown using the `getTableName` function of the `current` object of `GlideRecord`.

> It is always a good idea to give the Business Rule a meaningful name so you can easily identify it later. There is also a description field that you can add to the form to allow you to better describe what the script does.

From now on, whenever you create a **User** or **Guest** record, you will receive a message telling you which table has been used.

For **Guest** records, you get the following message:

And this is the one you get for **User** records:

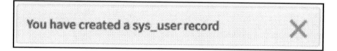

Conditioning your scripts

When records in a table are worked with, Business Rules are run. Each Business Rule has a condition that determines whether the script should run or not. The condition can be a JavaScript statement that is executed. If the result is `true`, then the main script is parsed and run. In addition, the **Filter conditions** and **Role conditions** fields can be used to specify when to execute.

It is good practice to always provide some sort of condition. Here's why:

- Code should only be run when appropriate. Since the **Script** field is only parsed if the statement passes, code that is not appropriate at that time is ignored, speeding up the execution.
- It provides easier debugging. Business Rule debugging tells you which scripts were run and when and whether the condition was met or not. Chapter 8, Securing Applications and Data, discusses this in more detail.

The condition has access to the current object of GlideRecord and the other predefined variables, where appropriate. This lets you check what is happening to the record, ensuring the Business Rule is running only at the right time. For example, for a Business Rule on the **Check-in** table, a condition can be added to run the script only if the value of the **Guest** field has been altered:

```
current.guest.changes()
```

This line of code uses several elements we've already seen: current, our GlideRecord object representing the record we are dealing with; guest, the GlideElement object for the field; and a function called changes, which returns true if someone (or something) has altered the value of that field.

In addition to always having a condition, it a good idea to always have a condition that includes a changes function call on a GlideElement object. It is common to see code like this:
current.guest == 'Bob'
This means that whenever guest is set to Bob, even if it hasn't changed, this Business Rule will run. For the majority of the time, you only want to run your rule when the value is changed:
current.guest.changesTo('Bob')

You may also want to use some of the other functions available in GlideSystem to limit Business Rules, such as the hasRole function. Roles and platform security is explored in – Import Sets, Web Services, and other Integrations">Chapter 7, *Exchanging Data – Import Sets, Web Services, and other Integrations*.

Having good conditions

When writing conditions, be careful with using the right JavaScript operators. Since the **Condition** field is a short line, the code can get quite compressed. If you have a very complex condition, consider the following:

- Split one Business Rule into many. This is always good practice anyway. Instead of having lots of OR conditions and writing one big Business Rule, have several, more targeted Business Rules with smaller conditions.
- Put the most important statements in the **Condition** field and place the rest in an if block in the **Script** field.
- Write a function and call it from the condition (the ideal place to store the function is in a **Script Include**, described later in this chapter).
- Expand the **Condition** field. It is possible to make the **Condition** field bigger by changing the dictionary settings. However, consider that this may just encourage you to write longer conditions, and longer conditions tend to go wrong!

Finally, lay out your conditions carefully, and test thoroughly. The most common confusion I see is around negative or conditions. If you want to test that several values aren't true, you must use and. In English, we often say "I don't want a, b, or c", which is short for "I don't want a, I don't want b, and I don't want c." We need the long format! In JavaScript, it would be this:

current.field != 'a' && current.field != 'b' && current.field != 'c'

Controlling the database

Business Rules run when there is database access. So, if you try to delete 20 records, a delete Business Rule will run 20 times. It is most common for Business Rules to run on insert and update, but you can select a combination of the options relatively freely.

As this diagram shows, when the instance does something with the database, it triggers the Business Rules to run against whatever record was worked with.

Controlling database queries with Business Rules

Query Business Rules are slightly different. These run before the user has a chance to interact with a particular record, and even before the database has received the results. In fact, they are designed to control exactly what the database returns. When a query Business Rules runs, the `current` object is still provided, but it is before the `query` function has been called. This gives you an opportunity to add conditions, such as when we manipulated our first `GlideRecord` object.

A great example is the baseline Business Rule called `user query` that makes inactive users invisible to everyone bar System Administrators. Let's examine its contents:

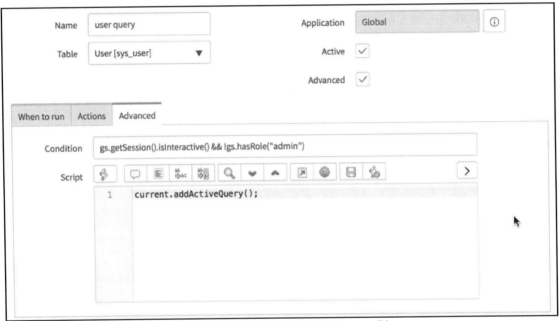

The first thing to look at is the following condition:

```
gs.getSession().isInteractive() && !gs.hasRole("admin")
```

The condition is split into two parts. Firstly, it checks to see how the user is logged in. `GlideSystem` provides session details through the `getSession` function, and the `isInteractive` function returns `true` if the user is using the web interface (other alternatives include accessing the platform via web services, as discussed in `Chapter 7`, *Exchanging Data – Import Sets, Web Services, and Other Integrations*).

Secondly, it determines whether the user has the admin role. So, if the user is accessing through the web interface and isn't an admin, the script will run.

If the condition matches, this one-line script does the work:

```
current.addActiveQuery();
```

This is equivalent to running the `addQuery` function you may be more familiar with:

```
current.addQuery('active', true);
```

It uses slightly fewer keystrokes!

This Business Rule will always ensure that (subject to the condition) only active users are returned when accessing the **User** table. Once a user is marked as inactive, they will effectively "disappear" from reference fields and lists alike. This technique is very useful for enforcing particular security rules, but it is worth remembering if you wonder why you can't access some records. The following diagram shows that the Query Business Rule runs before the database access.

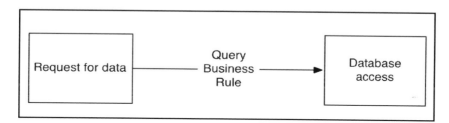

Choosing when to execute – before, after, and really after

In addition to the **Insert**, **Update**, **Delete**, and **Query** checkboxes, the **When to run** section in the business-rules form also contains the **When** and **Order** fields. These control exactly when your rule runs.

The **When** dropdown field controls the point during the database operation the Business Rule runs: **before** the data is sent to the database, or **after**. When inserting a record, you may want to programmatically set or alter default values. Any **before** Business Rules that run against this record can alter or check what data will be sent to the database. An **after** Business Rule is used when you want to update another table or system, since at that point you know the record has been successfully altered. This diagram shows this graphically, as well as the **aysnc** option, discussed in a moment.

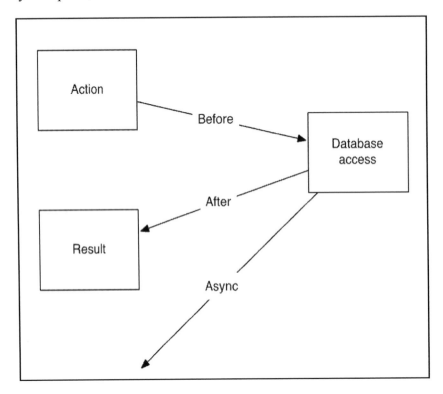

Defaulting data

Let's create a Business Rule that will automatically populate the floor number when you create or update a Room record. In most hotels, the first digit of the room number is the floor number. Follow these steps:

1. Create a new Business Rule (navigate to **System Definition** > **Business Rules**, and click **New**), and set the following information:

   - **Name:** Set default floor number
   - **Table:** Room [x_hotel_room]
   - **Advanced:** <ticked>
   - **Insert:** <ticked>
   - **Update:** <ticked>
   - **Condition:**

```
(current.number.changes() || current.floor.changes()) &&
current.floor.nil() && current.number.toString().length > 1
```

This fairly long condition checks several items. It'll only run when the **Number** or the **Room** field changes, and check that the floor field is not populated and that the number field, when converted to a string, has a length of at least one character.

This condition could also be specified using the Condition builder.

Script:

```
current.floor = current.number.substring(0, 1);
```

The script will take the first digit of the `number` value and assign it to the `floor` field. Remember to keep the `executeRule` method in place.

Notice that current.update() was not necessary. Since this is a before Business Rule, we are able to make changes before the record writes to the database. In other words, the reason why Business Rules are running is because something triggered the record to save. (Probably someone pressing the Submit or Save button in the UI.) We don't need to try to save it again, and in fact, you may cause loops by doing so. Wherever possible, the platform will detect and stop this from happening.

2. Save the business rule.
3. To test, try creating a room without the **Floor** field populated, but ensure **Number** is. When you save the record, the system will automatically provide a value for the **Floor** field. This will also happen if you try to clear out the floor, effectively providing a rule using which the system will ensure that a room number is generally always available.

When you test, you'll receive a message saying that access to `ScopedGlideElement` was granted. This is the first time you've accessed fields whilst in the Hotel scope.

As done here, if you are providing default values or calculating new ones, it is a good idea to ensure you have the data and that the user hasn't overridden the system. When possible, you should trust the users of your system to know what they are doing. There are usually exceptions to policies, and if the system is too locked down and only allows for foreseen circumstances, frustration will arise!

There are many other options for validation and checking data. In the next chapter, we'll explore client-side options, while later on in this chapter, we'll look at Data Policy.

Validating information

Another use of `before` business rules is to validate data. If you find information that is wrong or missing, you can tell the platform not to commit the action to the database.

One of the big issues with our hotel application is that you can check in to a room multiple times. There is nothing to prevent the allocation of the same room to several different people!

Let's expand the **Check-in** table slightly to include more information:

1. Navigate to **Hotel** > **Check-ins**, and click **New** to open the form.
2. Click the additional action menu icon and choose **Configure**, then **Form Design**.
3. Click the **Field** Types tab on the left, and drag in a new **Date** field. This represents the date on which the check-in happened. Click the cog next to it, and set the label and name as below:
   - **Label**: Date
   - **Name**: Date

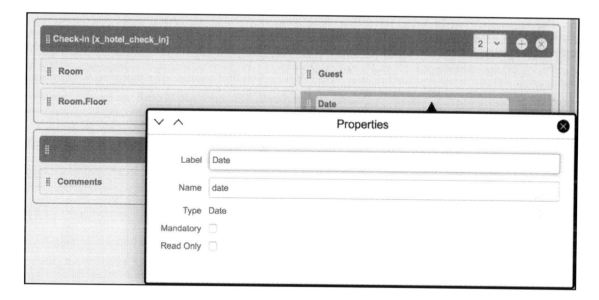

4. Click **Save.** If you navigate to **Hotel** > **Check-ins**, and click **New** again, the form should look like this:

5. Now, let's create a Business Rule that uses this date and the **Room** field to ensure collisions don't occur. Navigate to **System Definition** > **Business Rules** and click **New**. Fill in these fields, and Save.

   - **Name:** Stop duplicate check-ins
   - **Table:** Check-in [x_hotel_check_in]
   - **Advanced:**<ticked>
   - **Insert:** <ticked>
   - **Update:** <ticked>
   - **Condition:**

```
current.room.changes() || current.date.changes() || current.operation() ==
'insert'
```

This condition is shorter. This rule will fire if either the **Room** or **Date** fields change. Also, there is an additional check to see whether the record is being inserted. If you start with a completely blank record and insert it, then the **Date** and **Room** fields will both change (from nothing to something), but it is possible to "copy" a record (using **Insert and Stay**). In this edge case, you may end up with a record being inserted without any fields changing.

- **Script**: (Remember to insert this code inside the provided function)

```
var dup = new GlideRecord('x_hotel_check_in');
dup.addQuery('room', current.room);
dup.addQuery('date', current.date);
dup.setLimit(1);
dup.query();
if (dup.hasNext()) {
  gs.addErrorMessage('This room is already checked in on this date.');
  current.setAbortAction(true);
}
```

This script is longer than what we've seen before, but it reuses a lot of the functionality we've already seen. The bulk of the code sets up a `GlideRecord` query to find any **Check-in** records that have the same room and date as the record we are dealing with. We are only interested if there is at least one record, so a limit is added-a simple optimization.

Then, we query the database. Instead of looping round the results, we just ask the database whether there was a result. The `hasNext` function of `GlideRecord` will return `true` if there is.

If so, the script then call two new functions: the `addErrorMessage` function of `GlideSystem` gives the user a red error message, and, as the name suggests, `setAbortAction(true)` will stop the system in its tracks. This means the record is not inserted or updated.

Once the Business Rules has been saved, test it by creating some Check-in records. If you choose a date and a room that is the same as another record, when you click on **Submit**, you will be faced with the following error message:

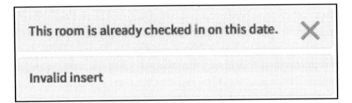

This room is already checked in on this date. ✕

Invalid insert

TIP

GlideAggregate could have been used instead of GlideRecord. This lets the database do more of the counting.

Working with dates

A common requirement is ensuring that dates make sense. Let's validate that the **Departure** field on the **Reservations** table has a value that's after the **Arrival** date. There are several ways to compare dates: ensure you check out all the functions available in GlideDateTime to find the date from a few days ago or the beginning of the next quarter:

1. Create a new Business Rule (**System Definition** | **Business Rules** and click **New**), and set the following information. Once done, Save.
   - **Name**: Sanity check dates
   - **Table**: Reservation [x_hotel_reservation]
   - **Advanced:**<ticked>
   - **Insert**: <ticked>
   - **Update**: <ticked>
   - **Condition**: current.arrival > current.departure
   - This very simple condition uses coercion to compare two dates against each other. The script runs if the arrival date is greater than (meaning after) departure. Most of the time, you can work with the GlideElement objects as you expect them to, but ensure you always test thoroughly.
   - **Script**:

```
gs.addErrorMessage('Departure date must be after arrival');
current.setAbortAction(true);
```

- Both these two function calls have already been use: they add an error message and stop the record from being saved.

2. Try out your script by creating or editing an **Arrival** date that is after the **Departure** date. You should get the error message, and the record should not be saved.

Updating information

The opposite to `before` is `after`. Rules with **When** set to `after` will run after the record has been committed to the database. This means that you cannot use them to set field values or stop the database write, since it has already happened. Indeed, knowing that the record has successfully been saved means that it is the perfect place to update other records.

We can use this to enforce a rule we have within Gardiner Hotels-ensuring there is only one lead passenger in a reservation:

1. Go to **System Definition** > **Business Rules** and click **New**. Set the following information, and Save.
   - **Name**: `Force single lead passenger`
   - **Table**: `Guest Reservations`
     `[x_hotel_m2m_guests_reservations]`
   - **Advanced**: `<ticked>`
   - **When**: `After`
   - **Insert**: `<ticked>`
   - **Update**: `<ticked>`
   - **Condition**:

```
current.lead.changesTo(true) || (current.lead && current.operation() ==
'insert')
```

This condition checks whether **Lead** has just been selected as `true` or whether it is a new record being inserted and the **Lead** field is `true`.

A true/false field in ServiceNow will always be either true or false; it cannot be null. And don't forget that the field will be a GlideElement object. This means that you shouldn't use current.lead === true to test for strict equality-it'll be false.

- **Script**:

```
var lead = new GlideRecord('x_hotel_m2m_guests_reservations');
lead.addQuery('reservation', current.reservation);
lead.addQuery('lead', true);
lead.addQuery('sys_id', '!=', current.sys_id);
lead.query();
while(lead.next()) {
   lead.lead = false;
   lead.update();
}
```

This is a fairly typical loop based on GlideRecord. It queries the many-to-many relationship table that relates guests to their reservations. It looks for the set of records that are for this reservation, and it finds every one that has the **Lead** field set to true. Of course, it should avoid working with the current record, so this is excluded by filtering out using sys_id.

The result set is looped around, with the script setting the **Lead** field of each to false, and finally, it saves the record.

2. Try creating a new **Reservation** record, and set more than one of the guests to have **Lead** marked as true. You will find that the script will change the records so that only the last one to be updated keeps it. All the others will have **Lead** set to false.

Running things later with system scheduling

Another way to execute a Business Rule is to run it **async**, meaning asynchronous. This is similar to an after Business Rule, but instead of running the script immediately after the record is saved and before the results are presented to the user, it runs it at some later time. The platform does this by creating a scheduled job.

If you wish to see these jobs, navigate to **System Scheduler** > **Scheduled Jobs**. Chapter 5, Getting Things Done with Tasks, explains these concepts in much more detail.

A scheduled job has a **Next Action** date, which tells the platform when the record can be run. Jobs will be run after this date, but in order and only when the system has the capacity. If the instance is busy, perhaps serving interactive (user) requests, then the scheduled jobs may queue up. An asynchronous Business Rule will be scheduled to run immediately, but it is not guaranteed to run within a specific timeframe.

 Asynchronous Business Rules are not run within the user's current session. When a scheduled job is picked up and is assigned to a specific user account, the platform creates a new session and impersonates the user. This does have an impact on some session-specific functionality, such as Field Encryption plugin. However, most of the time, you won't notice it.

Asynchronous Business Rules are therefore perfect for jobs that may take some time to run and don't need immediate feedback to be sent to the end user. A good example are integrations such as **eBonding**, where ServiceNow connects to a remote system using web services and exchanges information after an update in ServiceNow. E-mail notification are another. In general, you don't want to force the user to wait, blocking their browser session while these activites takes place.

 Apps using the scoped API are subject to restrictions on what they can do within Business Rules. For example, you must perform a REST call in an async Business Rule. The platform will not allow it in a before or after script. This is to protect system performance.

Display business rules

We've discussed Business Rules that control queries, manipulate data on the way to the database, and react to events such as deletion, but there is a final, less common option available: **display Business Rules**. Scripts marked to run on display will run after the record has been pulled from the database, but before it is displayed on a form. (Display Business Rules are not run for lists.)

Display Business Rules don't actually change the data that is stored, but only what is presented. So a script could, on every display, populate a field with a random number, and it'd be different every time. The database changes to the most recently generated number only if the record is saved.

However, the most important aspect of display Business Rules is the ability to pass data to the client. A special variable called `g_scratchpad` is available, allowing calculated information to be passed to the browser, making it is instantly available. We'll discuss this capability in the next chapter.

Global business rules

Sometimes, it is desirable to have code that runs all the time. You may have noticed that some business rules, have the **Table** field set `Global`. You may think of this as "all tables" instead, since a script written in a global Business Rule is executed regardless of which table is being updated, queried, inserted, or deleted.

As they stand today, global business rules have limited use due to the bluntness of their nature. If you want to run a script every time any record is deleted, then this is the way to achieve it. But this use case is not very frequent! In the past, a global business rule was the only way to define code that was always available, such as a utility function. However, Script Includes perform this job far more efficiently.

Instead, the rather large downside of a global business rule is that the code is parsed and executed very frequently-on every transaction or interaction with the platform. A function defined in a global Business Rule is parsed and stored in memory, cluttering the namespace, even if it is not used. This therefore means that global business rules are generally only used in very specific circumstances.

Business rules created in an application cannot create global Business Rules. They can only be created in the global scope; and even then it's a bad idea.

You may see lots of legacy global Business Rules in the out-of-the-box platform. Over time, these will be removed and replaced as Script Includes.

Script Includes

Business rules are inherently tied to a database action. However, often you want to write code that is available in multiple places, perhaps creating utility functions or even creating your own data structures. **Script Includes** are designed specifically for this situation. The big advantage, aside from the separation that encourages efficient reuse, is that the code is only accessed and parsed on demand, meaning that your scripts only run when they need to. This process is cached, optimized, and controlled, giving meaningful performance benefits.

When you create a Script Include, you give the record a name. This is very different to the name of a business rule. The name in a Business Rule is purely descriptive, enabling you to find the script more easily. For a Script Include, the **Name** field must have a value identical to the name of the function or class you are defining, since it is used by the platform to identify the code when you try to call it. This means your Script Include names should contain no spaces and should be in accordance with your convention. Use the **Description** field to document what the script is doing.

When deciding upon names for your functions, it is a good idea to use `CamelCase`, as is the general convention, but `underscore_case` is also acceptable, except for classes. Always use `CamelCase` there. However, the most important thing is consistency!

Creating classes

JavaScript is an object-based language, but it doesn't have a very strict class structure like Java. Using a variety of techniques, it allows you to simulate object-orientated behavior, such as inheritance. It is up to the coder to use an appropriate pattern. ServiceNow has a particular convention, which you should follow for ease of upgrading and maintainability.

This section does contain some technical specifics of how ServiceNow has implemented Script Includes, but just following the convention will get you most of the way.

When you create a Script Include, and after you've populated the name field, the platform automatically fills in the script field with the beginnings of a class. If you are familiar with the various JavaScript libraries, you may recognize it as the style that jQuery and the prototype JavaScript framework use. For example, consider the following lines of code:

```
var MyClass = Class.create();
MyClass.prototype = {
    initialize: function() {
    },

    type: 'MyClass'
}
```

ServiceNow includes some functionality to structure the definition of a class through the `Class` global variable. The `create` function returns a function, and you can then specify, through the prototype, the methods you want. This pattern is relatively common. John Resig, as always, has a very helpful article available, which uses the same methodology as ServiceNow. It can be read at `http://www.ejohn.org/blog/simple-class-instantiation/`.

Coding a class

Let's write some code to see how this works.

1. Create a new Script Include by navigating to **System Definition** > **Script Includes** and clicking on **New**. Fill out the fields, and Save.
   - **Name**: `SimpleAdd`
   - **Script**:

```
var SimpleAdd = Class.create();
SimpleAdd.prototype = {
    initialize: function (n) {
        gs.info('Creating new object');
        this.number = (n - 0) || 0;
    },

    increment: function () {
        this.number++;
        gs.info(this.number);
        return this;
    },

    type: 'SimpleAdd'
};
```

The first line creates a variable called `SimpleAdd` and executes the `Class.create` function. This starts the definition of the object.

The second line is where the prototype is edited in order to make the class actually do something. The prototype consists of two functions: `initialize`, which is called when the object is created, and `add`.

The `initialize` function provides a variable called `number` that attaches itself to the object by using the `this` keyword. If you pass through a value when creating the object, `number` will be set to it; otherwise, it will be zero. The double-bar `or` function checks to see whether the little expression in the brackets is `false`. If so, it provides a . A little JavaScript trick is used to ensure that `number` is indeed a number; by subtracting zero, JavaScript will try and turn n into a number. It will succeed for numbers as strings (such as `'100'`) and fail for things it can make no sense of (`'foo'`).

The end result of this ensures that when `initialize` runs, the `number` variable is indeed a number, or else, it is set to zero.

Every time you call the `increment` function, it increases `number` by one and then displays it. The function then returns itself, which is useful for chaining.

Finally, the `type` variable at the end is a convention; it allows you to easily identify which object you are dealing with.

The prototype definition has been accomplished by creating variables for every property. This includes defining the functions as function expressions, meaning `increment` is a variable with an anonymous function. The alternative function declaration (`function x() {}`) is a named function. Refer to these articles if you are interested in learning more:
http://javascriptweblog.wordpress.com/2010/07/06/function-declarations-vs-function-expressions/.
http://kangax.github.io/nfe/.

Once the class has been defined, you can try it by using the following code. Navigate to **System Definition > Script – Background**. Paste the following code in, and change the scope to be x_hotel. Then click **Run script**.

```
var sa = new SimpleAdd();
sa.increment().increment();
gs.info('Accessing the variable number ' + sa.number)
```

Together, this shows that the sa object is created from the SimpleAdd class, the increment function is called twice in a chain and how the number property can be accessed and logged.

Note that it is generally considered bad form to rely on public variables. In this example, number is accessed directly. This breaks the idea of encapsulation, which means that anything outside the class shouldn't worry about what is happening on the inside. Predefined functions that expose useful information (getters and setters) should generally be used.

Accessing across scope

Just like tables, Script Includes can be worked with from a different scope – if you allow it, and you use the right syntax.

To access a class from another scope, prefix the name with the scope and a period. This is shown in the API name in the Script Include record. For the SimpleAdd class, it is x_hotel.SimpleAdd.

It's best (and clearer) if you use this syntax all the time, even when you are running in scope. It also makes your code more portable.

You must also specify that this class is public by changing the **Accessible from** field. Setting it to **All application scopes** scripts running in different scopes can run this code.

1. Run the following (slightly altered) code in Background Scripts in the global scope, without changing the Script Include:

```
var sa = new x_hotel.SimpleAdd();
sa.increment().increment();
gs.info('Accessing the variable number ' + sa.number)
```

You should get an error message saying:

```
Illegal access to private script include SimpleAdd in scope x_hotel being
called from scope global
```

> 2. If you wish, edit the SimpleAdd Script Include, and change the Accessible from field. Note how this allows you to run the code.

There is also a Protection Policy field that defines if other admins can read the code. This is discussed further in `Chapter 10`, *Packaging with Applications, Update Sets, and Upgrades.*

Using classes to store and validate data

One of the judgments needed when designing a more complex ServiceNow application is whether to use a class to represent your data and provide validation and data manipulation or to use the `GlideRecord` objects, Business Rules, and other functionalities provided by ServiceNow.

For example, if you want to create a new **Room** in the **Hotel**, should you create a Script Include that takes in the parameters, validates it, and then creates the record?

Or should you use Business Rules to check the data once it has been submitted through the UI?

I suggest that in the majority of the situations, using Business Rules provides the most obvious, consistent, and scalable solution. If you decide to start accessing your data via web services, for instance, Business Rules will need little alteration, while a custom class will need to have access to it scripted. We've had to use several tricks in our `initialize` function to validate input, something the platform already does well. The overhead in maintaining a complex class is often not needed-it quickly gets frustrating to create getter and setter functions if you add a new field, for instance.

Having an API for scoped apps

The exception to this advice is for scoped apps. Here, if you have data you want to protect, it makes sense to access it only through an API. Use the controls on the Table record to deny other apps access, and instead force them to use a Script Include you create.

Perhaps we want to strictly control how other applications create guest records. The Guest table would be useful for the Theme Park app, but rather than changing the Application Access to allow any and all records to be created from all scopes, we could create a Script Include that has a function to accept data, validate it-perhaps applying security restrictions- and only then commit the record to the database.

Extending classes

As with other object-oriented systems, extending a class allows you to take advantage of its defined functionality while adding to or altering it. Again, ServiceNow has a specific convention to do this easily. Extra functions have been added to the Object object: extend, extendsObject, and clone.

Let's create a new Script Include through **System Definition** > **Script Includes,** and saving the following fields:

- **Name**: SimpleSubtract
- **Script**:

```
var SimpleSubtract = Class.create();SimpleSubtract.prototype =
Object.extendsObject(SimpleAdd, {
decrement: function () {
this.number--;
gs.info(this.number);
return this;
},
type: 'SimpleSubtract'
});
```

The definition for this extended class begins in a similar way to SimpleAdd, by calling the class.create function and then defining its prototype. However, instead of providing the variables directly, it passes them through the extendsObject function of Object. This simulates inheritance by cloning the SimpleAdd class prototype and then injecting all the new properties into the resulting object.

 These examples are rather artificial. You don't need to extend a class just to add another function.

This results in all the functions of `SimpleAdd`, including `initialize`, being part of any `SimpleSubtract` object when `new` is called:

```
var ss = new x_hotel.SimpleSubtract(2);
ss.decrement().increment();
```

Taking advantage of utility classes

The classes defined so far have needed to be initialized with the `new` operator to perform their job as a data structure. Sometimes, however, this is not appropriate. Code could be packaged up in a utility library, which contains functions without creating a new object. In other programming languages, you can achieve this using static functions or classes. JavaScript doesn't have static functions, but to avoid calling the `new` operator, it's possible to define functions directly on the class rather than in the prototype.

 ServiceNow provides several utility classes in the out-of-the-box platform. Try searching for Script Includes that contain `Util` in the name. `JSUtil` and `ArrayUtil` are especially helpful. The code search in Studio is excellent for dicovering the uses of these functions.

Providing utility classes

1. To create an example, navigate to **System Definition** > **Script Includes**, click New, set the following fields and Save:
   - **Name**: `SimpleMath`
   - **Script**:

```
var SimpleMath = Class.create();
SimpleMath.square = function(x) {
    return x * x;
};
```

Notice how the `square` function has been attached directly to `SimpleMath`, without altering the prototype. This means that you don't use the `new` operator.

2. Go to **System Definition** > **Scripts – Background**, and run this in the `x_hotel` scope:

```
gs.info(x_hotel.SimpleMath.square(10));
```

Storing functions

Often, you don't need the full structure of a class if you just want to store a single function. There is a lot of overhead code in the `SimpleMath` class. Instead, let's create another implementation to simplify it.

Having functions in Script Includes

1. Create another new Script Include, available at **System Definition** > **Script Includes**:
   - **Name**: square
   - **Script**:

```
function square (x) {
   return x * x;
}
```

Notice how `square` is written with an initial lowercase letter, since it is a single function. `SimpleMath` started with an upper case letter, since it is a class.

2. You can then run this in Background Scripts in the `x_hotel` scope very easily:

```
gs.info(x_hotel.square(10));
```

It is much better to group similar functions together in a single utility class. This will also give them a namespace, which means it is less likely there will be collisions or variables with the same name.

Client Callable Script Includes

While we've been making Script Includes, you may have noticed the **Client Callable** checkbox in the form. If this box remains unticked, then any request to run this code that is initiated from the client will not be served. This can happen in many scenarios, including **reference qualifiers**, first discussed in Chapter 1, *ServiceNow Foundations*.

Due to the damage that can be caused by calling code from the client, any such calls are made in a sandbox environment that prevents the modification of the database. For example, any attempt to delete records through `GlideRecord` will fail. This is discussed more in – Import Sets, Web Services, and other Integrations">Chapter 7, *Exchanging Data – Import Sets, Web Services, and other Integrations*. The next chapter discusses **GlideAjax**, a way of calling Script Includes from the browser.

Enforcing data

Earlier in this chapter, we explored how Business Rules can validate information, ensuring that data is consistent and appropriate. For example, we ensured that departure dates are always after arrivals. However, writing a script for every situation is an administrative overhead. Reduce it by using a data policy, which allows definitions to be made without writing a single line of code.

Data Policies are another of the point-and-click functionalities available. Try to data policies when possible, and use Business Rules otherwise.

Data policies enable you to specify whether fields in a table should be mandatory or read-only under certain conditions. The conditions can only apply to the current record, which means the script that checks for multiple lead passengers cannot easily be replicated with a data policy.

Forcing a comment using a data policy

Let's ensure that a user cannot change a **Check-in** record that is in the past unless there is a comment to explain the situation.

1. Navigate to **System Policy > Rules > Data Policies**. Click on **New**. Enter these values, then Save.
   - **Table:** `Check-in [x_hotel_check_in]`
   - **Short description:** `Must have a comment if in past`
   - **Use as UI Policy on client:** `<unchecked>`
   - **Conditions:** `Date - before - Today`

Once you saved, you can create **Data Policy Rules**. These specify exactly what is being controlled. Click on **New** in the **Data Policy Rules** related list and enter this information. Once done, click Submit.

- **Field name**: `Comments`
- **Mandatory**: `True`

2. Then, to try it out, change or create a new Check-In record (**Hotel** > **Check-Ins**, **New**) that has a date in the past.

    You should notice that if you try to save the record, you will get a message very similar to `addErrorMessage` used before, but without any code.

 In this example, we unticked the **UI Policy** option. This means the data policy will only be checked on the server. We'll explore UI Policies in `Chapter 3`, *Server-Side Control*, and security in – Import Sets, Web Services, and other Integrations">Chapter 7, Exchanging Data – Import Sets, Web Services, and other Integrations.

Specifying dynamic filters

Data policies, like many areas of ServiceNow, use condition fields as the basis for the logic. These are incredibly useful, but they don't solve every situation since they don't have context.

For example, if you want to have a data policy that allows only the guests themselves to change the **Check-in** record, you need to know who the current user is and compare that with the **Guest** field.

In older versions of ServiceNow, you needed to embed JavaScript directly in the condition builder. In the example given, the condition would be `Guest - is - javascript:gs.getUserID()`.

The condition field will show a red background while you enter the JavaScript code, indicating invalid data, but the system will let you save it.

This uses the `GlideSystem` functions again, this time returning the `sys_id` value of the currently logged-in user with the `getUserID` function. If the contents of the **Guest** field and this `sys_id` value match, the condition will pass. Again, **Script Includes** is a great place to create your own function to embed in the condition. Just remember to check the **Client Callable** box.

However, a more friendly method to do this is with dynamic filters, giving users a simple drop-down option menu. Dynamic filters can be used where there is a condition filter, including lists. Let's create a dynamic filter for **Guests** now, to see how it works.

Displaying guests that are Me

1. Navigate to**System Definition** > **Dynamic Filter Options**. Click on **New** and fill out the following information:
   - **Label**: `Me`
   - **Script**: `gs.getUserID()`
   - **Field type**: `Reference`
   - **Referenced Table**: `Guest [x_hotel_guest]`
   - **Available for filter**: `<ticked>`

2. After saving this, navigate to the **Hotel** > **Check-in** table list, and create a new filter. You should be able to create the following filter:

   `Guest - is (dynamic) - Me`

This will show the **Check-in** records made for the user you are currently logged in as. It's unlikely there is any for the System Administrator.

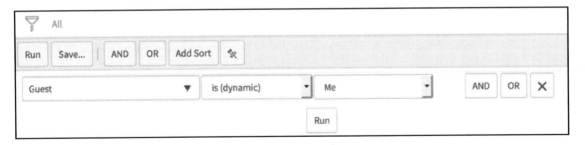

This functionality allows you to make a script that passes back whichever values you want. In theory, you could create a dynamic filter that returns a random guest, which while being a little useless, could be fun!

Scripting reference qualifiers

Chapter 1, *ServiceNow Foundations*, looked at **reference qualifiers**. Reference qualifiers filter the choices available in a referenced field. The three options (simple, dynamic, and advanced) all work in the same way under the hood. They provide an encoded query, which is used by the platform to find the records that can be selected. Scripted reference qualifiers use JavaScript to accomplish this in a Script Include, in two broad ways:

- They dynamically create an encoded query. For example, you may wish to filter out inactive guests if the currently logged-in user is not a system administrator.
- They dynamically create a list of multiple sys_id values, which is used as an encoded query. The function typically uses a more complicated method to obtain a valid list of records, and passes the list to the reference field. Users then pick an entry from this list.

Showing only guests with reservations

Let's improve the reference qualifier on the **Guest** field in the **Check-in** table so that only users who have a reservation can check in.

1. Firstly, create a new Script Include. Navigate to **System Definition** > **Script Includes** and click **New**.

   In this example, we'll create a single function for simplicity, but you could include it as part of a larger utility function.

   - **Name**: guestsWithReservations
   - **Script**:

```
function guestsWithReservations() {
var result = [];
var res = new GlideRecord('x_hotel_m2m_guests_reservations');
res.query();
while (res.next()) {
result.push(res.guest + '');
}
var au = new global.ArrayUtil();
return au.unique(result);
}
```

This script should be very familiar from the early part of the chapter. It does a `GlideRecord` lookup function call on the `x_hotel_m2m_guests_reservations` table, and loops round. Each result is put into an array, ensuring that it is converted into a string first. Then, the very useful `ArrayUtil` class is used. This provides a function called `unique`, which removes any duplicates in the result. Note that the global prefix is used, because the ArrayUtil class is in the global scope. Finally, the function returns the array containing the guest `sys_id` values.

2. Next, navigate to **System Definition** > **Dynamic Filter Options** and click **New**. While it is not strictly necessary to do this (an advanced reference qualifier could be used instead), it is a good idea for reusability and maintenance purposes. Fill out the field below, and Save.
   - **Label**: Guest has reservation
   - **Script**: 'sys_idIN'+x_hotel.guestsWithReservations()

- **Field type**: Reference
- **Referenced table**: Guest [x_hotel_guest]
- **Available for ref qual**: <ticked>

The **Script** field calls the function defined in the Script Include and prefixes the result with sys_idIN. This reference qualifier still provides the platform with an encoded query, but is now dynamic. The guestsWithReservations function may return a different result each time. The sys_idIN string tells the platform that the **Guest** records must have a sys_id value that matches one of these results.

It is a good idea to have a generic function that returns data in a useful format, such as an array, so that it can be reused elsewhere. In this example, JavaScript coerces the result into a comma-separated string.

3. Finally, we need to change the dictionary entry of the **Guest** field in the **Check-in** table. To find it, navigate to **System Definition** > **Dictionary**, and find the entry where Table is x_hotel_check_in, and Column name is guest. Then set the following fields, and Save.

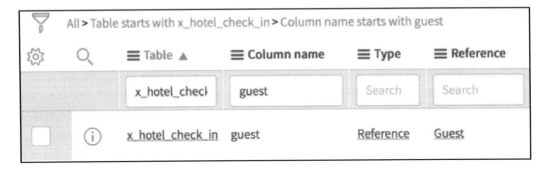

- **Use reference qualifier**: Dynamic
- **Dynamic ref qual**: Guest has reservation

4. Now, when you use the **Guest** reference field in the **Check-in** table, you can only select guests that have any sort of reservation (for any date and any room).

Filtering using the current record

This function could be improved by further filtering the records. We only want to select guests who have a reservation for the date that the check-in is for. Rather wonderfully, the script has access to current, which contains the values that are filled out on the form at the moment, even if the form isn't saved.

When you perform a type-ahead or use the magnifying glass on a reference field, the platform sends the current state of the form to the server to enable it to create the current object of GlideRecord.

1. Navigate back to System Definition > Script Includes, and find the guestsWithReservations record. Remove lines 3 and 4, and replace them with this snippet.

```
...
  var res = new GlideRecord('x_hotel_m2m_guests_reservations');
if (current.date) {
    res.addQuery('reservation.arrival', current.date);
}
res.query();
...
```

2. The script field should look like this screenshot. Once done, Save.

```
Script
 1  function guestsWithReservations() {
 2      var result = [];
 3      var res = new GlideRecord('x_hotel_m2m_guests_reservations');
 4      if (current.date) {
 5        res.addQuery('reservation.arrival', current.date);
 6      }
 7      res.query();
 8      while (res.next()) {
 9        result.push(res.guest + '');
10      }
11      var au = new global.ArrayUtil();
12      return au.unique(result);
13  }
14
```

The `GlideRecord` lookup is now more selective. If the **Date** field has been populated, then the arrival date of the reservation must match it. Notice that dot-walking has been used because we are querying the many-to-many table.

Try it out. Create a reservation for a particular date, and add a guest using the related list. Then, create a **Check-in** record. Set the **Date** field to the same date, and notice that the **Guest** field is constrained.

Reference qualifiers are incredibly useful and very powerful. They will help you show the right information in a reference field. But if you want to always constrain the results in a table, then a query Business Rules is a better fit.

Rhino – the JavaScript engine powering ServiceNow

JavaScript needs to be interpreted and executed in order for it to do useful work. The functionality that does this in each web browser is the JavaScript engine: it understands the code written on the web page and executes it to provide the functionality that the developer expects.

The ServiceNow server-side platform uses the Rhino JavaScript engine, which is managed by the Mozilla Foundation, the maintainers of Firefox. Rhino itself is written in Java, which provides a hint of the backend platform code ServiceNow is written in. Rhino provides a full implementation of the language, with the exception of some objects that only make sense to the client. It's relatively complete and standard-compliant, though ServiceNow has made some changes to make scripting more forgiving (including not altering on missing if the function doesn't exist.) All versions of ServiceNow prior to Helsinki include a version of Rhino that supports up to version ECMAScript 3 of JavaScript. From Helsinki onwards, the platform supports ES5-a significant upgrade and improvement.

 For more information, look at the *Improving scripting with ECMAScript 5* section earlier in the chapter.

Accessing Java

The ServiceNow platform is written in Java using the Apache Struts framework. In earlier versions of ServiceNow, scripts could, through the support in Rhino, access Java code and execute calls to backend functions. For example, you might find examples that use the `ftp4che` FTP library. This is built into the platform to enable the Import Sets functionality, which we'll explore in `Chapter 7`, *Exchanging Data – Import Sets, Web Services*, and other Integrations. Since Java code is organized in classes and then into packages, Rhino normally provides a global variable, called `Packages`, that enables the script writer to access any code they can find.

Since the Calgary version of ServiceNow, unfettered Java access has been curtailed and has been limited to a subset of classes and packages. Some Java functions are now marked as **scriptable**, meaning that JavaScript code can call it. There are several hundred classes currently accessible, but only a few are documented. ServiceNow recommends that only the classes listed on the developer portal be used:

Note that scoped apps are restricted to the smaller scoped subset:

> The full list of accessible objects is available at the following link, but this doesn't mean they are always the right ones to use!
> `http://wiki.servicenow.com/index.php?title=Packages_Call_Repla cement_Script_Objects`.

Summary

Since ServiceNow is a very data-oriented platform, `GlideRecord` plays a critical role. This chapter explored how each field is represented by a `GlideElement` object and what that means for dates and other areas of interest. `GlideAggregate` uses the database to perform calculations and so can perform much faster than alternative methods.

Business Rules are the home of scripting in ServiceNow. Since every item in ServiceNow is a database record and Business Rules allow you to alter queries and change the record itself, you get enormous power at your fingertips. We ran through several scenarios, including working with dates, validating data, and ensuring data integrity.

Script Includes are the perfect place to store commonly used code. By defining classes, you can create your own data structures, enabling you to extend ServiceNow in any way you require. The wide variety of Script Includes available out of the box should give you inspiration, but the background of each pattern and how it is used was explained.

Data policies and advanced reference qualifiers are another way to control data. Data policies ensure that fields are mandatory and read-only according to predefined conditions and reference qualifiers can be supercharged by using JavaScript.

ServiceNow provides a fantastic environment for script writers. Rhino is embedded into the heart of ServiceNow and is used throughout the platform, enabling you to make the data work how you want. Scoped apps use a newer, cleaner set of APIs than was originally available, and it also provides more flexibility and control around data access.

The next chapter will move on to the way the user interacts with ServiceNow. It will explore how the browser can improve user experience through client-side scripting, buttons, and validation controls.

4

Client-Side Interaction

In this chapter, we will explore how to control how the user works with our application. We started with the groundwork for this in Chapter 1, *ServiceNow Foundations*, where we looked at how data is stored in ServiceNow and displayed it on the screen using forms and lists. In the previous chapter, we looked at how scripts and other server-side functions are used by the instance to control and manipulate data flow.

Since ServiceNow is a web application, the majority of interactions happen on a user's web browser. This chapter focuses on how you can control the user experience through scripts, buttons, and data exchange. This includes the following:

- Using Client Scripts to manipulate forms dynamically, unleashing the power of the browser
- UI Policies, which provide simple functionality to guide the user without using scripts
- Improving the user's experience of working with lists with context menus and list editing
- UI Actions which enable you to add buttons that interact with the browser
- Communicating with the server using GlideAjax

 ServiceNow is embracing a client-side framework called AngularJS. This increasingly common framework allows you to build very reactive single-page apps. This library is discussed in more detail in Chapter 11.

Building a modern interface

There are two parts to a web-based platform such as ServiceNow: the **central server**, which is where most of the data is stored, and the **client browsers** that ask for the data, display it, and then push information back to the server.

ServiceNow takes advantage of modern web browsers to provide a simple-to-use and feature-rich interface. This is built with JavaScript, the language of the Web. JavaScript is very capable, giving you control over the whole interaction with the user.

Most ServiceNow system administrators have had some experience working with client-side JavaScript. So, writing scripts that interact with a web browser is often simple and familiar. The fact that ServiceNow also uses JavaScript on the server is a bonus: you only need to know one language.

The power and pitfalls of Ajax

Modern websites make heavy use of **asynchronous JavaScript and XML (Ajax)**, a technique built by Microsoft but popularized by Google. It is the key method for loading data from a server, independent of page loading, in order to improve user experience.

A typical web page consists of data, display information (such as text, CSS, or links to style sheets), and often JavaScript code as well. When Ajax is used, the browser can just ask for more data, keeping the rest of the page the same. This means that a web-based map can just return new map tiles when you zoom or scroll, and an e-mail application can check for new messages and keep the current ones on the screen.

But JavaScript is single-threaded. It can only do one thing at time. So, when the browser runs scripts, it doesn't interact with the user. To stop the frustrating freezing that occurs when you click and nothing happens, the browser supports the use of **callback functions**. A callback function essentially provides a way to continue processing after a delay. Instead of just staying there and waiting, you provide a function and the browser will call it when it's got the data that it's been asked for. It helps keep the page responsive.

An analogy is simple. When you want to speak to someone in a telephone call center, do you want to stay on the line in a queue or do you want them to call you back while you get on with other things in the meantime? Of course, you would prefer the latter. It's likewise with the browser, except it always keeps its promises, unlike many call centers!

Being in control

One of the reasons that the web has thrived is because it is an open system. ServiceNow uses standards like HTML, JavaScript and CSS to build web pages that your browser interprets and displays. It's important to realize that ServiceNow does not fully control how that browser uses the data generated by the instance. Depending on the browser, you can override many of ServiceNow's choices, perhaps by providing your own style sheets, or restricting the functionality it uses. Because the rest of the web is a wild place, web browsers help keep you secure by being in control.

But this means that a malicious user can instruct the browser to not follow the rules. If you use client scripting to disable writing to a field, another script, perhaps run with nefarious ideas in mind, can easily undo that instruction. Client-side scripting should never be considered security.

Using client-side code effectively

Client-side scripting lets you to provide an enhanced experience to the users of your system by providing instant feedback and a faster way to interact. It is often much quicker to validate information using the browser than asking the instance to do the work, simply because the instance may be located many hundreds or thousands of miles away, across several Internet links.

Most ServiceNow developers get very excited by the power that JavaScript brings. But this power and capability does come with downsides, and this enthusiasm can result in inappropriate usage, many of which we'll touch on in this chapter, and throughout the rest of the book. Specifically, we'll look at better ways to deal with these common scenarios that shouldn't be tackled with client-side scripting

- **Security** is most appropriately configured with access control rules
- Final **data validation** should be done with Business Rules and Data Policy
- **Automation** is accomplished with workflow and Business Rules
- A **custom look and feel** can be built with UI Pages and the Service Portal.

 We'll go through the reasons in this chapter. But the main reason is that you should not trust the client. It is under the control of someone else, and any automation or security that it attempts to do can be disabled or altered.

The familiarity and capability of using client-side JavaScript is alluring. During the rest of this chapter, I hope to help you to use this power effectively.

Choosing a UI Action

A **UI Action** is a rather grandiose name for a button. Using a button is possibly the simplest interaction that a user can make, and a UI Action runs a script after the click (or a tap, if using a touchscreen device!).

There are several different representations of UI Actions, each displayed in a different way, available in both the form and list views:

- Form buttons: These are the most accessible ones. They show up as more recognizable buttons and appear at two places: the top right and the bottom left of the form. The context bar in which the buttons are located is fixed and will always display at the top of the screen, even as you scroll down the form. This accessibility and visibility makes form buttons a great choice for important actions that will change the record that you are viewing. A form button looks like this:

 You can control some aspects of button display through properties, such as only displaying form buttons in the context bar and not at the bottom.

- Form links: UI Actions are represented as links. These are presented underneath the form with a title named **Related Links**. It is possible to display more text with form link UI Actions, making them helpful for less frequent actions that need more description. These UI Actions are also useful for navigating to other areas of the system, perhaps to launch a window or find a related record. Due to their disconnected nature compared to form data, they often do not alter the record.

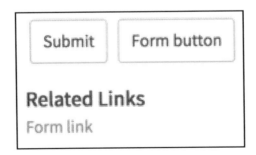

- Form context menus: These show up when you right-click on the form header or use the Additional actions menu button. These are unobvious and should be reserved for real power users such as the system administrator. The `Copy sys_id` UI Action is a great example of a useful functionality that doesn't need to be easily available to everyone. A form context menu looks like this:

- List links: These are displayed in a similar way to form links. In addition to being navigation links like the form version, they are used to manipulate the list itself.
- List banner and list bottom buttons: These show up at the top and bottom of a list and generally apply to selected records. They are not often used due to their visual separation from a record, though the **New** button is a list banner button. List bottom buttons are mostly used as a more obvious action on multiple records.

- List choices: These show up in the drop-down menu at the bottom of a list. It is fairly obvious that these affects items that have been selected in the list, though the choices themselves are hidden in the selection box. The platform controls the visibility and display of the options depending upon the properties that are set for the UI Action. If the UI Action only applies to a few of the selected records, the platform will confirm how many in a subsequent alert dialog. A list choice button looks like this:

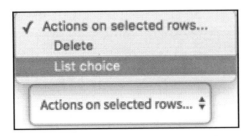

- List context menus: Just like form context menus, these adds an entry to a menu that appears when you right-click on a row. I recommend reserving this one for power users again due to its unobvious nature.

Finding the current table

In Chapter 3, *Server-Side Control*, you saw how a simple Business Rule could display which table was being manipulated. Let's make a UI Action that will show up on both User and Guest records, and tell you what the table name is.

1. Navigate to **System Definition** > **UI Action**, then click on **New**, and use the following values before choosing Save:
   - **Name:** Show table name
   - **Table:** User [sys_user]
   - **Form context menu:** <ticked>
   - **Script:**

```
gs.addInfoMessage('The current table name is ' + current.getTableName())
```

This script should be familiar. It uses `GlideSystem` to display a message, and `current` is available, too. This will output the table name whenever you choose the option. Try it out by finding it in the Additional actions on a Guest record. It will display the following message:

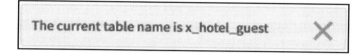

The current table name is x_hotel_guest

Note that the code is run on the server. Server-side UI Actions can leverage all of the functionality explored in `Chapter 2`, *Developing Custom Applications*.

Displaying UI Actions in the right place, at the right time

There are several mechanisms that control whether and where a UI Action will be displayed. They are as follows:

- The **Table** field works in a very similar way to the one in Business Rules. Table inheritance is supported (which means that as we just saw, when a UI Action is added to the **User** table, it'll show for **Guests** too).
- The **Order** field, as expected, controls what sequence the buttons are put in. Lower numbers mean farther to the left or top side of the window.

 Be consistent as you decide the ordering. It helps people use your application when buttons are in logical places. `Update` has been given an order of −100 to keep it in the left of all the buttons, while the order of `Delete` is 1,000, so it is always on the right.

- **Action name** serves as a unique identifier across table extensions. If you create a UI Action for the **User** table, you can override it by creating a button with the same action name but against the **Guest** table.

 This is especially helpful to change how global buttons (such as Save) work. If you don't want Insert and Stay to show on your table, create a UI Action with an action name of sysverb_insert_and_stay, and set the condition to false.

- The **Show insert** and **Show update** checkboxes are easy to control. Often, you only want to show buttons that are on previously saved records, perhaps to control related records.

- The much-overlooked **UI Action Visibility** list controls the views in which your UI Action will be shown. You might, for example, have an advanced view that gives users extra functionality with more UI Actions. A UI Action can even be used to switch between views on demand.

Using the Condition field

Just like a Business Rule, a UI Action has a **Condition** field. Any JavaScript put in here is always run on the server. If it returns `true` (in addition to the other options controlling when and where), the button will be shown.

The `current` object of `GlideRecord` is available in the condition as well as `gs` and the other global objects.

 Try to leverage access control rules when you write conditions. Rather than creating a long string of conditions, checking roles and fields, use `current.canWrite()` as a base. In most situations, if a user can write to the record, they can use a button. This is discussed further in Chapter 7, *Exchanging Data – Import Sets, Web Services, and other Integrations.*

In general, the same advice that applies to Business Rule conditions also applies to UI Action conditions: keep them simple and maintainable so that you are never surprised when a UI Action is available.

Running client- or server-side code

What is quite special (and confusing!) about a UI Action is that the code that it runs can be either server- or client-side. In the definition of the UI Action, you can choose the **Client** checkbox, which will make an **Onclick** field appear. Any code that is entered here is placed directly in the HTML element on the rendered page, unsurprisingly, in the `onclick` attribute.

Additionally, the contents of the **Script** field are copied onto the page and enclosed in a `<script>` tag each time the button is shown. This is often used to provide a client-side function for the button to use.

A simple client-side UI Action example would involve populating the **Onclick** field with a function call that is then defined in the script field. Let's try this out with simple example.

1. Navigate to **System Definition** > **UI Action**, then click on **New**, and use the following values. Save once done.
   - **Name:** Show table name (client)
   - **Table:** User [sys_user]
   - * **Form context menu:** <ticked>
   - * **Client:** <ticked>
   - **Onclick:**

```
sayHelloWorld()
```

   - **Script:**

```
function sayHelloWorld() {
   alert('This is ' + g_form.getTableName());
}
```

This script uses the standard alert function in JavaScript to pop a simple dialog. The name of the table is found by using the g_form global object. This is instantiated from GlideForm, which we'll discuss in the next few sections.

Client-side UI Actions are commonly used to control popup interfaces, such as custom dialogs. Some of the ways to do this, one of which is GlideDialogWindow, are explored in Chapter 10, *Packaging with Applications, Update Sets, and Upgrades.*

Due to a quirk of how the platform works, you can combine code that will be executed on the client and server in the **Script** field, by not wrapping it in a function. However, I strongly recommend this technique not be used since it can be very difficult to debug when scripts are running on both the browser and the instance.

Saving and redirecting

If the **Client** checkbox is not ticked, the code in the **Script** field is executed on the instance, as server-side JavaScript, just like a Business Rule. When the UI Action is clicked on, the form submits, and the code is executed before the next page loads. In this case, the usual server-side variables are available, including `current`. In addition, any changes to the fields in the record are reflected in the updated `GlideRecord` object.

It is the job of the UI Action script to save these changes. The script of a simple save UI Action would solely be `current.update()`. This would cause the database to be updated and trigger any Business Rules.

Try not to do too much in UI Actions; their purpose should be to help the user perform common actions by changing fields for them.

For example, in our hotel app, we could provide a button that extends all selected reservations by a day. The script in the UI Action in this case would change the **Departure date** fields and then save the record. The business rules can then pick up the job of validation and abort the update if it is not correct, rather than performing any checks in the UI Action script. This way, the server-side checks will be consistent, regardless of how the data enters the system: through a UI Action or a field entry.

When a button is clicked on, the platform defaults to returning you to the previous screen. For example, if you chose a record from a list and then clicked on a UI Action, the default action would be to return you to that list. While this is probably the most efficient navigation exercise, users often want validation that the command was successful, and they would also like to see the updated record. Therefore, it is very common to see the following statement in a UI Action:

```
action.setRedirectURL(current);
```

Despite the name, `setRedirectURL` is rather flexible as it accepts a `GlideRecord` object as well as a string that should contain a URL.

> The action variable does contain other functions, including `setReturnURL`. This allows you to specify where the platform will redirect the user after another click of a button.
> `GlideSystem` also provides `setRedirect` and `setReturn` which accept URLs. See the API docs for more information on both:
> https://developer.servicenow.com/app.do#!/api_doc?v=helsinki&type=server&scoped=false&to=method_class__unscoped_setredirect_object_uri__glidesystem__helsinki.

Converting a record from Reservation to Check-in

At the moment, our **Reservation** and **Check-in** tables are relatively unconnected. It's a manual copy-and-paste step at the moment to check in a guest when they arrive at reception. Let's address this with a UI Action that quickly makes a new **Check-in** record from **Reservation**.

1. Navigate to **System Definition > UI Action**, and click on **New**. Then, fill in the following values:
   - **Name:** `Check-in`
   - **Table:** `Reservation [x_hotel_reservation]`
   - **Form button:** `<ticked>`
   - **Action name:** `checkin`
   - **Condition:** `current.arrival > new GlideDate()`
   - **Script:**

```
current.update();

// Get lead passenger
var m2m = new GlideRecord('x_hotel_m2m_guests_reservations');
m2m.addQuery('reservation', current.sys_id);
m2m.setLimit(1);
m2m.orderByDesc('lead');
m2m.query();

// Create the new check-in record
var gr = new GlideRecord('x_hotel_check_in');
gr.newRecord();
gr.date = current.arrival;
gr.room = current.room;
if (m2m.next())
  gr.guest = m2m.guest;
gr.insert();

action.setRedirectURL(gr);
```

Let's walk through this script.

After saving the current record, the script uses `GlideRecord` to query the many-to-many table. Since the aim is to find the lead passenger, and we know there will only ever be a maximum of one lead passenger (due to our Business Rule), the script sets a limit in order to reduce the load on the database and the instance. By ordering the result set, the script ensures that a record that is marked as lead will float to the top.

The next block of code concentrates on creating a new Check-in record. It copies over the Date and Room, and if a lead passenger is found, it sets the Guest field. The record is then committed.

Finally, it asks the platform to display the new record on the screen.

Managing fields with UI Policy

In Chapter 3, *Server-Side Control*, we looked at Data Policies. These force a field to meet a condition by rejecting a database operation if it is necessary. The benefit of Data Policies is that it does not matter where the data came from. This will reject invalid updates from user entry, scripts, and even through web services, if the right options are set.

UI Policies have the same function, but they only work for browsers. They do have an advantage, however, since they work before the data is submitted to the instance, giving instant feedback to the user.

As discussed earlier, faster feedback to the user is often beneficial. However, UI Policies only request the browser to perform the check. While the ServiceNow admin controls the instance, we must assume that the user controls the browser. Later in this chapter, we will learn how a knowledgeable user can easily make the browser ignore any checks that you put in place.

Manipulating the form

In addition to making fields mandatory and read-only like Data Policies, a UI Policy action can also hide a field if a condition is met.

This power is often exploited by inexperienced admins as an opportunity to make very large forms and make UI Policies control the visibility of a large proportion of the fields. This is almost always the wrong thing to do. Having lots of UI Policies can quickly slow down the browser, as they perform lots of page changes and a multitude of checks each time a form changes. In addition, the browser would still need to load data and functionality that may never be seen or used-since the fields are hidden.

A good rule of thumb is that you should not hide more than 20 percent of the fields on page load using UI Policies. Instead, use other ways to control visibility, such as views.

Client-side conditioning

The way that a UI Policy deals with fields that aren't on the form depends on the UI version. In UI11 and below (Eureka and earlier), any condition that uses a field not in the form will evaluate to `false`. For UI15 and above, the field value will be copied from the database to the client, and the condition will work as expected.

A common way to make it work the same in all versions is to place the required fields in the form and then have a UI Policy that always hides them. However, this compounds the problem: there is now an extra field that needs to be rendered and an extra UI Policy-all to hide some fields that should not show up! Avoid this whenever possible.

Chapter 1, *ServiceNow Foundations*, showed you how views can be used to have different field layouts. That's often a better alternative.

Forcing a comment on reservations

In Chapter 2, *Server-Side Control*, a Data Policy rule was created to make a comment mandatory if the date was before the current day. One drawback of server-side checks is that the data must be submitted to the instance and the new page must be loaded in order to get the results. Instead, let's optimize the user experience by performing the checks on the client.

A Data Policy rule can generate the equivalent UI Policy for us, so you don't typically need to do both. However, to gives us the practice, we unchecked the **Use as UI Policy on client** field. There are even UI Actions to help you convert one to the other.

Navigate to **System UI > UI Policy**. Then, click on **New**, and use the following values:

- **Table:** Check-in [**x_hotel**_check_in]
- **Short description:** Force comment if in the past
- **Conditions:** Date - before - Today

    Save this (not Submit!) and create a new UI Policy Action in the related list by setting the following values, saving once done.

- **Mandatory:** True

- **Visible**: True
- **Field name**: Comments

Now, try to create a new **Check-in** record. The **Comments** field will not be shown by default now. If you select a date in the past, it will appear almost instantly and be set as a mandatory field.

 This example also highlights one of the differences between the client and the server. Try submitting a completely blank Check-in record. The client-side checks will not fire (and thus not force you to enter a comment), while the data policy will, even though the condition on the UI Policy and the Data Policy are exactly the same. This is because a blank Date field on the server is considered to be the Unix epoch (1 Jan 1970), and so, it will be considered before now, while on the client, it is seen as not valid and will not be checked.

Controlling UI Policies

The majority of UI Policies do not use any of the extra options available in the **Advanced** view of the UI Policy form. The defaults are generally appropriate, and I especially recommend leaving the **Reverse if false** and **On Load** fields checked.

UI Policies are always evaluated when the field to which they are attached changes, and this normally happens when the form loads (the browser "changes" the field when it is first displayed). Having **On Load** checked means the condition will always be evaluated. Otherwise, it is terribly confusing if the UI Policy only kicks in at certain times.

Reverse if false means that when the condition is false, the UI Policy actions are applied, but with the opposite action. This means that if you are displaying the **Comment** field when the date is before the current day, *it will be hidden at other times*. This is often what you want, but it can catch you unawares. This also makes conflicts much more likely since each UI Policy does two things: it makes changes when the condition is either true or false.

UI Policy conflicts occur when two actions for the same field are subjected to different conditions and the two conditions can both be true at the same time. The situation should be avoided to prevent unpredictable behavior, and the platform does a good job of warning you if this occurs. The simplest way to deal with this is to use the **Order** field: set more important UI Policies to have a higher number, and they will take precedence. Regardless, it is simplest to ensure that each field is only attached to one rule and make the condition very clear with multiple OR conditions if necessary to cover each situation.

The other options are straightforward. Perhaps the **Inherit** checkbox should be ticked by default, to be more similar with business rules and allow UI Policies to apply to extended tables. A nice feature is that you can use views to only apply UI Policies to certain circumstances.

Running client-side scripts

It would be inappropriate to have any chapter on client-side JavaScript without having a `Hello, world!` example at some point.

ServiceNow has a very simple JavaScript executor that is the equivalent of Background Scripts, but for the browser. On almost any page, pressing *Ctrl* + *Shift* + J will launch the JavaScript execution window:

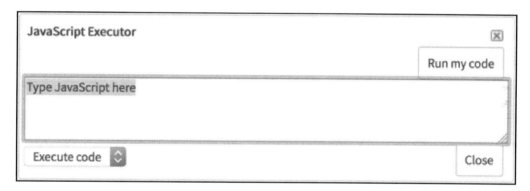

Let's run some code:

```
alert('Hello, world!');
```

Once you press the **Run my code** button, you should see the little pop-up alert box, as you may expect.

Your web browser executes the very simple JavaScript that you put in the window. Virtually every browser has a JavaScript console that provides the same functionality, which you will probably prefer, but it is helpful that ServiceNow gives you a simple alternative for every browser.

Scope on the client

The JavaScript executor will always run code outside of any scope. But as we journey through the platform, we'll find several places where only certain functionality is allowed, just like the server.

Scripts that are attached to a scoped app, such as Client Scripts and those in UI Policies, will not have access to mechanisms deemed inefficient.

Remembering client-side GlideRecord

Originally, ServiceNow provided a client-side class called GlideRecord. As you may suspect, it allows you to access the database from the browser. Whilst this seems wonderful in theory, the result was a lot of inefficient code. Inexperienced admins wrote scripts that ran on the load of a form, attempted to loop through hundreds or even thousands of records to process data, and performed all this without using callbacks. Together this caused the browser to freeze, and be unresponsive meaning users got frustrated. No-one was really happy.

While there are way to make it more efficient, ServiceNow has cut its losses and disabled the use of client-side GlideRecord in scoped applications. You may see it used in legacy code, and you may be tempted to use it if you are working in the global scope, but there are many better ways to achieve the same thing, (like GlideAjax) as we'll find out.

In addition, ServiceNow has also enforced the use of callbacks in any other functionality that communicates to the instance.

Understanding callbacks

As mentioned at the beginning of the chapter, a callback is a mechanism of freeing the browser up. Alternatively called a promise (especially in Angular), a callback is a function passed as a parameter that will take some time to return. The callback itself will take a parameter that contains the result of this processing. A good example is the `getReference` function of the GlideForm API we are about to see.

 If callbacks confuse you, try this nice explanation about the same concept in Angular: `http://andyshora.com/promises-angularjs-explained-as-cartoon.html`.

The defined function

Perhaps the more obvious way to do this is to create a new function and pass the reference as a parameter to the getReference function. The dealWithIt function is called when the data has been returned.

```
g_form.getReference(<field>, dealWithIt(data));

function dealWithIt (data) {
// do stuff with data
}
```

The results will be returned in the first parameter of your defined function.

The anonymous function

In the next example, an anonymous function is defined directly in the getReference method:

```
g_form.getReference(<field>, (function(gr) {
  // do stuff with gr
});
```

While this form may not be as familiar, it has the advantage of keeping all the code together in one place. This is typically the style that Angular and other libraries use.

Manipulating forms with GlideForm

A UI Policy conditionally performs a limited set of actions on a form, such as making a field mandatory or hiding it from view. Internally, this uses a client-side class called GlideForm, which is also available for use by the system administrator.

Just like business rules, ServiceNow provides some global variables that smooth the interaction with the platform. On every form, you'll find a g_form object.

For more information, check out the developer site:
https://developer.servicenow.com/app.do#!/api_doc?v=genev a&type=client&scoped=null&to=class__client_glideform__gen eva.

Using GlideForm

GlideForm provides getter and setter methods that provide access to the record as it is displayed on the screen. Let's run some code in the JavaScript executor in order to understand what options are available.

1. Navigate to a new **Check-in** record (**Hotel** > **Check-ins**, then press **New**). Populate the form as follows, but you don't need to save.
   - **Room**: 301 (you may need to create it)

2. The aim is to ensure the floor field is populated. Once done, press Ctrl + Shift + J to launch the JavaScript Executor.

3. Use the following code, then click on **Run**:

```
var floor = g_form.getValue('room.floor');
if (floor > 2) {
g_form.showFieldMsg('room.floor', 'This is a high floor!');
g_form.setDisplay('comments', true);
g_form.setValue('comments', 'Is the customer okay with high floors?');
g_form.flash('comments', 'lightyellow', 0);
}
```

4. You should see the comments field flash, get filled in, and a little blue field message appear, as per the following screenshot:

Let's look at the code in more detail. It is quite artificial, but it does show some of the important available functions:

1. The very first line uses a getter method of g_form. You pass it the field that you are interested in, and it returns the value that it finds. Note that this will always return a string, and it will always return what would be saved in a particular field in the database. For a reference field, it will return a sys_id value.

> Notice how we've used dot notation in this function. Since floor is a derived field, we needed to use the full path to the field to note that we access it through the Room field.

2. The next line is standard JavaScript. It runs the provided statements if the room number is more than 2. We are rather afraid of heights at Gardiner Hotels, so we have chosen a low number here!

3. The showFieldMsg function is a useful part of GlideForm. It puts a little message underneath the field that you specify, which is really helpful for drawing attention to invalid values. The platform will scroll to the field if it can. While the native alert function is useful for getting attention, it is also annoying and aggressive. A field message is a more gentle and persuasive method. There is also showErrorBox, which presents a more ominous warning.

4. The setDisplay function is an echo of the UI Policy. The first parameter specifies the field, while the second parameter lets you choose whether the field should be hidden or shown. If it is hidden, the function removes the field entirely from the form, and fields move around to fill the gap. There is also a function called setVisible that is very similar, but instead of removing the field completely, it fills the gaps with whitespace.

5. The setter in GlideForm is setValue. Pass a string value to this. For fields with a label on a data item, such as **Choice** fields, you must set the database value. For reference fields, this means that you must provide the sys_id value.

> Be aware that in order to provide the display value, the platform runs an Ajax call to find the display value. This may cause unexpected traffic if you are setting many reference fields. Instead, there is an optional third parameter to setValue that lets you specify the display value. Use this, if possible, to reduce network traffic.

6. The final line of significance uses the `flash` function. This draws even more attention to a field by performing a modicum of animation. The second parameter gives the color that the label should have, while the third parameter gives an indication of how many times it will flash.

For a guide to what the numbers mean, go to the API documentation:
`https://developer.servicenow.com/app.do#!/api_doc?v=helsi`
`nki&type=client&scoped=null&to=method_class_client_flash_`
`string_widgetname_string_color_number_count_glideform_hel`
`sinki`.

Choosing a UI Policy

`GlideForm` lets you duplicate the functions of a UI Policy exactly. In addition to the functions that we explored in the preceding section, `setMandatory` forces the platform to check for population before submission, and `setReadOnly` prevents you from easily typing in the field. This means that there is a tendency to use `GlideForm` as the primary method for manipulating the field layout, but this is not a good idea. If possible, use a UI Policy and then fall back to using `GlideForm` if you need to.

UI Policies have a number of advantages:

- They are optimized by the platform to be less resource intensive by storing the details in a format that can be easily parsed by the Client Scripts.
- They are more likely to be upgrade safe. Upgrades of ServiceNow may include further benefits, and UI Policies will easily be transferred to the new version.
- Other interfaces, such as mobile devices and tablets, are much more likely to work. While the desktop interface is by far the most used, alternative device types should not be forgotten.

Some `GlideForm` methods are unavailable on mobile devices, such as those that return HTML elements. Refer to the product documentation for more information:
`https://docs.servicenow.com/script/client_scripts/reference/r_`
`MobilePlatformMigrationImpacts.html`.

Client-side scripting

In many ways, Client Scripts are very similar to business rules, which, as we saw in the previous chapter, run in the instance. Both Client Scripts and Business Rules run JavaScript against a specific table, one record at a time. However, instead of triggering at database access, Client Scripts add interactivity to a form. When specific events happen on the page, such when a field changes, when the form loads, or when a UI Action is clicked on, the Client Scripts will be evaluated. These actions can all cause the JavaScript code of your choice to run. In the majority of cases, the scripts will use the `GlideForm` functions.

Client Scripts can run in four different scenarios:

- **onChange**: When a field is edited in a form
- **onLoad**: When the form is displayed in the browser
- **onSubmit**: When a UI Action is clicked on in the form
- **onCellEdit**: When a field is edited in a list

As with business rules and Script Includes, the platform gives a script template to use.

Client Scripts are supported for mobile devices, with some caveats. You must explicitly tell the platform that a particular script should be applied to a mobile device. Some API calls are also not available, specifically the ones that involve manipulating the DOM. The Product Documentation has more here: `https://docs.servicenow.com/script/client_scripts/concept/c_MobileClientGlideFormScripting.html`.

Sending alerts for VIP guests

Lets enforce a new rule at Gardiner Hotels: when a guest is checked in, the system should flag whether they would need special attention. To do so, we can reuse the VIP field that exists on the User table.

1. Start by navigating to **Hotel** > **Guests**, and select an example record.
2. Using the Additional actions menu, choose **Configure** > **Form Design**.

3. Remove all the fields, apart from User ID, First name, Last name and Membership number by clicking the x against one. Drag VIP from the left pane into the form, and rearrange everything to make it look nice. You should get something like the screenshot below. Save once done.

4. Finally, navigate back to **Hotel** > **Guests**, and ensure that some of the test **Guest** records have the **VIP** flag ticked.

5. To show a message in the form, we need a client script. To create this, navigate to **System Definition** > **Client Scripts**, and click on **New**. Then, use the following values:

- **Name:** Alert for VIP
- **Table:** Check-in [x_hotel_check_in]
- **Type:** onChange
- **Field name:** Guest

- **Script**:

```
function onChange(control, oldValue, newValue, isLoading, isTemplate) {
if (!isLoading) {
g_form.hideFieldMsg('guest');
}
if (newValue == '') {
return;
}
g_form.getReference('guest', function(g) {
if (g.vip == 'true') {
g_form.showFieldMsg('guest', 'Guest is a VIP!');
}
});
}
```

 This client script will be improved later in this chapter. It currently runs an Ajax call (through the `getReference` call) when a form loads, which is inefficient.

When you create a new client script, pick what type it needs to be first, since a typical function template will be given to you in the **Script** field. `onLoad` Client Scripts will have an `onLoad` function. Don't ignore or remove this! Before the script is inserted into the page, the platform renames the function so that it is unique and is run at the appropriate time.

 This is useful if you use the debugging tools in your browser.

Client Scripts do not have a condition field. Instead, you must include them in your script. The default template for an `onChange` script is quite typical, in that you generally do not have to run code if the user empties the field (represented by `newValue == ''`) or if the reason for the change in field value is that the form is loading.

 The `oldValue` variable is always the value that was in the database when the form was loaded. Perhaps it should be called `savedValue` instead!

In this code, the script uses `hideFieldMsg` to remove any messages put up. It does not remove messages when the script is loading, since there is no point in doing this. If the value of the field is empty, the script stops.

A useful function call for onSubmit scripts is getActionName in the g_form object. This returns the action name of the button that was clicked. When we created the button for **Check-in**, we used checkin.

The final part of the script uses getReference to query the database on the instance to get all the fields of the guest record that is referred to in the Guest field. An anonymous function is passed in as the second parameter, which then checks the value of the VIP field. Note that even though VIP is a boolean field, GlideRecord only returns strings. Therefore, it must be checked as such.

Remember that only guests with a reservation record will show up in the Guest field due to the Reference Qualifier added in the previous chapter.

The disappearance of current

What confuses many new system administrators is that current is not available on the client. They see the many similarities between the two environments and assume that their code will be completely portable. However, client-side code is often quite different, since it cannot assume that there is a fast link to the database.

On the server, the current object of GlideRecord is available in business rules, UI Actions, and many others. On the client, g_form is available as its closest functional equivalent; an object to manipulate the data with which the user is working. Since the two classes are focused on different things, there are quite a few differences: GlideForm focuses on the form, while GlideRecord is more about the data.

Check out the developer site for all the details:
https://developer.servicenow.com/app.do#!/api_doc?v=helsi nki&type=client&scoped=null&to=class__client_glideform__h elsinki

Unfortunately, the simple dot notation (current.name = 'Bob') is not possible using GlideForm, and longer getter and setter functions must be used (g_form.setValue('name', 'Bob')). Moreover, g_form can only change values that are in the form. In addition, to send the data to the instance and reload the window, g_form.save() is used instead of current.update() to commit to the database.

Changing, submitting, loading, and more

The most common use of a Client Script is to run JavaScript when a field changes. It allows the validation of fields as the form is being filled out. Alternatively, Client Scripts can validate fields right before the form is submitted to the server. Returning `false` in an `onSubmit` script will cancel the button click.

Client Scripts that run when a page loads should be avoided. For the vast majority of use cases, a **display** business rule is more appropriate since it avoids the browser needing to parse and work with the form right when the user is waiting. Any Ajax that runs when a page loads is heretical!

While every Client Script must keep the function that is provided in the template, it does not need to contain any code. Some `onLoad` functions are empty and have functions stored outside. For example, the following `onLoad` client script is storing a function that is accessible from other Client Scripts in the same table. The `onLoad` function itself is empty and has no purpose other than to keep the platform happy:

```
function onLoad() { }

function ratherUseless() {
    alert("I don't do anything, but I could be accessed by other Client
Scripts!");
}
```

UI Scripts is a better place to store libraries, as discussed in the next section.

Client Scripts marked as `onCellEdit` are the only ones that are relevant to lists. They allow the validation of changes made via list editing, where the user double-clicks on a field to alter the value. To reject a change and keep the value of the field as it was earlier, the callback function should be passed `false`. You are provided an array of the `sys_id` strings of the records that are being changed, though the `g_form` object of `GlideForm` is not available.

Validating the contents of fields

One important use of client-side scripts is their ability to validate information before it is submitted to the server. It's straightforward to write a Client Script to check a form, as we've just seen. In contrast, validation scripts are associated with a particular field type, such as strings, dates, or choices.

A topic of frustration is that **Date** fields are not validated on the client side. It is possible to enter any sort of text into a **Date** field and save the record. If it is nonsensical, the platform will ignore the value change with no error message.

Let's improve the situation with a few undocumented functions.

1. Navigate to **System Definition** > **Validation Scripts** and click on **New**. Then, use the following values, and Save once done.
   - **Type**: Date
   - **Validator**:

```
function validate(value) {
  if (!value) {
    return true;
  }
  if (getDateFromFormat(value, g_user_date_format) != 0)
    return true;
  return "Invalid date format. Please use " + g_user_date_format;
}
```

A validator script should return `true` if the `value` parameter is appropriate. Otherwise, it should return `false` to display a generic error message or pass a string to supply a custom one.

This short script firstly ignores any blank values. The `getDateFromFormat` function is an undocumented function that will return the number of milliseconds since the epoch, as long as it is passed a string that presents a date/time and the format of that date/time. If it cannot convert the time, it will return . The default format is `yyyy-MM-dd` (for example, `2016-12-25` represents Christmas Day in 2016). ServiceNow stores the user's date/time preference in another undocumented variable called `g_user_date_format`.

To validate **Date/Time** fields, use the `g_user_date_time_format` variable.

2. To try this out, navigate to **Hotel** > **Reservation** and click **New**. Type in a nonsensical date in the **Arrival** field. If you try to save the record, a field error message will appear with the message stating that the date format is invalid. The script will also fire on any other **Date** field, such as **Date** in **Check-in**. The following screenshot shows the output message that is displayed:

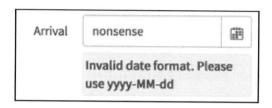

Storing code in UI Scripts

Client scripts are associated with a particular table, just like Business Rules. So it may not surprise you that there is an equivalent to Script Includes for the client: UI Scripts. However, unlike Script Includes, UI Scripts are only useful in very narrow circumstances. The majority of applications will not need them, so you may skip this small section if you wish.

UI Scripts allow you to store the equivalent of a JavaScript source file in ServiceNow, so are useful for scripts that will be accessible by multiple pages, or when you are building a custom interface, and therefore don't have access to Client Scripts.

A UI Script has a name that is used to reference the script by. To include a UI Script in a page, you can use a standard HTML script tag.

```
<script src="<UI Script Name>.jsdbx" />
```

Ensure you include the jsx suffix. The x denotes a cached, database sourced file.

Alternatively, the UI Script form includes a checkbox called Global. When ticked, the platform includes the script on every single page that is delivered to every user, regardless of table or type. You could create your own library of helper functions, and use them in Client Scripts. However, this is often not a good idea: there is the potential to impact browsing speed, and to conflict. Why include code you may only use a fraction of the time, causing the browser to spend time unnecessarily parsing it? But as ever with ServiceNow, the capability is there.

Efficiently transferring data to the client

Moving information from the instance to the browser is one of the most time consuming operations that you will need to do. The information you want could be many thousands of miles away, or it may take some time for the instance to process it. The users will not be impressed if their browser freezes while they wait.

We've already seen how the `getReference` function of GlideForm allows you to pull data from the instance through a reference field. This retrieves all the fields of a single record. But, it doesn't give very much control over what is sent and received.

`GlideAjax` is a technique that allows you to craft specific communication between the server and client, ensuring that only relevant data is transferred. Let's create a reusable way of grabbing the value of a single field of a record.

Since `GlideRecord` is not available to scoped apps, `GlideAjax` is the only way to get data from the client. However, it is also recommended to use it in non-scoped apps due to its performance benefits.

Writing a script include for GlideAjax

GlideAjax comes in two parts: a Client Script and a server-side script. A Script Include script should be written that extends the global AbstractAjaxProcessor.

1. Firstly, navigate to **System UI** > **Script Includes**. Click New and enter the following fields, before saving.
   - **Name**: QuickQuery
   - **Client callable**: <ticked>

This flag means that the scriptwriter understands that this code can be executed from the browser. Unless you are careful, you could create a data leak, and this is very possible with this script.

   - **Script**:

```
var QuickQuery = Class.create();

QuickQuery.prototype = Object.extendsObject(global.AbstractAjaxProcessor, {

  getField : function() {
    var table = this.getParameter('sysparm_table');
    var sys_id = this.getParameter('sysparm_sys_id');
    var field = this.getParameter('sysparm_field');
    var gr = new GlideRecordSecure(table);
    gr.get(sys_id);
    if (gr.isValidRecord())
      return gr[field];
    else return null;
  },

  type: "QuickQuery"
});
```

This script uses a few new tricks. You may have noticed that when you ticked the **Client callable** field, the template changes. The aim of this is to create a class that extends `AbstractAjaxProcessor`. It is in the global scope, hence the prefix. The class provides several helpful functions to ease the creation of a GlideAjax script. The `getParameter` function will get data that was sent from the client, while `setParameter` will send data back. Alternatively, as here, simply return a value to populate the `answer` parameter.

 To send multiple values, you can use the `newItem` function. On the client side, you would use `getElementsByTagName` to create an array of the values. Alternatively, you could create and return a JSON object.

`GlideRecordSecure` is an extension of `GlideRecord`, as you might expect. If it exists in the database, `GlideRecord` will generally find and return the data. It ignores all access control rules and is only affected by business rules and domain separation. In contrast, `GlideRecordSecure` respects access control rules. This means that you must have the right role or some other condition must be met. Access controls rules are discussed in `Chapter 7`, *Exchanging Data – Import Sets, Web Services, and other Integrations*.

For scripts that are accessible by the client, by not using `GlideRecordSecure`, you can open a security hole: a malicious user would be able to get any data they wanted from the platform. It would be especially bad if the script wrote or deleted records. However, `GlideRecordSecure` will not stop all malicious access, so ensure that the script includes that delete records are well protected with appropriate conditions and checks.

Using GlideAjax

In order to take advantage of this new Script Include, the **Alert for VIP** Client Script must be altered.

1. Navigate to **System Definition > Client Scripts** and open up the Alert for VIP record.
2. Remove the `getReference` function call, and replace it with this code snippet. It should look like the screenshot below. Save once done..

```
var ga = new GlideAjax('QuickQuery');
ga.addParam('sysparm_name', 'getField');
ga.addParam('sysparm_table', 'x_hotel_guest');
ga.addParam('sysparm_sys_id', newValue);
ga.addParam('sysparm_field', 'vip');
ga.getXMLAnswer(function(answer) {
  if (answer == 'true') {
```

```
        g_form.showFieldMsg('guest', 'Guest is a VIP!');
    }
});
```

Script

```
 1 ▾   function onChange(control, oldValue, newValue, isLoading, isTemplate) {
 2 ▾       if (!isLoading) {
 3             g_form.hideFieldMsg('guest');
 4         }
 5
 6 ▾       if (newValue == '') {
 7             return;
 8         }
 9
10         var ga = new GlideAjax('x_hotel.QuickQuery');
11         ga.addParam('sysparm_name', 'getField');
12         ga.addParam('sysparm_table', 'x_hotel_guest');
13         ga.addParam('sysparm_sys_id', newValue);
14         ga.addParam('sysparm_field', 'vip');
15 ▾       ga.getXMLAnswer(function(answer) {
16 ▾           if (answer == 'true') {
17                 g_form.showFieldMsg('guest', 'Guest is a VIP!');
18             }
19         });
20
21     }
22
```

The majority of the code sets the parameters that the Script Include will extract. Most are hardcoded, except for the parameter that contains the `sys_id` value of the guest whose record we want to check.

There are several other functions of GlideAjax that send the request and get the data. The `getXML` function of `GlideAjax` accepts a callback function in order to run the script asynchronously. It provides an unprocessed XML document to the function as its first parameter. The data can then be extracted using standard parsing methods such as `getElementsByTagName`.

Since the script is only getting a single data point from the instance, using `getXMLAnswer` saves us a few steps: it will unpack the XML document for us and give us a simple string from an attribute called `answer`. The script uses the result to determine whether the field message should be shown.

Using `GlideAjax` in this simple example is 50 percent faster than using `getReference` of `GlideForm`, with a data reduction of 90 percent! But this improvement doesn't mean you should use `GlideAjax` many times on a page; there is still come impact.

Passing data when the form loads

`Chapter 2`, *Developing Custom Applications*, introduced `g_scratchpad`. This is a mechanism to include arbitrary data as part of the page generation. At the moment, after the form loads, the client script runs an Ajax call, asking the instance for data. If we use the `g_scratchpad` object, we remove the need to contact the instance within milliseconds of the page being on screen-an obvious performance benefit.

1. Firstly, navigate to **System Definition** > **Business Rules**, and click **New**. Fill in the following fields, and Save.
   - **Name**: `Get VIP flag`
   - **Table**: `Check-in` [**x_hotel**`_check_in`]
   - **Advanced**: `<ticked>`
   - **When**: `display`
   - **Script**: Paste this into the provided function

```
g_scratchpad.vip = current.guest.vip;
```

The `g_scratchpad` variable is a global object that is initially empty. The platform turns it into JSON and injects it right before any Client Scripts are included on the page.

One of the benefits of server-side code is the extra flexibility that you get. The VIP field is accessed via dot-walking through the **Guest** field. This is much more convenient than the equivalent client-side `getReference` function!

Using scratchpad on the client

The `g_scratchpad` object is reconstructed on the client side as a global variable.

Edit the **Alert for VIP** client script again to take advantage of this data. The following reworked code includes the `GlideAjax` calls that we discussed previously:

1. Navigate to **System Definition** > **Client Scripts** and open up the Alert for VIP record. Update the **Script** field and Save.
   - **Script**:

```
function onChange(control, oldValue, newValue, isLoading, isTemplate) {
  var showVIP = function() {
    g_form.showFieldMsg('guest', 'Guest is a VIP!');
  };
  // Check the scratchpad. Regardless, leave if the form is being loaded
  if (isLoading) {
    if (g_scratchpad.vip == "true") {
      showVIP();
    }
    return;
  }
  // Always clear the flag if the field is changing
  g_form.hideFieldMsg('guest');
  // Do nothing if the field is empty
  if (newValue == '') {
    return;
  }
  // Check the database
  var ga = new GlideAjax('QuickQuery');
  ga.addParam('sysparm_name', 'getField');
  ga.addParam('sysparm_table', 'x_hotel_guest');
  ga.addParam('sysparm_sys_id', newValue);
  ga.addParam('sysparm_field', 'vip');
  ga.getXMLAnswer(function(answer) {
    if (answer == 'true') {
      showVIP();
    }
  });
}
```

The Client Script has changed a little. There are now two places where the system displays the message: one using the result of the scratchpad, when the form loads, and the other when the field changes. A `showVIP` function is used to reduce duplication. The code is otherwise largely the same, though some parts have been reordered to be as efficient as possible.

Storing data in the session

When a display business rule sets the `g_scratchpad` variable, the data is transferred to the client for that form. What if you had some data that you'd like to be available on every page?

Rather wonderfully, ServiceNow allows you to add data to the currently logged-in user's session, which is then accessible everywhere, on the client and on the server, at any time.

1. To try this out, go to **System Definition** > **Script – Background**, and run the following code in the global scope.:

```
gs.getSession().putClientData('myData', 'Hello, world!');
```

2. Now, visit another page and open the client-side JavaScript executor by pressing , press *Ctrl* + *Shift* + *J*. Then, run this code:

```
alert(g_user.getClientData('myData'));
```

Once you run the code, an alert box will appear on the screen that will show the text:

The data will stay available until your session ends, typically when you log out, or if the session times out. The default is 60 minutes.

In addition to `putClientData`, the server can also access data with the `getClientData` function call. The client-side `g_user` object does have a function called `setClientData` (notice the difference in names!), but it does not update the information on the instance; therefore, it only lasts for that page load.

 The `g_user` object also contains other items of data in addition to the custom session data. Try the properties of `userName`, `userID`, and `lastName` as well as methods such as `hasRole`. More information is available here:
`https://developer.servicenow.com/app.do#!/api_doc?v=helsi nki&type=client&scoped=null&to=class__client_glideuser__h elsinki`

This technique is an excellent way to have information easily at hand. Any data that may be used during the user's interaction with ServiceNow can easily be stored, meaning it does not need to be repetitively computed or pulled from the database. Indeed, it would be very useful even if it did not copy the data to the client.

 One useful mechanism is to use a Script Action (discussed in `Chapter` 6, *Developing Custom Applications*) to populate useful variables with information at login.

Controlling lists with Context Menus

It is not common for lists to be controlled with Client Scripts. In the majority of applications, users spend most of their time on a form and interact with a single record. We've already discussed UI Actions, which can be placed onto a list to affect multiple records at once. In addition to these, Context Menus provide even more choice. All the follow options provide controls that run client-side:

 Context Menus don't currently work with ListV3, which is the next generation of lists, and is optionally installed in Helsinki, and standard in Istanbul.

- **List title**: This provides filters for the table. It is visible when you click on a table's label at the top-left corner of the list. A list title generally affects the whole list in some way, perhaps by limiting the number of records on screen. The following screenshot shows an example of a list title:

- **List header**: This provides options for a particular field. It may include choosing a column to sort or enable grouping. These are visible when you right-click on a column heading. In addition to affecting particular fields, they also provide options to import and export data. The following screenshot shows a list header example:

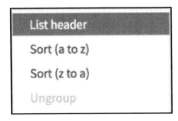

- **List row**: This is very similar to the **List context menu** UI Action. However, it provides more advanced functionality, such as submenus. These show up when you right-click on a row. The following screenshot shows an example of a list row:

Context Menus provide a great deal of flexibility in terms of how the items are laid out. All these types can create submenus to nest information and prevent options that may create a long list. Labels and separators allow you to provide a more controlled interface.

In addition to a standard condition field, Context Menus allow the use of dynamically controlled options. The platform allows you to add an arbitrary number of actions into each menu.

Finding out about the list

A context menu entry has access to several predefined variables. These are available everywhere a list can be found, even in Related Lists. The one that is most useful is `g_list`. The `g_list` variable is an instance of `GlideList2`, which is equivalent to `GlideForm`. It provides several help properties and methods. These are mainly used within the **Action** script field that defines what the item will do, but they are also available in other script boxes.

> `GlideList2` shouldn't be confused with the **Glide List** field type. `GlideList2` is used to customize the lists to only grab data but not formatting markup in order to improve navigation speed. Refer to the documentation here, where you can also see documentation for `GlideList3`:
> `https://developer.servicenow.com/app.do#!/api_doc?v=helsi nki&type=client&scoped=null&to=class__client_glidelist2__ g_list___helsinki.`

Some of the supported methods are as follows:

- getQuery: This provides the current encoded filter that the list displays. It accepts an object that uses flags to control what is returned. Use g_list.getQuery({all : true }); to return the group by, order by, and fixed parameter fields.
- setFilterAndRefresh: This changes which query will be run and refreshes the list to show the resulting records. It accepts an encoded query.
- getChecked: This returns a comma-separated list of the sys_id values of the checked records.

Opening a new tab

Context menus have a variety of uses, but they are not very common. Let's look at two simple examples to show the power that is available with them.

1. First, navigate to **System UI > UI Context Menus**. Then, click on **New**, and use the following values before saving.
   - **Table:** Global [global]

 This will affect all tables! An unusual power for scoped applications...

   - **Menu:** List title
   - **Type:** Action
   - **Name:** Open in new tab
   - **Action script:**

```
var url = new GlideURL(g_list.tableName + '_list.do');
url.addParam('sysparm_query', g_list.getQuery({all: true}));
url.addParam('sysparm_view', g_list.getView());

window.open(url.getURL());
```

To see the results of this addition, navigate to a list and then click on the menu icon at the top-left corner. Then select **Open in new tab** – and you should see a new window pop open. This script uses GlideURL to construct the address, using GlideList to grab the query and the view.

1. For another example, navigate to **System UI > UI Context Menus**, click **New** and fill out the form using the following values. Once done, Save.

   - **Table**: `Global [global]`
   - **Menu**: `List row`
   - **Type**: `Action`
   - **Name**: `Open in new tab`
   - **Action script**:

```
window.open('/' + g_list.getTableName() + '.do?sys_id=' + g_sysId);
```

When you right-click on a record in a list, you should now see a new option to open the record in a new tab:

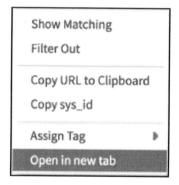

Customizing and extending the platform

Sometimes, administrators want to perform manipulations that `GlideForm` cannot do. This might include supporting additional events, such as `onmouseover`, or altering the layout of the page. Although I'll tell you how you can achieve this, I recommend that you don't use this technique in your production instance!

This section assumes that you have a basic understanding of dynamic HTML.

Firing on more events

Client Scripts allow you to run code when a field changes or when the form is loaded or submitted. However, the browser can inform JavaScript code about many more events, such as zooming the view, moving a mouse, or dragging files.

One way is to create an onLoad client script that sets up these events manually. The following code uses some undocumented functions of the ServiceNow platform to run scripts when the mouse moves over the **Departure** field on the **Reservation** form. Let's try this out:

1. **Navigate to System Definition > Client Scripts**. Then, click on **New**, and use the following values before saving:
    - **Name: Watch departure**
    - **Table: Reservation** [x_hotel_reservation]
    - **Type:** onLoad

```
function onLoad() {
var control = g_form.getControl('departure');
Event.observe(control, 'mouseover', function() {
g_form.hideFieldMsg(control);
g_form.showFieldMsg(control, 'in');
});
Event.observe(control, 'mouseout', function() {
g_form.hideFieldMsg(control);
g_form.showFieldMsg(control, 'out');
});
}
```

To test, move your mouse over the **Departure** field. You should get a little message saying **in**.

Firstly, `GlideForm` is used to get the field object by calling `getControl`. This is the HTML element that is displayed on the page. It is passed to a global function called `Event`, which accepts several parameters: the element in question, the event to react to, and the code that should run. Here, anonymous functions use some standard `g_form` functions.

> The Event.observe method is from the Prototype library, making standard functionality work across browsers. If ServiceNow stop using Prototype, this script will stop working too. Be warned!
> Read more here: `http://prototypejs.org/doc/latest/dom/Event/obse rve/`.

Additionally, you can create your own events. These are more useful if you are building a large client-side application, but these events also give an indication of how ServiceNow works under the hood. Consider the following script:

```
CustomEvent.observe('sayHello', function() {
  alert('Hello, world!');
});
CustomEvent.fire('sayHello');
```

Custom events are a way of passing information between different scripts, without creating very interlinked code. You can have many listeners all reacting on a single event, making it modular and reusable.

> This functionality is not documented on the ServiceNow Product Documentation. It should be considered unsupported.

Using built-in libraries

ServiceNow has historically been built on the Prototype JavaScript library. It is used to provide helpful shortcuts and remove browser inconsistencies; therefore, it provides a much smoother base on which to build `GlideForm`. However, Prototype's method of achieving this helpful functionality is now generally agreed to be the wrong way: it extends object classes, thus changing their definition. This causes cross-browser incompatibilities and potential performance problems among others. Other libraries, such as jQuery, wrap objects instead. This has been accepted as the better approach. As we'll see in Chapter 11, other libraries are gaining traction in ServiceNow, especially Angular.

Nonetheless, Prototype gives quick access to the DOM-the hierarchy of elements that the browser uses to understand and display the page on the screen. It then allows you to manipulate them very easily.

 Access to Prototype (and other libraries) is not allowed in a scoped app. This will work in the JavaScript Executor because the code runs in global.

To see what Prototype can do, follow these steps:

1. Navigate to **Hotel** > **Guests**, and select a record.
2. Once in the form, press Ctrl + Shift + J to open the JavaScript Executor.
3. Enter the following script, then click **Run my code**.

```
$$('input').invoke('observe', 'mouseover', function(event) {
    this.setStyle({fontSize: '30px', color: 'red'});
});
```

Close the dialog, then move the cursor over some text fields like First name. You should notice the font size increases, and the color goes red, just like this screenshot:

This code is quite impenetrable to someone who isn't familiar with Prototype or other JavaScript libraries. First, the code searches for all input fields through the $$ shortcut. It then runs a function called observe on each one. It passes the mouseover event name and a function that will be called when that event occurs. This function then increases the size and color of the font of the element, so you will get a supersized text when the mouse hovers over it. This code could easily be made part of a client script-as long as it is not in a scoped app.

While this example is just a nice trick, you could use similar techniques to really customize the way ServiceNow looks and feels. For example, you may want to change the background color of field labels dynamically or alter how the screen is laid out. However, this comes with some serious disadvantages, as mentioned in the next subsection.

What could go wrong

When you manipulate the layout of a document, you must make some assumptions about how that document will be laid out. An example is to alter the label of a field to include an icon. This is possible to achieve by setting a CSS style for the table cell. In order to do this, you need to know the way in which the text is oriented-is it right or left aligned? This will determine where the icon will fit best.

The ServiceNow development team is constantly looking to improve the look and feel of the interface. An upgrade of the ServiceNow platform may entail changes to assumptions that a script may be relying on. In the preceding example, the label's alignment may move from left to right.

Additionally, new techniques for accessing web applications are constantly being developed. Mobile devices are capturing an ever-increasing share of browsing habits. ServiceNow has an interface focused on tablets and mobile phones, where different assumptions than the desktop environment are made.

Scripts will break when assumptions are wrong. Any script that goes wrong may have unintended consequences, and non-functional scripts normally need to be fixed. This means that scripts that alter the layout must be tested after an upgrade to ServiceNow or when a new method of accessing ServiceNow is introduced. Since many customers want seamless upgrades with minimal testing and as little rework as possible, this means that scripts that alter the layout of a document through CSS, DOM manipulation, or otherwise should be avoided.

Taking control of the browser

Client-side code is executed by the browser. This means that, in many respects, it should be considered to be a polite request only! A technical user can easily undo the setting of a mandatory field that was achieved through a UI Policy or by `GlideForm`, as we'll see in this example:

1. Open the **Check-in** form in a new window. Do this by typing `x_hotel_check_in.FORM` in the application navigator filter text and pressing enter.

You must do this in a new window to escape the frames that interfere with the script.

2. Populate the fields as you wish, but ensure you set the **Date** field to a value in the past. This means the **Comments** field will be shown and made mandatory.

> Because of the UI Policy created earlier in the chapter, if you try to submit the form without a comment, the platform will notice and present an alert box. It won't let you send the data to the instance without filling in the comments.
>
> Now, pretend to be a malicious user. In the address bar of your browser, enter the following online script and press enter:

```
javascript:g_form.setMandatory('comments', false);
```

You may need to type this in rather than being able to copy and paste it. Some browsers attempt to protect against common attacks by removing the javascript prefix.

As you might expect, the **Comments** field loses its red mandatory indicator, and the form can now be submitted without a value. This means a user has subverted our controls!

Data Policies save the day

Luckily, Chapter 2, *Developing Custom Applications*, showed you a way to protect against such an attack. We've already put a Data Policy in place that captures the error. The familiar red error message is displayed, and the record is not committed to the database. We've been saved by the server-side check. If you wish, try disabling the Data Policy to prove that this is the only thing that is stopping the error from being shown.

This scenario is possible regardless of your role in the instance. You do not need to be an admin to disable mandatory fields in this way. With the right knowledge, a malicious user can instruct the browser to change the status of fields, setting read-only fields to writeable or mandatory fields to optional. Code need not be used at all, since most browsers have developer tools that allow the manipulation of fields directly. This method even allows the population of fields that are not on the form, by changing the name of input fields in the DOM.

This once again underlines the importance of having strong server-side controls to properly validate client-side data.

Summary

Most ServiceNow system administrators have had some experience working with client-side JavaScript. It is often very obvious and familiar to write scripts that interact with the web browser. Validating information using the browser will mean that your users can generally work more quickly with the application rather than clicking and waiting.

However, client-side scripts do have significant drawbacks. They should not be used to guarantee data integrity and enforce security controls since a malicious user can easily manipulate the browser to disable the checks. Client-side scripts can easily start to slow the browser down in situations such as when there are dozens of fields that are being hidden by a UI Policy.

However, there are many other ways of providing a great user experience. UI Actions are a great way to carry out complex actions in a single click. They can run code on the server, or in the browser, and can be placed on a form or in a list. Use them to simplify the interface for your users. In the same way, context menus let you manipulate lists and add additional buttons and functionality, mainly for power users.

If you need to communicate with the instance, `GlideAjax` is a relatively efficient mechanism, allowing you to grab precisely what is needed and leverage the database-processing power of the instance. However, this power doesn't come for free: doing this in tight loops will just cause the user frustration.

The next chapter focuses on the **Task** table. This important table begins our ascent out of the foundations of ServiceNow and into the building of a workflow-based solution that is designed to get stuff done.

5
Getting Things Done with Tasks

The first few chapters focused heavily on the underpinnings of the ServiceNow platform: how data is stored, manipulated, processed, and displayed. With these tools, you can create almost any forms-based application. But building from the foundations up each time would be time consuming and repetitive. To help with this, the ServiceNow platform provides baseline functionality that allows you to concentrate on the parts that matter.

If business rules, tables, Client Scripts, and fields are the foundations of ServiceNow, the **Task** table, approvals, and the service catalog are the readymade lintels, elevator shafts, and staircases-the essential, tried and tested components that make up the bulk of the building.

This chapter looks at the standard components behind many applications:

- The **Task** table is probably the most frequently used and important table in a ServiceNow instance. The functionality it provides is explored in this chapter, and several gotchas are outlined.
- How do you control these tasks? Using business rules is one way, but **Graphical Workflow** provides a drag-and-drop option to control your application.
- While you can bake in rules, you often need personal judgment. **Approval workflows** lets you decide whom to ask and lets them respond easily.
- The **Service Catalog** application is the go-to place to work with the applications that are hosted in ServiceNow. It provides the main interface for end users to interact with your applications. We will also briefly explore request fulfillment, which enables users to respond to queries quickly and effectively.
- **Service Level Management** lets you monitor the effectiveness of your services by setting timers and controlling breaches.

Introducing tasks

ServiceNow is a forms-based workflow platform. The majority of applications running on ServiceNow can be reduced to a single, simple concept: *the management of tasks*.

A task in ServiceNow is work that is assigned to someone. You may ask your colleague to make you a cup of tea, or you may need to fix a leaking tap in a hotel guest's bedroom. Both of these are tasks. There are several parts to each of these tasks:

- A **requester** is someone who specifies the work. This could be a guest or even yourself.
- A **fulfiller** is someone who completes the work. This may, less frequently, be the same person as the requester.
- The fulfiller is often part of a **group** of people. Perhaps someone among them could work on the task.
- Information about the task itself is included-perhaps a **description** or a **priority**, indicating how important the task is.
- The **status** of the task-is it complete? Or is the fulfiller still working on it?
- There is a place to store **notes** to record what has happened.
- An **identifier** is a unique number to represent the task. The `sys_id` parameter is an identifier that is very specific and unique, but not very friendly!
- Links, references, and **relationships** to other records are present. Is this task a subdivision of another task, or is it connected to others? Perhaps you are moving house-that's a big job! But this could be broken down into separate individual tasks.

Sometimes, a task may be as a simple as the equivalent of a Post-it note. Many of us have had something similar to "Frank called, could you ring him back?" attached to our desk. But you often need something that's more permanent, reportable, automated, and doesn't fall to the floor when someone walks by.

Looking at the Task table

The Task table in ServiceNow is designed to store, manage, and process tasks. It contains fields to capture all the details and a way to access them consistently and reliably. In addition, there is a whole host of functionality described in this chapter for automating and processing tasks more efficiently.

The product documentation has an introductory article to the Task table: `https://docs.servicenow.com/bundle/helsinki-servicenow-platform/page/administer/task-table/concept/c_TaskTable.html`. It also covers some of the lesser-used elements, such as the task interceptor.

To begin our journey, let's inspect the record representing the **Task** table. Navigate to **System Definition > Tables**, and then find the entry labelled `Task`.

In the Helsinki version of ServiceNow, there are 65 fields in the **Task** table. There are also many other associated scripts, UI Actions, and linked tables. What do they all do?

The **Task** table is designed to be extended, so you can of course add your own fields to capture the information you want. We'll do just that in a later example.

The important fields

It is often instructive to view the fields that have been placed in the form by default.

Click on the **Show Form** related link to take a look.

- **Number**: A unique identifier, it's a seven-digit number prefixed by TASK. This is constructed using a script specified in the dictionary entry.

The script uses details in the **Numbers** [`sys_number`] table, accessible via **System Definition > Number Maintenance**.

- **Assigned to**: This field represents the fulfiller-the person who is working on the task. It is a reference field that points to the User table. It has a reference qualifier that lets only users with the itil role be selected. Roles are explored further in Chapter 7, *Exchanging Data – Import Sets, Web Services, and other Integrations* but it will suffice to say that itil is usually necessary to work on tasks.

    The Assigned to field is also dependent on the Assignment group field. This means that if the Assignment group field is populated, you can only select users that belong to that particular group.

- **Assignment group**: This field is not in the **Task** form by default. You would typically want to add it using the Form Designer. Groups and users are discussed further in the chapter, but in short, it shows the team of people responsible for the task.

    Assignment group has been made a tree picker field. The Group table has a parent field, which allows groups to be nested in a hierarchical structure. If you click on the Reference Lookup icon (the magnifying glass), it will present a different interface to the usual list. This is controlled via an attribute in the dictionary.

    The following screenshot shows how an hierarchical group structure would be displayed using the tree picker:

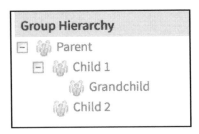

- **Active**: This field represents whether a task is "operational". Closed tickets are not active, nor are tasks that are due to start. Tasks that are being worked on *are* active. There is a direct correlation between the state of a task and whether it is active.

If you change the choices available for the State field, you may be tempted to write business rules to control the Active flag. Don't. There is a script called `TaskStateUtil` that does just this. Try not to cause a fight between the business rules! Refer to the wiki for more information on this:
`https://docs.servicenow.com/bundle/helsinki-servicenow-platfor m/page/app-store/dev_portal/API_reference/TaskStateUtil/concep t/c_TaskActiveStateMgmtBusRule.html`.

- **Priority**: This is a choice field designed to give the person working on the task some idea as to which task they should complete first. It has a default value of 4.

- **State**: This is probably the most complex field in the table–so much so that it has its own section later in this chapter! It provides more details than the Active flag as to how the task is currently being processed.

- **Parent**: This is a reference field to another task record. A parent-to-child relationship is a one-to-many relationship. A child is generally taken to be a subdivision of a parent; a child task breaks down the parent task. A parent task may also represent a master task if there are several related tasks that need to be grouped together.

Breadcrumbs can be added to a form to represent the parent relationship more visually. You can read up more about this here:
`https://docs.servicenow.com/bundle/helsinki-servicenow-platfor m/page/administer/form-administration/task/t_TaskParentBreadcr umbsFormatter.html`.

- **Short description**: Provide a quick summary of the task here. It is free text, but it should be kept short since it has an attribute in the dictionary that prevents it from being truncated in a list view. It is often used for reporting and e-mail notifications.

Short description is a suggestion field. It will attempt to autocomplete when you begin typing: type in "issue" as an example. While you are free to add your own suggestions, it is not usually done. Check out the product documentation for more details:
`https://docs.servicenow.com/bundle/helsinki-servicenow-platfor m/page/administer/field-administration/concept/c_SuggestionFie lds.html`.

- **Description**: Here, you provide a longer description of the task. It is a simple large text field.

- **Work notes**: This field is one of the most well-used fields in the form. It is a `journal_input` field that always presents an empty text box. When the form is saved, the contents of a journal field are saved in a separate table called `sys_journal_field`. The `journal_output` fields such as **Comments** and **Work notes** are used to display them.

 Work notes and Comments are heavily integrated into Connect. When you follow and subsequently chat about a task, the appropriate field is automatically updated. We'll cover more about this later.

Populating fields automatically

The majority of the fields in the **Task** table aren't directly used. Instead, many fields are auto-populated, through logic actions such as business rules and as default values. Others are optional, available to be filled in if appropriate. All the data is then available for reporting or to drive processes.

Some of the more notable fields are explained here, but this list is not exhaustive!

- The **Approval** field is discussed in more detail later in the chapter. There are several automatic fields, such as **Approval set**, that represent when a decision was made.
- A business rule populates **Duration** when the task becomes inactive. It records how long the task took in "calendar" time.

 There is also a **Business Duration** field to perform the same calculation in working hours, but it uses calendars, which are deprecated. The more modern equivalent is Service Levels, discussed at the end of this chapter.

- When a task is first created, a business rule records the logged-in user who performed the action and populates **Opened by**. When the task is set to inactive, it populates the **Closed by** field. **Opened at** and **Closed at** are date/time fields that also get populated.

- **Company** and **Location** are reference fields that provide extra detail about who the task is for and where it is. **Location** is dependent upon **Company**: if you populate the **Company** field, it will only show locations for that company. **Location** is also a tree picker field, like **Assignment group**.

- **Due date** is a date/time field to represent until when a task should be completed.

- **Time worked** is a specialized duration field that records how long the form has been on the screen for. If it is added to the form, a timer is shown. On saving, a business rule then populates the **Time Worked** [task_time_worked] table with the current user, how long it took, and any added comments.

- A formatter is an element that is added to a form (such as a field), but it uses a custom interface to present information. The activity formatter uses the **Audit** tables to present the changes made to fields on the task: who changed something, what they changed, and when.

Chapter 9, *Diagnosing ServiceNow – Knowing What Is Going On*, discusses the **Audit** tables in much more detail. The product documentation also has more information on the activity formatter: https://docs.servicenow.com/bundle/helsinki-servicenow-platform/page/administer/form-administration/concept/c_ActivityFormatter.html.

Recording room maintenance tasks

At Gardiner Hotels, we have the highest standards of quality. Rooms must be clean and tidy, with all the light bulbs working, and no dripping taps! Let's create a table that will contain jobs for our helpful staff to complete.

The process for dealing with a maintenance issue at Gardiner Hotels is straightforward; the need gets recorded in ServiceNow, and it gets assigned to the right team, who then work on it till it is resolved. Sometimes, a more complex issue will require the assistance of Cornell Hotel Services, a service company that will come equipped with the necessary tools. But to ensure that the team isn't used unnecessarily, management needs to approve any of their assignments.

Have a look at the following figure, which represents what the process is:

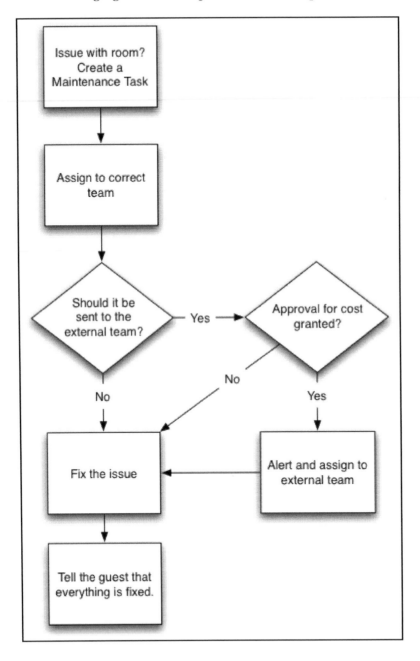

These requirements suggest the use of the Task table. In order to take advantage of its functionality, a new **Maintenance** table should be extended from it. All of the fields from Task, its business rules, and other functions will be available there. Chapter 1, *ServiceNow Foundations*, explains how table extension works.

Any time that a record is to be assigned to a person or a team, consider using the Task table as a base. There are other indicators too, such as the need for approvals.

In general, you should always extend the Task table when supporting a new process. Table extension gives natural separation for different types of records, with the ability to create specific logic yet with inheritance.

Now, let's create the **Maintenance** table by performing the following steps:

1. Navigate to **System Definition** > **Tables**. Click **New**.
2. Fill out the form with the following details, and Save when done:
   - **Label**: Maintenance
   - **Extends table**: Task
   - **Auto-number**: <ticked> (In the Controls tab)

3. Then, using the **Columns** related list, create a new field using this data. Save when done.
   - **Column label**: Room
   - **Type**: Reference
   - **Reference**: Room

4. Click on **Design Form** in **Related Links**, and do the following:
   - Add the **Assignment Group**, **Approval**, and **Room** fields and **Activities (Filtered) Formatter** from the selection of fields on the left.
   - Remove the **Configuration Item**, **Parent**, and **Active** fields

- Rearrange the form to make it look good! (Think about the suggestions in `Chapter 1`, *ServiceNow Foundations* - or make it similar to this screenshot.)

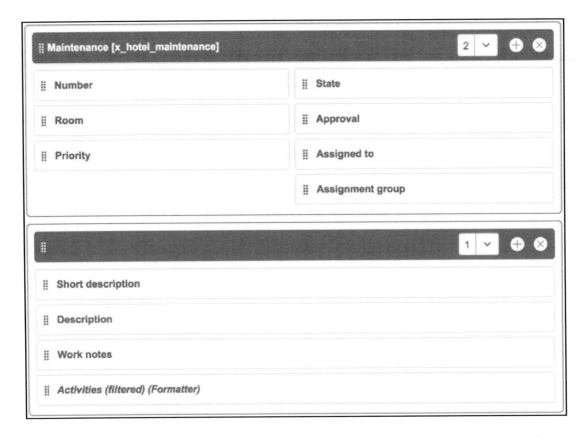

- Click the **Save** button, then close the Form Design window once done.

5. We want scripts to control the **Approval** field. So let's make that read-only. You should be in the Maintenance Table record. Find the Approval field in the Columns related list, and click on it.

6. Once in the Dictionary record, you will notice the form is read-only and there is a message at the top of the screen saying you can't edit this record since it is in a different scope. We do not want to take ownership of this field.

This record is in the Global application, but Hotel is the current application. To edit this record click here.

Changing the settings of a field in the Task table will change it for *all* tables extended from Task. This is often not what you want! Contrarily, a **Dictionary Override** will only affect the selected table. Read more about this here:`https://docs.servicenow.com/bundle/helsinki-servicenow -platform/page/administer/data-dictionary-tables/concept/c_Dic tionaryOverrides.html`

7. Instead, find the **Dictionary Override** tab, and click on **New**. Fill out the form with the following details, and Save.
    - **Table**: `Maintenance [x_hotel_maintenance]`
    - **Override read only**: `<ticked>`
    - **Read only**: `<ticked>`

There are better ways to make fields read-only. This configuration setting won't be enforced through scripts or a web service. `Chapter 7`, *Exchanging Data – Import Sets, Web Services, and other* Integrations, shows how ACLs can make fields read-only. We've done it this way for speed – and to show you how Dictionary Overrides work.

8. If you navigate to **Hotel** > **Maintenances** and click **New,** the Maintenance form should now look something like this:

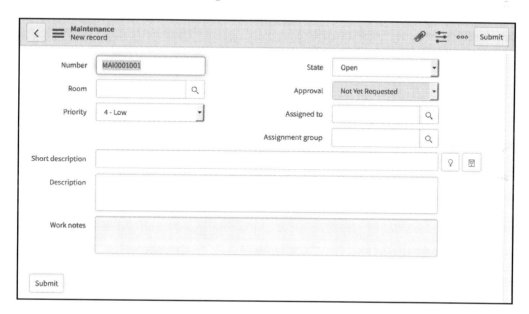

Working with tasks

You may be familiar with a work queue. It provides a list of items that you should complete, perhaps representing your work for the day. Often, this is achieved by assigning the item to a particular group. The members of that group then have access to the ticket and should do the necessary work to close it.

In ServiceNow, this concept is represented in the **Service Desk** application menu.

Open up the **Service Desk** Application Menu. You will find these options: **My Work** and **My Groups Work**. The former is a simple list view of the **Task** table with the following filters:

- Active is true. This filters out closed tasks.
- Assigned to is the current user, so if you are logged in as the user called System Administrator, you see tasks where the Assigned to field is set to System Administrator.
- State is not Pending, which filters out tasks that should not be worked on right now.
- The **My Groups Work** entry is very similar, but it shows tasks that haven't been given to a fulfiller and are still something that your group should deal with. It does this by showing tasks where the Assigned to field is empty and the Assignment group field is one of your groups. This means that when the My Work list is empty, you probably should get more work from My Groups Work.

The **My Work** list shows all records that are derived from the **Task** table. This means you will see a mixture of records from many tables in this list. It is incredibly useful to have a "single pane of glass", where all your activities are in a single place, with consistent fields and data values. They can be manipulated easily and effectively: assign all your tickets to your colleague when you go on leave with a couple of clicks!

Working without a queue

Some platforms make the use of a work queue mandatory; the only way to look at a task is through your work queue. It is important to realize that ServiceNow does not have this restriction. The **My Work** list is a filtered list like any other. You do not have to be "assigned" the work before you can update or comment on it.

It may be a policy restriction in your organization that you must be assigned the ticket before you can update it. If you want to enforce this behavior in ServiceNow, it is possible through security rules and business rules. However, this discourages collaborative working and information sharing. As mentioned in Chapter 1, *ServiceNow Foundations*, UI16 provides live updates of forms (if another user updates a record you are looking at, your form will update). which is a neater way to ensure the latest information is being viewed:
https://docs.servicenow.com/bundle/helsinki-servicenow-platform/page/use/using-forms/task/t_EditingInForms.html

There are many ways to find tasks to work on. This usually involves creating filters on lists. This may include tasks that have been marked as high priority or those that have been open for more than two weeks.

In many IT organizations, a central service desk team is the single point of contact. They have the responsibility of ensuring tasks are completed quickly and effectively, regardless of who they are currently assigned to. ServiceNow makes this easy by ensuring tasks can be accessed in a variety of ways and not just through a work queue.

Working socially

Social media concepts are infiltrating many aspects of the IT industry, and ServiceNow is not immune. Some useful ideas have been pulled into the platform in an attempt to make working on tasks a more collaborative experience, ensuring the right people are involved.

Chatting with Connect

Connect Chat focuses on bringing fulfillers together. As discussed in Chapter 1, *ServiceNow Foundations*, you can start chats with other users individually or as a group, bringing people into the conversation as needed. The UI16 Connect sidebar is easy to activate and use, letting you swap text, pictures, videos, and links easily and efficiently.

As discussed in Chapter 1, *ServiceNow Foundations*, the real benefit that ServiceNow brings with Connect is the ability to create a **record conversation** especially around tasks. This allows you to have a chat session that is connected to a particular record, allowing your conversation to be recorded and embedded. In Gardiner Hotels, the experienced staff probably already know how to deal with common maintenance tasks, and so by giving a newer team member easy access to them, our guests get better service.

The Follow button is already available on every table extended from Task. But what's special about Connect with the Task table is that the messages are added either as comments or work notes. While this is very useful for monitoring the progress of multiple tasks at the same time, record conversations are far less private: many users will have access to the activity log that shows the chat conversation. It probably isn't a good idea to share a meme in the work notes of a high-priority task.

> Additional comments and work notes are discussed later in the chapter

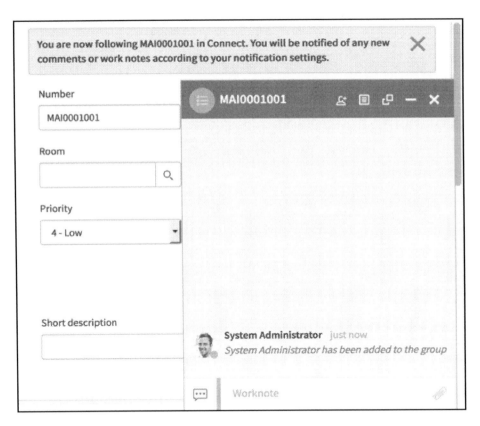

Communicating some more

In addition to Connect Chat, ServiceNow provides several other options to share information.

- **Connect Support** allows requesters to ask for help via chat. Generally, the requester initiates the session through a self-service portal, by clicking on a button and entering a queue. A Service Desk Agent can then work with multiple fulfillers in the Connect window.
- Older versions of ServiceNow had chat functionality, but it was limited in capability-it did not support in-browser notifications, for instance. Help Desk Chat was also limited by having to use a custom page rather than having it integrated into the main interface.

 Both Chat and Connect use the same tables to store the message; they should not be used at the same time. More information is available in the Product Documentation
https://docs.servicenow.com/bundle/helsinki-servicenow-platform/page/use/using-social-it/concept/c_HelpDeskChat.html.

- **Live Feed** gives a Facebook-wall type interaction, where all types of users can read and add messages. This can be used as a self-service system, since the messages are searchable and referenceable by copying a link. It is a communication mechanism that allows users to be as involved as they'd like. Unlike e-mail, Live Feed is pull-style communication, where users must go to the right place to receive information. To ensure it gets checked regularly and is therefore most beneficial, the right culture must be cultivated in a company. Navigate to **Collaborate** > **Live Feed** to use it.
- **Table Notification** creates Chat and Live Feed messages automatically based on conditions and configurations. For example, during a service outage, the service desk may want an automatic communication to be sent out, alerting people proactively. Check out **Collaborate** > **Feed Administration** > **Table Notifications**.

Organizing groups and users

In Chapter 2, *Developing Custom Applications*, the **User** table was extended to create the home for the **Guest** records. It is generally a good idea to keep all your users in the **User** [sys_user] table, since it lets you use things such as notifications and Connect easily and effectively.

To organize users, put them into groups. Groups and users have a many-to-many relationship. One person can be a member of many groups, and a group can have many members.

Groups are stored in the `sys_user_group` table. The relationship between groups is stored in the **Group Members**[`sys_user_grmember`] table.

Groups are also hierarchical. A group has a reference field pointing to the group table, letting you build up a parent-child structure. A person in a child group is also treated as a member of the parent group in most circumstances.

There are many different uses for groups. To help sort them, there is a list field called Types, though it is not on the form by default. This points to the **Group Types** [`sys_user_group_type`] table, which allows you to identify what this group is being used for.

Another way to achieve this is just to add boolean true/false representing the different options fields to the table. It is then very easy to check this in scripts and reference qualifiers.

Some of the common uses of groups include:

- **Assignment groups** will be completing tasks. There is a default Reference Qualifier on the Assignment group field that ensures that must have a type of itil (or be blank).
- The **organizational structure** of the company may be represented in groups. Departments and companies are mentioned in the next section.
- As discussed in the security-oriented Chapter 7, *Developing Custom Applications,* you may want groups designed to **distribute roles**-perhaps a Managers group that will have extra privileges.
- **Distributing reports** and **e-mails** via groups is very useful.
- Sending **approval requests** to a group rather than a user avoids making a process dependent on a single person.

Creating a room-maintenance team

In order for our room-maintenance system to be effective, we need some groups that will work on the tasks. First, let's create a new field in the **Group** table. We'll need to create a new view, since the Group table is global.

1. Navigate to **User Administration > Groups**, and click **New**. Use the menu button to select **Configure, Form Design**.

2. In the **Default view** drop down, select **New**. Type the following name, then click OK.
   - **View name:** `Maintenance`

3. Click **Save**.

4. Select Maintenance from the view drop down.

5. Drag in the **Name**, **Type**, **Manager** and **Parent** fields onto the form, so it looks like below.

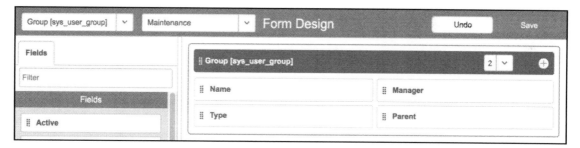

6. Click **Save,** and close the window.

7. Let's add a new Group Type. Unfortunately, there isn't a module for easy access. So type `sys_user_group_type.list` into the Application Navigator filter and press enter. This will open up the Group Types list.

8. Click **New**, fill out the following fields, and Save.
    - **Name:** maintenance
    - **Description:** Groups who do maintenance tasks

9. Now let's add a new module so we can access the maintenance groups more easily. Navigate to **System Definition** > **Modules**, and click **New**. Fill out the form using the following values, and Save.
    - **Title:** Maintenance groups
    - **Application menu:** Hotel
    - **Table:** Group [sys_user_group]
    - **View name:** maintenance
    - **Filter:** Type - contains - maintenance

10. Now the data structure is set up, navigate to **Hotel** > **Maintenance groups**, and click on **New**. Use these details, and be ensure to Save.
    - **Name:** Maintenance
    - **Manager:** Howard Johnson
    - **Type:** maintenance

11. Once saved, the **Groups** related list becomes available. Click on **New** to create a new child group with the following data:
    - **Name:** Housekeeping
    - **Parent:** Maintenance (should be populated already)
    - **Type:** maintenance

12. Finally, make another child group for **Maintenance**, with these details:
    - **Name:** Cornell Hotel Services
    - **Parent:** Maintenance
    - **Type:** maintenance

The **Maintenance** group should look as follows:

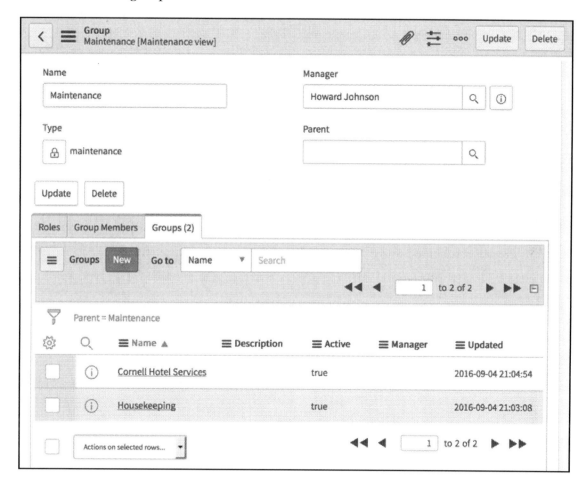

Creating a property

As briefly mentioned in `Chapter 1`, *ServiceNow Foundations*, properties are used throughout ServiceNow. These provide a simple way of altering how the system works in a very controlled manner without hardcoding choices. To organize them, go to **System Properties > Categories** and group the items together.

Let's make our own property to specify that Cornell Hotel Services is the external team that we should use when we need to call in the outside experts:

1. Navigate to **System Properties > Categories** and click on **New**. Fill out the form using the values below and once done, Save.
    - **Name**: `Room Maintenance`

2. This property is going to store the name of our external team. Click on **New** in the **Properties** related list. Use these details, and Save once done.
    - **Suffix**: `maintenance.external_group`
    - **Description**: `The group that gets approved maintenance requests`

3. Now, create another module. Navigate to **System Definition > Modules**. Click **New**, use the following details, and Save.
    - **Title**: `Room maintenance properties`
    - **Application menu**: `Hotel`
    - **Link type**: `URL (from Arguments:)`
    - **Arguments**: `/system_properties_ui.do?sysparm_title=Room Maintenance properties&sysparm_category=Room Maintenance`
    - The URL points to a UI page called `system_properties_ui`. It accepts two parameters: a category of the properties we are interested in and a title to display at the top of the page.

4. Once the module has been saved, the application navigator will refresh. Click on **Hotel > Room maintenance properties** link to see the simple interface, and populate the property as follows, then Save.

The group that gets approved maintenance requests: `Cornell Hotel Services`

 Using the name of a group in this way does mean that you cannot rename the group without updating this property.

The **Room Maintenance properties** page should look like the following screenshot:

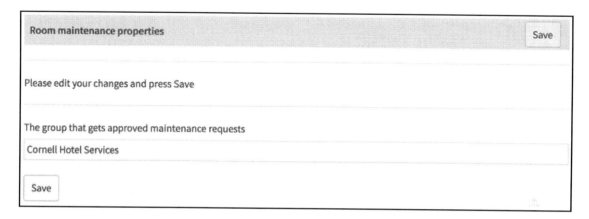

Using departments and companies

In addition to groups, ServiceNow also lets you associate users with departments and companies.

The **Department** `[cmn_department]` and **Company** `[core_company]` tables are slightly different to groups in that they have a one-to-many relationship with users; a user is only ever a member of a single department and company.

Each of these tables records relevant information: a department has a cost code and a manager, and a company may be a vendor, manufacturer, a customer or a mixture of all. Both tables are hierarchical and have a parent field.

Using additional comments and work notes

The central purpose of a Task record in ServiceNow is to record and communicate. There are two main ways to enter information in the **Task** table: **Additional comments** and **Work notes**. They provide a space to enter free-text information that will be presented in the activity formatter or in a Journal Output field, as an ongoing commentary on how the task is progressing.

In UI16, the two fields are typically combined into one to save space. There is a check-box to toggle between the two. A button lets you control this behavior.

You may wonder why there are two:

- **Additional comments** is provided for communication with the requester. Often, they are progress updates, giving the requester insight into how the work is going. They are made available to everyone.
- **Work notes** is targeted at notes for fulfillers. These are likely to be technical or sensitive in nature and should not be shared with the requester.

Work notes are highlighted with yellow, as per the screenshot above, to try to differentiate between the two.

As we'll explore later in Chapter 7, *Exchanging Data – Import Sets, Web Services, and other Integrations*, the **Work notes** field is protected by access control rules, which means that requesters cannot see any of these entries.

There are two other fields not yet mentioned: the **Watch** and **Work notes** lists. These are often tied to the journal fields through notifications. When an entry is made in the **Additional comments** field, the requester and the users in the **Watch** list are sent an e-mail. When you save a record with **Work notes**, the contents get sent to the **Work notes** list and the user in the **Assigned to** field. E-mail notifications are discussed in detail in the next chapter.

The **Watch list** and **Work notes** lists can contain e-mail addresses in addition to a `sys_id` value representing a user record. This means you can send updates to people who do not have a record in the **User** table in ServiceNow.

Understanding the State field

The state of a task drives a tremendous amount of business logic in a typical ServiceNow application. It represents how a task is progressing-whether it should be worked on, whether it actually is being worked on, and when the task is done. This may drive e-mail notifications, be a trigger for service-level monitoring, or be a condition for a security rule, to name but a few.

The **State** field in the **Task** table is an integer choice field. This means a number is stored in the database, while the available options are given labels. In general, scripts use the number value while the UI displays the label. This table details the relationship between the two:

Label	Number	Description
Pending	-5	**The task exists, but it shouldn't be worked on yet. It may have been created for planning reasons. The convention is that any number less than 0 represents a state that hasn't yet started.**
Open	1	The task has been created, but no one is working on it yet.
Work in Progress	2	The task is being worked on. This usually means that the **Assigned to** and **Assignment group** fields have been populated. This indicates who is responsible for, or who currently owns, the work.
Closed Complete	3	The task was finished successfully, and no further work needs to be done.
Closed Incomplete	4	The work has been attempted, but it was not considered a success. It might be that the task was impossible, that this section of the work failed, or that it was only partially finished. It is no longer being worked on.
Closed Skipped	7	The task isn't complete, but it is no longer relevant. Perhaps it has been canceled or a predecessor task has failed, meaning this task will not be worked on.

One benefit of having the State field backed by an integer is that you can create a filter using greater-than or less-than conditions. For example, you could have State > Closed Complete to get all the closed states in one go.

Also, you know you are a ServiceNow master when you can remember all the state numbers!

 These states are the default for tasks. Most tables that extend the **Task** table provide their own choices, as we'll see.

Configuring different states

Many task-based applications add, remove, and relabel state choices in order to better represent the specific type of work that the task represents. A very typical addition is Awaiting Requester. This usually means that the fulfiller, the user in the Assigned to field, is asking for clarification about the task-perhaps not enough detail was provided, or there are multiple ways to complete the task, and a choice should be given to the requester.

If the states are changed in an extended table, it is important to align them correctly. For instance, if you remove Closed Skipped and add Awaiting Requester, do not give Awaiting Requester a number value of 7. Otherwise, it can be confusing when comparing different ticket types.

Representing progress

The **progress** of a task is stored in lots of fields, not just State. State is often used for particular milestones, but other fields such as **Approval** also provide information about what is happening.

Don't try to cram too much into the State field. Break down information into logical chunks, avoiding a cluttered, unorganized choice field. If necessary, create a Substate field to provide more options-make it dependent upon State so that for each state, you can have multiple substates. The Incident Management application does this for the state of **On Hold** – a new field is made available called **On hold reason**.

There are three different closed states in the default configuration. I like to have a single **Closed** state and then a separate dependent **Substate** field that gives you further options to refine.

Navigating between states

It is very frustrating when you want to do something but, inexplicably, some system says **No**. Perhaps you are moving outside of the norm or are a power user-you know what you are doing is right, even if it is different. This is very often the case with states in a task. You may have a typical flow, moving from New to Open to Closed Complete, but are you allowed to move from New directly to Closed Complete?

In order to get a more visual representation of the **State** field, you can add a process flow formatter to the form. Find out more here:
`https://docs.servicenow.com/bundle/helsinki-servicenow-platfor`
`m/page/administer/form-administration/reference/r_ProcessFlowF`
`ormatter.html`.

ServiceNow is usually a permissive platform by default. This extends to the states. It is a choice field that allows you to select whichever state you'd like. You simply choose the one you want from the drop-down selection list and click on **Save** or **Submit**.

However, sometimes this isn't quite right. For example, there may be a business decision that means that once you have closed the task, it should be completely read-only; otherwise, it messes up reporting. If you reactivate tasks, your statistics may go backwards.

One way to fix this is to make the record read-only when the active flag is `false`. This is straightforward, as we'll find out when we discuss security in `Chapter 8`, *Securing Applications and Data*.

But what happens if you want to allow movement to **Closed Complete** only from the **Open** state? There are several ways to achieve this:

- Validate using a business rule with a script that uses `current.state.changes()` and check the `previous` and `current` values. This will work fine, but it only works on the server side. It is frustrating to click on **Submit** and have the system tell you your previous update wasn't valid!

- Have a client script dynamically add and remove options from the **State** field. This is more user friendly, but as we've seen in the previous chapter, it can be overridden quite easily. We could combine this and the previous option, but it involves a fair amount of scripting. There are some solutions out there that involve a data-driven approach, letting you populate a table that provides each allowed combination, but this is a heavyweight option.

> This option is used in the updated Change Request application available in Geneva. Look at the `Show valid states values` client script.

- My usual preference is to always make the state field read-only and then provide UI Actions to those that change the state for the user. This is secure, but it does involve potentially quite a few buttons. I also believe it provides a more intuitive action-instead of clicking on the dropdown menu, selecting the option you want, and then clicking on **Save**, you just click on the relevant button.

The biggest disadvantage is that a UI Policy that makes a field mandatory on a state change is harder to implement since no fields are changing. One way is to create an on submit Client Script that detect which button you've clicked (using `g_form.getActionName()`), use `g_form.setMandatory()` on the fields you want filled in, and then call `g_form.mandatoryCheck()` to determine whether they are filled out.

- All of these options are achievable without scripting by using State Flows. They let you specify which states are valid at each point and then create Business Rules, UI Actions, and Client Scripts automatically. It will even make fields mandatory, visible, or read-only. This functionality is enabled using a plugin.

To use **State Flows** [sf_state_flow], create a record for each valid transition. For example, if moving from **Open** to **Closed Complete** is appropriate, create an entry with a **Starting state** of **Open** and an **Ending state** of **Closed Complete**. You will likely need a few entries to cover every combination.

Then, decide how the transition should work: automatically when conditions are met (click on **Create Business Rule**), on a button press (click on **Create UI Action**), or manually (ensure the field is writeable, and then click on **Create Client Script** to limit the **State** selection box).

> The product documentation has more information on state flows:
> https://docs.servicenow.com/bundle/helsinki-servicenow-platfor
> m/page/administer/state-flows/concept/c_StateFlows.html

Ultimately, though, the design depends on how much freedom you wish to give the users of your application. If they need hand-holding, then it's useful to have a more controlled way of working. But experienced users may become frustrated if they are prevented from achieving what they want in an efficient manner.

Creating room maintenance states

Let's change the default states to be a little more relevant for the hotel application. It should represent when the outside repair team is required. Also, three different closed states are unnecessary. Follow these steps:

1. Navigate to **Hotel > Maintenances** and click **New**. Right-click on the **State** field label. Choose **Configure Choices**.

> You could use the **Show Choice List** option and do the work manually, but for extended tables, you need to be careful not to upset the default options. Use **Configure Choices** to add and remove options and **Show Choice List** if you need to change the values or labels of the options.

2. Remove **Closed Incomplete** and **Closed Skipped**, and add a new option with the following details, and Save.
    - **New item text**: External repair
    - **Numeric value**: 10

 It is a good idea to set numeric values to above 10, since you can then be sure they won't conflict with the default options. Be aware that the value is what is used to sort lists.

The choices should look as follows:

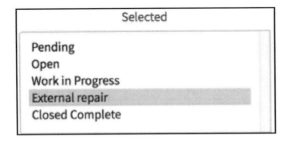

Although the Gardiner Hotels team is trustworthy, some control is needed behind the **External repair** option. Since it will involve a financial outlay, this state should be tracked and controlled. So, setting values should only be possible after appropriate approvals.

 State Flows remove the need for some of this scripting. But configuring this manually will make the steps clearer.

Enforcing on the server

To make our system secure, we should enforce the decision to set the state on the server:

1. Navigate to **System Definition** > **Business Rules**, click **New**. Use the following details and Save:
   - **Name:** `Secure external repair state`
   - **Table:** `Maintenance [x_hotel_maintenance]`
   - **Insert:** `<ticked>`
   - **Update:** `<ticked>`
   - **Filter condition:**

```
State - changes to - External repair AND
Approval - is not - Approved
```

   - **Abort action:** `<ticked>`

The condition means the business rule will run if a user tries to set the **State** field to **External repair** without the **Approval** field being set to **Approved**. It simply stops the update and ensures the database remains unchanged, just like `current.setAbortAction(true)`.

Adding a reference qualifier

Right now, a user could manually select Cornell Hotel Services. To fix that, let's filter out the group entirely using a reference qualifier. And for extra validation, let's show only the **Maintenance** groups.

> A Reference Qualifier only controls the user interface. Any sort of script can still set whichever group they wish, both on the client and the server.

1. First step is to write the Script Include. Navigate to **System UI > Script Includes**, click on **New**, fill out the form, and Save.
   - **Name:** maintenanceGroups
   - **Script:**

```
function maintenanceGroups() {
var gt = new GlideRecord('sys_user_group_type');
gt.get('maintenance');
return gt.sys_id;
}
```

This short script grabs the sys_id of the Group Type that has the name of maintenance. This does mean that the name cannot be changed without updating this script; it would be better to store it in a property.

2. Next, we need to add a Dictionary Override. Navigate to **Hotel > Maintenances** and click New. Right click on the Assignment group label, and choose **Configure Dictionary**.
3. Note there is already an entry for the Ref qual condition for the Task table. We want to override this, so choose New under the Dictionary Overrides tab. Fill out the field as follows, and Save.
   - **Table:** Maintenance [x_hotel_maintenance]
   - **Override reference qualifier:** <ticked>
   - **Reference qualifier:**

```
javascript:'typeLIKE'+x_hotel.maintenanceGroups()+'^name!='+gs.getProperty(
'x_hotel.maintenance.external_group')
```

This is an Advanced Reference Qualifier, as mentioned in Chapter 1, *ServiceNow Foundations*. It uses a short server-side JavaScript snippet to stop the user from picking a group with a name that has been saved in the property. In addition, it also uses our script to show only groups where the type field is populated.

 Unfortunately, Dynamic Filters can't be used in conjunction with Dictionary Overrides.

Test it out by trying to pick a group through the reference field. Navigate to **Hotel** > **Maintenances** and click New. Only **Maintenance** and **Housekeeping** should be available. If you are having trouble, ensure the groups have the right field values. The following screenshot shows what the tree picker should look like:

The reference qualifier controls the Assignment group field via the user interface. However, it doesn't stop updates via web services or via a Client Script. Therefore, if the data or process is particularly sensitive, write a Business Rule, Access Control Rule, or Data Policy to protect the data. It is good practice to have multiple layers of security.

Removing states with client scripts

Next, make the option unavailable in the **State** choice list. While the Business Rule will abort any update if the Approval field isn't set correctly, it's nice to stop users getting confused and thinking they can set it themselves.

1. Navigate to **System Definition** > **Client Scripts**, and click **New**. Fill out the form with the following data, and Save.
   - **Name:** Remove External Repair state
   - **Table:** Maintenance [x_hotel_maintenance]
   - **Type:** onLoad
   - **Script:**

```
function onLoad() {
if (g_form.getValue('state') != '10')
g_form.removeOption('state', 10);
}
```

This script uses the `GlideForm` object to remove the **External repair** option from the choice list, but only if the state is not already selected.

> This will only take effect in the form view. If you try editing the state field through the list, you can still choose External Repair. The **State** field could also still be set with web services or other client scripts. But our business rule won't let it be saved!

Automating an assignment based on state

There are several ways to set the Assignment group and Assigned to fields. We could use Business Rules or Graphical Workflow, for example. But there are built-in ways to do this without any scripting.

Using Data Lookup

Data Lookup is a way to populate information based on rules. It works by storing a matrix of several combinations in a data lookup table that you build. When a record or field is inserted or updated, the platform searches this table for matches. If one is found, data is set.

For example, a data lookup table could contain rules about the type of Maintenance request that has come in. If it is about a room that needs refreshing, then it could be assigned to housekeeping. If the air conditioning is broken, it will go to Cornell Hotel Services.

Data lookup works on entire field values and only on a single table. Inheritance is not supported, so rules on the Task table don't apply to Maintenance. However, a clever trick is performing matching and assignment on both client and server sides so that fields are immediately and dynamically populated, but your rule will also be enforced by the instance.

> For more information on data lookup, check out the Product Documentation:
> `https://docs.servicenow.com/bundle/helsinki-servicenow-platfor`
> `m/page/administer/task-table/concept/c_DataLookupRules.html`.

Setting the Assignment group with Assignment Rules

Assignment Rules are a simpler alternative to Data Lookup. While Data Lookup is very powerful, allowing you to set any field, it does involve a quite a bit of configuration, including creating a new table.

In contrast, an Assignment Rule uses the simpler condition builder to specify when it should run. If it matches, then it'll either populate the Assigned to and Assignment group fields with a hardcoded value, or you can use a script. We have got the group we want to use in a property, so this option is perfect. Follow these steps:

1. Navigate to **System Policy** > **Rules** > **Assignment**, and click on **New**. Use the following values, and Save.
   - **Name**: Assign to External Team
   - **Table**: Maintenance [x_hotel_maintenance]
   - **Conditions**:

```
Approval - is - Approved AND
State - is - External repair
```

   - **Script**:

```
gs.getProperty('x_hotel.maintenance.external_group');
```

Once saved, the Assignment Rule will be active. When the condition matches, the script will set the Assignment group field to the one specified in the property. Assignment Rules only work on the server, so the Maintenance record will need to be saved before the change in assignment takes effect. Also, Assignment Rules only run if the Assigned to and Assignment group fields are empty-they won't overwrite an existing value.

2. Now, make a second assignment rule to provide a default value for the Assignment group field. Navigate again to **System Policy** > **Rules** > **Assignment**, and click on **New**. Fill out the form as below, and Save.
   - **Name**: Default assignment
   - **Table**: Maintenance [x_hotel_maintenance]
   - **Group**: Maintenance

Assignment rules will run in the sequence of the Order field, smallest first. The Order field is not in the form by default (though you can, of course, add it), but is shown in the list. Try list-editing it.

Drag-and-drop automation with Graphical Workflows

Chapter 2, *Developing Custom Applications*, discussed how Business Rules validate data and automate functionality. But, as always in ServiceNow, there is another way. The Graphical Workflow editor provide a drag-and-drop interface to quickly and easily run a series of automated steps, much like an automated flowchart.

Workflows consist of blocks called **activities**. An activity has outputs, usually representing the result of the activity. The outputs then connect to the next activity. The connections are called **transitions**. More than one activity can be running at any instant, as a single activity may have multiple output transitions. The outputs may be conditional: you often want a different path for failure than what you want for success. You could then choose to retry or simply give up and send a notification.

A workflow uses **stages** to summarize progress. Each activity can be associated with a stage, and the value of the stage is copied into a field of your choice. A stage gives the user an indication of how the workflow is moving, letting him or her know what is happening at the moment. Most of the time, the stage of the workflow is copied into the state field.

If you have several complex workflows, each following different paths, consider creating a field on the target table with a type of **Workflow** . It will dynamically contain the right options, based on the current workflow. To learn more about stages, refer to the Product Documentation: https:// docs.servicenow.com/bundle/helsinki-servicenow-platform/page/a dminister/using-workflows/concept/c_WorkflowStages.html.

Running a workflow

Just like much of the other functionality in ServiceNow, a workflow is set against a table with a condition. When the condition matches, the workflow runs against that record.

When you edit a workflow, it's in one of two states: **checked out** or **published**. For a workflow to be available for everyone to run, it must be published, while if you wish to edit the activities or transitions, it must be checked out.

The execution of a workflow typically lasts for a while, often as long as the record is active. The platform may run several activities and pause until a task is closed, an approval decision made, or a field changed.

Workflows are best suited for very controlled processes that step through activities in a linear, ordered manner, especially if there is automation. Tasks that jump from step to step, giving the users a lot of control with regard to what to do next, are not a great match. While you can have multiple branches and routing logic, it quickly becomes too complex to handle successfully, and your workflow becomes a nest of conditions and transitions. In such circumstances, you must consider carefully whether a workflow is the right approach-you may want to use Business Rules to accomplish the same functionality with a script.

It is also possible to run multiple workflows at the same time. This is appropriate for automating short, specific flows, but be careful not to have hundreds running against each record. Each workflow instance does consume resources and is far more intensive than a simple Business Rule.

Exploring under the hood

When a workflow starts running, it creates a record in the **Workflow Contexts** [wf_context] table. This contains reference fields to the record that started it, what stage it is currently at, and which workflow version it is using. Each time you check out a workflow, it creates a new version, stored in the **Workflow Version** table. Linked to this record are copies of all the activities and transitions that are used in this workflow.

 There is a good overview of graphical workflows in this wiki:
https://docs.servicenow.com/administer/using_workflows/concept
/c_WorkflowConcepts.html.

By navigating to **Workflow** > **Live Workflows** > **Active Contexts**, you can look at the running workflows. You get some helpful UI actions, such as **Show Timeline** and **Show Workflow**. The latter shows the workflow interface, but in a read-only fashion. The activity headers are color coded-green for running and blue for finished-which gives you an excellent overview of how the workflow is progressing.

The activities themselves are stored in **Workflow** > **Administration** > **Activity Definitions** [wf_activity_definition]. They consist of a script that extends WFActivityHandler with functions such as initialize (which runs when the workflow starts) and onExecute (which is called when the activity is run). The script has access to variables, which are displayed when you add the activity to the workflow. Perhaps the simplest activity is **Run Script**. It has a single variable, called script, and the workflow definition script simply runs eval on the contents.

Sometimes, you may want to alter activity definitions. Copy the original before making your changes to ensure that upgrades are more successful.

Exploring the activities

The activities available to the workflow are listed on the extreme right-hand pane of the graphical workflow editor. Some are dependent on the table the workflow is running against. For example, task activities are only available to a workflow from a table extended from Task.

The following activities are more commonly used:

- The **Approvals** group provides several activities that are mostly only available to Task tables. Workflow allows complex scenarios to be determined using the **Approval Coordinator** activity. The **Group Approvals** functionality allows us to involve multiple people easily. The next section dives into this topic in much more detail.

- The **Conditions** group allows logic to be made in the workflow through **If** and **Switch** activities. By looking at the value of fields, the workflow engine can go down different routes. Alternatively, you can add conditions that are based on the activities themselves by right-clicking on an activity and choosing **Add Condition**.

- **Wait for condition** will hold the flow until a field changes to a desired value. This is very useful in a branched workflow, perhaps to detect a canceled state.

Wait for Condition will only check its condition after the record is updated in the database. Unless the record is saved, changing a field on a form will not trigger anything. Note that the workflow is only evaluated when the record itself is updated; you may need to write script to broadcast the update event if you want the workflow to move on from other situations.

- Another way to hold up a workflow is through a **Timer**. It is very flexible, offering percentages, scripts, schedules, and time zones to work out how long it should wait. This activity is not dependent on the record being updated.
- You can send out e-mail notifications with the **Create Event** notification. Don't use the **Notification** activity directly, since it is very confusing to try to find the right definition for an e-mail message when it is in a Workflow step.

Chapter 6, *Events, Notifications, and Reporting*, discusses e-mail notifications in much more detail.

- **Create Task** is available for Task table workflows. It will create another task and link it to the current record through the parent field. If **Wait for completion** is ticked, the workflow will pause until the task is inactive. If you then add an exit condition, you can route on the success (or otherwise) of that task. The **Utilities** section brings you **Script** activities, the ability to easily send **REST** and **SOAP** messages, and other helpful options, such as **Turnstiles**, **Branch**, and **Join**. These three options help with workflow branching and having multiple activities valid at the same time. For example, **Turnstiles** is useful when retrying something several times while ensuring that the workflow doesn't enter an infinite loop.

Workflow activities run just like the *before* Business Rule, with an order of 1000. You don't need to call `current.update()` in a script.

- **Sub-workflows** allow you to call other workflows. Each can return values, letting you compartmentalize functionality for easy reuse.

A bigger list of activities is also available in the ServiceNow product documentation:
`https://docs.servicenow.com/bundle/helsinki-servicenow-platfor m/page/administer/using-workflows/concept/c_WorkflowActivities .html`.

Orchestrating your datacentre

ServiceNow Orchestration extends the base Graphical Workflow functionality to new levels. Rather than focus on automating tasks, Orchestration automates things outside of a ServiceNow instances, to affect remote services, servers and applications.

It provides several additional features, including:

- Pre-built activity packs, including ways to integrate easily with Active Directory, run PowerShell on remote servers, use SSH to copy files and execute commands, and more.
- Build your own activities much more easily, perhaps without scripting. It parses and maps data, checks output, shares information between activities.

Activities you build can also be shared (or sold!) on the ServiceNow store.

- The Orchestration databus provides a better way to share information between activities. It lets you drag outputs from one activity to the inputs of another. The databus is available for activities built with it in mind.

The extensions that Orchestration provides are very useful if you will be developing many workflows. However, it is sold separately as a separate ServiceNow application.

Using data-driven workflows

Since workflows are so powerful with the ability to run scripts, any updates to them are usually part of a development / test / release regime. While this reduces the risk of mistakes, it may mean that changes cannot be implemented as quickly.

The functionality and strategies used to manage testing are discussed in
`Chapter 10`, *Packaging with Applications, Update Sets, and Upgrades.*

To ensure that changes can be made quickly in production, a common strategy is to create
data tables that are used by the workflow or use platform functionality to drive the process.
For example, what should the Assignment group be for a new task? If this information is
hardcoded into the workflow, it is difficult to change. Instead, store it in a property or use
Data Lookup to populate the values.

Another common store of information is the **Configuration Management Database**
(**CMDB**). The CMDB is often used in implementations, and **Assignment group** information
could be stored there.

A common and useful script for the **Create Task** activity is to copy the
Assignment group from the parent task:
task.assignment_group = current.assignment_group;

Approving tasks

An important step in many applications is obtaining the approval to proceed. This may be
due to a financial outlay, risk to the business, or simply getting the validation that you are
doing the right thing.

There are several ways to get approval in ServiceNow. **Workflow** is the most powerful. For
very simple scenarios, however, Approval Rules may be sufficient (available under **System
Policy** > **Rules** > **Approval**). These allow you to hardcode a specific user or group or use a
script to determine who will be asked to make a decision if the condition matches.

When an **Approval** record is generated, it is always associated with a single person. That
person has two choices: to approve or reject. The decision of that person is taken into
account when deciding what should happen next.

It is common to want to customize the Approval activity to add options than such as **Need more information** or **Defer decision**. This may stem from the language of **Reject**, which is often taken to mean "everything should be cancelled" rather than "I don't support this in its current form." A rejection in an approval does not necessarily mean the whole request should be stopped. It just gives an alternative option to **Approve**. Instead, if you must change the Approval form, try just adding UI Actions and leave the workflow side alone.

If you ask a group of people for approval, each person in that group will have an Approval record generated for them. A **Group Approval**activity in Workflow gives you several options to determine what happens during an approval request. This includes the following:

- **An approval from each group**: If several groups have been asked, we need a positive decision from every group. We should wait until we get that.
- **An approval from any group**: It is good enough that one person approves.
- **An approval from everyone**: It must be unanimous.
- **The first response from each group**: Whoever answers first makes the decision for that group.
- **The first response from any group**: Whoever answers first makes the decision for everyone.

If anyone rejects, you can decide what happens:

- Mark the overall decision as rejected.
- Wait to see what others say. Majority may rule.

Alternatively, by using an **Approval Coordinator**, you can even make the decision through scripts. Maybe you want a majority decision-first to 50 percent wins!

Making the decision

When an approval request is sent out, the approver is sent an e-mail. In the e-mail are several links: one to view the approval request, another to see the record that is being approved, and two further links that open up a new e-mail-one to approve and one to reject. The approver therefore has a choice to approve via the web interface or using e-mail.

The next chapter, which looks at notifications in more detail, explores how this is actually achieved.

The web interface contains two form UI actions: **Approve** and **Reject**. The **Reject** button checks whether the **Comments** have been filled out-but it doesn't verify whether comments have been added via e-mail.

This is a great example of how you must think about all the methods of interaction, not just the web interface.

Understanding what you are approving

Approval records are stored in the **Approvals**[sysapproval_approver] table. The table contains a special reference field that can point to any table. This means that a workflow can create user approvals for any type of record.

This means that there is a single central store of all approval requests in ServiceNow. It may be an order for some new IT hardware or, as in our situation, a desire to bring in a team to fix a leaky tap in a hotel room.

This generic approach, although great for consistency and having convenience for the approved user, presents some challenges for the UI. If every approval request is handled the same, how can the approver know the specific details of the request? When you approve an order, you want to know how much it'll cost. When you approve a maintenance request, you need to know what's wrong. How do we show the relevant information?

In order to solve this conundrum, the **Approval** form has a formatter included, called **Approval Summarizer**. This pulls information from other tables to present relevant information in one place.

If you navigate to **System UI > UI Macros**, you can filter the list to show all the records that start with approval_summarizer. There is a specific UI macro for each table that needs a custom summary. The name of the table adds a suffix to the name. If there is no specific UI macro, the default is used instead, which embeds the pop-up summary window in the form instead.

Type in `approval_summarizer%` into the **Go to Name** box on the **UI Macro** list. The percentage sign after the search term means **Starts With**, while as a prefix it means **Ends With**.

Asking for approval for the repair team

When a big maintenance job comes about, we need to call in the experts. In order to understand costs, we want to put a streamlined approval process in place. We'll do this using the following graphical workflow:

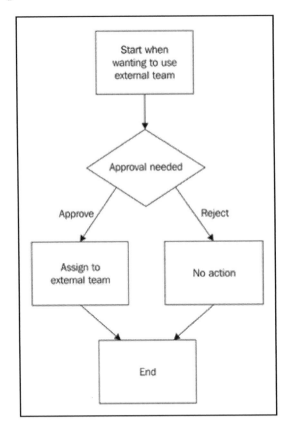

Performing the approval

Let's create the workflow. The workflow will create an approval request for the manager of the group, letting them decide whether a **Maintenance** task should be assigned to the external Cornell Hotel Services group.

1. Navigate to **Workflow > Workflow Editor** to launch the Graphical Workflow Editor. Click on the plus icon under the Workflows tab on the right. Use these details:

    - **Name:** `Ask approval for external team`
    - **Table:** `Maintenance [x_hotel_maintenance]`
    - **If condition matches:** `Run the workflow`

    There are three options:
    — **None** — means the workflow will not automatically run, but will only be triggered through scripts or other workflows.
    Run if no other workflows matched yet won't allow multiple running workflows. The order field is useful here.
    The default, **Run the workflow,** simply starts the workflow when the condition matches.

    - **Condition:** `Approval - is - Requested`

    Click **Submit** to see an empty workflow canvas with the `Begin` and `End` activities set out on the screen:

2. Then, add the **Approval – User** activity. Switch to the Core tab on the right, and find the activity in the **Approvals** group. Drag it into the workflow or double-click to add it automatically. We want to send the request to the manager of the group, so fill out these details and click **Submit**.

    - **Name:** `Manager approval`

```
Users: ${assignment_group.manager},
${assignment_group.parent.manager}
```

For **Users**, use the field selector to dot-walk to the manager of the **Assignment** group and the manager of the parent of the **Assignment** group.

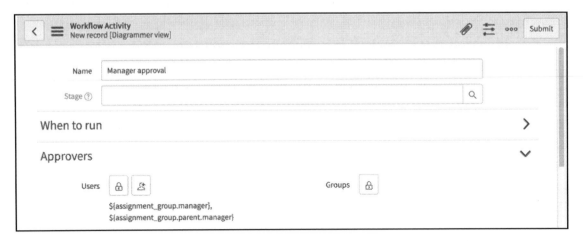

 This strategy of adding the manager of the parent and the group works because we know that one of the three groups we added will be the **Assignment** group, and only one has a manager.

3. Add a **Set Values** activity from the **Utilities** group, following the same technique of dragging it in.
   - **Name:** `Rejected`
   - **Set these values:** `Approval – Rejected`

4. Add another **Set Values** activity:
   - **Name:** `Approved`
   - **Set these values:**

```
Approval - Approved
State - External repair
Assignment group - <blank>
```

The status fields of Approval and State are set to the correct values and the Assignment group field is blanked out. This forces the Assignment Rule to run.

5. Remove the transition between **Begin** and **End** and then create the transitions:
   - From **Begin** to **Approval – User**
   - From **Approval – User: Approved** to **Set Values: Approved**
   - From **Approval – User: Rejected** to **Set Values: Rejected**
   - From **Set Values: Rejected** to **End**
   - From **Set Values: Approved** to **End**

6. Arrange the activities so the flow is clear like the screenshot below.

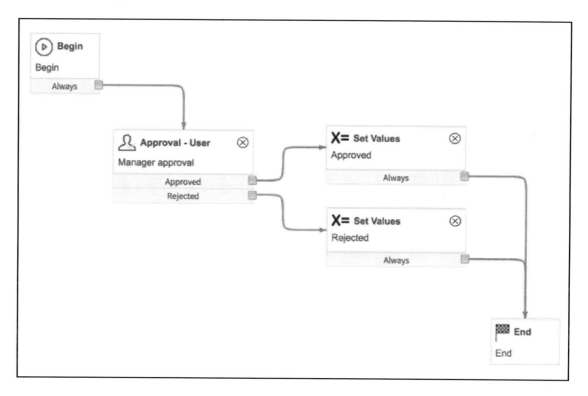

7. Click on the menu button, then choose **Publish**.

Starting up the workflow

The workflow starts when the **Approval** field is set to **Requested**. But the **Approval** field is read-only in the **Maintenance** form.

1. Navigate to **System Definition > UI Actions**. Click New, fill out the form, and Save.

   - **Name:** `Send to External`
   - **Table:** `Maintenance [x_hotel_maintenance]`
   - **Form button:** `<ticked>`
   - **Condition:** `current.active && current.canWrite()`

     The condition ensures the button only shows up when the task is active and the user has permission to write to the table.

   - **Script:**

```
if (current.approval == 'approved') {
current.assignment_group = '';
current.state = 10;
} else {
current.approval = 'requested';
}
current.update();
```

The script checks to see whether approval has already been granted. If it has, it doesn't run the workflow again, but instead sets the state and clears the Assignment group field, in the same way as the script in the workflow. Otherwise, it triggers the workflow to set by setting Approval to Requested.

> Of course, the Assignment group field could be set directly, using code such as
> `current.assignment_group.setDisplayValue(gs.getProperty('x_hotel.maintenance.external_group'));`.
> But it is a good idea to have a single place for setting fields. We are using Assignment Rules. Otherwise, it is confusing to determine which function is setting what and when!

Monitoring progress

When a workflow is running, it creates an entry in the workflow contexts table, available under **Workflow** > **Live Workflows** > **Active Contexts**. This lets you visualize the progress of the workflow. But this is hard to get to. Instead, the platform provides us with a very useful UI Action that gives a one-click visualization. Let's copy it for our purposes.

1. Navigate to **System Definition** > **UI Actions**, and find **Show Workflow** entry against the **Change Request** [change_request] table.
2. Choose **Insert and Stay** from the Additional actions menu to make a copy.
3. Change the fields as shown here, and Save.

```
Condition: !current.isNewRecord() && (new
global.Workflow().hasWorkflow(current))
Table: Maintenance [x_hotel_maintenance]
```

4. Navigate to **Hotel** > **Maintenances**, and select (or create) a new record.
5. Use the Additional actions menu, and select **Configure**, then **Related Lists**. Add the **Approvers** related list and click **Save**.
6. To test, click on the **Send to External** button.

7. Use the **Show Workflow** link to visualize progress, and as an admin, approve it on Howard's behalf by clicking on the **Approve** button

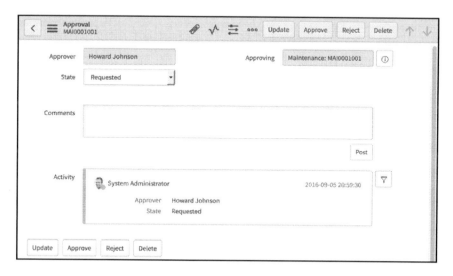

8. When you click on the Approve button, you should find the Maintenance record is change. State becomes External repair and the Assignment group is Cornell Hotel Services, as per the screenshot below.

Using the Service Catalog

The **Service Catalog** in ServiceNow is often the backbone of an IT portal. It makes it easy for end users to submit requests to fulfillers by providing a one-stop shop for ordering new equipment, creating tasks, and monitoring their progress with a simple and straightforward interface. It is designed to reduce distraction and be similar to systems that they are already familiar with.

Chapter 11, *Making ServiceNow Beautiful with Service Portal and Custom Interfaces,* builds a self-service interface with the Service Portal. It makes the Service Catalog much more beautiful and easy to use.

The Service Catalog is split into two main parts: a shopping-style interface (with a cart, items to order, and a more graphical interface than we've seen so far) and a fulfillment backend that uses workflows to control how the orders are processed. Often, the two are conflated, even though they are aimed at two different audiences and achieve very different purposes.

The different types of Catalog Items

The **Service Catalog** frontend can do more than just create orders. When you navigate to **Self Service** > **Service Catalog**, you will see many categories full of **Catalog Items**. A Catalog Item provides some sort of service to the end user, and as such there are several different types:

- A standard Catalog Item is an item that has a workflow attached. It is often a mechanism to order something new-such as a new keyboard or laptop-but may also be a request for a service. Once ordered, the items are processed using the **Request Fulfillment** tables. Unfortunately, there is no distinction between an orderable catalog item and the more specialized alternatives listed here, so I will refer to these as **Catalog Request Items**.

 Catalog Request Items could use execution plans instead of **Workflow**, but this is an older, less powerful alternative. In almost every situation, **Workflow** is the better choice.

- A **Content Item** can be a simple HTML page or a link to a knowledge base article or any other URL. It cannot be ordered or manipulated by the end user but does give read-only information.
- An **Order Guide** is a mechanism to order multiple catalog request items. By answering some initial questions, the order guide can bundle together several catalog request items and put them all in the cart.
- A **Record Producer** creates a record in a table of your choice. It provides an alternative friendly interface, which means that end users do not need to see the standard form. Record Producers could create reservations, guests, maintenance tasks, or any other record, which in ServiceNow means anything!

One of the defining features of a catalog item is that it is more graphical, with pictures and icons for each item, and HTML-formatted descriptions that allow the use of colors, fonts, and more. Together, these elements provide a more appealing interface than the typical stark form.

Using Service Creator

Service Creator is a streamlined way of populating the Service Catalog. It is designed to allow departments within a company take responsibility for their own services, giving them a step-by-step way to create all the items necessary. In fact, a self-service requester can request the functionality for their group or department. It doesn't give ServiceNow masters any new functionality, but does reduce the burden of administration.

 Again, we aren't going to use Service Creator in this chapter, since it hides many useful concepts from you. In any case, we've already done much of the work! The steps are summarized in the next paragraph, or take a look at the product documentation:

`https://docs.servicenow.com/bundle/helsinki-application-development/page/build/service-creator/concept/c_ServiceCreator.html`

The process for using Service Creator looks like this:

1. Create a new service category. You select which group or department this is for.
2. With a button click, the platform create a new category for the Service Catalog and a table extended from Task. Roles, modules, and other necessary items are also created.
3. By clicking on **Create New Service**, use the Service Creator to create a record producer. Using a simple drag and drop interface, you can add fields and pictures to make a system for your self-service users to submit work for the group or department to work on.

Creating a record producer

At Gardiner Hotels, it should be easy for our guests to communicate with us. Occasionally, there might be a problem, and it should be sorted out right away. Of course, our guests can pick up the phone and talk to someone at reception, but we also want to give them the choice of doing it via the new guest portal we are designing. Let's build a record producer to make it easier to create a **Maintenance** task. That way, our guests can tell us about a leaky tap very easily.

1. Navigate to **System Definition** > **Tables** and find the **Maintenance** table.
2. Click on the **Add to Service Catalog** link at the bottom of the table definition. It gives an interface that does a few steps for you.

This could be made manually through **Service Catalog** > **Record Producers**.

Enter these values into the form, and Save.

- **Name:** Room Maintenance
- **Short Description:** Submit a Room Maintenance issue
- **Category:** Can We Help You?

Pick **Short Description**, **Room**, and **Description** from the slush bucket.

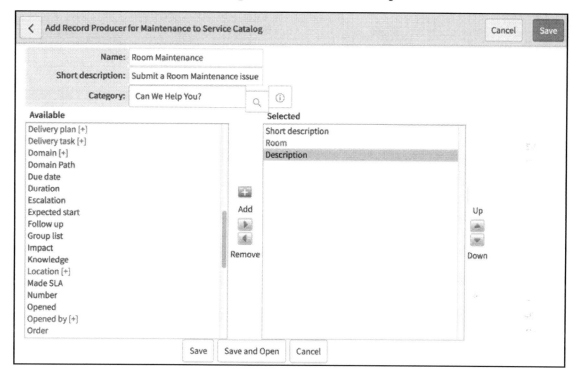

Picking these fields will cause three variables to be created. Variables are the way requesters specify what they want done. We are creating a maintenance form, and we would want to know which room the leaky tap is in.

There is more information about variables in the next section.

When you create a record producer, you often align the variables to the fields in the table. By naming the variables the same as fields, the record producer will copy data directly into the field when the record is created. This way, fulfillers can see what data was entered.

When you create variables, you can save yourself some time by using the **Map to field** checkbox. This automates this for you.

3. Click on **Save and Open** to see what was made.

Adding more information

The record producer that has been created is ready to go. But a few changes could be made to make it friendlier.

1. Add this information to the Record Producer form, and Save once done.
   - **Description**:

```
Are you having problems with your room? Please fill out this form, and
click the Submit button to send through a maintenance alert. One of our
team will be with you right away to fix the issue!
```

   - **Script**:

```
gs.addInfoMessage ('Your maintenance request has been received. The
reference number is ' + current.number + '. A member of the team will
contact you shortly!');
```

This simple code has a single purpose: when the record producer is submitted, it will display an informational message on the screen, giving the user some feedback. The `current` object is available and references the record you are making. The `producer` object gives access to variables and other data, though that isn't used here.

Additionally, let's take full advantage of the layout to give better text for the variables.

2. Click on each variable in turn in the **Variables** related list. Use these details to populate the form, and click Submit once done to return to the Record Producer.
    - **Short Description**:
        - **Question**: `What issue are you facing? Please give a brief summary`
        - **Mandatory**: `<ticked>`
    - **Room**:
        - **Mandatory**: `<ticked>`

    - **Description**:
        - **Question**: `Please enter a longer description that outlines the issue you are having.`
        - **Show help**: `<ticked>`
        - **Help text**: `For example, which tap is leaking?`

Routing the submitted request with templates

The next step is to tell the platform to route any of these requests to the housekeeping team created earlier. An Assignment Rule sets the Maintenance team by default, but the majority of end-user requests could be about cleaning. There are a number of ways to send the request to them instead, such as Graphical Workflow, more Assignment Rules, and other options, but we'll use a very simple template. This means it can be edited easily whenever necessary directly in a production instance instead of altering the script.

A template is an easy way to fill out fields of a form, like a typing macro. If you have the `template_editor` role, you can click on the **More Options** menu to see the **Toggle Template Bar** option.

1. Navigate to **System Definition** > **Templates**, and click on **New**. Use the following data, and Save:
   - **Name**: `Assign to Maintenance`
   - **Table**: `Maintenance [x_hotel_maintenance]`
   - **Template**:
   - **Assignment group**: `Maintenance`

The data in a template is actually stored in the database as a string, in the same format as an encoded query. This has the `field1=value1^field2=value2` format. It is displayed in the user interface in a much more accessible manner.

2. Navigate back to the record producer by going to **Service Catalog** > **Catalog Definitions** > **Record Producers**. Look for **Room Maintenance**, populate the following field, and Save.
   - **Template**: `Assign to Maintenance`

Testing the record producer

Try out the record producer and see how requesters could report an issue about a room.

1. Try either of these:

   Click on the **Try It** button in the record producer

   Navigate to **Self-Service** > **Service Catalog** > **Can We Help You?** and then choose **Room Maintenance**

2. Fill out the form with any details you'd like, and then click on **Submit**:

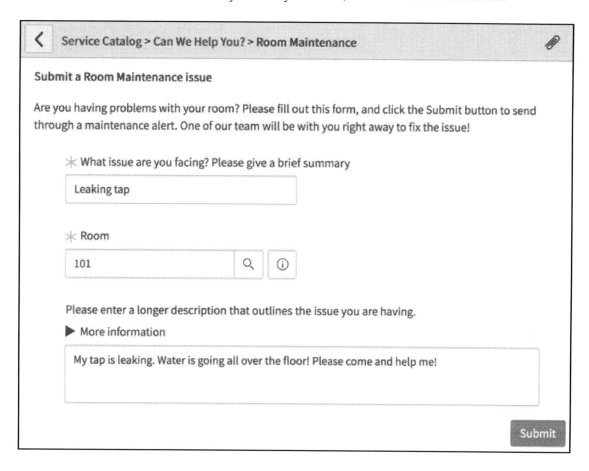

You will get an informational message at the top of the form, with the newly created record displayed. Check that it is assigned to the Housekeeping team. If you impersonate a member of the Maintenance team, you will see that it shows when you click on **My Work**.

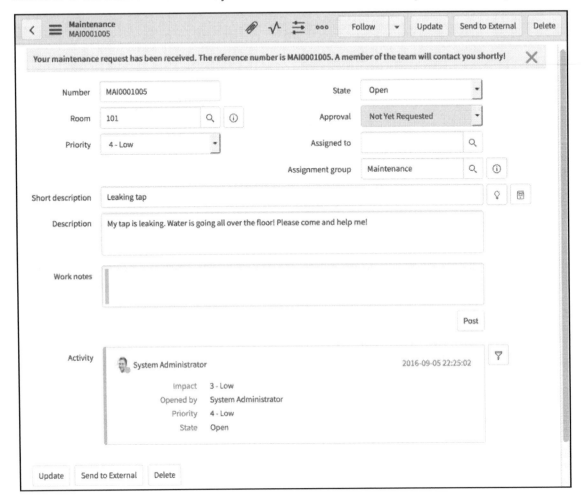

Understanding the data behind Service Catalog

Service Catalog items are stored in the `sc_cat_item` table. The different types, such as Record Producers, extend this table. They all contain a description of the item, its title, and perhaps how much it costs. For Service Request Items, there is a reference field to a workflow. The workflow is started once the item is ordered in order to control its fulfillment. For example, the workflow may say that a request needs approval before fulfillment, followed by two tasks, to two separate groups.

A Catalog Item is almost always associated with **variables**. Variables are the questions that are presented to the user while they are using the **Service Catalog**. They give a means for the end user to provide extra information and choices. In that sense, they are similar to fields on a table, but their implementation is very different.

As we saw in `Chapter 1`, *ServiceNow Foundations*, ServiceNow is built on a foundation of data. The vast majority of applications is built on top of a table that stores its data, and with which the business rules, client scripts, and security rules are all associated. When viewing a form, you see a database record. A list shows multiple records.

The **Service Catalog** does not use the same foundations. Instead, **Service Catalog** items are displayed much more dynamically, using multiple sources of information. Variables are stored in the **Variables** [`item_option_new`] table. Each variable has a **Name** (which is used in scripting), a **Question** label, and a **Type** (which is similar to the one for fields). You can create reference variables that point to a record in a table, date variables, and more, including radio-button choice variables that are not available as standard in a form.

 The product documentation has a list of all the variable types with examples:
`https://docs.servicenow.com/bundle/helsinki-it-service-managem`
`ent/page/product/service-catalog-management/reference/r_Variab`
`leTypes.html`.

Variables can either be associated with a single catalog item or with a **Variable Set**. A **Variable Set** [`item_option_new_set`] is a reusable grouping of variables that has a many-to-many relationship with variables and catalog items. Once in a **Variable Set**, a variable can then be associated with several catalog items.

When the Catalog Item is displayed in the **Service Catalog** interface, the system combines the information from these tables. Every Catalog Item, of which there may be hundreds or even thousands, may have different variables and thus different prompts for the end user, and different workflows to fulfill the request.

Configuring the Service Catalog

The difference in the data model means that many of the fundamentals explored in the first few chapters don't directly apply to the **Service Catalog**.

Business rules do not run against a catalog item, and Access Control Rules (explored in Chapter 7, *Exchanging Data – Import Sets, Web Services, and other Integrations*) are not applied. **Catalog Client Scripts** and **Catalog UI Policy** are similar to their form-based cousins, but are specially adapted. They are attached to a catalog item or a variable set instead of a table.

To control who can see and use a catalog item, use User Criteria. Navigate to **Service Catalog** > **Catalog Definitions** > **User Criteria** to see the options. As you set up your Catalog Items, you can decide whether group or department membership gives them access. Locations, companies, roles and even scripts can be used to determine whether a user gets access. You can even add your own fields to filter on.

User Criteria replaces **Catalog Entitlements**, which was used in older versions of ServiceNow. While performance has been improved, I still recommend avoiding scripts when possible. If you have thousands of catalog items and complex scripted entitlements, performance can be affected.

One addition that is only for Catalog Request Items is that of a cart. Similar to an online shopping system such as Amazon, the shopping cart allows the user to submit many items at once. You may order several laptops, some software, and perhaps a password reset, all at the same time. Note that Record Producers are not integrated into the cart; it is only relevant for Service Request Items that use the **Service Catalog** request-fulfillment system.

There are also quite a few system properties that control the **Service Catalog**. One includes having a two-stage checkout, which gives you a final opportunity to edit the variables and confirm any cost before submission. Have a look under **Service Catalog** > **Catalog Policy** > **Properties**.

The layout of the **Service Catalog** interface is highly configurable in recent versions of ServiceNow. Everything from the way the cart looks and works to the order of items in the checkout screen can be edited by navigating to **Service Catalog** > **Catalog Definitions** > **Maintain Cart Layouts**. Despite the name, all the checkout screens are also defined here. It also links to the UI Macros that actually generate the HTML, which allows you to have total control over the output. The UI Macros that control how the list and catalog items themselves are displayed are in **Service Catalog** > **Catalog Definitions** > **Renderers**. UI Macros are discussed more in Chapter 11, *Making ServiceNow Beautiful with Service Portal and Custom Interfaces*.

Understanding Request Fulfilment

The **Request Fulfilment** functionality in ServiceNow is a way to deal with requests created from a catalog request item submitted through the Service Catalog. This could be anything from a laptop order to a facilities complaint or asking HR a question. However, as we've already explored, the Service Catalog can also provide an interface to any other table through a record producer, such as our Maintenance request. That allows us to build a more custom system.

So, which should we use?

- **Request Fulfillment**: Catalog Request Items are useful for lower-volume, simpler requests or for requests that are highly aligned to orders. Workflow is used to create tasks or approvals.

  The **Catalog Item Designer** is a great way to quickly build out independent catalog request items in a guided manner. Since it doesn't use variable sets or custom workflows, it doesn't allow reusability but instead allows teams of people to maintain hundreds or even thousands of catalog request items directly in a production environment with minimal training. Check out the Product Documentation for more:
  https://docs.servicenow.com/bundle/helsinki-it-service-managem
  ent/page/product/service-catalog-management/reference/r_Catalo
  gItemDesigner.html.

- **Custom table**: Record Producers create a record in any table you specify. The use of a dedicated table gives more flexibility around custom fields, business rules, and other task functionalities. This provides the ability to implement the data structure that is most appropriate for the application. It is the more powerful option, but does require more configuration.

As your use of ServiceNow grows, you may decide to migrate from request fulfillment to a dedicated data table. If you start dealing with HR questions using request fulfillment, you may decide to use a dedicated table in the future, letting you categorize and manage your tickets in whatever way you'd prefer.

Checking out

The user of the Service Request Catalog goes through a few steps. Firstly, they find the Catalog Request Items they want, fill out the variables with the appropriate information, then put them in a cart. Once they are finished, they check out. The checkout process takes all the data and starts the request-fulfillment process.

The platform keeps a record of who is browsing the service catalog in the **Shopping Cart** [sc_cart] table. These records have a relationship with the **Catalog Item** [sc_cart_item] table, which references the data the user has given to the variables and what the catalog item it is.

Checking out is a conversion exercise for the instance, turning the cart into actionable tasks that can then get fulfilled. The three tables are the core of the request fulfillment process:

- A new record is created in the **Request** [sc_request] table. It acts as a container and a mirror for the cart-who ordered it, when, and what the total cost is.
- **Requested Item** [sc_req_item] records are made for each catalog item in the cart. It has reference fields to the Request table and to the catalog request item. Through the **Variable Ownership** [sc_item_option_mtom] table, requested items are associated with the answers that the user gave to the variables.
- **Catalog Tasks** [sc_task] are generated according to the Catalog Request Item workflow. These drive the implementation process. Usually, the Catalog Tasks represent the individual steps that are necessary to deliver the service; they are often assigned to a variety of teams who each need to do their part.

This graphic visualizes the relationship between each of the tables:

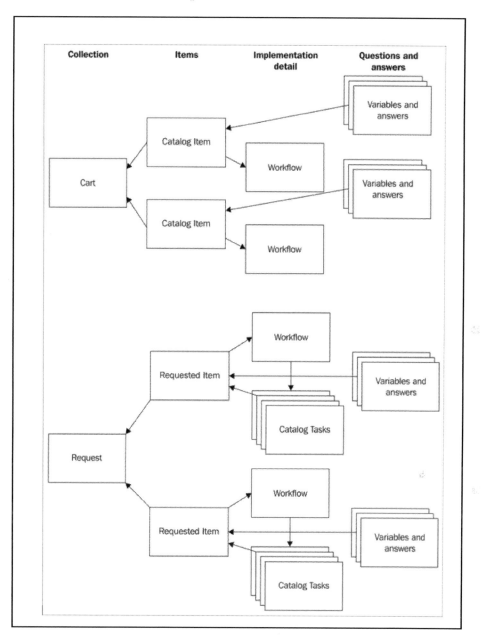

Using the request tables

All three of the request fulfillment tables extend the Task table. However, only Catalog Tasks are routinely assigned to fulfillers and their groups. A Service Desk may monitor the progress of Requested Items, while end users (the requesters) are more interested in the Request.

The three tables are generic. They always show the same fields no matter which catalog item has been selected. But the workflow allows per-item automation to occur. This may involve the creation of tasks and approval records. The progress of the workflow is recorded in a field on the request item table called **Stage**.

In order to see the information that the end user provides, the Requested Item form has a formatter called **Variable Editor**. This is a custom UI macro that queries the **Variable Ownership** [sc_item_option_mtom] table to find the answers and the variables that were entered when the Catalog Item was ordered.

Scripting variables

Whilst Business Rules can't run on catalog items, they can run on the Request Fulfillment tables (such as Requested Item and Catalog Tasks). This means you can control the delivery of items using normal ServiceNow business logic.

Business Rules and Client Scripts have access to variables once the Requested Item has been made. They are available through a global object called variables.

A Client Script (running on the Requested Item page) can use the following script to hide a variable called name:

```
g_form.setDisplay('variables.name', false);
```

The variables property is also added to the current object for Business Rules to access, as follows:

```
gs.addInfoMessage(current.variables.name);
```

Finally, you can also script the adding of items to the cart, and then the resulting generation of the fulfillment records:

```
var cart = new Cart(); // Clears the user's current cart
var item = cart.addItem(<sys_id of catalog item>, <optional quantity>);
cart.setVariable(item, <variable name>, <answer to variable>);
var rc = cart.placeOrder();
gs.addInfoMessage(rc.number); //rc is the Request GlideRecord
```

Service Level Management

When someone requests work, it needs to get done. The **Service Level Management** functionality specifies target times for how long a task should take and then uses Graphical Workflow to trigger notification reminders or perform automated actions. The results (success or failure) can also be reported or worked against.

The **Service Level Agreement** (**SLA**) engine in ServiceNow monitors effectiveness by comparing how long it takes to move between two conditions against a predefined goal. The main focus is on measuring time. For example, Gardiner Hotels may have a target of fixing all maintenance tasks within 2 hours, day or night.

This definition may be different to what you were expecting. In business terms, you may define a service level without a mention of times at all (such as reliability or uptime). These service levels may be recorded in ServiceNow using **Service Portfolio Management** or **Service 360**.

In addition, there are other ways to measure time, including metrics and using business rules to populate date/time fields. Metrics are discussed in Chapter 6, *Events, Notifications, and Reporting*.

Exploring the SLA data structure

The definition of the SLA is done in the **SLA Definitions** [contract_sla] table. You can see the list by navigating to **Service Level Management** > **SLA** > **SLA Definitions**. This table provides the key information that the platform needs to perform the calculations: when to start, when to stop, when to pause, and what the target time is.

> There is a field on the SLA called **Type**, with the choices **SLA**, **OLA**, and **Underpinning Contract**. These are only for reference, and selecting one does not impact how the system works.

An SLA can only be registered against a table extended from a task, such as Maintenance. When an SLA starts, it creates a record in the **Task SLA** [task_sla] table, which has a reference field joining the SLA and the task. In addition, there are fields that contain estimated and actual times and information such as the percentage complete. It also has a state field that is controlled by the SLA engine.

Timing an SLA

While many options are in an SLA Definition, probably the most important are the main condition fields: **Start**, **Stop**, and **Pause**. These are used by the SLA engine to manipulate the elapsed duration timer that is on the **Task SLA** record.

It is common for the SLA timer to start when a task becomes active and stop when it becomes inactive. This would be implemented by setting the **Start** condition to `Active - is - true` and the **Stop** condition to `Active - is - false`. The elapsed time would then be how long it took to transition between these two conditions.

There are optionally other condition fields, including the **Cancel** and **Resume** conditions, and the **When to cancel** options. These let you tailor how the platform responds when the Start and Pause conditions are not true. Often, you want to select `Start conditions are not met`. This means it is more accurate to think of the **Start** condition as "valid while" instead. If, at any point, the start condition is evaluated to false, the state is set to Cancelled. This means that the start condition must continue to be true all the time the SLA is running.

In addition, the timer does not increment as long as the **Pause** condition is met. This means that often the SLA elapsed time is only part of the actual calendar elapsed time.

To illustrate this, consider this simple example, where the target time is 15 minutes:

Event	Calendar time	Current timer
Start condition becomes true	09:00	0 mins
Pause condition becomes true	09:05	5 mins
Pause condition is no longer true	09:10	5 mins
Stop condition becomes true	09:15	10 mins

This would result in a completed **Task SLA** record with an elapsed time of 10 minutes and an elapsed percentage of 66 percent.

Finally, the **Reset condition** field will clear the elapsed time if met, meaning the timer starts from 0 again.

Travelling through time

There may be multiple SLAs registered against a single table. Priority-based SLAs are very common, where a high-priority task must be completed in a few hours, but a lower-priority task may take several days. In this situation, the priority is included in the condition. If the priority changes, the start condition no longer matches, and the Task SLA is set to cancelled. Usually, another condition matches and it starts running.

Often, in this situation, the elapsed timer should not be 0. Ticking the **Retroactive start** checkbox allows the selection of a date/time field that will be used as the starting point. In this example, setting the start time to Created means the timer will be populated as if the SLA started from the creation of the task.

> The platform is clever enough to use the audit history of the record to factor in pause times, even if the SLA wasn't actually running at that point.

This functionality is also employed in the **SLA Repair** UI actions that show on relevant task lists and forms. It reruns the current SLA definition from the beginning, allowing you to tweak or adjust parameters and see how they affect the calculations.

This functionality can be used to retroactively run SLAs on records that were created before an SLA definition was created, providing consistency across all records. However, since it relies upon the audit history, be very cautious about using it for imported data.

Enjoying relativity

The majority of SLAs have a specific, predetermined endpoint: maybe 4 hours or 4 days. But the platform also allows durations to be calculated. For a promise to do it "next day by 10 am", use a relative duration. The length of the timer will be dependent on when the SLA started. Relative Durations are defined by going to **System Scheduler** > **Schedules** > **Relative Durations** and writing a script. There are several examples in the baseline build.

> A Relative Duration is only ever calculated once, at the start. Don't expect it to keep recalculating throughout the life of the SLA.

Scheduling and time zones

An SLA can also take working hours into account during calculations. By specifying a Schedule (defined under **System Scheduler** > **Schedules** > **Schedules**), the timer will effectively be paused when appropriate. This is very useful for holiday periods. If a schedule isn't specified, the SLA runs all the time, 24/7.

Time zones are usually needed when a schedule is specified. When exactly 9 am-5 pm occurs depends on the time zone.

Both of these items can be specified in the SLA itself, or they can be derived from other parts of the system. If a task has a location and the location is associated with a time zone, the SLA may use this for calculations.

Customizing condition rules

The majority of SLAs run fine with the default condition rules; that is, they use the start condition to begin or cancel running, stop to finish, and so on. This logic is stored in a script include called `SLAConditionBase`.

A custom SLA condition rule will give you complete control over how SLAs work. Most often, you create a Script Include that extends `SLAConditionBase` and change the functions that control how the **Task SLA** states are changed.

For example, in `SLAConditionBase`, there is a function called `cancel`. When this function returns `true`, the **Task SLA** has **State** changed to **Cancelled**. In `SLAConditionBase`, this occurs when the stop and pause conditions are both `true`.

This allows you to alter the logic and even add in extra fields on the SLA definition page. For example, you may want to create a more data-driven approach to starting the SLA rather than relying on the conditions. For instance, you may want to have the SLA dependent on the Assignment group field, and create a lookup table to start at the right time.

You may wonder what is calling your new code. There is another Script Include called `TaskSLAController`, which is run by a series of Business Rules. I strongly recommend that you do not edit this script. It handles a variety of tricky situations in order to prevent race conditions, collisions, and several other events. It is often updated by the ServiceNow development team. If you edit it, you won't take advantage of the improvements!

Once you have defined an SLA Condition Rule, you can make it the default rule through **SLA Properties** or use a field in the **SLA Definition** table called **Condition Type** that lets you specify it per record.

> The Product Documentation has some very useful pages on custom condition rules, including state diagrams:
> `https://docs.servicenow.com/bundle/helsinki-it-service-managem`
> `ent/page/product/service-level-management/concept/c_SLAConditi`
> `onRules.html`.

Avoiding a breach

Having the timings of a task being calculated and recorded is very useful, but what makes the system especially powerful is the ability to run workflows. A workflow that is built against the Task SLA table has an extra activity called SLA Percentage Timer. This activity will have the workflow wait for a given percentage of the target time. This makes it very easy to have a generic workflow that can be attached to an SLA and makes it convenient to run commands at appropriate points. A reminder e-mail may be sent to the assignee of a task when the timer gets to 80 percent of the target time, and a manager may be informed in the case of a breach.

> An SLA percentage timer activity can have a separate flow that runs for SLA repairs, thus avoiding lots of e-mails that are sent out inappropriately.

Workflows offer more options than just e-mailing, however. The task could be reassigned to the service desk or another team, or a message could be sent to another system-anything a workflow can do.

Working SLAs

Additionally, the baseline configuration provides modules under the **Service Desk** application menu for working SLAs. Navigate to them by going to **Service Desk > SLAs > My Work**. This view looks at the Task SLA table, with field styles being used to highlight records that are paused and near to breach. Since the list can show information that is dot-walked through the Task reference field, it can show any information on the Task table, such as Short description or State.

The Task SLA table can be used as an alternative to looking directly at the Task table. This slight shift in perspective may have a dramatic impact on how fulfillers work: instead of attempting to close the ticket, they would be trying to stop the SLA. This may give better service to the requesters, or it may focus them towards gaming the system!

Ensuring maintenance is quick

Let's create an SLA to monitor the performance of our room maintenance. We have high expectations for our staff, and we want to be able to prove how good a job they are doing.

1. Navigate to **Service Level Management** > **Administration** > **Workflow Editor**. This module provides exactly the same link as the one in the Workflow Editor. Click on the plus icon under the Workflow tab to create a new one. Use the following information:
   - **Name:** Notify and reassign
   - **Table:** Task SLA [task_sla]
   - **If condition matches:** -- None --

   Click Submit, and create the workflow as follows:

2. Add the **SLA Percentage Timer** activity in the **Timers** group to the canvas:
   - **Name:** Wait for 75%
   - **Percentage:** 75

The SLA Percentage Timer has two exit points; one used during normal operation, and one used when the SLA is repaired. This lets you avoid email notifications and the like when SLAs are being recalculated.

3. Add **Create Event** from **Notifications** to the canvas:
   - **Name:** Give assignee a warning
   - **Event name:** sla.warning

Events are covered in the next chapter, Chapter 6, *Events, Notifications, and Reporting*.

4. Add the **SLA Percentage Timer** activity in the **Timers** group to the canvas:
   - **Name:** Wait for 25%
   - **Percentage:** 25

Note that the percentage timers are cumulative. Having 25 percent after 75 percent will be when the SLA breaches.

5. Drag **Create Event** from **Notifications** to the canvas:
   - **Name:** Notify manager of breach
   - **Event name:** sla.warning.breach

6. Finally, add a new **Run script** activity from **Utilities**:
   - **Name:** Reassign to default team
   - **Script:**

```
                    var tsk = current.task.getRefRecord();
tsk.assignment_group = '';
tsk.update();
```

This code follows the **Task** reference field in the **Task SLA** table using getRefRecord. This returns a GlideRecord. Then, the **Assignment group** field is blanked out and the record saved.

7. Remove the transition between Begin and End, and connect up the activities as follows:

- From **Begin** to **SLA Percentage Timer: Wait for 75%**
- Then to **Create Event: Give assignee a warning**
- Then to **SLA Percentage Timer: Wait 25%**
- Then to **Create Event: Notify manager of breach**
- Then to **Run Script: Reassign to default team**
- Then to **End**

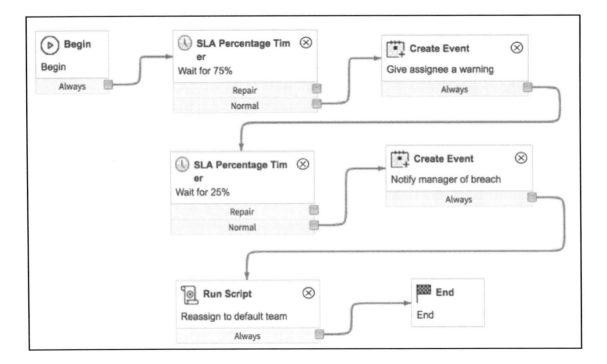

8. Click the Workflow Actions menu, and select **Publish**. You will get a warning because not all the outputs are connected, but that's okay; we are only testing. Click **OK** and close the window.

9. Navigate to **Service Level Management** > **SLA** > **SLA Definitions** and click on **New**. Use the following data, and Save once done.

- **Name:** `Priority 1`
- **Table:**
  `Maintenance [x_hotel_maintenance]`
- **Workflow:** `Notify and reassign`
- **Duration:** `00 : 05 : 00` (5 minutes-just for our testing purposes!)
- **Schedule source:** `No schedule`
- **Start condition:**

```
Active - is - true AND
Priority - is - 1 - Critical
```

- **Retroactive start:** `<ticked>`
- **When to cancel:**
  `Start conditions are not met`
- **Set start to:** `Created`

- **Stop condition:**

```
Active - is - false
```

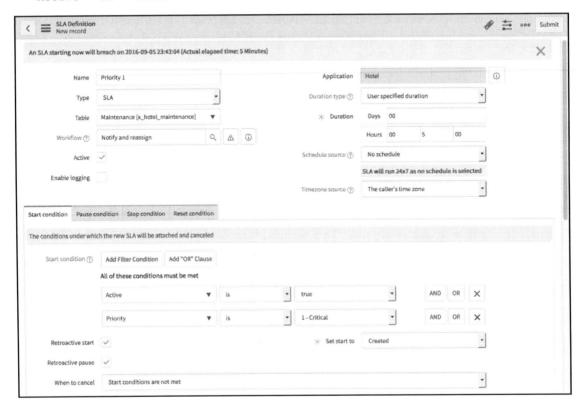

10. Once it's saved, make the following changes and use **Insert and Stay** in the Additional Actions menu to create an altered copy:
    - **Name:** Other priorities
    - **Duration:** 00 : 10 : 00
    - **Start condition:**

```
Active - is - true
Priority - is not - 1 - Critical
```

11. To test this out, navigate to **Hotel** > **Maintenances**, and create a new record with some sample data. Then use the Additional Actions menu and choose Configure, Related Lists. Add the **Task SLA->Task** related list. Click Save.

12. You should see the 10-minute SLA running against it. If you change the **Priority** field to 1 - Critical and save, you will see the SLA cancel and another one start. Keep refreshing the form using the **Reload form** context menu option to see the **Actual elapsed time** and percentage changing.

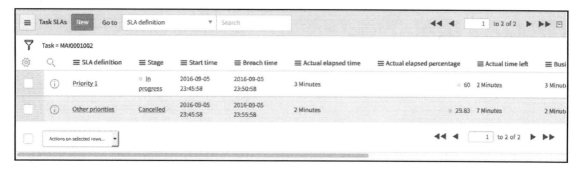

 The entries in the **Task SLAs** record are refreshed using a display Business Rule by default. This means that whenever you look at the form of a task, the related list will be updated, but it does put a load on the platform. There are many different options in SLA properties to control how they work.

Summary

This long chapter moved away from the foundations of ServiceNow and dealt with understanding how you can get work done in ServiceNow in more detail. The **Task** table is the basis of most applications-it provides the single place that all tickets are stored in. Over 60 fields have already been created, with logic built around them. This means reporting is much easier, consistency is improved, and implementation time is reduced.

The Graphical Workflow can control any table but is especially useful for Tasks. It provides a drag-and-drop interface, allowing you to chain activities together. It is integrated into the SLA system and is the best way to deal with approvals. Users and groups can be asked for their opinion, which the workflow can then use to decide the course of a task.

The **Service Catalog** presents a different interface to end users. Record Producers can collect information that then gets turned into a task or any other record.

Some **Service Catalog** items also make heavy use of workflow. We touched on how to perform request fulfillment in ServiceNow, which uses three tables, all derived from **Task**. Together, it gives you a prebuilt application that can easily be used to implement a simple process.

SLAs are used to time the progress of a task. By defining start, stop, and pause conditions, it enables you to monitor how well the team is completing tasks.

Altogether, ServiceNow is a great place to build a task-focused application. The platform provides lots of helpful functionality to build a very powerful application in a very short amount of time. We built a fairly fully featured maintenance application in the space of a chapter!

The next chapter looks at how to communicate from ServiceNow. This includes e-mails and reports and explores some more of the automation features of the platform, including scheduled jobs and events.

6
Events, Notifications, and Reporting

Communication is a key part of any business application. Not only does the boss need to have an updated report by Monday, but your customers and users also want to be kept informed. This can take up a lot of time – so wouldn't it be better if was made easy?

ServiceNow helps users to know what's going on, automatically and quickly. In this chapter, we'll explore the functionality available. The platform can notify and provide information to people in a variety of ways:

- Registering events and creating **scheduled jobs** to automate functionality
- Sending out informational **e-mails** when something happens
- **Live dashboards** and home pages showing the latest reports and statistics
- **Scheduled reports** that help with handover between shifts
- Capturing information with **metrics**
- Presenting a single set of consolidated data with **database views**

Dealing with events

Firing an **event** is a way to tell the platform that something happened. Since ServiceNow is a data-driven system, in many cases, this means that a record has been updated in some way. For instance, maybe a guest has been made a VIP or has made 20 reservations.

Several parts of the system may be listening for an event to happen. When it does, they perform an action. One of these actions may be sending an e-mail to thank our guest for their continued business.

You don't need to create an event to fire e-mail notifications. However, it is a good example to work through.

Events are fired using server-side code. Each includes a `GlideRecord` object and up to two string parameters. The item receiving this data can then use it as necessary, so if we want to send an e-mail confirming a hotel booking, we have the **Reservation** record to refer to during processing.

Registering events

Before an event can be fired, it should be known to the system. (This is mandatory in scoped apps.) Do this by creating a record in the **Event Registry** [`sysevent_register`] table, which can be accessed by navigating to **System Policy** > **Events** > **Registry**. It's a good idea to check whether there is an existing one you can use before you add a new one.

An event registration record consists of several fields, but the event name is the most important. An event can be called anything, but by convention, it is in dotted-namespace format. Often, it starts with the table name and then by the activity that occurred. An example is `task.approved`, which, perhaps surprisingly, is fired after a task has been approved.

As with other types of configuration, events created in an application will have a prefix.

Firing an event

Most often, a script in a business rule will notice that something happened and will add an event to the **Event** [sysevent] queue using the eventQueue function of GlideSystem. It accepts four parameters: the name of the event, a GlideRecord object, and two runtime parameters. These can be any text strings, but most often are related to the user that caused the event.

The **Event** table stores all of the events that have been fired, whether one has been processed, and what page the user was on when it happened. The platform deals with them in a *first in, first out* order by default. It finds everything that is listening for a specific event and executes it. This may be an e-mail notification or a script. By navigating to **System Policy** > **Events** > **Event Log,** you can view the state of an event, when it was added to the queue, and when it was processed.

Sending an e-mail for new reservations

Let's create an event that will fire when a **Maintenance** task has been assigned to one of our teams. We'll pick this up later when we perform e-mail processing.

1. Navigate to **System Policy** > **Events** > **Registry.** Click on **New,** set the following fields:

```
Suffix: maintenance.assigned
Table: Maintenance [x_hotel_maintenance]
```

2. Next, we need to add the event to the Event Queue. This is easily done with a simple Business Rule. Navigate to **System Definition** > **Business Rules**, click **New**, fill out these fields, and then Save.
    *   **Title:** Maintenance assignment events
    *   **Table:** Maintenance [x_hotel_maintenance]
    *   **Advanced:** <ticked>
    *   **When:** after

Make sure to always fire events after the record has been written to the database. This stops the possibility of processing an event even though another script has since aborted the action.

- **Insert**: `<ticked>`
- **Update**: `<ticked>`
- **Filter Conditions**:

```
Assignment group - changes AND
Assignment group - is not empty AND
Assigned to - is empty
```

This filter represents when a task is sent to a new group but someone hasn't yet been identified to own the work.

- **Script**: `gs.eventQueue('x_hotel.maintenance.assigned', current, gs.getUserID(), gs.getUserName());`

This script follows the standard convention when firing events: passing the event name, then current, which contains the `GlideRecord` object the business rule is working with, and finally some details about the user who is logged in.

We'll pick this event up later and use it to send an e-mail whenever it is fired.

There are several events, such as `<table_name>.view`, that are fired automatically. A very useful one is the `login` event. Take a look at the **Event Log** to see this happening.

Scheduling jobs

You may be wondering how the platform processes the event queue. What picks them up? How often are they processed? In order to make things happen automatically, ServiceNow has a **system scheduler**. Processing the event queue is one job that is done on a repeated basis.

ServiceNow sometimes creates extra nodes that only process events. These concentrate on the processing of things such as e-mails, enabling the other application nodes to better serve user interactions.

To see what is going on, navigate to **System Scheduler** > **Scheduled Jobs** > **Today's Scheduled Jobs**. This is a link to the **Schedule Item** [sys_trigger] table, a list of everything the system is doing in the background. You will see a job that collects database statistics, another that upgrades the instance (if appropriate), and others that send and receive e-mails or SMS messages. You should also spot one called **Events Process**, which deals with the event queue.

A schedule item has a **Next action** Date and **T**ime field. This is when the platform will next run the job. Exactly what will happen is specified through the **Job ID** field. This is a reference to the Java class in the platform that will actually do the work. The majority of the time, this is RunScriptJob, which will execute some JavaScript code.

The **Trigger type** field specifies how often the job will repeat. Most jobs are run repetitively, with **Events Process** set to run every 30 seconds. Others run when the instance is started-perhaps to preload the cache.

Another job that is run on a periodic basis is **SMTP Sender**. Once an e-mail has been generated and placed in the **Email** [sys_email] table, the SMTP Sender job performs the same function as many desktop e-mail clients: it connects to an e-mail server and asks it to deliver the message. It runs every minute by default.

This schedule has a direct impact on how quickly our e-mail will be sent out. There may be a delay of up to 30 seconds in generating the e-mail from an event and a further delay of up to a minute before the e-mail is actually sent.
Other jobs may process a particular event queue differently. Events placed into the metric queue will be worked with after 5 seconds.

Adding your own jobs

The sys_trigger table is a backend data store. It is possible to add your own jobs and edit what is already there, but I don't recommend it. Instead, there is a more appropriate frontend: the **Scheduled Job** [sysauto] table.

Once you create an entry in the sysauto table, the platform creates the appropriate record in the sys_trigger table. This is done through a call in the **Automation Synchronizer** business rule.

The `sysauto` table is designed to be extended. There are many things that are run on a periodic basis in ServiceNow, including data imports, sending reports, and creating records, and they each have a table extended from `sysauto`.

Each table extended from `sysauto` contains fields that are relevant to its automation. For example, a **Scheduled Email of Report** [`sysauto_report`] requires e-mail addresses and reports to be specified.

Creating events every day

Let's keep our Gardiner Hotel rooms spick and span. Our aim is to ensure that a Maintenance task gets created at the end of a hotel stay, ensuring that each room then gets cleaned. There are several ways to achieve this, but let's fire an event to get the most control. Schedule this for midday to give our guests plenty of time to check out.

1. To begin, create an entry in **System Policy** > **Events** > **Event Registry**. Click **New**, fill out the form and Save.
    *   **Suffix**: `room.reservation_end`
    *   **Table**: `Room [x_hotel_room]`

2. Then navigate to **System Definition** > **Scheduled Jobs**.

    Unfortunately, the `sys_trigger` and `sysauto` tables have very similar module names. Be sure to pick the right one.

3. Click on **New**, and an interceptor will fire, asking you to choose what you want to automate. Choose **Automatically run a script of your choosing**.
4. Set the following fields, then Save.
    *   **Name**: `Clean on end of reservation`
    *   **Time**: `12:00:00`
    *   **Run this script**:

```
var res = new GlideRecord('x_hotel_reservation');
res.addQuery('departure', gs.now());
res.addNotNullQuery('room');
res.query();
while (res.next()) {
gs.eventQueue('x_hotel.room.reservation_end', res.room.getRefRecord());
}
```

Our reliable friend, `GlideRecord`, is employed to get reservation records. The first filter ensures that only reservations that are ending today will be returned, while the second filter ignores reservations that don't have a room.

Once the database has been queried, the records are looped round. For each one, the `eventQueue` function of `GlideSystem` is used to add in an event to the event queue. The record that is being passed into the event queue is actually the **Room** record. The `getRefRecord` function of `GlideElement` dot-walks through a reference field and returns a `GlideRecord` object rather than more `GlideElement` objects.

Once the scheduled job has been saved, it'll generate the events at midday. But for testing, there is a handy **Execute Now** UI action. Ensure there is test data that fits the code (ie, a reservation with a departure date of today, and a room record, and click on the button. Navigate to **System Policy** > **Events** > **Event Log** to see the entries.

 There is a **Conditional** checkbox with a separate **Condition script** field. However, I don't often use this; instead, I provide any conditions (like checking a property) inline in the script that I'm writing, just like we did here. For anything more than a few lines, a Script Include should be used for modularity and efficiency.

Running scripts on events

The ServiceNow platform has several items that listen for events. E-mail notifications are one, which we'll explore soon. Another is Script Actions.

Script Actions are pieces of server-side code that are associated with a table and run against a record, just like a Business Rule. But instead of being triggered by a database action, a Script Action is started with an event.

There are similarities between a Script Action and an asynchronous Business Rule. They both run server-side, asynchronous code. Unless there is a particular reason, stick to Business Rules for ease and familiarity.

Just like a business rule, the GlideRecord variable called current is available. This is the same record that was passed into the second parameter when gs.eventQueue was called.

Additionally, another GlideRecord variable called event is provided. It is initialized against the appropriate record stored in the **Event** [sysevent] table. This gives you access to the other parameters (event.param1 and event.param2) as well as who created the event, when, and more.

Creating tasks automatically

Let's create the new Script Action that reacts to our new event.

1. Go to **System Policy > Events > Script Actions**, click **New,** use the following details and Save:
    - **Name:** Produce maintenance tasks
    - **Event name:** x_hotel.room.reservation_end
    - **Active:** <ticked>
    - **Script:**

```
var tsk = new GlideRecord('x_hotel_maintenance');
tsk.newRecord();
tsk.room = current.sys_id;
tsk.assignment_group.setDisplayValue("Housekeeping");
tsk.short_description = "End of reservation room cleaning";
tsk.insert();
```

This script is fairly straightforward. It creates a new GlideRecord object that represents a record in the **Maintenance** table. The fields are initialized through newRecord, and the **Room** field is populated with the sys_id value of current-which is the **Room** record that the event is associated with. Then a few fields are set. That sets the fields of the new **Maintenance** record to be those stored in the template.

It would be much better to use properties here instead of hardcoding the details. Even better would be using a template – but the `applyTemplate` method of `GlideRecord` doesn't work for scoped apps.

Now, the following items should occur every day:

1. At midday, a scheduled job looks for any reservations that are ending today
2. For each one, the `room.reservation_end` event is fired
3. A Script Action will be called, which creates a new Maintenance task
4. The Maintenance task is assigned to the Housekeeping group.

But how does housekeeping know that this task has been created? Let's send them an e-mail!

Sending e-mail notifications

E-mail is ubiquitous. It is often the primary form of communication in business, so it is important that ServiceNow has good support. It is easy to configure ServiceNow to send out communications to whoever needs to know.

 ServiceNow also supports push notifications for the ServiceNow mobile apps. This isn't as widely used, but it can be a useful alternative to email overload.

There are a few general use cases for e-mail notifications:

- **Action**: Asking the receiver to do some work
- **Informational**: Giving the receiver an update or some data
- **Approval**: Asking for a decision

While this is similar enough to an action e-mail, it is a common enough scenario to make it independent.

We'll work through these scenarios in order to understand how ServiceNow can help.

There are obviously many more ways you can use e-mails. One of them is for a machine-to-machine integration, such as ticket e-bonding. It is possible to do this in ServiceNow, but it is not the best solution. `Chapter` `7`, *Exchanging Data – Import Sets, Web Services, and other Integrations*, discusses integrations in more detail.

Setting e-mail properties

A ServiceNow instance uses standard protocols to send and receive e-mail. E-mails are sent by connecting to an SMTP server with a username and password, just like Outlook or any other e-mail client.

When ServiceNow sets up an instance that is provisioned, it also gets an e-mail account. If your instance is available at `instance.service-now.com` through the Web, it has an e-mail address of `instance@service-now.com`.

This e-mail account is not unusual. It is accessible via POP to receive e-mail and uses SMTP to send it. Indeed, any standard e-mail account can be used with an instance.

The modules underneath **System Mailboxes** > **Administration** show you the options. The most useful page is **Email Diagnostics**, which gives a useful overview of how the instance is configured and how the jobs are performing. Before you spend time configuring e-mail notifications, make sure the basics work! More accounts can be set up in **Email Accounts**, while **Email Properties** lets you tweak various options.

ServiceNow will only use one e-mail account to send out e-mails. Sometimes, there is a need to have multiple incoming addresses. This is discussed later in the chapter.

Assigning work

Our Housekeeping team is equipped with the most modern technology. Not only are they users of ServiceNow, but they have mobile phones that will send and receive e-mails! They have better things to do than constantly refresh the web interface, so let's ensure that ServiceNow will come to them.

The previous chapters mentioned Connect. If you follow a Task you can receive updates with notifications through your web browser or via the ServiceNow mobile app.

One of the most common e-mail notifications is to inform people when they have been assigned a task. The e-mail usually gives an overview of that task and a link to view more details. The inference is that the user needs to pick the work and that the system should be updated with progress.

Sending an e-mail notification on assignment

When our Maintenance tasks have the **Assignment group** field populated, we need the appropriate team members to be aware. We are going to achieve this by sending an e-mail to everyone in that group. At Gardiner Hotels, we empower our staff: they know that one member of the team should pick the task up and own it by setting the **Assigned to** field to themselves and then get it done. Here's how to send e-mail notifications:

1. Navigate to **System Notification** > **Email** > **Notifications**. You will see several examples that are useful to understand the basic configuration, but we'll create our own. Click on **New**.
2. The **Email Notifications** form is split into three main sections: **When to send**, **Who will receive**, and **What it will contain**. Some options are hidden by default.
3. Click on **Advanced view** to see all the options, and fill out the form as follows, using Save when done.
   - **Name**: `Group assignment`
   - **Table**: `Maintenance [x_hotel_maintenance]`
   - **Send when**: `Event is fired`
   - **Event name**: `x_hotel.maintenance.assigned`
   - **Users/Groups in fields**: `Assignment group` (in **Who will receive** tab)
   - **Send to event creator**: `<checked>`
   - **Subject**: `Maintenance task assigned to your group` (in **What it will contain** tab)

- **Message HTML**:

```
Hello ${assignment_group}.
Maintenance task ${number} has been assigned to your group, for room:
${room}.
Description: ${description}
Please assign to a team member here: ${URI}
Thanks!
```

Now, let's inspect each section of the **Email Notifications** form to understand what all this means.

To create push notifications that are sent to a mobile device, navigate to **System Notification** > **Push** > **Create Push Notification**. The form sections (and the concepts) are the same for both e-mail and push notifications.

When to send

This section gives you a choice of either using an event to determine which record should be worked with or for the e-mail notification system to monitor the table directly. Either way, the **Conditions** and **Advanced condition** fields let you provide a filter or script to ensure you only send e-mails at the right time. If you are using an event, the event must be fired and the condition fields satisfied for the e-mail to be sent.

The **Weight** field is often overlooked. A single event or record update may satisfy the condition of multiple e-mail notifications. For example, a common scenario is to send an e-mail to Assignment group when it is populated and to send an e-mail to the Assigned to person when that is filled out. But what if they both happen at the same time? You probably don't want Assignment group being told to pick up a task if it has already been assigned. One way is to give the Assignment group e-mail a higher weight: if two e-mails are being generated, only the one with the lower weight will be sent. The other will be marked as skipped. If they have the same weight, both are sent.

Another way to achieve this scenario is through conditions. Only send the assignment group e-mail if the **Assigned to** field is empty.

Since we've already created an event, we've used it. And because of the careful use of conditions in the Business Rule, it only sends out the event in the appropriate circumstances. That means no condition is necessary in this e-mail notification.

Who will receive

Once we've determined when an e-mail should be sent, we need to know who it will go to. The majority of the time, it'll be driven by data on the record. This scenario is exactly that: the people who will receive the e-mail are those in the **Assignment group** field on the **Maintenance** task. Of course, it is possible to hardcode recipients, and the system can also deliver e-mails to users and groups that have been sent as a parameter when creating the event.

> You can also use scripts to specify the **From**, **To**, **Cc**, and **Bcc** of an e-mail. The product documentation contains more information:
> `https://docs.servicenow.com/bundle/helsinki-servicenow-platfor`
> `m/page/script/server-scripting/concept/c_ScriptingForEmailNoti`
> `fications.html`

Send to event creator

When someone comes to me and says, "Martin, I've set up the e-mail notification, but it isn't working. Do you know why?" I like to put money on the reason. I very often win, and you can too. Just answer with "Ensure **Send to event creator** is ticked and try again."

> You can test various combinations of users by using the **Preview Notification** button. Select a user and a record, and it will show you who will get it, and what it looks like.

The Send to event creator field is only visible in the Advanced view, but is the cause of this problem. So tick Send to event creator. Make sure this field is ticked, at least for now. If you do not, when you test your e-mail notifications, you will not receive your e-mail.

Why? This option stops confirmation e-mails. If you are the person to update a record and it causes e-mails to be sent, and it turns out that you are one of the recipients, it'll go to everyone other than you. The reasoning is straightforward: you carried out the action, so why do you need to be informed that it happened? This cuts down on unnecessary e-mails and so is a good thing. But it confuses everyone who first comes across it.

> The default has changed in the Helsinki version of ServiceNow, and now Send to event creator is ticked by default. But it is still important to know!

What it will contain

The last section is probably the simplest to understand, but the one that takes the most time: deciding what to send.

The standard view contains just a few fields: a space to enter your message and a subject line. Additionally, there is an **Email template** field, which isn't often used but is useful if you want to deliver the same content in multiple e-mail messages. View them by navigating to **System Policy** > **Email** > **Templates**.

These fields all support variable substitution. This is a special syntax that instructs the instance to insert data from the record that the e-mail is triggered for. This Maintenance e-mail contains data from the **Maintenance** task, like the description and number.

This lets you create data-driven e-mails. I like to compare it to a mail-merge system: you have some fixed text, some placeholders, and some data, and the platform puts them all of it together to produce a personalized e-mail.

There is also the option to associate to a push notification, giving users the choice of either e-mail or receiving a message on their mobile device using subscriptions.

Using variable substitution

The format for substitution is `${variable}`. All of the fields in the record are available as variables, so to include the Short description field in an e-mail, use `${short_description}`. Additionally, you can dot-walk. So by having `${assigned_to.email}` in the message, you insert the e-mail address of the user whom the task is assigned to.

To make this easier, there is a **Select variables** section in the Message HTML field that will create the syntax in a single click. But don't forget that variable substitution is available for the Subject field, too.

In addition to adding the value of fields, variable substitutions like the following ones also make it easy to add HTML links:

- `${<reference field>.URI}` will create an HTML link to the reference field, with the text LINK
- `${<reference field>.URI_REF}` will create an HTML link, but with the display value of the record as the text

Running scripts in e-mail messages

If the variables aren't giving you enough control, like everywhere else in ServiceNow, you can add a script. To do so, create a new entry in the **Email Scripts** [sys_script_email] table, available under **System Notification > Email > Notification Email Scripts**. Typical server-side capability is present, including the currentGlideRecord variable. To output text, use the print function of the template object, like this, for example:

```
template.print('Hello, world!');
```

Like a script include, the **Name** field is important. Call the script by placing ${mail_script:<name>} in the **Message HTML** field in the e-mail.

> An object called email is also available. This gives much more control over the resulting e-mail, giving you methods such as setImportance, addAddress, and setReplyTo.
> The product documentation has more details:
> https://docs.servicenow.com/bundle/helsinki-servicenow-platform/page/script/server-scripting/reference/r_MailScriptAPI.html.

Controlling the e-mail more

There are several other options to control how an e-mail is processed:

- **Include Attachments**: It will copy any attachments from the record into the e-mail. There is no selection available: it simply duplicates each one every time. You probably wouldn't want this option ticked on many notifications, since otherwise you will fill up the recipient's' inboxes quickly!

> The attach_links e-mail script is a good alternative: it provides HTML links that will let an interested recipient download the file from the instance.

- **Importance**: This allows a low or high priority flag to be set on an e-mail.
- **From** and **Reply-To** fields: They'll let you configure who the e-mail purports to be from, for every e-mail. It is important to realize that this is **e-mail spoofing**: while the e-mail protocols accept this, it is often used by spammers to forge a false address.

Sending informational updates

Many people rely on e-mails to know what is going on. In addition to telling users when they need to do work, ServiceNow can keep everyone informed about the current situation.

This often takes the form of one of these scenarios:

- Automatic e-mails, often based on a change of the **State** field
- Completely freeform text, with or without a template
- A combination of the preceding two: a textual update given by a person, but in a structured template

Sending a custom e-mail

Sometimes, you need to send an e-mail that doesn't fit into a template. Perhaps you need to attach a file, copy in additional people, or want more control over formatting. In many cases, you would turn to your normal e-mail client, such as Outlook or Gmail. But the big disadvantage is that your message won't be part of the task. You could save the e-mail and upload it as an attachment, but that isn't as good as it being part of the audit history.

ServiceNow comes with a basic e-mail client built in. In fact, it is just shortcutting the process. When you use the e-mail client, you are doing exactly the same as the **Email Notifications** engine would, by generating an entry in the sys_email table.

Enabling the e-mail client

The e-mail client is accessed by a little icon in the form header of a record. In order to show it, a property must be set in the **Dictionary Entry** of the table. Here's what you need to do:

1. Navigate to **System Definition** > **Tables** and select the entry for the Maintenance table.
2. Using the Additional Actions menu, click **Show Dictionary Record**.
3. Click on **Advanced view**. Set the following field, and Save.
   - **Attributes**: email_client

4. Navigate to **Hotel** > **Maintenances**, select a record, and in the More Option menu will be the envelope icon. Click on it to open the e-mail client window:

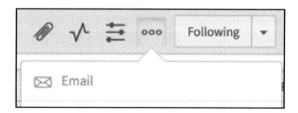

The e-mail client is a simple window, and the fields should be obvious. Simply fill them out and click on **Send** to deliver the e-mail.

You may have noticed that some of the fields were prepopulated. You can control what each field initially contains by creating an **e-mail client template**. Navigate to **System Policy** > **Email** > **Client Templates**, click on **New**, and save a template for the appropriate table. You can use the variable substitution syntax to place the contents of fields in the e-mail. There is a **Conditions** field you can add to the form to have the right template used.

Quick messages are a way to let the sender populate the message text, similar to a record template. Navigate to **System Policy** > **Email** > **Quick Messages** and set some text. These are then available in a dropdown selection field at the top of the e-mail client.

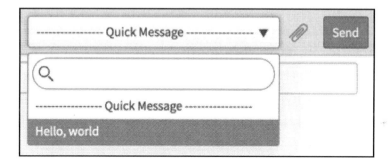

The e-mail client is often seized upon by customers who send a lot of e-mail. However, it is a simple solution and does not have the depth of functionality that is often expected. I've found that this gap can be frustrating. For example, there isn't an easy way to include attachments from the parent record.

Instead, I recommend using a more automated way to send custom text.

Sending e-mails with additional comments and work notes

The journal fields in the Task table are useful enough, allowing you to type notes that are then displayed on the activity log in a *who, what, when* fashion. But sending out the contents via e-mail makes them especially helpful. This lets you combine two actions in one:

- Documenting information against the ticket
- Giving an update to interested parties

The Task table has two fields, **Watch list** and **Work notes list**, that let you specify who will receive the e-mails.

Sending out work notes

First, change the **Maintenance** form to include the elements we need. The **Work notes** field should already be in the **Maintenance** form.

1. Navigate to **System Definition** > **Tables**, and select the **Maintenance** entry. Click on **Design Form**.
2. Use the designer to include the **Work notes list** field, placing it somewhere appropriate, such as underneath the **Assignment group** field. Once done, click **Save**.

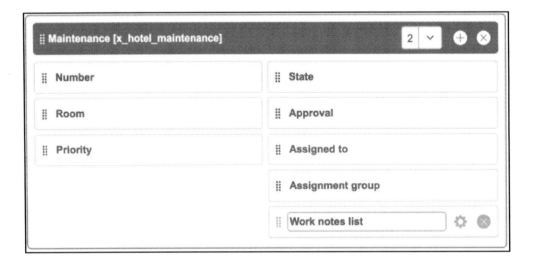

Both **Watch list** and **Work notest** list are list fields (often referred to as **Glide Lists**). What is special about these lists is that although they point towards the sys_user table and store the sys_id values of user records, they also store e-mail addresses in the same database field. The e-mail notification system knows all about this. It will run through the following logic when determining how to send an e-mail:

- If it is a sys_id value, the user record is looked up. The e-mail address in the user record is used.
- If it is an e-mail address, the user record is searched for. If one is found, any notification settings they have are respected.

A user may turn off e-mails, for example, by setting the Notification field to Disabled in their user record. More options are mentioned later.

- If a user record is not found, the e-mail is sent directly to the e-mail address.

Let's try this out and create a new e-mail notification:

1. Navigate to **System Notifications** > **Email** > **Notifications**, click on **New**, fill out the following fields, then Save:
   - **Name:** Work notes update
   - **Table:** Maintenance [x_hotel_maintenance]
   - **Inserted:** <ticked>
   - **Updated:** <ticked>
   - **Conditions:** Work notes – changes
   - **Users/Groups in fields:** Work notes list
   - **Subject:** New work notes update on ${number}

   - **Message HTML:**

```
${number} - ${short_description} has a new work note added.
${work_notes}
```

This simple message would normally be expanded and made to fit into the corporate style guidelines-use appropriate colors and styles. By default, the last three entries in the Work notes field would be included. If this were not appropriate, the appropriate property could be updated or a mail script could use getJournalEntry(1) to grab the latest one.

2. To test, navigate to **Hotel** > **Maintenances**, click **New**, add an e-mail address or a user into **Work notes list**, enter something into the **Work notes** field, and save.

Approving via e-mail

Chapter 5, *Getting Things Done with Tasks,* spoke about approvals for tasks and how Graphical Workflow generates records that someone will need to evaluate and make a decision on. Most often, approvers will want to receive an e-mail notification to alert them to the situation.

There are two approaches to sending out an e-mail when an approval is needed. An e-mail is associated with a particular record, and with approvals, there are two records to choose from:

- The **Approval** record, asking for your decision. The response will be processed by Graphical Workflow. The system will send out one e-mail to each person that is requested to approve it. This is more flexible but more complicated.
- The **Task** record that generated the Approval request. The system will send out one e-mail in total, but may have several recipients. Typically, this is used when you don't want to use the approval activity in Graphical Workflow, but its simpler to set up, such as giving you access to all the fields in the task without dot-walking.

Using the Approval table

An e-mail that is sent out from the Approval table often contains the same elements:

- Some text describing what needs approving: perhaps Short description or Priority. This is often achieved by dot-walking to the data through the Approval for reference field.
- A link to view the task that needs approval.

- A link to the approval record.
- Two `mailto` links that allow the user to approve or reject through e-mail.

This style is captured in the e-mail template named `change.itil.approve.role` and is used in an e-mail notification called **Approval Request** that is against the **Approval** [`sys_approver`] table.

The `mailto` links are generated through a special syntax: `${mailto:mailto.approval}` and `${mailto:mailto.rejection}`. These actually refer to e-mail templates themselves (navigate to **System Policy** > **Email** > **Templates** and find the template called `mailto.approval`). Altogether, these generate HTML code in the e-mail message that looks something like this:

```
<a href="mailto:<instance>@service-now.com?subject=Re:MAI0001001 -
approve&body=Ref:MSG0000001">Click here to approve MAI0001001</a>
```

 Normally, this URL would be encoded, but I've removed the characters for clarity.

When this link is clicked in the receiver's e-mail client, it creates a new e-mail message addressed to the instance, with `Re:MAI0001001 - approve` in the subject line and `Ref:MSG0000001` in the body. If this generated e-mail were sent, the instance would receive it and after processing would approve the approval record. The later section called Receiving e-mails, describes in detail how this happens.

Testing the default approval e-mail

In the baseline system, there is an e-mail notification called **Approval Request**. It is sent when an approval event is fired, which happens in a business rule on the Approval table. It uses the e-mail template mentioned earlier, giving the recipient information and an opportunity to approve it either in their web browser or using their e-mail client.

To see how this works, follow these steps:

1. Set your user account as the manager of the Maintenance group. Navigate to **Hotels** > **Maintenance groups**, and select Maintenance.
2. Fill out the following fields and Save.
   - **Manager**: `System Administrator` (or whoever you are logged in as)

3. Once saved, click on the Reference icon of the Manager, and ensure the email address of the user record is one you have access to. If you need to, update it, and save.

4. Navigate to **Hotel** > **Maintenances** and select a task. Click on the **Send to External** button. You should receive an e-mail after some time.

If you have trouble, navigate to **System Diagnostics** > **Email Diagnostics** and look for errors. You should see the e-mail recorded in **System Logs** > **Emails**.

Specifying notification preferences

Every user that has access to the ServiceNow web interface can configure their e-mail preferences through the **Subscription Notification** functionality. Navigate to **Self-Service** > **My Notification Preferences** to explore what is available.

To never receive a notification again, just toggle it **Off**. This is useful if you are bombarded by e-mails and would rather use the web interface to see updates!

 If you want to ensure a user cannot unsubscribe, check the **Mandatory** field in the **Email Notification** definition record. You may need to add it to the form.

Subscribing to e-mail notifications

The Email Notifications table has a field labeled **Subscribable**. If this is checked, then users can choose to receive a message every time the Email Notification record's conditions are met. This offers a different way of working: someone can decide whether they want more information, rather than the administrator deciding.

Let's copy our work notes e-mail notification to allow users to opt in to receiving all work note notifications:

1. Find the **Work notes update** e-mail notification in **System Notification > Email > Notifications**. Switch to the **Advanced** view.
2. From the Additional Actions menu, choose Insert and Stay to make a copy.
3. Now make the following changes, and Save once done.
   - **Name**: `Work notes update (Subscribable)`
   - **Users/Groups in fields**: `<blank>`
   - **Subscribable**: `<ticked>`

4. Go to **Self Service > My Notification Preferences**, and click on **Subscriptions** and then on **Add Personal Subscription**. Fill out the form, as follows:
   - **Name**: `All work notes`
   - **Notification**: `Work notes update (Subscribable)`

5. Now, every time a work note is added to any **Maintenance** record, a notification will be sent to the subscriber.

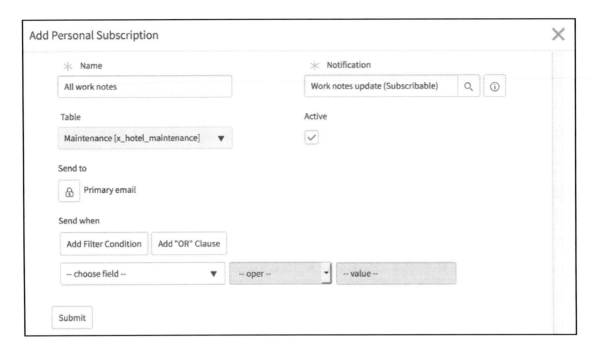

The user can also choose to only receive a subset of the messages by using the Send when filter. Perhaps you only want to receive work notes for high-priority Maintenance tasks.

There is an additional option to choose when to receive emails but you will have to alter the field shown on the **Notification Subscription** [sys_notif_subscription] form to see it. The **Schedule** field lets specify a timeframe to receive these notifications: perhaps only during working hours

Creating a new device

The **Notification Devices** [cmn_notif_device] table stores e-mail addresses for users. It allows every user to have multiple e-mail addresses or even register mobile phones for text messages.

When a User record is created, a business rule named **Create primary email device** inserts a record in the Notification Devices table. The value in the Email field in the User table is just copied to this table by another business rule named Update Email Devices.

1. Navigate to **Self-Service** > **My Notification Preferences** and click on **Create New Device**.
2. The Notification Device form allows you to enter the details of your device supporting e-mail or SMS. **Service provider** is a reference field to the **Notification Service Provider** [cmn_notif_service_provider] table, which specifies how an SMS message should be sent. If you have an account with one of the providers listed, enter your details.

> There are many hundreds of inactive providers in the **Notification Service Provider** [cmn_notif_service_provider] table. You may want to try enabling some, though many do not work for reasons discussed soon.

3. Installing the ServiceNow mobile application and agreeing to accept push notifications will automatically create a device called **ServiceNow Mobile Application**. Try it now! Download the ServiceNow app from your app store.

Once a device has been added, it can be set up to receive messages through Notification Preferences. For example, a user can choose to receive approval requests via a text message by adding the Approval Request Notification Message entry and associating their SMS device. Alternatively, they could have two e-mail addresses, perhaps one for an assistant.

> If a notification is sent to a SMS device, the contents of the **SMS alternate** field hidden on the Email Notification record is used. Remember that a text message can only be 160 characters at maximum.

The Notification Device table has a field called Primary Email. This determines which device is used for a notification that has not been sent to this user before. Despite the name, Primary Email can be ticked for an SMS device.

Sending text messages

Many mobile phone networks in the US supply e-mail-to-SMS gateways. AT&T gives every subscriber an e-mail address in the form of `5551234567@txt.att.net`. This allows the ServiceNow instance to actually send an e-mail and have the gateway convert it into an SMS. The Notification Service Provider form provides several options to construct the appropriate e-mail address. In this scheme, the recipient pays for the text message, so the sending of text messages is free.

Many providers do not provide such functionality, since the sender is responsible for paying. Therefore, it is more common to use the Web to deliver the message to the gateway-perhaps using REST or SOAP. This gives an authenticated method of communication, which allows charging.

 Chapter 7, *Exchanging Data – Import Sets, Web Services, and other Integrations*, discusses these integration techniques in more detail.

The Notifications Service Provider table also provides an Advanced notification checkbox, which enables a script field. The code is run whenever the instance needs to send out an e-mail. This is a great place to call a script include that does the actual work, providing it with the appropriate parameters. One way to do this is with ServiceNow Notify's integration with Twilio.

 Some global variables are present: `email.SMSText` contains the **SMS alternate** text, and `device` is the `GlideRecord` value of the notification device. This means `device.phone_number` and `device.user` are very useful values to access. To send SMS messages with Twilio, check out the product documentation: `https://docs.servicenow.com/bundle/helsinki-servicenow-platform/page/product/notify2/concept/c_NotifySMS.html`.

Delivering an e-mail

As you can see from the following list, there are a great many steps that the instance goes through to send an e-mail. Some may be skipped or delivered as a shortcut, depending on the situation, but an e-mail may not be sent if any one goes wrong!

1. **A record is updated**: Most notifications are triggered when a task changes state or a comment is added. Use the debugging techniques discussed in `Chapter 9`, *Diagnosing ServiceNow – Knowing What Is Going On,* to determine what is changing.

> The next two steps may not be used if the notification does not use events.

2. **An event is fired**: A business rule may fire an event. Look under **System Policy > Events > Event Log** to see whether it was fired.
3. **The event is processed**: A scheduled job will process each event in turn. Look in the Event Log and ensure that all events have their state changed to Processed.
4. **An e-mail notification is processed**: The event is associated with an e-mail notification or the e-mail notification uses the Inserted and Updated checkboxes to monitor a table directly.
5. **Conditions are evaluated**: The platform checks the associated record and ensures the conditions are met. If not, no further processing occurs.
6. **The receivers are evaluated**: The recipients are determined from the logic in the e-mail notification.

> The use of Send to event creator makes a big impact on this step.

7. **The notification device is determined**: The **Notification Messages** table is queried. The appropriate notification device is then found. If **Notification Device** is set to inactive, the recipient is dropped.

> The Notification field on the User record will control the Active flag of the Notification Devices.

8. **Any notification device filters are applied**: Any further conditions set in the **Notification Preferences** interface are evaluated, such as **Schedule** and **Filter**.

9. **An e-mail record is generated**: Variable substitution takes place on the message text and a record is saved into the sys_email table, with details of the messages in the outbox. The e-mail client starts at this point.

> Business Rules are respected on the sys_email table, allowing you to customize further what the email does.

10. **The weight is evaluated**: If an e-mail notification with a lower weight has already been generated for the same event, the e-mail has the **Mailbox** field set to **Skipped**.

11. **The email is sent**: The **SMTP Sender** scheduled job runs every minute. It picks up all messages in the outbox, generates the message ID, and connects to the SMTP server specified in **Email properties**. This only occurs if **Mail sending** is enabled in the properties. Errors will be visible under **System Mailboxes > Outbound > Failed**.

> The generated e-mails can be monitored in the **System Mailboxes** application menu or through **System Logs > Emails**. They are categorized into mailboxes, just like an e-mail client. This should be considered a backend table, though some customers who want more control over e-mail notifications make this more accessible.

Knowing who the e-mail is from

ServiceNow uses one account when sending e-mails. This account is usually the one provided by ServiceNow, but it can be anything that supports SMTP: Exchange, Sendmail, NetMail, or even Gmail.

The SMTP protocol lets the sender specify who the e-mail is from. By default, no checks are done to ensure that the sender is allowed to send from that address. Every e-mail client lets you specify who the e-mail address is from, so I could change the settings in Outlook to say my e-mail address is `president@whitehouse.gov` or `primeminister@number10.gov.uk`.

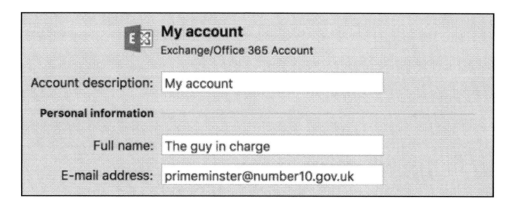

Spammers and virus writers have taken advantage of this situation to fill our mailboxes with unwanted e-mails. Therefore, e-mail systems are doing more authentication and checking of addresses when the message is received. You may have seen some e-mails saying an e-mail has been delivered on behalf of another when this validation fails, or it even falling into the spam directly.

ServiceNow uses SPF to specify which IP addresses can deliver `service-now.com` e-mails. Spam filters often use this to check whether a sender is authorized. If you spoof the e-mail address, you may need to make an exception for ServiceNow. Read up more about it here: `http://en.wikipedia.org/wiki/Sender_Policy_Framework`

You may want to change the e-mail addresses on the instance to be your corporate domain. That means that your ServiceNow instance will send the message but will pretend that it is coming from another source. This runs the real risk of the e-mails being marked as spam. Instead, think about only changing the **From** display (not the e-mail address), or use your own e-mail account.

Receiving e-mails

Many systems can send e-mails. But isn't it annoying when they are broadcast only? When I get sent a message, I want to be able to reply to it. E-mail should be a conversation, not a fire-and-forget distribution mechanism.

So what happens when you reply to a ServiceNow e-mail? It gets categorized and then processed according to the settings in **Inbound Email Actions**.

Lots of information is available in the product documentation: https://docs.servicenow.com/bundle/helsinki-servicenow-platform/page/administer/notification/concept/c_InboundEmailActions.html.

Determining what an inbound e-mail is

Every two minutes, the platform runs the POP Reader scheduled job. It connects to the e-mail account specified in the properties and pulls them all into the Email table, setting the Mailbox to be Inbox.

Despite the name, the **POP Reader** job also supports IMAP accounts.

This fires an event called `email.read`, which in turn starts the classification of the e-mail. It uses a series of logic decisions to determine how it should respond. The concept is that an inbound e-mail can be a *reply* to something that the platform has already sent out, is an e-mail that someone *forwarded*, or is part of an e-mail chain that the platform has not seen before; that is, it is a *new* e-mail. Each of these are handled differently, with different assumptions:

1. As the first step in processing the e-mail, the platform attempts to find the sender in the User table. It takes the address that the e-mail was sent from as the key to search for. If it cannot find a user, it either creates a new User record (if the `Automatically create users` property is set), or uses the Guest account.

2. Should this e-mail be processed at all? If either of the following conditions matches, then the e-mail has the Mailbox set to skipped, and no further processing takes place:

    - Does the subject line start with recognized text such as "out of office autoreply"?
    - Is the User account locked out?

3. Is this a *forward*? Both of the following conditions must match, else the e-mail will be checked as a reply:

    - Does the subject line start with a recognized prefix (such as FW)?
    - Does the string **From** appear anywhere in the body?

4. Is this a *reply*? One of the following conditions must match, else the e-mail will be processed as new:

    - Is there a valid, appropriate watermark that matches an existing record?
    - Is there an In-Reply-To header in the e-mail that references an e-mail sent by the instance?
    - Does the subject line start with a recognized prefix (such as RE) and contain a number prefix (such as MAI000100)?

5. If none of these are affirmative, the e-mail is treated as a new e-mail.

The prefixes and recognized text are controlled with properties available under System Properties > Email Properties.

This order of processing and logic cannot be changed. It is hardcoded into the platform. However, clever manipulation of the properties and prefixes allows great control over what will happen. One common request is to evaluate forwarded e-mails like replies. To accomplish this, a nonsensical string should be added into forward_subject_prefix, and the standard values added to the reply_subject prefix property. For example, the following values could be used:

- Forward prefix: xxxxxxxxxx
- Reply prefix: re:, aw:, r:, fw:, fwd:, and so on

This will ensure that a match with the forwarding prefixes is very unlikely, while the reply logic checks will be met.

Creating inbound email actions

Once an e-mail has been categorized, it will run through the appropriate **Inbound Email Action** [sysevent_in_email_action]. Navigate to **System Policy** > **Email** > **Inbound Actions** to see and create them.

The main purpose of an inbound email action is to run JavaScript that manipulates a target record in some way. The target record depends upon what the e-mail has been classified as:

- A forwarded or new e-mail will create a new record
- A reply will update an existing record

Every inbound email action is associated with a table and a condition, just like business rules. Since a reply must be associated with an existing record (usually found using the watermark), the platform will only look for inbound email actions that are against the same table. The platform initializes the GlideRecord object current as the existing record.

An e-mail classified as Reply must have an associated record, which can be found via the watermark or the In-Reply-To header or by running a search for a prefix stored in the sys_number table, or else it will not proceed.

Forwarded and new e-mails will create new records. They will use the first inbound email action that meets the condition, regardless of the table. It will then initialize a new GlideRecord object called current, expecting it to be inserted into the table.

In order to make the scripting easier, the platform parses the e-mail and populates the properties of an object called email. The product documentation has a list of the variables:
https://docs.servicenow.com/bundle/helsinki-servicenow-platform/page/administer/notification/reference/r_AccessingEmailObjsWithVars.html.

Approving e-mails using Inbound Email Actions

The previous section looked at how the platform can generate mailto links, ready for a user to select. They generate an e-mail that has the word `approve` or `reject` in the subject line and watermark in the body.

This is a great example of process automation in ServiceNow. Approving via e-mail is often much quicker than logging in to the instance and clicking on buttons, especially if you are working remotely and are on the road. It means approvals happen faster, which in turn provides better service to the requesters and reduces the effort for our approvers-win-win!

Navigate to **System Policy** > **Email** > **Inbound Actions** and select the **Update Approval Request** Inbound Email Action. We'll inspect a few lines of the code to get a feel for what is possible when automating actions with incoming e-mails.

Understanding the code in Update Approval Request

Whilst the script is quite long, it boils down to a few simple steps.

One of the first actions is to run the `validUser` function which performs a check to ensure the sender is allowed to update this approval. They must either be a delegate or the user themselves. Some companies prefer to use an e-signature method to perform approval, where a password must be entered. This check is not up to that level, but does go some way to helping.

 E-mail addresses (and From strings) can be spoofed in an e-mail client.

Assuming the validation passes, the Comments field of the Approval record is updated with the body of the e-mail:

```
current.comments = "reply from: " + email.from + "\n\n" + email.body_text;
```

In order to set the State field, and thus make the decision on the approval request, the script simply runs a search for the existence of **approve** or **reject** within the subject line of the e-mail using the standard `indexOf` string function. If it is found, the state is set.

```
if (email.subject.indexOf("approve") >= 0)
  current.state = "approved";
if (email.subject.indexOf("reject") >= 0)
  current.state = "rejected";
```

Once the fields have been updated, it saves the record. This triggers the standard Business Rules and will run the workflow as though this were done in the web interface.

Updating the work notes of a Maintenance task

Most often, a reply to an e-mail is to add Additional comments or Work notes to a task. Using scripting, you could differentiate between the two scenarios by seeing who has sent the e-mail: a requester would provide additional comments and a fulfiller may give either, but it is safer to assume work notes.

Let's make a simple inbound email action to process e-mails and populate the Work notes field.

1. Navigate to **System Policy** > **Email** > **Inbound Actions**, and click on **New**. Use these details and Save when done:
   - **Name:** Work notes for Maintenance task
   - **Target table**: Maintenance [x_hotel_maintenance]
   - **Active**: <ticked>
   - **Type**: Reply (In the **When to run** section)
   - **Script**:

```
current.work_notes = "Reply from: " + email.origemail + "\n\n" +
email.body_text;
current.update();
```

Insert the script inside the provided function, just like in a Business Rule.

This script is very simple: it just updates our task record after setting the **Work notes** field with the e-mail address of the sender and the text they sent. It is separated out with a few new lines. The platform impersonates the sender, so the activity log will show the update as though it were done in the web interface.

Inbound email actions run Business Rules run as normal. This includes ServiceNow sending out e-mails, so this means anyone who is in Work notes list will be notified. If Send to event creator is ticked, it means the person who sent the e-mail may receive another in return, telling them they updated the task!

Having multiple incoming e-mail addresses

Many customers want to have logic based upon inbound e-mail addresses. For example, sending a new e-mail to `invoices@gardiner-hotels.com` would create a task for the finance team, while `wifi@gardiner-hotels.com` creates a ticket for the networking group. These are easy to remember and work with, and implementing ServiceNow should not mean that this simplicity be removed.

ServiceNow provides a single e-mail account that is in the `instance@service-now.com` format, and it is not able to provide multiple or custom e-mail addresses. There are two broad options for meeting this requirement:

- Checking multiple external accounts
- Redirecting e-mails

Using the Email Accounts plugin

While ServiceNow only provides a single e-mail address, it has the ability to pull in e-mails from multiple external e-mail accounts. Navigate to **System Mailboxes** > **Administration** > **Email Accounts** to set them up.

Since ServiceNow does not provide multiple e-mail accounts, it is the customer's responsibility to create, maintain, and configure the instance with the details, including the username and passwords. The instance will need to connect to the e-mail account, which is often hosted within the customer's datacenter. This means that firewall rules or other security mechanisms may need to be configured.

ServiceNow does support the use of a VPN tunnel. This allows ServiceNow to connect into a customer's datacenter, which helps with getting access to things like email servers.
See the product documentation here for more details: `https://docs.serv icenow.com/bundle/helsinki-servicenow-platform/page/administer /encryption/concept/c_SetUpAVPN4SNowBusNet.html`.

Redirecting e-mails

Instead of having the instance check multiple e-mail accounts, it is often easier to work with a single e-mail address. Any additional e-mail addresses can be redirected to the one that ServiceNow provides.

The majority of e-mail platforms, such as Microsoft Exchange, make it possible to redirect e-mail accounts. When an e-mail is received by the e-mail system, it is resent to the ServiceNow account. This process differs from e-mail forwarding:

- **Forwarding** involves adding the **FW:** prefix to the subject line, altering the message body, and changing the **From** address.
- **Redirection** sends the message unaltered, with the original **To** address, to the new address. There is little indication that the message has not come directly from the original sender.

Redirection is often an easier method to work with than having multiple e-mail accounts. It gives more flexibility to the customer's IT team since they do not need to provide account details to the instance, and it enables them to change the redirection details easily. If a new e-mail address has to be added or an existing one decommissioned, only the e-mail platform needs to be involved. It also reduces the configuration on the ServiceNow instance; nothing needs to change.

Processing multiple e-mail addresses

Once the e-mails have been brought into ServiceNow, the platform will need to examine who the e-mail was sent to and make some decisions. This will allow the e-mails sent to `wifi@gardiner-hotels.com` to be routed as tasks to the networking team.

The easiest method to deal with this is to copy the email address into a new field in the task. Standard routing techniques, such as **Assignment Rules** and **Data Lookup**, could be used to examine the new field and populate the assignment group.

Seeing progress being made

ServiceNow has great support for processing emails. The previous few sections looked at how you can embed the sending of emails at key parts during a process. In the Hotel app, we've notified our staff whenever a task is assigned, or Work notes added, and then included any replies. This is great for seeing how the task is unfolding through your email client – but wouldn't it be better if ServiceNow recorded some statistics automatically? Metrics let you do just that.

Recording metrics

Metrics are a way to record information. It allows the analysis and improvement of a process by measuring statistics, based upon particular defined criteria. Most often, these are time based. One of the most common metrics is how long it takes to complete a task-from when the record was created to the moment the Active flag became `false`. The duration can then be averaged out and compared over time, helping answer questions such as "Are we getting quicker at completing tasks?"

 Metrics provide a great alternative to creating lots of extra fields and Business Rules on a table. Of course, these can do calculations too, but what's the point in creating lots of code and fields that clutter up the table when you have a pre-built system to help?

Other metrics are more complex and may involve getting more than one result per task:

- How long does each assignment group take to deal with the ticket?
- How long does an SLA get paused for?
- How many times does the incident get reassigned?

 Performance Analytics can also perform calculations to gather insight into your processes, as discussed later.

The difference between metrics and SLAs

At first glance, a metric appears to be very similar to an SLA, since they both record time.

 Service Level Agreements (SLAs) were covered in `Chapter 5`, *Getting Things Done with Tasks*.

However, there are some key differences between metrics and SLAs:

- There is no *target* or aim defined in a metric. It cannot be breached; the duration is simply recorded.
- A metric cannot be paused or made to work to a schedule.
- There is no workflow associated with a metric.

In general, a metric is a more straightforward measurement, designed for collecting statistics rather than being in the forefront when processing a task.

Running metrics

Every time the Task table gets updated, the `metrics events` Business Rule fires an event called `metric.update`. A Script Action named `Metric Update` is associated with the event and calls the appropriate metric definitions.

> If you define a metric on a non-task-based table, make sure you fire the `metric.update` event through a Business Rule.

The **Metric Definition** [`metric_definition`] table specifies how a metric should be recorded, while the **Metric Instance** [`metric_instance`] table records the results. As ever, each metric definition is applied to a specific table.

The **Type** field of a metric definition refers to two situations:

- **Field value duration** is associated with a field in the table. Each time the field changes value, the platform creates a new Metric Instance record. The duration for which that value was present is recorded. No code is required, but if some is given, it is used as a condition.
- **Script calculation** uses JavaScript to determine what the metric instance contains.

Scripting a metric definition

There are several predefined variables available to a metric definition: `current` refers to the `GlideRecord` value under examination and `definition` is a `GlideRecord` value of the metric definition.

The `MetricInstance` script include provides some helpful functions, including `startDuration` and `endDuration`, but it is really only relevant for time-based metrics. Metrics can be used to calculate many statistics (such as the number of times a task is reopened), but code must be written to accomplish this.

Monitoring the duration of maintenance tasks

Lets monitor how quickly Maintenance tasks are dealt with.

1. Navigate to **Metrics** > **Definitions** and click on **New**. Set the following fields, saving once done:
    - **Name**: Maintenance states
    - **Table**: Maintenance [x_hotel_maintenance]
    - **Field**: State
    - **Timeline**: <ticked>

2. Test it by changing the State field on a Maintenance record to several different values. Navigate to **Hotel** > **Maintenances** to find the records. Make sure to wait 30 seconds or so between each State change so that the scheduled job has time to fire.

3. Use the Additional actions menu and choose **Metrics Timeline** to visualize the changes in the State field.

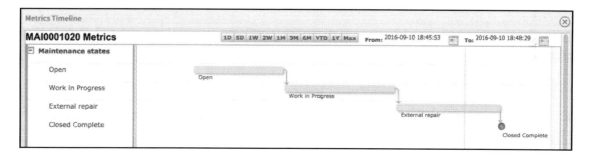

 Adding the **Metrics** related list to the **Maintenance** form will display all the captured data. Another related list is available in the **Metrics Definition** form.

Flattening data with Database Views

Database Views take information as it is stored and present it in a different way, often combining two different data sources. They appear as a standard table to the user, albeit read-only.

In most situations, Database Views are not strictly necessary. Dot-walking can achieve many requirements. In the background, ServiceNow performs the appropriate joins on the database tables, giving you the data that is needed. Nonetheless, you may need to use them when data is difficult to get to.

If you wish to provide a predefined data set in reporting, consider using a Report Source. This helps ensure everyone is using a standard set of filters. The product documentation has more:
`https://docs.servicenow.com/bundle/helsinki-performance-analytic`
`s-and-`
`reporting/page/use/reporting/task/t_CreateAReportSource.html`.

Creating a Metric Instance Database View

Database Views are useful when working with metric instance records. A Metric Instances table does not contain a regular Reference field, but instead a document ID and a Table field. Together, they can point to any record in any table in the system. This flexibility comes with a price: dot-walking is not possible.

So let's use a database view!

1. Navigate to **System Definition** > **Database Views** and click on **New**. Use the following details:
   - **Name**: `x_hotel_maintenance_metric`
   - **Label**: `Maintenance Metric`
   - **Plural**: `Maintenance Metrics`

   Once saved, a related list will be available. This specifies which tables to join together.

2. Click on **New** on the **View Tables** related list and set the following fields. Once done, click Submit to return to the Database View.
   - **Table**: `Metric Definition [metric_definition]`
   - **Variable prefix**: md

As you define each table, you have the opportunity to specify which fields you want from the table. If none are specified, all are used. Every field that is included will have its name prefixed with the variable prefix, followed by an underscore. Therefore, in this example, the fields will be `md_active`, `md_description`, `md_field`, and so on.

Do not make the variable prefix too long-keep it to a couple of characters at most. It is easy to go over the maximum field length.

3. Create another new **View Table** record. Set the following fields, and click **Submit** when done.

   - **Table**: `Metric [metric_instance]`
   - **Variable prefix**: `mi`
   - **Order**: `200`
   - **Where clause**: `mi_definition = md_sys_id`

   The `where` **clause** is what selects what records appear in the resulting Database View, but it does *not* work exactly the same as SQL `where` clause. Two different tables, with different fields, will be combined together. Every row from one table will be joined to every row of the other. Then this combined set will have the `where` clause applied. Any combinations that match the clause will be kept.

In general, you want to match the sys_id of one table with a reference field from the other table.

This example says that the **Definition** field from the Metric Instance table (the foreign key) will contain the same value as the `sys_id` unique identifier that is on the Metric Definition table. So we'll get a list of all metric instances with the appropriate Metric Definition fields alongside.

The default join in ServiceNow is an inner join. A left join can be made by adding the Left join field to the form and checking it. In this instance, it will include entries where a metric definition doesn't have any metric instances. This is not what we want.

4. Finally, we want to join the metric information to the Maintenance table. Set the following fields on another new **View Table** record, and click **Submit** when done.

- **Table**: `Maintenance [x_hotel_maintenance]`
- **Variable prefix**: `m`
- **Order**: `300`
- **Where clause**: `m_sys_id = mi_id`

5. When you click on the **Try it** UI action on the **Database View** form, you should see the result. We see every Metric Instance that is associated with a Maintenance task and a metric definition.

A Database View will behave in a similar fashion to normal tables. Each one can have a form designed, fields chosen for a list, and views for both. As we'll see in the next section, it gives us everything we need to create a report.

Reporting

You've already run reports in ServiceNow. Choosing what data you get, by picking the columns you want and adding the filters you need, is all part of using lists. Sometimes, this is all you need. Want to know how many maintenance requests there have been today? Create the appropriate filter and then have a look at the record count. Easy!

Do you want to keep this data somewhere? From the standard list interface, click on the menu button and choose **Export**. You'll have a choice of **Excel**, **CSV**, **XML**, and several different PDF formats. The detailed versions of the PDF exports not only include the list, but also the forms of each record. There is even a Print icon if you go into the System Settings menu in the top right.

The columns included in a download are the same as the list. Add in additional columns or use views to easily switch between what you export.

Many people like Excel documents or PDF files. But my advice is to right-click on the filter, choose **Copy URL**, and distribute that. That way, a recipient always gets the latest information just by clicking on the link. No out-of-date information!

It is easy to save a list you particularly like. In the filter builder, there is a **Save** button that asks for a name as well as who can select it: just yourself, everyone, or a particular group. Access to these filters is controlled by role. Alternatively, just add it to your favorites list in the Application Navigator.

The functionality of a list

The list interface provides more than just a list. Right-clicking on the column headings displays several options. Some of them are as follows:

- **Group By ...** will collect all the records with the same field value together, and fold them together. This is really useful for a choice field, like State or Priority, or for a reference field like Assignment group.
- There are also two self-explanatory options: **Pie chart** and **Bar chart**. Choosing either of these options on a column brings up the chart in the reporting interface. Using the option on choice list fields such as **State** usually work well.

Using reports elsewhere

A report is created through a custom interface. Access it by going to **Reports** > **CreateNew**. It provides several chart types, with many of the options dependent on what you select.

The product documentation provides lots of details about the options available for each report type:
`https://docs.servicenow.com/bundle/helsinki-performance-analytics-and-reporting/page/use/reporting/reference/r_ReportTypes.html`.

Once a report has been saved, quite a few buttons are made available. Most are obvious, but some are worthy of further explanation:

- **Publish** makes the report available via URL. When you click on the button, the URL is shown at the top of the page. This can be distributed to anyone inside or outside of the company. No one who visits the URL will be prompted for a username or password, since the page has been declared public. The data itself is live and is subject to access control rules.
- Homepages are made from widgets and gauges. Clicking on the **Make Gauge** button makes the report available for selection on a homepage. Homepages are discussed further in the next section.
- The **Add to homepage** button shortcuts the process by making a gauge and adding it to the homepage in one step.
- **Schedule** will e-mail the contents of a report automatically on a regular basis.

> Note that setting who the report is **Visible to** only changes who can see the report, not what the report contains. The data is controlled by normal access control rules. Remember though that if you export the data (perhaps by using the schedule option), the data is now uncontrolled. You could be emailing data outside of your organization very easily.

Sending a shift handover report

The **Scheduled Email of Report** [sysauto_report] table extends sysauto. Earlier in the chapter, we saw how the platform will run jobs automatically, given a time and something to do. A scheduled report has several options in order to make it easy to automate report distribution.

One common use of a scheduled report is to produce a report showing the activity of yesterday or last week. This is very easy with the relative time conditions. Let's build a list to show what Maintenance tasks were created yesterday, to give the incoming team a heads-up on what happened.

The quickest way is to create a report in the reporting interface:

1. Navigate to **Reports** > **Create New**. Set the following information:
    - **Report title**: `Shift handover` (at the top of the page)
    - **Data table**: `Maintenance [x_hotel_maintenance]`
    - **Type**: `List`
    - **Group by**: `State`
    - **Add Filter Condition**: `Created - on - Yesterday`

2. Click the **Save** button, then click on the down arrow next to **Save**, and click on **Schedule**.

 While you are there, look at all the options you have with the report, including publishing, export options, and saving as a Report Source.

3. The **Scheduled Email of Report** form should be straightforward. Set the following fields as an example. If you want to test it, save it and click on **Execute Now**.
    - **Groups**: `Maintenance`
    - **Subject**: `Daily handover report`
    - **Run**: `Daily`
    - **Time**: `05:00:00`
    - **Omit if no records**: `<ticked>`
    - **Introductory message**: `Enjoy the attached report!`

 The Include with field and related list are useful. They allow several reports to be linked together, rather than having multiple e-mails with a single attachment each.

Analytics with ServiceNow

The basic reporting engine built into ServiceNow is focused on transactional operational reporting. It reports on a single table at once, with little support for calculating values. Since each report is focused on individual records, trending is difficult. Comparing data from two tables is not possible.

Basic trending with line charts

One report that goes some way to determining how things change over time is the line chart. To see how this works, follow these steps:

1. Navigate to **Reports** > **Create New**. Use the following options, and click **Save**:
   - **Name:** Tasks opened per day
   - **Data table:** Maintenance [x_hotel_maintenance]
   - **Type:** Line
   - **Group by:** -- None --
   - **Trend by:** Opened
   - **Per:** Date

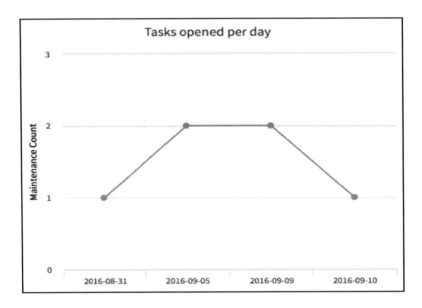

This report gives a good indication of how demand for your service varies. However, the x-axis is not consistent and will not render zero when there are no Maintenance tasks opened on that day.

Performance Analytics

In order to provide better trending functionality, ServiceNow offers **Performance Analytics** as an additional service. It provides a more capable system to define and report on key performance indicators, especially around processes analysis.

A version of **Performance Analytics** is available for free for Incident Management. It does not allow you to create new indicators, and is restricted in how much data it keeps. To unlock its potential and use it for other apps, such as hotel apps, extra licenses are needed.

Some of the features of Performance Analytics include:

- Data-collection jobs run on a scheduled basis to capture the indicator information. For example, the number of open tasks is counted every day, providing the ability to compare over time
- Formulas can calculate statistics, such as the average age of a ticket or the backlog growth.
- Each indicator can be broken down, letting you view how these numbers differ between assignment groups or departments.
- E-mail summaries can be sent when large changes in indicators occur.
- Targets and trend lines can be given for indicators, such as having less than 10 percent of your tasks as high priority.

The Product Documentation has a great deal of information on Performance Analytics:
`https://docs.servicenow.com/bundle/helsinki-performance-analytic`
`s-and-reporting/page/use/performance-`
`analytics/reference/r_PALandingPage.html.`

Making sense of reports

ServiceNow makes easy reporting available to everyone. The reporting functionality is available to fulfillers, letting them pick any table they want to look at, and requesters can create a bar or pie chart from a list. However, that doesn't mean they get useful information from it!

> The Reports application menu is restricted to the `itil` and `asset` roles, but this can easily be changed. Chapter 7, *Exchanging Data – Import Sets, Web Services, and other Integrations*, talks more about roles and access.

As an example, consider a report that shows the number of tasks closed on a particular day, similar to how the example line chart we just saw shows opened tasks. What this report may do is count how many tasks have the same Closed date. In this example, we'll start with the data set shown in this table:

Number	Closed
TSK001	**1 May**
TSK002	2 May
TSK003	1 May
TSK004	3 May

If a report on this data is run, it'll say that two tasks were closed on 1 May and one each on 2 and 3 May. Simple, right?

Now consider that TSK003 was reopened on 3 May. It had its State changed from Complete to Active since, in fact, the work had not been finished. Later that day, it was closed again. We now have a table like this:

Number	Closed
TSK001	1 May
TSK002	2 May
TSK003	3 May
TSK004	3 May

Now, if the same report were run again, it would give a different result. Only one task was closed on 1 May. This may surprise some people! Having a Closed date that has changed is a simple example, but one that is common and frustrating.

Performance Analytics deals with this by capturing the count and storing it, rather than calculating it fresh each time. Of course, it may be that logic and security rules in ServiceNow stops a task from being reopened, so this situation never arises. This is a common configuration, and we'll explore how to achieve this in Chapter 8, *Securing Applications and Data*.

Ensuring consistency

The example we just saw shows that reports need to be thought about carefully:

- Should you use the Active flag or Closed states?
- Which table should I start with to give me the right information?
- Will dot-walking give me the right information, or do I need a database view?
- Is reporting on the Transaction table on a busy instance a good idea, where only a Contains filter is applied on the URL field across all dates?

The answer to that last question, by the way, is no. It will perform very badly!

ServiceNow offers several roles to control access, including report_group and report_global. These control the Visible to option when defining a report, and the guage_maker role specifies who can see the **Add to Homepage** and **Make Gauge** buttons. It is important to control these reports appropriately: not only do the reports need to make sense, but they should also be quick to run. Train report writers effectively, and make sure they understand the data they are producing.

A good practice is to use Report Sources. These allow you to specify a base position, and use that for similar reports. For example, create a Report Source to decide if the Active flag or the State field should define what *Open* means.

I have often seen multiple reports, all answering the same question but with different approaches and therefore different results. Consistency is important, especially with items such as SLA reporting.

Remember that 69.7 percent of statistics are made up on the spot. Are yours?

Using outside tools

As we'll see in Chapter 9, *Diagnosing ServiceNow – Knowing What Is Going On*, ServiceNow has great support for integrating with external systems. Sometimes, therefore, it is most appropriate to use dedicated reporting tools. ServiceNow provides an **ODBC driver** that allows tools such as **Tableau, Microsoft SQL Service**, or even **Excel** to connect to the instance and generate the reports. If an organization already uses a reporting tool, then it often makes sense to have ServiceNow feed into it. These may allow the use of more complex analysis techniques that just aren't possible in ServiceNow.

The ODBC driver uses SOAP web services to grab the data. ServiceNow does not allow direct connections to the underlying database for security reasons-all communication must go through the platform. Queries you write using the ODBC driver will be converted into GlideRecord queries, which may mean you get different results than you expect. It may also be slow! Finally, it means that all security rules, as we will discuss in Chapter 8, *Securing Applications and Data*, will also be respected.

Other tools such as **ServiceNow Data Mart Loader** (or **SnowMirror**) allow you to create a replica of all the ServiceNow data locally. This is useful for a data warehouse solution, where multiple systems all contribute data. Use this to compare and contrast data sets: does an increase in phone calls to the Service Desk result in slower resolution of tasks? Refer to these links for more information:

- http://sourceforge.net/projects/servicenowpump/
- http://www.snow-mirror.com/

Building homepages

When you log in to ServiceNow, the first thing you see is a homepage. These are built out of reports. They are often used as dashboards, providing a quick overview- perhaps showing high-priority tasks or SLAs that have been missed. It is how you get multiple reports on the same page.

A homepage is organized through a layout. A homepage is made up of dropzones-areas that items can be added to. The vast majority of homepages use the same layout, with a header, two columns, and a footer. This design uses HTML tables to position the elements.

You can make your own custom layouts using Jelly. Check out the product documentation for more:
`https://docs.servicenow.com/bundle/helsinki-servicenow-platform/page/administer/homepage-administration/concept/c_CustomLayouts.html`.

Content in the form of widgets is added to each dropzone. The different types of widgets are listed under **System UI** > **Widgets**. A widget has to provide two things: how it should be rendered, and a list of options. These are defined by making appropriately named functions, `render` and `sections`, respectively.

It is unlikely that the widgets themselves will need to be edited or added unless a particularly customized homepage is desired. The **Gadgets** and **Cool Clock** widgets serve as an example of how custom widgets are often made: make a UI page that is then rendered when the homepage is displayed. UI pages are discussed in `Chapter 11`, *Making ServiceNow Beautiful with Service Portal and Custom Interfaces*.

The Gadgets widget is an example of how a homepage doesn't have to just have reports but can also provide useful navigation and other tools. It provides a little sticky-note scratch pad and a way to search the knowledge base-all from the homepage.

Some widgets can interact with others. Interactive filters let you change what data is shown directly on the homepage. Look at the **Example Interactive Filters** page to see how changing the options on the right affect all the reports.

Creating a Maintenance homepage

Homepages are stored in the **Portal Pages** [sys_portal_page] table, but most of the time, you don't need to access the table directly.

Instead, you can work directly with the homepage interface:

1. Navigate to the homepage via **Self-Service** > **Homepage**. Click the plus icon in the top left, next to the dropdown menu, to create a new page.
2. The **My Homepage** text is actually editable. Alter it to say **Maintenance**, and remove the default scrolling widget.
3. Click on the **Add content** button, and select **Reports**, **Maintenance**, and then **Shift Handover**. Choose somewhere in the layout to add it.

 Another, sometimes easier way is to use the **Add to Dashboard** option in the report screen. Before Helsinki, you needed to create the widget from the report screen, but this is no longer necessary.

Making global homepages

A personal homepage is one associated with a user. When a homepage not belonging to the user is edited, the system makes a new page and copies over all the widgets. Editing could mean adding a new widget, repositioning a widget, or renaming the homepage by overtyping the title. You can often distinguish when a personal homepage has been created, since the platform adds the text **My** to the front of the title.

The majority of the time, this is desirable, since otherwise a user could ruin your carefully curated page with a single click! But how do you publish a standard homepage that everyone can see as a default?

1. To make our new homepage global, find the Maintenance homepage by navigating to **Homepage Admin** > **Pages**, and make the following changes. Once done, Save.
   - **Selectable**: <ticked>
   - The **Selectable** checkbox ensures that it is listed in the drop-down box on the homepage.
   - **View**: maintenance
   - **User**: <empty>

2. Once saved, an **Edit Homepage** link becomes available. This is because the **View** field has been populated. Use this link to edit the master copy of the homepage.

Because the **User** field has been cleared, other users can now select the homepage-but only because the **Selectable** checkbox is ticked. If you wish to restrict who can see the homepage, use the **Read roles** field. Unless someone has made a personal homepage, they will see the homepage with the lowest-order value that their roles allow.

Editing homepages

Accessing a homepage can either occur by using the **Switch to page...** field or through a link. There are two different types of links. Each handles the editing of pages slightly differently.

- A link that includes a `view` parameter will show and edit the master copy. This view uses **Write roles** to determine whether a page can be edited. If the user doesn't have the role, they cannot change the page. The format used is `/home.do?sysparm_view=<view name, like maintenance>`.

- Otherwise, a link can be created that uses the `sys_id` of the homepage. Any edits to this page will create a personal homepage copy. The **Switch to page...** selection also uses this style:
`/home.do?sysparm_userpref_homepage=<sys_id of homepage>`

Counting on a homepage

In addition to reports, **Count** gauges provide a quick insight into some important numbers. As with reports, the numbers are run on demand, so they are often used to say how many high-priority tasks are still open or how many tasks are assigned to you. They use a simple condition that is run against a table, from which the number of matching records is returned.

1. Navigate to **System UI** > **Gauges** and click on **New**. This record will be used to group the Count gauges together. Use these details, then Save.
    - **Name:** `Maintenance counts`
    - **Type:** `Counts`
    - **Table:** `Maintenance [x_hotel_maintenance]`

2. Click on **New** under **Count Gauges**. Let's return how many tasks are currently open and how many are higher priority. Use this data:
   - **Name:** `Open Maintenance Tasks`
   - **Table:** `Maintenance [x_hotel_maintenance]`
   - **Short description:** `How many maintenance tasks still need to be closed`
   - **Order:** `10`
   - **Query:** `Active - is - true`

3. Click on Submit when done, then create another Count Gauge with these options:
   - **Name:** `High priority tasks`
   - **Table:** `Maintenance [x_hotel_maintenance]`
   - **Short description:** `Of those, how many are higher priority`
   - **Order:** `20`
   - **Omit seperator:** `<ticked>`

   If you tick this on the last entry, it makes the list look neater.

   - **Query:** `Active - is - true AND Priority - greater than - 2 - High`

   This gauge can then be added to the homepage.

4. Navigate to **Homepage Admin** > **Pages**, select Maintenance and use the Edit Homepage link so that you don't create a personal copy. Use the Add content button and then select Gauges, Maintenance, and Maintenance Count. Position it nicely.

 Gauge Counts can also use a script to determine a number. You can run any script in the provided field, with the return value providing what is displayed. It doesn't even need to be a number.

Gauge Counts show you data that is correct upon the load of homepage. There is an alternative type of report that shows you information that is correct to within a few seconds, without needing a reload!

To see an example, follow these steps:

1. Navigate to **Reports** > **View / Run**.
2. Click **Create a Report**, the fill it out the following information:
   - **Name**: Reservations for today
   - **Data table**: Reservation [x_hotel_reservation]
   - **Type**: Single Score
   - **Add Filter Condition**: Arrival - on - Today

3. Click Save. Use the dropdown selection of the Save button and then click Add to Dashboard. Set the following choices, then choose a position.
   - **Add to**: Homepage
   - **Homepage**: Maintenance

This will create a personal copy of the homepage as previously discussed.

4. Finally, hover over the newly added **Reservations for today** widget and select the gear shaped **Edit widget** option.
5. Select the following option, then click Done.
   - **Real-time**: <ticked>

6. You should see a little blue icon appear. Now in another browser, navigate to **Hotel** > **Reservations**, click New, populate the **Arrival** field with today's date, the **Departure** field with tomorrow's date and click Submit. The Reservations for Today widget should update within seconds showing the new count. Cool, eh?

We explore Real-time counts more in `Chapter 11`, *Making ServiceNow Beautiful with Service Portal and Custom Interfaces.*

The following screenshot shows the final result of the homepage:

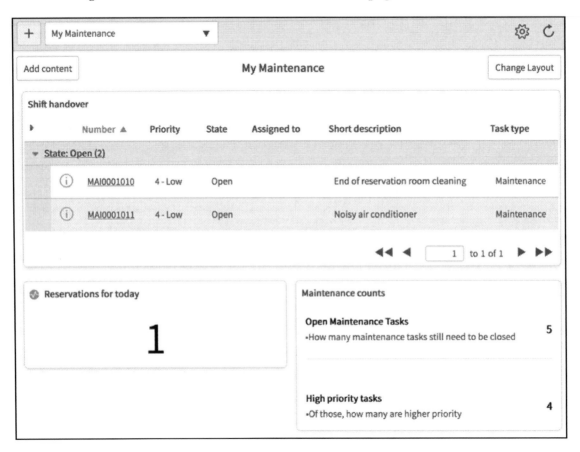

Optimizing homepages

Homepages seem innocuous. However, they frequently end up being a significant influence on the overall performance of an instance. Consider this scenario:

- 50 people in the same team have the same homepage.
- The homepage contains 10 reports, with several using inefficient queries.
- Everyone logs in at the same time, at 9 a.m., when work starts.
- Even then, they all ignore the homepage, since it isn't relevant to them, and click on My Work. (Many of the reports actually aren't even seen, since they are beyond the '"fold"', or only visible after scrolling.)

This gives the system a great deal of work to do: 500 graphs to show, all at the same time, but for no benefit! A series of optimizing strategies is used by the instance, including caching, to mitigate this scenario, but it is most important to be considerate about the reports and the conditions they contain. Perhaps only show tasks that have been updated in the last month, for example, instead of reporting on every record.

Caching can be controlled by going to **Homepage Admin** > **Properties**.

Summary

This chapter showed you how to deal with all the data collected in ServiceNow. The key to this is the automated processing of information. We started with exploring events. When things happen in ServiceNow, the platform can notice and set a flag for processing later. This keeps the system responsive for the user, while ensuring all the work that needs to get done, does get done.

Scheduled jobs are the background for a variety of functions: scheduled reports, scripts, and even task generation. They run on a periodic basis, such as every day or hour. They are often used for the automatic closure of tasks if the requester hasn't responded recently.

E-mail notifications are a critical part of any business application. We explored how e-mails are used to let requesters know when they've got work to do, to give requesters a useful update, or when an approver must make a decision. We even saw how approvers can make that decision using only e-mail.

Every user has a great deal of control over how they receive these notifications. The Notification Preferences interface lets them add multiple devices, including mobile devices, to receive push notifications.

The e-mail client in ServiceNow provides a simple, straightforward interface to send out e-mails, but the **Additional comments** and **Work notes** fields are often better and quicker to use. Every e-mail can include the contents of fields and even the output of scripts.

Every two minutes, ServiceNow checks for e-mails sent to its account. If it finds any, the e-mail is categorized into being a reply, forward, or new, and it runs inbound e-mail actions to update or create new records.

Metrics are useful to capture additional information about a particular record, such as how long it took to close. Reports can then use this information, especially if a database view has been used to flatten the structure.

Finally, homepages were looked at. These display information for a user to see when they log in or any time they click on the home icon. Most often, they contain reports, but any widget can be made and added, providing great flexibility. You can even add some clocks!

The next chapter, explores how an instance can get data from other systems, how to synchronize important information such as who the users are, and also very easily extract information out from ServiceNow. Learn how to get the right data in the right place at the right time.

7

Exchanging Data – Import Sets, Web Services, and other Integrations

So far, our journey through ServiceNow has focused on configuring the platform and creating a new application with scripts, data structures, and workflow functionality. But a ServiceNow instance that doesn't exchange data, requires manual interaction every time an employee joins or leaves, or needs task information copy-pasted into another system is a ServiceNow instance not being used to its full capability.

This chapter explores how ServiceNow can make it easy to exchange data with almost any other system. There are quite a few ways to make this happen:

- Let other systems pull information using Direct Web Services with no configuration in ServiceNow
- Import and export flat files such as CSV, XML, or Excel spreadsheets manually or automatically
- Shape, control, and manage the flow of data with Import Sets and Transform Maps
- Get user and group data from Active Directory or other LDAP servers
- Utilize the MID Server to easily communicate from behind firewalls, send and receive data and run custom scripts.
- Use Web Service Import Sets to connect to push and pull data using REST and SOAP quickly and easily.
- Gain more control with Scripted REST APIs

Beginning the web service journey

ServiceNow was born in the cloud. Every instance has native capability to share all its information in a variety of formats, without any configuration, directly over the Web.

People are often most comfortable browsing the Web when they see words, pictures, and some nice formatting. So ServiceNow uses forms, lists, and various widgets to make sense of the data in the instance.

But pictures don't mean much to a computer, nor do reams of text. So ServiceNow can output the same information you see in a form or a list in many other formats. It is your data-you can decide what to do with it.

Pulling data out of ServiceNow

ServiceNow can output in many different formats, all transferred via the Web. We'll explore each one of these, and more, in this chapter:

- Among file-based data, we will discuss CSV, XML, PDF, and Excel documents
- Among Web-based data, we will cover RSS, JSON, REST, and SOAP

Downloading file-based data

Chapter 6, *Events, Notifications, and Reporting,* explained how you could export any list in a variety of formats. You simply go to a list menu, right click on the list headings and choose **Export**. And Chapter 1 explored how we could navigate to pages without using the frameset. Open a new browser window and set the path as the table name suffixed by `_list.do`.

Let's imagine you may want a list of every Maintenance task in a format that Excel can use.

1. Navigate to `http://<instance>.service-now.com/x_hotel_maintenance_list.do` in your browser, replacing `<instance>` with your instance name.

Make sure you do this in all the examples I give – there are many occasions in this chapter.

2. You will be presented with the Maintenance task list, and you can choose **Export** > **Excel (.xlsx)** from the list menu to be prompted with a file to download.

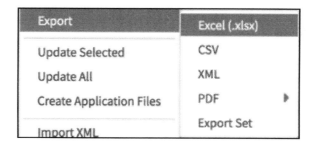

That's all very well, but it still takes a few clicks. By adding a URL parameter, we can skip those clicks.

3. Add the suffix `?EXCEL` to the URL like this: `<instance>.service-now.com/x_hotel_maintenance_list.do?EXCEL`.

Now, the file is downloaded immediately without any clicking. Of course, ServiceNow supports several URL parameters:

- **Comma-separated values (CSV)**: This is a plaintext file, with the field values separated by commas (as you'd expect!)
- **Portable Document Format (PDF)**: This format is often associated with Adobe Acrobat and Reader. Since it is a more presentational format, it contains headers, footers, and even colors.
- **Extensible Markup Language (XML)**: This is a ubiquitous and powerful format that many applications support. It has many features, including the use of complex types that allow the grouping of elements; for example, the street, city, and country may be part of a postal address. ServiceNow exports in a very flat structure, similar to a spreadsheet.
- **Excel**: This is the proprietary format used in Microsoft Excel, part of the Office suite. ServiceNow produces the original Excel binary file format (XLS), used primarily up until Excel 2007.

There are other parameters, like `JSONv2`, to get JSON data. But it is better to use the REST API mentioned later. (The REST API also delivers XML, as we'll see.)

The diagram below shows how the connection is initiated by the remote system (perhaps your web browser), and sent from ServiceNow.

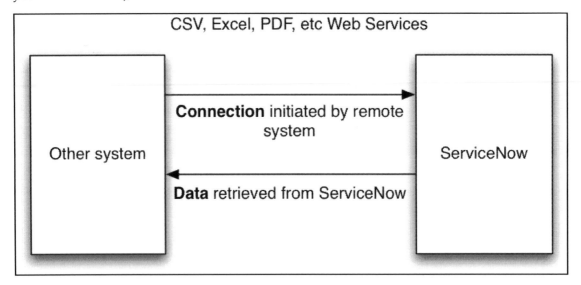

Automatically download data using cURL

ServiceNow is all about choice and flexibility. Chapter 6, *Events, Notifications, and Reporting,* looked at how scheduled reports could be used to send out an e-mail containing an Excel document on a periodic basis. But instead of filling everyone's mailbox, why not download it to a file share instead?

cURL is free, open source software that downloads data from almost anything, for basically every operating system. It doesn't use a graphical interface; you just pass it a URL and it saves it to disk.

- **Windows**: Download the binary from: http://curl.haxx.se/download.html. The **Win64** version is probably the one you should pick.
- **Linux**: Most distributions include cURL in their package manager. It is most likely already installed.
- **OS X**: cURL is already installed.

To download the Excel version of a document, use the following command:

```
curl --user <username> https://<instance>.service-
now.com/x_hotel_maintenance_list.do?EXCEL --output MaintenanceList.xls
```

Replace `<username>` and `<instance>` appropriately. You will be prompted for your password and the download will begin.

> The next chapter discusses authentication in more detail. For now, just use your normal username and password, as you would in a normal web interface.

This mechanism allows systems to grab whatever data they want to, without any configuration in ServiceNow. It is fairly straightforward to create a script and then combine it with a scheduler, such as Windows Task Scheduler or `cron`.

Being more specific with URL parameters

Part of the appeal of the ServiceNow API is its simplicity. Nonetheless, the platform lets you specify more parameters in order to control what you see. Some of the web services, such as the REST interface that we explore in detail later, support more parameters than the simpler CSV and XML interfaces. All, however, have a basic subset.

> The product documentation provides more examples of how to jump directly to the data you want:
> `https://docs.servicenow.com/bundle/helsinki-servicenow-platfor`
> `m/page/use/navigation/reference/r_NavigatingByURLExamples.html`

Choosing the fields

The Excel files that are downloaded from the instance have the same columns that are shown in the web interface. Often, this is a limited subset of the total number available. To see more, or have more control, two options are available:

- Use a database view
- Create a list view

Database views were explored in `Chapter 6`, *Events, Notifications, and Reporting*. Their main purpose is to join multiple tables together, but they can be used to control the available fields. The URL would be constructed using the database view, like so:

`<instance>.service-now.com/x_hotel_maintenance_metric_list.do?CSV`

`Chapter 1`, ServiceNow Fundamentals, covered how views can be created for lists and forms. Try creating an `All` view for the list, and include every field. Specifying a view gives better reliability-if you don't select a view, the default is used, which is highly likely to be changed by another system admin.

To select a view, use the `sysparm_view` URL parameter. An example URL would be this:

```
<instance>.service-
now.com/x_hotel_maintenance_list.do?sysparm_view=all&CSV
```

> These are the form and list views mentioned in `Chapter 1`, *ServiceNow Foundations*, where you select the fields you are interested in seeing, and not Database Views. It's useful to have an view that has the fields you want to present to the remote system, like this.

Specifying records

As we saw in Chapter 1, an encoded query lets you specify which records you are interested in. It is a simple field, operator, and value notation, with ^ representing an `AND`. An encoded query can be presented to the list using the `sysparm_query` parameter. To see the higher-priority tasks that are still active, you could use this example:

```
<instance>.service-
now.com/x_hotel_maintenance_list.do?sysparm_query=active=true^priority<
2&CSV
```

To get a filter, it is often easiest to copy it from the list. There are several operators, such as `LIKE`, `!=`, `NOT LIKE`, and `IN`. The Product Documentation has a section on creating encoded query strings:

```
https://docs.servicenow.com/bundle/helsinki-servicenow-platform/page/use/usi
ng-lists/concept/c_EncodedQueryStrings.html
```

> Rather than downloading all the data all the time, it is best to use the automatic date fields to create deltas. Pass through an encoded query to use the `sys_updated_on` field, like this:

```
<instance>.service-now.com/u_maintenance_list.do?sysparm_query=sys_created_
on><last run time>
```

Getting my stuff

When you build an encoded query, you often want to get a personalized list. For example, some people may want a constantly updated list of tasks available at their desktop without launching the ServiceNow web interface. There are several ways to achieve this.

Prefix each example with the instance domain name: `https://<instance>.service-now.com`. You will need to be logged in to the instance; otherwise, you will be prompted to enter a password. These examples are extracted in CSV, but you can of course change this.

- **Hardcoding a username in the URL**: This is dot-walking to the user ID in the User table through the Assigned to field:

```
/x_hotel_maintenance_list.do?sysparm_query=assigned_to.user_name=admin&CSV
```

- **Using a dynamic filter**: As discussed in `Chapter 2`, *Developing Custom Applications*, this is created by using the `Assigned to - is (dynamic) - Me` query. The records that are returned depend on which username and password is used to log in:

```
/x_hotel_maintenance_list.do?sysparm_query=assigned_toDYNAMIC90d1921e5f5
10100a9ad2572f2b477fe&CSV
```

- **Using a scripted query**: Passing JavaScript to a filter is just like an advanced reference qualifier. Again, it will depend on the username and password used to access the system to decide which user is taken:

```
/x_hotel_maintenance_list.do?sysparm_query=assigned_to=javascript:gs.getUse
rID()&CSV
```

For these to return some records, you must have some records that meet the criteria! For you to set System Administrator (or another user) into the Assigned to field, it means putting that user in a Maintenance group and it having the `itil` role for the Reference Qualifier to succeed.

Pulling data designed for the Web

In addition to the file-based formats of XML and CSV, ServiceNow lets you grab information that is often directly usable by other applications. RSS and JSON are formats that are often only produced by websites. SOAP is an industry-standard interchange format for integrations. Let's take a brief look at them all:

- **Rich Site Summary** (**RSS**): This is an XML file that has a specific schema to provide information about articles and items that are frequently updated. It can be used to very quickly integrate with Slack, with new items being added to the channel. To grab an RSS feed, just add RSS to the URL, exactly the same as the CSV examples above.

- **Simple Object Access Protocol** (**SOAP**): (Though SOAP is now just a name.) SOAP is a specification for requesting and receiving structured data, usually over the Web. It uses XML as its underlying format, so it is relatively human readable. However, its power and capability often make it difficult to use.

- **JavaScript Object Notation** (**JSON**): This is a lightweight name-value pair format. It uses the same notation as JavaScript, making it easy for web browsers to parse, though many other languages now offer support.

- **Representational State Transfer** (**REST**): This is a mechanism of transferring data, usually XML or JSON, over the web. It uses HTTP, taking advantage of the same methods (GET, POST, and so on) that web browsers use. While there is no official standard, it has rapidly gained popularity since it's a simpler, more efficient alternative to the rather more verbose, structured, and complex SOAP protocol.

Cleaning up with SOAP

SOAP is designed to be self-describing. A Web Services Description Language (WSDL) is an XML document that tells a system what data it can request, what data it can send, and what it will receive in return.

Armed with the WSDL, a system can create the right XML message and send it to the instance. The instance should understand it and respond with an XML message containing the results.

ServiceNow produces a WSDL for every table. You've probably guessed how you can access it: the URL parameter is WSDL. To view the data for the Maintenance table, navigate to `<instance>.service-now.com/x_hotel_maintenance_list.do?WSDL`.

You will be presented with a big XML document. There are plenty of resources on the Web that will give you an understanding of what it all means! Some of the basics are listed in this chapter. But most of the time, you would just take the WSDL and put it in an IDE such as Eclipse.

The WSDL describes the methods or operations that ServiceNow provides for each table. They are your typical **Create, Read, Update, and Delete (CRUD)** activities, letting you interact with the records in a fashion akin to database interaction.

- The `insert` method lets you create new records in the table. The parameters it accepts are fields, letting the calling system provide all the data necessary to create a record. No parameters are necessary. The `sys_id` of the created record is returned as well as the field containing the display value.

To add an additional `insertMultiple` method, activate the Insert Multiple Web Service plugin. It allows you to create multiple records at the same time, as you'd expect.

- The **update** method accepts all fields, but requires a `sys_id` value. The matching record has its records set to the values provided. It returns the `sys_id` value of the updated record.

It is best practice to not use the `insert` and `update` methods on tables directly. Instead, use an Import Set, as we will explore in the upcoming sections.

- The **get** method accepts a `sys_id` value and returns all the fields for that record.
- The **deleteRecord** method accepts only a `sys_id` value. If it exists, it is deleted. It returns the number of records that have been deleted.
- The **getKeys** method accepts all fields and performs a query on the data. A list of `sys_id` values is returned, along with a count of how many records are present.
- The **getRecords** method combines `getKeys` and `get`. It accepts all fields and uses them to query the table. It returns all the records that match.

The instance provides these methods for every table. It allows a calling system to connect to the instance and create, read, update, and delete records in any table-as long as it has the right permissions.

The diagram below shows how SOAP Direct Web Services (and REST, discussed later) are initiated from another system, and these other systems can retrieve from, or insert or change data in ServiceNow.

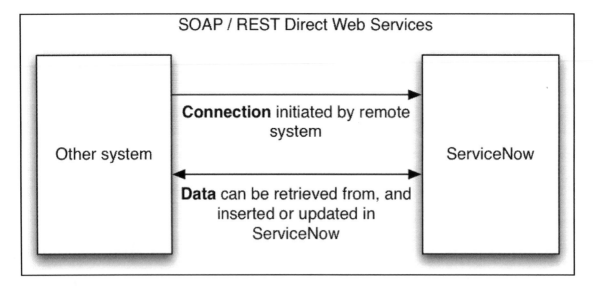

Using direct web services

SoapUI is a great tool to test out web services in ServiceNow. It reads the WSDL, generates sample messages, and lets you send them to the instance in only a few clicks. SoapUI is open source and available for Windows, OS X, and Linux:

```
https://www.soapui.org/downloads/latest-release.html
```

Let's use SoapUI to get a list of Maintenance tasks. Follow these instructions to see how.

1. Launch the program, and create a new SOAP project using the File menu.
2. In the dialog, use
   `https://<instance>.service-now.com/x_hotel_maintenance_list.do?`
   `WSDL` as the **Initial WSDL**. When you click OK, a a series of sample requests will be automatically generated, one for each method.

3. Expand **getRecords** and double-click on **Request 1**:

4. The request will open in another window, showing the XML message that will be sent to the instance. SoapUI provides an element for each field as well as some extra parameters that we'll explore later. In general, the majority of these elements should be removed, except for the ones you want to use as queries.

5. As a simple example, remove all the elements other than the `active` tag. Then, replace the `?` parameter with `true`. The resulting XML should look something like the following:

```
<soapenv:Envelope xmlns:soapenv="http://schemas.xmlsoap.org/soap/envelope/"
xmlns:x="http://www.service-now.com/x_hotel_maintenance">
    <soapenv:Header/>
    <soapenv:Body>
        <x:getRecords>
            <active>true</active>
        </x:getRecords>
    </soapenv:Body>
</soapenv:Envelope>
```

6. Before the message is sent to the instance, your username and password to be given to SoapUI. Click on the **Authorization** button at the bottom of the request window. In the **Authorization** selection field, choose **Add New Authorization**. Click on **OK** when **Authorization** is set to **Basic** and then fill out the **Username** and **Password** fields.

7. To send the request, click on the green play button in the window. After just a moment, the right-hand pane will be populated with the response from the instance, just like the screenshot below:

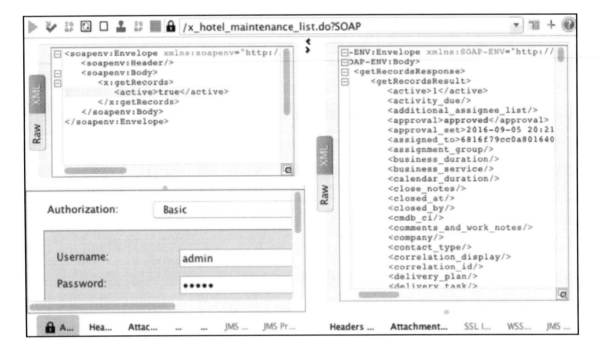

Filtering the response

Creating AND-based queries is easy, by simply populating the getRecords node with the fields you want to filter on. The following XML snippet will look for high-priority Maintenance tasks for room 201:

```
<room>201</room>
<priority>1</priority>
```

As this example shows, you can query the using display (as per the room field) or database value (as with priority).

To perform more complex queries, and control how many results you return, there are several other parameters available, beyond those named after the fields. They all start with a double underscore (__) to keep them separate:

- __encoded_query lets you specify a more complex query, using conjunctions other than equal to. It does require an understanding of the ServiceNow query syntax (for example, ^OR), which means it is not self-describing – and therefore more complex for someone not used to ServiceNow.
- __limit, along with __first_row, is useful for paging through results. An alternative is __last_row. Only the data that you want is returned. If __limit is not specified, it defaults to 250. Use with __order_by for consistency.
- __use_view lets you restrict which fields are returned. By default, a view called soap_response is used. If it doesn't exist in the table, all available data is returned. A URL parameter of sysparm_view is also accepted.

> Specifying a view is a great way to include derived (dot-walked) fields.

- __order_by and __order_by_desc let you specify a comma-separated list of fields to sort the results.

Returning display values

By default, the content of the database column is returned for reference, choice, and other fields that have a display value. This means that a sys_id value will be returned for the Assignment group field. The displayvalue parameter gives alternative options:

- To have the display value instead of the database value, set displayvalue to true.
- To have the display value as well as the database value, set displayvalue to all. This will cause an extra field to be added, prefixed with dv_. The Assignment group field would have two nodes in any response: assignment_group (containing the sys_id value) and dv_assignment_group (containing the group name).

> The property can be set either as a URL parameter (for example, x_hotel_maintenance_list.do?SOAP&displayvalue=all), or through the glide.soap.return_displayValue property with either false, true, or all.

> Be consistent. If you grab the WSDL with `displayvalue=true` but send
> the SOAP message without it, the SOAP response will not conform to the
> WSDL, and some systems may reject it as invalid. Its best to set the
> property to `all` if you like this feature and leave it at that.

Having a REST

RESTful web services have quickly established themselves as the primary mechanism of
exchanging information across the Web. **REST** is not a fully defined standard, but uses
commonly accepted mechanisms to simplify the way of asking for information in a
machine-readable format. If you thought that SOAP was too complicated, you aren't alone!

The ServiceNow REST API provides everything that SOAP does, and more. Instead of using
bespoke methods, REST uses the standard HTTP `GET`, `POST`, `PUT`, `PATCH`, and `DELETE`
methods to manipulate data, just like your web browser. To retrieve information, use the
`GET` method (as you would while browsing the Web for cat pictures), and to send
information, use the `POST` method (which is also used for updating your status on
Facebook).

To select the content, REST primarily uses information in a URL. Collections are lists or
groups of information. So when using the Table API, you can retrieve all users by accessing
`https://<instance>.service-now.com/api/now/table/sys_user`. To select a
specific element (in this case, a single user), append the URL with the `sys_id` value, like
this: `api/now/table/sys_user/5137153cc611227c000bbd1bd8cd2005`.

Using the REST Explorer

To make it really easy to understand the capabilities available in the REST APIs,
ServiceNow provides the REST Explorer. It is a specialized client interface that understands
the options available, and presents them in a point-and-click UI. It makes it far easy to
quickly create the right commands than experimenting in SoapUI.

Use it to craft the request you want, then generate sample code in Python, Ruby, Powershell, or even a cURL command. Follow these steps:

1. Navigate to **System Web Services** > **REST** > **REST API Explorer**, and for the first time only, click on **Explore**.
2. To retrieve a list of users, with all the defaults, make the following selections:
   - **Namespace**: `now`
   - **API Name**: `Table API`

     These two options are the defaults, but together select the ServiceNow APIs (as opposed to ones you can create yourself), and the ability to directly query the table, just like we did with SOAP earlier.

   - **Retrieve records from a table (GET)**: `<selected>`
   - **tableName**: `User (sys_user)`

3. At the bottom of the page, click on **Send**. You should then see a user record with all the fields in the response body section. As mentioned, you can copy code to generate the same result using the appropriate links.

```
Response Body

{
  "result": [
    {
      "calendar_integration": "1",
      "country": "",
      "user_password": "",
      "last_login_time": "",
```

GETting it your way

The REST Explorer makes it easy to set options. These are either sent to the instance as parameters or in the header, depending on REST convention. Let's explore some of the more useful options:

- To choose between receiving XML or JSON, set the **Response format** option to change the **Accept** header. You can also specify what type of data you are sending through the **Content-Type** header.

```
Response Body

<?xml version="1.0" encoding="UTF-8"?>
<response>
    <result>
        <calendar_integration>1</calendar_integration>
        <country/>
        <user_password/>
        <last_login_time/>
```

 Unfortunately, the XML response is not formatted nicely. I've altered it here to make it more readable. The key point is that the information is the same, just the format is different.

The following URL parameters can be set:

- `sysparm_query`: This accepts an encoded query, like in the other web services
- `sysparm_display_value`: This works in the same manner as the `displayvalue` URL parameter in a SOAP endpoint
- `sysparm_view`: This is the same as the `__use_view` parameter
- `sysparm_fields`: This is a simpler method to directly specify a comma-separated list of fields. It takes priority over the view
- `sysparm_limit`: This specifies the pagination limit, such as `__limit`, in the SOAP message

There are very few default options applied by the REST Explorer. The most important one to remember is that only one record is returned by default (`sysparm_limit` is set to 1). This is to stop you returning thousands of records when you just wanted to test things out.

There is also sysparm_offset, but this is not displayed in the REST Explorer. You can always add it manually by clicking **Add query parameter**. The REST API documentation lists everything. View it here:

For example, the following cURL command retrieves a single active Maintenance record, specifying three fields and the data to be in JSON format:

```
curl --user <username> --header "Accept: application/json"
"https://<instance>.service-
now.com/api/now/table/x_hotel_maintenance?sysparm_fields=number,short
_description,assignment_group&sysparm_display_value=true&sysparm_limi
t=1&sysparm_query=active=true&sysparm_exclude_reference_link=true"
```

This returns the following output from my instance, formatted nicely.

```
{
    "result": [{
        "number": "MAI0001001",
        "short_description": "",
        "assignment_group": ""
    }]
}
```

Using the right method

The REST API is very powerful: in addition to retrieving data, it can update, create, and delete records. While most web queries use the GET method (to retrieve data), you can ask web servers to do other activities too. You may, for example, use your browser to post a new photo on Facebook, or send message using Twitter. Both these activities send data – and use the POST method.

The following methods are typically used in a REST API – and ServiceNow follows the conventions nicely.

- GET – retrieves data
- POST – creates a new item
- PUT / PATCH – updates (or replaces) data
- DELETE – removes the data item

This article gives a more detailed overview on generic REST principles: `ht tp://www.restapitutorial.com/lessons/httpmethods.html`

Typically, these actions happen against a collection, or an individual element.

For the Table API, think of the collection as being the list of the table; and the element as the record. So Table API supports GET on both lists and records, PUT, PATCH and DELETE work on individual records, and POST is for lists.

The Table API gives examples on every operation here: `https://developer.servicenow.com/app.do#!/rest_api_doc?v= helsinki&to=class__rest_c_tableapi__helsinki`

Selecting the right content

These methods work alongside the URL presented to the API. Let's break apart this example URL to see each component:

```
<instance>.service-now.com
/api/now/v2/table/sys_user/5137153cc611227c000bbd1bd8cd2005
```

- **api** specifies to the instance you want to work with the REST API.
- **now** is the namespace. Most of the ServiceNow APIs are in the now namespace, but there are others. If you create a Scripted REST API, the namespace will be that of your application – x_hotel in our case.
- **v2** represents the version. This parameter is optional. The platform uses versioning of the APIs to ensure that every request is handled exactly the same way even across different releases of the API.

For example, v2 of the Table API responds differently to a GET request that returns no records, returning an HTTP 200 response with an empty dataset, as opposed to HTTP 404. This was done to be more similar to other REST APIs.

- **table** is the API name. For the Table API, it will be table. There are other APIs, including Import Sets, discussed later.

The rest of the parameters are dependent upon the API.

- **sys_user** in the case of the Table API is the table name. It specifies the collection you are working with.
- Finally, the `sys_id` specifies what individual element, or record, you want to work with. For the Table API, this is again optional.

So if you wanted to create a user, you would POST the data to the following URL snippet: `/api/now/table/sys_user`.

Or to update an existing user, PUT the data you want to change to: `/api/now/v2/table/sys_user/5137153cc611227c000bbd1bd8cd2007`.

> Postman is a very popular tool for interacting with REST APIs. Download it at `https://www.getpostman.com/` and try out these APIs.

Updating and inserting data

Let's use the REST Explorer to see how a new Maintenance record could be submitted by an external system:

1. Navigate to the REST Explorer (available at **System Web Services** > **REST** > **REST API Explorer**).
2. Make the following selections:
    - **Namespace**: `now`
    - **API Name**: `Table API`
    - **Create a record (POST)**: `<selected>` (click on the link)
    - **tableName**: `Maintenance (x_hotel_maintenance)`

3. In the **Request Body** section, click on the **Add a field** button. Fill out the fields as follows, using the plus button to add more. Note the data being built out in JSON format underneath.

Make sure you do this in the Request Body section, as per the screenshot below!)

- **Short Description**: `Creaky floorboard`
- **Room**: `101`
- **State**: 2 (This represents Work in Progress)

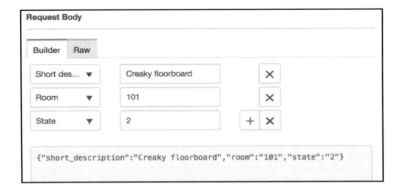

4. Finally, click on **Send**. After confirming using the **OK** button, you should see the new record's details in the **Response Body** section, including the `sys_id` value and the number that was generated for it. Verify the creation of the record by navigating to **Hotel** > **Maintenances**.

Exploring other APIs

Each release of ServiceNow comes with more APIs, allowing interaction with the instance from other systems. As we will see in `Chapter 11`, *Making ServiceNow Beautiful with Service Portal and Custom Interfaces,* other parts of the ServiceNow platform like Service Portal uses several of them.

Try exploring some of these APIs:

- The Aggregate API lets you query for some basic statistics against a table: counting records and returning max and min values. It is the equivalent of `GlideAggregate`.

- The Attachment API gives you a much improved way to deal with binary data. Use it to retrieve, delete, or upload attachments to records without resorting to Base64 encoding.
- The Import Set API, discussed in more detail later, provides much more control when bringing information into the system. It allows you to manipulate, reject, and script data during uploads.

The Product Documentation provides more information about all the endpoints and parameters and provides sample messages and responses:
`https://docs.servicenow.com/bundle/helsinki-servicenow-platform/page/integrate/inbound-rest/concept/c_RESTAPI.html`
`https://docs.servicenow.com/bundle/helsinki-servicenow-platform/page/integrate/inbound-rest/concept/c_TableAPI.html`
The Developer portal is an alternative source of information:

Bringing it in using Import Sets

SOAP and REST direct web services allow you to insert or update table data directly. It is like having all the fields available in a form, without any UI Policy, Client Scripts, or other browser-based checks. This means it is very easy to create and edit data using a SOAP or REST application-but also uncontrolled and unchecked. Business Rules are run to provide an element of validation, but the data format or schema must still match that of ServiceNow. For example, when populating the Priority field for a Maintenance task, one of the choice values must be supplied.

Import Sets is a set of technologies that work together to bring data into ServiceNow. It follows a particular pattern:

1. The data is imported from a **Data Source**, which specifies what the data is and where it is stored. This can be a file or information retrieved from a database or web server. After parsing, it is stored unaltered in a staging table.
2. The data is run through a **Transform Map**. This bridges the staging table and the target table. The target table can be any table in ServiceNow-anything from users to tasks or even configuration. The Transform Map specifies how data should be copied from the staging table to the target table. A record in the staging table often results in a record in the target table, but the data can be checked or manipulated as it is transferred. Scripts can be run during the transform.
3. This process can be **scheduled**, running as often as necessary-or on demand.

Import gives you a predefined template that you fill out and upload to ServiceNow. If you don't want to bother with mapping fields and just want to get data in quick, use Easy Import. Read up on this further at https://docs.servicenow.com/bundle/helsinki-servicenow-platform/page/administer/import-sets/concept/c_EasyImport.html

Easy Import gives you a predefined template that you fill out and upload to ServiceNow. If you don't want to bother with mapping fields and just want to get data in quick, use Easy Import. Read up on this further at https://docs.servicenow.com/bundle/helsinki-servicenow-platform/page/administer/import-sets/concept/c_EasyImport.html This diagram provides an overview of the steps:

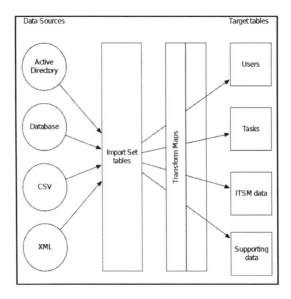

Specifying the data source

Each entry in the **Data Source** [sys_data_source] table contains the information that ServiceNow needs to pick the file up or connect to the server. Navigate to **System Import Sets** > **Administration** > **Data Sources** to see some examples.

As you select the different types and options, UI Policies show or hide other fields. Some of the most important items are discussed in this section.

The product documentation explains all the options in more detail-files can be unzipped, deleted after collection, and much more: `https://docs.servicenow.com/bundle/helsinki-servicenow-platfor m/page/administer/import-sets/concept/c_DataSources.html`

Several data sources, such as the following, are supported:

- **CSV, XML,**and **XLS** or **XLSX** Excel files. Ensure the **Type** field in the data source has **File** selected before selecting the type of data. Typically these files are retrieved from a file server, using **FTPS**, **SFTP**, **HTTPS** or **SCP**.

Custom separators can be used for CSV files. Just add the CSV delimiter field to the form. The pipe symbol (|) is quite common.

- Databases that can be accessed via **JDBC**.
- **LDAP servers**, such as **Active Directory**. They often store user and group information.

Once the data is retrieved from its source, it will be copied into a table in the instance, called an Import Set table. It is often referred to as a staging table. It is a standard database table, extended from **Import Set Row** [sys_import_set_row]. Therefore, the data to be imported cannot be hierarchical and needs to be in a simple row-column format. Excel files shouldn't have merged cells, and the column headings must be on a single row.

I like to prefix all the **Import Set table label** fields with IMP. Otherwise, it is difficult to know whether a table is a staging table or a standard table when creating reports or looking at the Dictionary.

The platform creates a field for each data point. For a CSV or Excel file, one is made for every column heading in the data source. By default, the column headings are assumed to be the first row. If the schema in the data source changes (such as a new column being added), the platform will create a new field in the table.

This process can cause severe performance problems if the Import Set tables are very large. Set the `glide.import_set_row.dynamically_add_fields` property to `false` to prevent this. A second property, `com.glide.loader.verify_target_field_size`, will increase the size of a field if it is too small. It is `false` by default.

For CSV and Excel files, the **Load Data** module within **System Import Sets** will guide you through the process very easily. It creates a data source, attaches the file to the record, creates an import set table, and brings in the data. It also creates an easy-to-access menu module to the table on the left-hand-side menu, under **System Import Sets** > **Import Set Tables**.

Cleaning up Import Set tables

Import Set tables can get pretty big very quickly. Each time an import runs, it stores more data. This is useful for debugging and testing, but can quickly slow the platform down during imports. There is a Scheduled Job that trims the data, removing records older than a week. The **Cleanup** module under **System Import Sets** > **Import Set Tables** lets you do this when you want.

Make sure Import Sets are kept trimmed. Since every import set table is extended from the Import Set Row table, the base table can easily contain millions of records. Performance issues will then impact all imports.

Getting data

CSV, XML, XLS, and XLSX data can be retrieved from file servers using the HTTP, SFTP, FTPS, and SCP protocols. Data can also be retrieved from LDAP and database servers. Regardless of where it comes from, the data is always placed in an import set table. Once configured, try grabbing data by clicking on the **Test Load 20 Records** related link to see whether it works.

Every time the **Load All Records** (or the **Test Load 20 Records**) related link is clicked on, a new **Import Set** [`sys_import_set`] record is created. This records when the load happened, how long it took, which data source it came from, and what data was pulled in. Every entry in an import set table will reference an import set, providing a link back to how it was originally brought into the system.

Navigate to **System Import Sets** > **Advanced** > **Import Sets** to see the list.

There are several data source options available:

- **Attachment** simply collects the file that is attached to the Data Source record. It is a good idea to build up an import in steps, and an attachment is often the place to begin.
- **FTP** is the easiest, though not secure. Try to avoid it when possible. It is useful for proof-of-concept purposes, however.
- **FTPS** and **SFTP**are secure file-transfer protocols. Despite their similar names, they are quite different. Check carefully which protocol your server uses.

It is very important to note that an FTP/SFTP/FTPS Data Source is tied to a single filename. You cannot use wildcards or expect the instance to find the latest file in a directory. When placing files on an FTP server for a scheduled pickup, it must always be in exactly the same location, with exactly the same filename. The instance can be configured to remove a file once imported. This is a useful option, since it gives an indication as to success, however unsophisticated.

- ServiceNow can also retrieve data over the web through **HTTP** and **HTTPS**.

A ServiceNow-to-ServiceNow integration can take advantage of the XML-generation capabilities of ServiceNow. If you want to import users from another instance, you can set the **File** path to be /sys_user.do?XML, with **Type** as File and **Format** as XML.

- The instance can also pull data in through a **JDBC** connection. Many databases are supported: **MySQL**, **SQL Server**, **Oracle**, **Sybase**, and **DB2**.

The Use last run datetime option allows the SQL query to be filtered and only return the records that have changed-a delta. Use this if possible, since it will accelerate the import and the transformation dramatically. Since database connections are not encrypted, use either a MID server or a VPN tunnel. Both will be discussed later.

- **LDAP** is used to pull in users and groups from a corporate address list, such as **Active Directory**. Importing data through a MID server is also possible. The next section explores LDAP servers in much more detail.

When importing data, ServiceNow initiates the connection and pulls back information from the source:

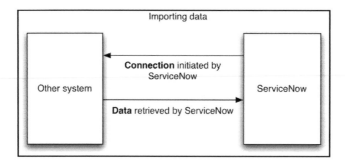

Dealing with XML files

Importing CSV files is usually pretty straightforward. Comma separated data is very similar to a database table, with a header and then rows of information.

In contrast, XML files are typically hierarchical. To fit into a database table, ServiceNow uses XPath to find the data you want, then flattening anything in that node.

Consider the following XML file that contains a list of hotel rooms. It is also hosted at http://www.gardiner-hotels.com/import/hotelrooms.xml

```xml
<xml>
  <produced_on>2016-07-01</produced_on>
  <room>
    <number>123</number>
    <location>
      <corridor>A5</corridor>
      <floor>1</floor>
    </location>
  </room>
  <room>
    <number>124</number>
    <location>
      <corridor>A5</corridor>
      <floor>1</floor>
    </location>
  </room>
</xml>
```

An XPath expression of /xml/room will return anything under an xml node and a room node. The produced_on node is ignored.

 //room will give functionally the same result in this example, but will search the whole document for room nodes. It means the instance must keep a list of processed nodes, making the import vastly more inefficient. Test your XPath expressions at http://www.xpathtester.com/.

Let's import these rooms into our Hotel app.

1. Firstly, lets create a Data Source. The XML file is stored on a web server, so it is easy to get it into the instance. Navigate to **System Import Sets** > **Administration** > **Data Sources** and click **New**.

2. Fill out the following fields, then Save:
   - **Name**: IMP XML Rooms
   - **Import set table label**: IMP XML Rooms

 Don't remove the u_ prefix from the Import set table name. Whilst this may seem unusual in a scoped application, it prevents you from deleting the table cleanly.

   - **Format**: XML
   - **XPath for each row**: /xml/room
   - **Expand node children**: <ticked>
   - **File retrieval method**: HTTPS
   - **File path**: /import/hotelrooms.xml
   - **Server**: www.gardiner-hotels.com

3. After you've saved the Data Source, click on **Load All Records**. The instance will then retrieve the file, create the IMP XML Room table, extending it from Import Set Table, and then create as many records as there are room nodes.

4. Once the import has succeeded, click on **Loaded data** to see what you brought in.

Any nodes that are nested will have the XML snippet placed in a new field. Because **Expand node children** was ticked, the instance created two more fields, **location/corridor** and **location/floor**.

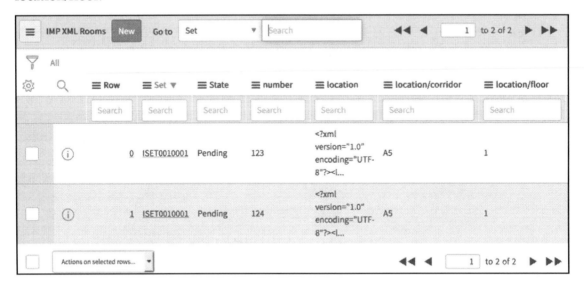

Transforming the data

Once the data has been brought into an Import Set table, it needs to be transferred to its final destination. Transform Maps do exactly that. By creating field maps and scripts, Transform Maps will validate, check, and copy data to the appropriate place. A Transform Map is always associated with a source Import Set table and a target table. The configuration is contained in a **Table Transform Map** [sys_transform_map] record, accessible under **System Import Sets** > **Administration** > **Transform Maps**.

The basic element of a transform map is a **field map**. It is an association between a particular field in an import set table and one in the target table. There cannot be more than one field map for a particular field on a target table. When the Transform Map runs, each field map is looped through in order to populate the fields in the target table.

Field maps can be created in three ways. The Related Links on a Transform Map link to the first two of the following:

- Automatically, through **Auto Map Matching Fields**. If a field with the same name or label exists on both the import set table and the target table, a field map is created.

- **Mapping Assist** provides a drag-and-drop interface to create associations between the import set table and the target table.
- Field map records can be created manually. This allows full control of all the features of a field map.

Creating a field map

A field map created by either Auto Map Matching Fields or Mapping Assist will have only the basics – a relationship between the source and the target. However, there are other options. **Coalesce** is one of the most important ones.

A Transform Map takes in data and attempts to apply it to a target table. Every row in the Import Set table may become a new record in the target table. However, this isn't always desirable, especially for repeated or scheduled imports. Instead, you often want the platform to **update** existing records. Specifying whether the platform will insert or update is the job of the Coalesce flag.

Any field map can be marked with the Coalesce flag. This means the target field will be used as a unique key. If the value being imported matches an existing row, that record will be updated. Otherwise, an insert will happen. This is directly comparable to the SQL MERGE (sometimes referred to as upsert) statement.

If multiple field mappings have the Coalesce flag set, then the platform will search for a record in the target table where *all* the field values match. For instance, matching on a person's name and address is more likely to find the right record to update than using the name alone.

Almost every Transform Map should have at least one field map marked with Coalesce. Otherwise, it will create duplicate records!

Once the Coalesce field is selected, you can refine how it works. Should it match only with case sensitivity? Should empty fields be matched?

Enabling scripting in transform maps

The **Use source script** checkbox provides a **Source script** field that can be used instead of a source field. This allows JavaScript to supply a value for the target field by setting the answer variable. There are several other global variables that are mentioned in the next section.

Creating new values

When the target field is a reference or choice fields, you get to determine what happens if the source value doesn't exist in the the target selection. For example, say you were importing Maintenance tasks, and one of the items to be imported had a priority value of 0 – `Super important`. This doesn't exist as an option. What should happen?

- **create** will provide a new option to choose from in the **Choice List** field

I don't like that this is the default option. It is unlikely that you want to create lots of new entries in your choice lists.

- **ignore** will do nothing and won't set the field
- **reject** will stop the insertion of the entire row

If you wanted to change certain source values, you will need to write a source script. For example, you could try this simple script to map those odd priorities:
if (source.u_priority == "") target.priority = "1";
The variables are discussed in the next section.

Dealing with times

The data in an Import Set table is stored as text. So, when importing date and time fields, the transform map will need to convert it. ServiceNow takes Java date formatting strings to tell the system how to deal with it. The **Date format** suggestion field gives several common patterns.

Importing into reference fields

Reference fields provide the **Referenced value field name** option. Normally, reference fields will find the right record using the display value, but any field in the table can be specified here. Use a unique value whenever possible.

For example, if you are inserting Maintenance tasks, you may want to specify whom it is assigned to. But specifying the name of the person, the default display field, isn't likely to be successful. What if there are two people with the same name? Using something unique, such as an e-mail address, will provide a better match. Specify `email` in the **Reference value field name** field to do this.

Moving in the rooms

Let's continue our example, and create a Transform Map for the room data we've brought into the instance.

1. Navigate to **System Import Sets** > **Create Transform Map**. File out the fields as below, and be sure to choose Save.
    - **Name**: Rooms
    - **Source table**: IMP XML Rooms [u_imp_xml_rooms]
    - **Target table**: Room [x_hotel_room]

2. For the easiest creation of the field maps, click **Auto Map Matching Fields**. You should see the Field Map list be populated with a new entry for the number field.

Notice how all the source fields are prefixed with u_, as if you were creating global configuration. This is because Import Sets sit in a strange place between scoped and global. A little more is discussed about global configuration in Chapter 10, *Packaging with Applications, Update Sets, and Upgrades.*

3. Click on the u_number Field Map entry, and update the fields as below, then click Update to return to the Transform Map.
    - **Coalesce**: <ticked>

4. Setting the **Coalesce** field means that repeated imports won't create lots of duplicate Room records with the same Room number.

5. When you return to the Transform Map, you will get a message saying: **None of fields configured to coalesce are indexed on the target table**. Click **OK,** select **Do not notify me**, then **OK** twice again.

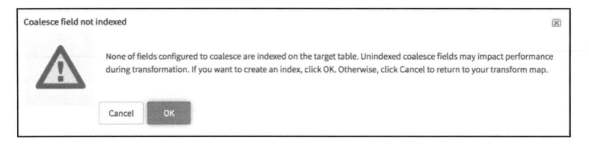

6. This will create an index on the Number field on the Room table. This helps the coalescing process so that imports are as fast as possible.
7. You should then have the field maps set up like this:

8. Finally, click **Transform**, then **Transform** again. When it completes, navigate to **Hotel > Rooms** to see the records that have been created. Rooms 123 and 124 have been created, and because **Run Business Rules** is ticked in the Transform Map (mentioned in the next section), the floor field is populated too.

Scripting in Transform Maps

Transform Scripts are just like Business Rules, but simpler. There is no condition field, instead just a simple **Type** field that chooses when it should run:

- Before (**onBefore**) or after (**onAfter**) a record is inserted or updated in the target table
- When the transform map starts processing (**onStart**) or when it stops (**onComplete**)

- When choices or reference values are created (**onChoiceCreate**, **onForeignInsert**, **onReject**). These are rarely used.

You can create a new Transform Script by clicking on New in the Related List of the Transform Map record. There is also a Script field in the Transform Map table itself.

All the scripts in a Transform Map have access to the following global variables:

- `source`: The `GlideRecord` object of the import set table that is currently being processed
- `target`: The `GlideRecord` object that is being inserted or updated in the target table
- `log`: Lets you add to the Import Log using the `info`, `warn`, and `error` functions
- `action`: A string that is either `insert` or `update`, depending on how the **Coalesce** operation has worked
- `ignore` and `error`: Will abort the current row or the whole Import Set transformation, respectively, if set to `true`

The Product Documentation has examples and more information on each object:
`https://docs.servicenow.com/bundle/helsinki-servicenow-platform/page/script/server-scripting/reference/r_TransformationScriptVariables.html`

Knowing when scripting will run

Since there are so many opportunities to run scripts, it is not immediately obvious when the code will be called. The list that follows shows the order that the scripts will be run in every time a record in the Table Transform Map table is evaluated. Within each section, the Order field of the transform script is used. The following order will be followed:

1. The scripts in any field maps marked for **Coalesce**.

The platform will determine at this point whether it is an `insert` or an `update`.

2. The `onBefore` transform scripts.
3. The other field map scripts.
4. The `onForeignInsert` transform scripts.

5. The Script field in the transform map.

 The write happens to the database between these steps.

6. The `onAfter` transform scripts.

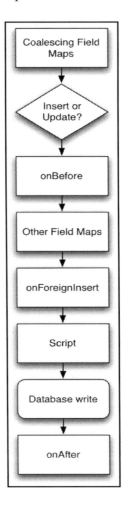

The Script field in the transform map is therefore a great place to perform any error checking or validation. Every field should have been populated at this point, and the database write is just about to happen.

The user account that runs the transform will be recorded in the audit log when changes to the records are made. To impersonate another user, use `gs.getSession().impersonate(<username>);` in the Script field. The Run As field in a scheduled import can be used to specify which account is used.

Keeping import sets running

It is common to have scheduled imports running every day, processing hundreds of thousands of records. To ensure that the instance does more than just import data, make Transform Maps as efficient as possible. Their processing speed depends on a great deal of things, including how much data there is, what format it is in, and what the target table looks like.

The product documentation has an article on **Troubleshooting Import Set Performance**. It provides some useful advice if things are getting slow. `https://docs.servicenow.com/bundle/helsinki-servicenow-platform/page/administer/technical-best-practice/concept/c_TroubleshootImportSetPerformance.html`

One of the most important items is the checkbox on the transform map, labeled **Run Business Rules**. If it is unchecked, scripts and workflows won't be run for each inserted or imported record. It is often much quicker to turn this off, but be aware that you are then avoiding the automatic population and data-validation capabilities of business rules. In our previous example, the Floor field is populated via a Business Rule, and so wouldn't have been populated.

Having the coalesce fields indexed is also critical. Click on Index Coalesce Fields on the Transform Map form to have the instance check this for you.

The platform can import data going up to many millions of records. Since it runs in the background, it'll crunch through the data, bringing in useful information. As long as the data is in a workable format, it is likely you'll be able to transform it.

Garbage in, garbage out is still true for ServiceNow. Think carefully about where the best source of data is in your company.

Importing users and groups with LDAP

An **Lightweight Directory Access Protocol (LDAP)** server is just another data source. In theory, it could store any information, meaning an LDAP server can be used like a database. However, LDAP most commonly stores user data, including information such as their phone number, e-mail address, and location.

 Microsoft **Active Directory** is the most commonly used LDAP server that ServiceNow customers use, and is probably the most common integration target. It is usually the most obvious source of user data in a company, but it's often badly maintained! Before integrating it without question, consider whether you have a better source of user information, such as an HR database.

An LDAP server also has the extra capability of authentication. In ServiceNow, these two functions are distinct and operate independently of each other, though they are obviously connected. Many LDAP servers, such as Active Directory, will also have the capability for **single sign-on (SSO)**

 In this chapter, we will focus on how the data is retrieved. Chapter 8, *Securing Applications and Data*, looks at authentication in more detail.

The structure of the data in an LDAP server is usually highly hierarchical. An object, such as a user, can be organized in many different ways. For example, users may be organized by location, team structure, or job role. Active Directory commonly uses the **Organizational Unit (OU)** attribute to group objects together and apply Group Policy. In addition, users are very often organized into groups. This structure can easily be mirrored in ServiceNow.

 This section uses LDAP terminology. There isn't space to explain it in great detail, but there are many great tutorials and books available on LDAP technology if you are interested.

Importing users from an LDAP server

Since connecting to an LDAP server is so common, ServiceNow provides a record producer to prompt you for the right information.

1. Navigate to **System LDAP > Create New Server**, and populate these fields:
   - **Type of LDAP Server**: Other
   - **Server name**: Gardiner Hotels
   - **Server URL**: ldap://ldap.gardiner-hotels.com/

This LDAP server provides a few test user records and a few groups. There are other example systems provided as a free service on the Internet.

   - **Starting search directory**: dc=gardiner-hotels,dc=com

LDAP queries need a starting point: the top of the tree. Domain names like this are most commonly used, where dc stands for domain component.

2. Click on **Submit**.
3. In the LDAP Server record that is shown next, populate the following fields, then Save.
   - **Login distinguished name**: cn=readonly,cn=staff,dc=gardiner-hotels,dc=com
   - **Login password**: password

ServiceNow will never update an LDAP server. It is often a good idea to create a user object that has read-only access to the objects you want.

Reviewing the configuration

The LDAP Record Producer creates several different records necessary to pull in and processuser and group information from this LDAP source. The default settings for these records are different depending on whether you choose `Active Directory` or `Other` in **Record Producers**:

- The **LDAP Server** record contains the information about which server to connect to and what username and password is needed.
- Linked to these are two **LDAP OU Definition** fields, one for **Users** and another for **Groups**. These provide filters and further search criteria to select the appropriate objects.
- The object from the LDAP OU definitions is linked to a data source. This provides the link to the **Import Set** functionality, specifying which import set table the table should be placed in.

> The ServiceNow instance will connect to the LDAP server over the Internet. Ensure you use LDAPS to protect the data. If your LDAP server is not available, a MID server can be used as an intermediary. This is discussed later in the chapter. A final option is to create a VPN tunnel, as mentioned at the end of the chapter.

- Finally, a **Scheduled Data Import** is made for the data sources. They are created inactive, so once tested, remember to turn them on to run every day.

> Some LDAP servers, such as Active Directory, support a persistent connection. In ServiceNow, this is termed as a **listener**. This is essentially a search query imitated from the instance that is constantly open, reconnecting if it drops. The search query from the instance asks the LDAP server to return any changed information. This means that the creation or update of a user record will be noticed within a few seconds, and the updated data will be pulled directly into ServiceNow. A scheduled job is recommended to be run nightly anyway, to cover anything that has been missed.

For all these records, you may need to make some alterations, for example, mapping extra fields or altering search criteria depending on the schema of the data.

> If you are not familiar with LDAP, some of these terms may be confusing. Work with the appropriate LDAP technical contact to find the right configuration for each server.

When finding objects, the value of the **RDN** (relative distinguished name) field is used along with the value of the Starting search directory field. (It can help to think about the RDN in ServiceNow as a folder or directory).

Additionally, a Filter can be used to select the object you are interested in. Often this is done on the `ObjectType` attribute, which specifies what the object is.

Our test server needs a few adjustments to find the correct items. We are only interested in getting guest information, so while the default configuration also includes groups, we won't import those, too.

1. Navigate to **System LDAP** > **LDAP Servers**, and select Gardiner Hotels.
2. When you enter the page, the instance performs a quick connectivity check. You should get a **Connected Successfully** message at the top of the screen. If you have problems, confirm the URL is correct, and ensure that SSL is turned off.
3. Since we are only bothering with users, let's delete the Groups LDAP OU Definition. Select it using the checkbox in the Related List, then choose **Delete** from the **Actions on selected rows** dropdown box. Confirm that you want to delete it.
4. Next, lets adjust the Users LDAP OU Definition. Select it from the Related List, change the following field, and click **Update**.
   - **RDN**: <blank>

5. Your changes should look like the screenshot below:

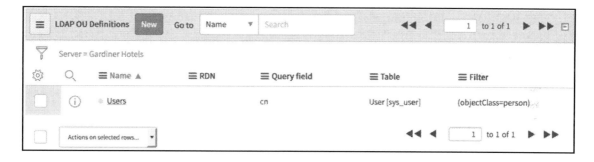

Once complete, use the **Browse** button to explore what information the instance has access to.

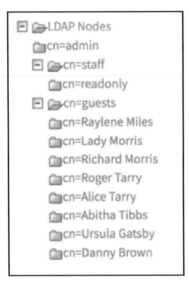

Altering the Transform Maps

As with a standard Import Set, a Transform Map is necessary to copy the data into the target tables. The provided Transform Maps are useful for Active Directory servers, but will need modification for anything else. Additionally, since they are in global, they won't directly work with our scoped tables. So we'll create our own, copying some of the best bits.

First, let's load some data into the Import Set tables:

1. Navigate to **System LDAP > Data Sources**. Firstly, delete the **Gardiner Hotels/Groups** entry by selecting it with the checkbox, then choosing **Delete** from the Action on selected rows dropdown.

2. Select the **Gardiner Hotels/Users** and click on **Load All Records**. This will create the `ldap_import` staging table.

3. Then, navigate to **System LDAP > Transform Maps**. You should see the example ones there, but click **New**. Set the following fields.
   - **Name:** Gardiner Users
   - **Source table:** Gardiner Hotels/Users [ldap_import]
   - **Target table:** Guest [x_hotel_guest]

> If you wanted to log in with these users using the password stored in the LDAP server, you would need to populate the LDAP server and Source fields on the User table. We aren't doing this, but it can be done with this script:
>
> ```
> target.source = source.u_source; target.ldap_server =
> source.sys_import_set.data_source.ldap_target.server;
> ```

4. Save once done, and then click **Mapping Assist**.

5. Drag **cn** and **uid** from the source column, and match it with **Name** and **User ID** from the target, so it looks like the following screenshot:

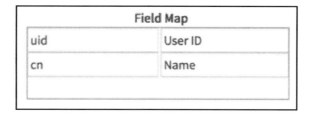

6. Click **Save**.

7. Now, on the Transform Map form, use list editing (or another mechanism) and toggle the **Coalesce** flag to `true` on the **u_uid** Field Maps. This means we won't get multiple Guests imported with same User ID.

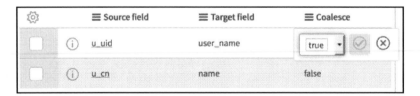

The data structure used by the LDAP server has a big impact on what field to use to coalesce on. An employee ID is often unique and is usually good choice. But cautious of values that change. For example, a username may be altered if a user changes their name – and that may mean one person has multiple user accounts.

8. Let's try this out. Click on **Transform**, and ensure the Selected maps only contains the Gardiner Users Transform Map. When happy, click **Transform**. You should see a message saying it was successful.

9. To validate, navigate to **Hotel** > **Guests**. You should see eight new members, as per the screenshot below:

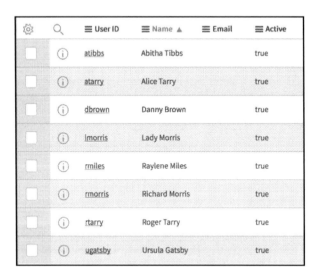

10. Finally, navigate to **System Import Sets** > **Advanced** > **Transform History** and select the most recent entry to see the logging available. You should see the statistics to say that 8 records were inserted, hopefully with no errors!

 You can choose to transform data again without repeatedly pulling it from the LDAP server. Just navigate to **System Import Sets** > **Administration** > **Import Sets**, select the set you are interested in, then click **Reprocess**. This will make it available for transformation again by resetting the state field of the rows in the Import Set table.

Importing in a scoped application

Import Sets and Transform Maps do work in a scoped application, but there are a few things to be aware of, especially when importing into shared tables:

- When the system performs the transform, both when using the Transform button and when scheduled, it actually uses impersonation. This means the user selected must have the rights to write to the tables.
- By default, scoped applications cannot write to the **Group** [sys_user_group] table. You will need to alter the Application Access settings in the Table record for a scoped application to import into them.
- The provided LDAP Transform Maps use a Script Include called LDAPUtils. This helps to manage group membership. It is by default inaccessible from scoped applications.
- The status of the transform process may be misleading in scoped applications when scripting: ensure you check the system logs frequently.

Whilst these, and other issues are certainly surmountable, consider keeping the configuration needed for shared data sets global, and manage it using Update Sets. *Chapter 10, Packaging with Applications, Update Sets, and Upgrades,* discusses Update Sets in more detail.

Building web service Import Sets

Both the SOAP and REST APIs can use Import Sets. The majority of scenarios would benefit from an Import Set providing the extra control and validation during a data upload-even if that is simply the extra logging that is provided. Most of the time, it's easiest to simply use an existing Import Set table. Simply use the /<Import Set table>.do?WSDL URL for SOAP, or POST to /api/now/import/<Import Set table> for REST.

However, if you want to create a new Import Set table, there is an easier way than manually making lots of fields in an Import Set table.

Instead, the form available at **System Web Services** > **Inbound** > **Create New** has functionality to create a Transform Map and associated Field Maps by copying the target table. It then provides a simple related list to allow other data to be sent to it.

The rest of the setup of a web service Import Set is standard, but remember that the direction of data has changed: the remote system pushes the data to ServiceNow rather than ServiceNow pulling the data, as in a regular scheduled data source Import Set:

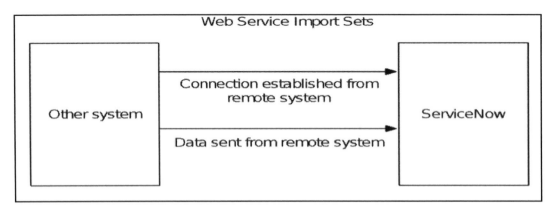

Using a web service Import Sets

Although an Import Set is a regular table, the ServiceNow web services handle it a little differently. While the REST API supports the GET method and the SOAP API has all the standard methods, you typically only need one for each: POST and insert. This creates the record in the import set table, triggering the transform map to process the data and copy it over to the target table.

The response back from an import set is a little different to the Table API. Instead of just the `sys_id` value, it gives more information, as follows:

- **table**: The table name (for example, `x_hotel_maintenance`) that the record was created in. Note that this is the target table, not the Import Set table.
- **display_name**: The field that contains the display value. This will be `number` value for a task-derived record.
- **display_value**: The contents of that display value, for example, `MAI0001001`.
- **status**: Returns what happened: whether the record was created or updated, whether there was an error, and so on.
- **sys_id**: The `sys_id` value of the record in the target table.

Connecting to web services

So far, this chapter has concentrated on how other systems can connect to a ServiceNow instance. But communication works both ways! Here's how:

- Creating an outbound SOAP message is achieved in just a few clicks. When the platform is provided with a WSDL, it scans it, automatically building the relevant methods. This process of consuming the WSDL means that the configuration of a SOAP message is very straightforward.
- Building an outbound REST integration won't be automatic, but since the majority of REST services follow conventions, defaults and assumptions usually work pretty well: POST to create, GET to retrieve, and so on.

However, regardless of the connection mechanism, to send a message, you must write some code, usually to include in a business rule. But the platform will generate a starting point for you!

Using SOAP to send tasks

One common use of SOAP web services is to send information about a task to a remote system. This often occurs when work is outsourced, to people who use their own systems to manage their work. In Gardiner Hotels, we've subcontracted complex maintenance work to Cornell Hotel Services and created an approval workflow to control it. But how do we send it to them?

An easy way is to simply send an e-mail. This is a straightforward solution that can be quickly implemented by all parties. However, as is discussed in more detail later, e-mail should not be relied upon, since it is not a guaranteed protocol. There is no way of knowing when or even *whether* an e-mail has reached its final destination. In addition, since the e-mail is unstructured, it is often difficult to send more complex data.

Instead, Cornell Hotel Services provides a very simple web service so that their customers can reliably submit information. Let's use this in our application:

1. Navigate to **System Web Services** > **Outbound** > **SOAP Message**, and click on **New**. Use these values, then Save.
   - **Name:** CHS SOAP
   - **WSDL:** http://www.gardiner-hotels.com/chs/soap/?wsdl

 This web service is useful only for testing. Apart from some basic error checking, it randomly creates responses, and will not be consistent.

2. Click on **Generate sample SOAP messages**. This causes the platform to download the given WSDL, place it into the **WSDL XML** field, and parse it. If a WSDL is not available to the instance, you can paste the XML directly into the field and uncheck **Download WSDL**.

3. In the **SOAP Message Functions** related list, two entries are shown. These are the methods that the web services support: **create** and **status**. Click on **create** to see which parameters it takes.

4. In the SOAP message function, the envelope contains what ServiceNow will send to the web service, just like the request in SoapUI. By inspecting the XML, we can see that ServiceNow has found three parameters, and for each one added variable placeholders:

```
<number>${number}</number>
<room>${room}</room>
<description>${description}</description>
```

5. When sending a message, you should specify the contents of these variables. This is typically done in a script using the `setStringParameter` function of `SOAPMessageV2`, as shown later.

Testing the web service

Let's experiment a little with this web service, and see what it does. Follow these steps:

1. Click on the **Test** Related Link to see what the web service does. A new **SOAP Message Test** record will be created and will show the results.

2. The **Request** field contains the information that was sent to the web service, while the **HTTP Status** and **Response** XML fields show you what was received. An HTTP status of 500 is an error, and we can find out the reason for this by looking at the Response field.

3. Click on the orange XML button to format the XML nicely. You should see that the `faultstring` node contains the text `Task number and room are mandatory`, which provides a great hint as to what we need to do next.

```
- <SOAP-ENV:Envelope SOAP-ENV:encodingStyle="http://schemas.xmlsoap.org/soap/encoding/">
  - <SOAP-ENV:Body>
    - <SOAP-ENV:Fault>
        <faultcode xsi:type="xsd:string">Client</faultcode>
        <faultactor xsi:type="xsd:string"/>
        <faultstring xsi:type="xsd:string">Task number and room are mandatory</faultstring>
        <detail xsi:type="xsd:string"/>
      </SOAP-ENV:Fault>
  </SOAP-ENV:Body>
</SOAP-ENV:Envelope>
```

This web service doesn't indicate in the WSDL that some fields are mandatory. It is possible to do so using the `minOccurs` attribute. When using Direct Web Services, ServiceNow uses this attribute if you have marked the field as mandatory in the dictionary

4. Close the window, then click back in your browser to return to the SOAP Message Function.

5. In order to send the web service the number and room, we need to create variables. Click **New** on the **Variable Substitutions** Related List, use the following values, and click Submit.

- **Name**: `number`
- **Test value**: `MAI0001`

6. Repeat step 4 again, creating another Variable Substitutions entry, but with the following information

- **Name**: `room`
- **Test value**: `1010`

The **Auto-generate variables** link should do some of this work for you, but it doesn't work in scoped applications up to Helsinki. For instances using Istanbul or later, this link will save you some time!

7. You should end up with the Related List looking like this:

8. **Click Test to try this out again.** Now the web service should receive the values it needs, and it will generate a different response. The HTTP status will be **200** (OK) and the return result from the web service should say something along the lines of **Task accepted. Sending engineer to room 1010**.

Sending the message

Once test messages are working, it is appropriate to integrate them into the application workflow. Once the Maintenance task is approved (which happens in a workflow), an assignment rule sets the Assignment group field to Cornell Hotel Services. That sounds like a good point to fire off the SOAP message using a Business Rule. To help, ServiceNow will generate the code for you.

Follow these steps to make this happen:

1. Click back in your browser to return to the `create` SOAP Message Function of CHS SOAP.

2. Click on **Preview Script Usage**. It will pop up a window with a code snippet that we'll use as a basis, using with examples provided by the variable substitutions:

```
Preview SOAP message script usage                                    ✕

try {
 var s = new sn_ws.SOAPMessageV2('x_hotel.CHS SOAP', 'create');

//override authentication profile
//authentication type ='basic'
//r.setAuthentication(authentication type,profile name);

 s.setStringParameter('room', '1010');
 s.setStringParameter('number', 'MAI0001');
 var response = s.execute();
 var responseBody = response.getBody();
 var status = response.getStatusCode();
}
catch(ex) {
 var message = ex.getMessage();
}
```

 This code could be run in Background Scripts as is, which is useful for further testing.

3. Navigate to **System Definition** > **Business Rules,** and click **New**. Fill out the following fields and Save.
   - **Name:** `Send to CHS Web Service`
   - **Table:** `Maintenance [x_hotel_maintenance]`
   - **Advanced:** `<ticked>`
   - **Condition:**

```
current.assignment_group.getDisplayValue() ==
gs.getProperty('x_hotel.maintenance.external_group') &&
previous.assignment_group != current.assignment_group
```

   - **When:** `async`
   - **Insert:** `<ticked>`
   - **Update:** `<ticked>`
   - **Script:** (Remember to insert it inside the provided function.)

```
var s = new sn_ws.SOAPMessageV2('x_hotel.CHS SOAP', 'create');
s.setStringParameter('room', current.room.getDisplayValue());
s.setStringParameter('number', current.number.getDisplayValue());
s.setStringParameter('description', current.description);
var response = s.execute();
var responseBody = response.getBody();
var status = response.getStatusCode();
var xmldoc = new XMLDocument2();
xmldoc.parseXML(responseBody);
if (status == 200) {
// 200 is success
current.correlation_id = xmldoc.getNodeText("//data");
current.work_notes = 'Successfully sent to external team';
} else {
current.work_notes = 'Did not successfully send to external team. ' +
xmldoc.getNodeText("//faultstring");
}
current.update();
```

This Business Rule will run when the Assignment group field is to the same one in the `maintenance.external_group` property. Using properties, as described in Chapter 5, *Getting Things Done with Tasks,* is great for situations like this, since it avoids hard-coding a group name. To ensure it only runs on the first assignment, a second condition ensures that the Assignment group in `previous` is not the same as the one in `current`.

The main script takes the code example and builds on it. First, a new SOAPMessageV2 object is constructed, specifying the SOAP message name and the required method. Then, a series of parameters is set from the current `GlideRecord` object.

When populating parameters with `SOAPMessageV2`, use either the `setStringParameter` or `setStringParameterNoEscape` functions. These provide the data for the variable substitution of the message. Any values passed via `setStringParameter` will encode characters such as the ampersand (`&`), which would otherwise cause errors.

Once the parameters are set, the message is sent using the `execute` method of `SOAPMessageV2`. As we have it here, the script blocks until the response is returned. It returns an XML string called `response`.

To find out whether the message was successfully processed, the `getStatusCode` method is used to see whether the HTTP status code is `200`. If so, it is assumed that everything worked. A more robust check may search for the data that was returned.

The `response` variable is then used to create another object called `xmldoc`. This results from a class called `XMLDocument2`, which provides several helpful functions for working with XML. The `getNodeText` function of `XMLDocument2` is used to pull out the `data` node. This contains a reference number that the web service provides. It's saved in the **Correlation ID** field on the Task table.

The `XMLDocument2` Script Include is detailed in the Developer portal:

Another very helpful Script Include is `XMLHelper`. It has a function called `toObject` that converts XML to JSON. I recommend using JSON rather than XML if you need to iterate in loops or for manipulation. Unfortunately, it is only available in the global scope.

Finally, regardless of whether the call was a success or not, an entry was made in work notes and the record saved. If there is an error, the text is included as part of the note.

When testing, ensure the Room field is populated. Otherwise, the web service will throw an error. It may be better to preclude this by adding another condition in the Business Rule or using a Data Policy to force the population of this field.

Building REST messages

Creating an outbound REST Message is almost as simple as using SOAP. Since REST does not have a schema like a WSDL, it does not autogenerate; however, it uses a very similar interface and concepts.

Each REST message can have four methods: PUT, DELETE, GET, and POST. The latter two are most commonly used. While all four are created when a new REST message is made, redundant ones can be removed. Unfortunately, you can only have one entry for each method, which may mean some creative use of variables, or multiple REST messages.

Within each method, there are several options to help you specify what data should be sent:

- The **REST endpoint** specifies the domain and path that the method should be sent to. It may contain variables in the typical form: ${variable_name}.
- **HTTP headers** specify what is sent in the HTTP header. This may specify which output format you want (for example, JSON or XML).
- **HTTP query parameters** contain the parameters that the instance will append to the endpoint. For example, if the endpoint field were populated with /endpoint/${number} and there were two parameters, the final URL generated by the platform may be /endpoint/1?param1=hello&param2=world.
- For PUT and POST methods, the platform will show another field, **Content**. This should contain whatever data you want to send to the system. As with all the fields, variable replacements will be made.

If a parameter is defined, it is sent. Optional parameters are not easily dealt with, since the parameter name will be sent with a blank value, for example, name=; . Instead, try just adding another endpoint variable, and then create the query parameters yourself.

Sending REST messages to CHS

In addition to the SOAP API, Cornell Hotel Services also has a REST API. Let's build an alternative to see how it works-and to spot the similarities with SOAP:

1. Navigate to **System Web Services** > **Outbound** > **REST Message** and click on **New**. Once done, Save. Use these values:
   - **Name**: CHS REST
   - **Endpoint**: http://www.gardiner-hotels.com/chs/rest

 This web service is useful only for testing. Apart from some basic error checking, it randomly creates responses, and will not be consistent.

2. Four standard HTTP methods are created. If you'd like, delete the put and delete HTTP methods.

3. Select the get HTTP method, modify the **Endpoint** value, as per below, and **Save:**
   - **Endpoint**:
     http://www.gardiner-hotels.com/chs/rest/${number}

4. Click on New under Variable Substitutions, fill out the following fields, then click **Submit**.
   - **Name**: number
   - **Test value**: MAI0001

5. Click on **Test**, and you should get a successful test run, with an **HTTP status** value of 200.

6. For the POST method, navigate back to **System Web Services** > **Outbound** > **REST Message** and select CHS REST. There, choose the post HTTP Method, and modify the **Content** field as follows. Save when done.
   - **Content**: (In the HTTP Request tab)

```
{"room": "${room}", "number": "${number}", "description": "${description}"}
```

7. Now, create a Variable Substitution record by click on the New button in the relevant Related List. Fill out these fields, and click **Submit**.
    - **Name:** number
    - **Test value:** MAI0001

8. Repeat step 7, but for the following values. Click **Submit** when done.
    - **Name:** room
    - **Test value:** 1010

9. Click on **Test,** and you should get a successful test run, with an HTTP status of 200.

10. Try generating the script, and compare it to the SOAP code. You should see that they are very similar.

> The biggest difference is that the REST response is typically in JSON and therefore much simpler to parse using the standard JSON stringify and parse functions.

Building custom interfaces

Web Service Import Sets and Direct Web Services provide a simple way to have a remote system send or retrieve data from your instance. However, beyond specifying the fields in import sets, the methods and schema are not configurable. What if you wanted a more flexible system?

Creating scripted services

ServiceNow supports both SOAP and REST scripted web services:

- SOAP scripted web services have two related lists, which contain the input and output parameters. These are used to generate a WSDL with a single method. A single script field determines the processing. In it, the input parameters are represented with a variable called request, while the output parameters with a variable called response.

- REST scripted APIs are more sophisticated. They support functionality such as versioning and flexible security and can work with information supplied in headers, the body, parameters, and much more-make as many methods as you want! As before, the scripts use the `request` and `response` variables. Once created, the REST scripted APIs can be tested out in the REST Explorer, just like all the other APIs.

> There is lots of information about scripted REST APIs in the product documentation:
> `https://docs.servicenow.com/bundle/helsinki-servicenow-platform/`
> `page/integrate/custom-web-`
> `services/concept/c_CustomWebServices.html`

Scripted Web Services are great when more processing needs to happen in ServiceNow, and especially when the data does not map directly on to a table. For example, ordering an item from the Service Catalog to initiate request fulfillment involves using variables and creating a number of records. This is a great candidate for a scripted web service.

Doing multiplication with a scripted REST API

Lets create a simple REST API to explore the concept:

1. Navigate to **System Web Services** > **Scripted Web Services** > **Scripted REST APIs** and create a new record. Use these details, and Save.
   - **Name**: Math

2. In the **Resources** related list, click on **New**. Set the following fields:
   - **Name**: Multiply
   - **HTTP method**: get
   - **Relative path**: /multiply/{a}/{b}
   - **Script**: (Insert inside the provided function)

```
var body = {};
body.answer = request.pathParams.a * request.pathParams.b;
response.setBody(body);
```

> This very simple script looks at two input variables, multiplies them, and sends the response back.

3. Once saved, click on **Explore REST API**. Give a numerical value for a and b, click on **Send**, and the instance will do some math for you! Note how the system will deal with things like XML formatting for you.

> Scripted REST APIs are not only useful for external systems to access ServiceNow but also for internal, single-page apps. Chapter 11, *Making ServiceNow Beautiful with Service Portal and Custom Interfaces,* explores this in more detail.

Working inside the data center – introducing the MID server

The **Management, Instrumentation, and Discovery (MID)** server is designed to ease communication with external systems that sit inside a customer's data center. While ServiceNow can easily integrate with cloud-based systems without one, integrating with systems behind a firewall requires extra help.

The MID server is not a device, and does not run on the instance-it is installable Java software that runs on customer infrastructure. This provides the following capabilities:

- The MID server has direct communication with other systems, since it is in the customer's network. This is very useful for communicating via unencrypted protocols, such as JDBC.
- Scripts that run on the MID server have access to the filesystem and can include custom Java code in JAR packages.
- The MID server only initiates connections. It does not accept inbound communication and does not open any ports. This makes it more acceptable to security teams.
- It offloads work from the instance, enabling integrations to scale out horizontally.

> The MID server is used heavily in ServiceNow's IT Operations products. Read more about its capabilities here:
> https://docs.servicenow.com/bundle/helsinki-it-operations-mana gement/page/product/mid-server/concept/c_MIDServer.html

Integrating with the ECC queue

The **ECC Queue** [ecc_queue] table, where **ECC** stands for **External Communications Channel**, is designed to communicate with other systems, such as the MID server. It has several fields that categorize the data, letting the right system pick it up and process it or post results back. The fields are generic, letting it be a storage area for any type of integration data, but their intended purpose is listed as follows:

- **Agent** is the external system that the instance is communicating with.
- **Topic**, **Name**, and **Source** depend on what the integration is. They can be used for anything, but often contain what the system should be doing and where it came from.
- **Response to** is used to relate two ECC queue records together. Often, it is used in a reply to a particular command. The field itself is a reference field.
- **Queue** is either input or output. An input record is created when another system gives information to the instance. Output is something designed to be sent.
- **State** tracks how the message is being processed. The value moves from the initial value of ready, optionally to processing, and then to either processed or error. This is typically controlled by a Business Rule.
- **Payload** contains the data itself.

Picking up jobs

The MID server architecture is straightforward, though often misunderstood. It isn't a physical machine that ServiceNow provides, but should be installed on a customer's own hardware or, more likely, in a virtual machine. Its design is such that it only ever connects outwards. The MID server opens no ports, and nothing connects in.

You may argue, therefore, that the MID server is not actually a server, in that no client connects to it!

In order to do work, the MID server relies upon the ECC queue. It watches for jobs constantly, by opening a persistent connection with the instance. If it is told to-and every few seconds regardless-it polls the ECC queue. The MID server picks up jobs that are assigned to it, using the **Agent** field to find the right ones. It runs the script or worker job and posts the result back to the ECC queue. All communication with the instance is done securely over SOAP using HTTPS. It can even use a proxy server. The graphical representation of the process is as follows:

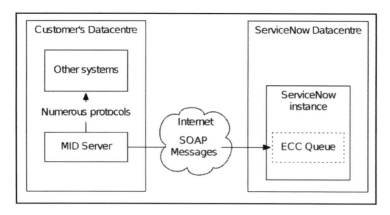

Installing the MID server

The MID server can be installed on either a Windows or Linux host, and in 32- or 64-bit versions. The MID server needs at least 4 GB of RAM with a multicore CPU over 2 GHz. It is often hosted in a virtual machine.

Setting up the server

For the purpose of these examples, try installing the MID server on your desktop or a spare machine. Use these steps:

1. Navigate to **MID Server** > **Downloads** and click on the required package. It is downloaded as a ZIP file from a ServiceNow web server. The instance will direct you to the right version.
2. Once downloaded, unzip it to a directory of your choice. The package includes the correct version of Java, so it is relatively self contained-no compilation required!

If you are installing it in a GUI, run the installer (`installer.sh` in Linux, `installer.bat` for Windows).

Otherwise, open the `config.xml` configuration file and set at least the URL, username, and password values. Note that the password will be encrypted on startup to ensure it isn't kept in plaintext. If you like, you can also give a name. The examples later in the chapter use `midserver`. Otherwise, blank it out, and a name will be generated for you.

It is a good idea to create a user dedicated to the MID server. In the User form, tick the **Web service access only** checkbox so the account cannot access the web interface, and tick **Internal Integration User**. Grant the `mid_server` role to the user account.
More detailed instructions are given in the Product Documentation:
`https://docs.servicenow.com/bundle/helsinki-it-operations-manage`
`ment/page/product/mid-`
`server/concept/c_MIDServerInstallation.html`

3. Run the `start.sh` or `start.bat` scripts to get the MID server working.

4. Navigate to **MID Server > Servers**; after a few seconds, you should see a record indicating that the MID server has checked in and registered itself. If things have gone wrong, look at the MID server log files and those on the instance.

5. Once it is listed, open up the MID Server form, and click **Validate**. This confirms that this MID server is available for use with this instance. You should see then a MID server that has a Status of Up, and Validated is Yes.

Using the MID server

A MID server's job is to execute the jobs that it collects. It constantly monitors the ECC queue, picking up output commands and executing them. By using the **Topic** field in the ECC queue record, the MID server knows what to do. The MID server has several **probes**, one of which should be handling the job.

Running a custom command

A simple example of this is running a shell script on the MID server. You will need to know the name of the MID server. Mine is called `midserver`.

Follow these steps to as an example:

1. Navigate to **ECC** > **Queue** and click on **New**. Use these details, and then Save:
   - **Agent**: `mid.server.<name>` (for example, `mid.server.midserver`)
   - **Topic**: `Command`
   - **Name**: `whoami`
   - **Queue**: `output`

2. This will run the `whoami` command on the MID server. It will return who the currently logged-in user is. This command is an easy example, since it works on both Windows and Linux hosts!

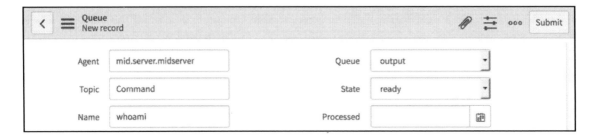

3. Navigate back to the ECC queue and set up a filter to look for all records where the value of **Topic** is `Command` and the value of **Queue** is `input`. Soon enough, a record will appear, though you may need to refresh a few times until you see it:

4. Open up the record and inspect the **Payload** field by clicking on the orange XML icon. Among some other items, there should be a result node, giving you what the command resulted in:

```
<result command="whoami">
<stdout>martin</stdout>
<stderr/>
</result>
```

5. In this example, the `whoami` command returned `martin`. This is the name of the user who is running the MID server agent.

This technique can be used to run whatever code you'd like on the MID server, whenever you'd like. It is therefore very simple to integrate with an esoteric system that can only be communicated with via a command prompt.

To send longer commands, keep the Name field blank and instead use the Payload field with the information in a couple of XML tags, as follows:

```
<parameters>
  <parameter name="name" value="./this_is_a_long_command
with_quite_a_few parameters"/>
</parameters>
```

Running JavaScript on the MID server

In addition to running shell commands, the MID server can also run JavaScript, just like the instance. There are a couple of key differences, however:

- The MID server does not have direct access to the database, and global variables (such as `gs`) are not defined. It also cannot access standard Script Includes.
- Instead, access to Java packages is allowed, enabling you to access lower-level functions within the extensive Java libraries.
- You can also add Java packages of your choice and distribute them from the instance.

Interacting with the ECC queue

MID server background scripts use the ECC Queue. To understand what they do, and potentially replicate them, just write a record to the **ECC Queue** table in the same way. Use `JavascriptProbe` as **Topic** and use **Payload** to pass through an XML snippet with a script parameter. Follow these steps:

1. Navigate to **ECC** > **Queue**, and click on **New**. Use these values:
   - **Agent**: `mid.server.<name>` (Mine is `mid.server.midserver`)
   - **Topic**: `JavascriptProbe`
   - **Queue**: `output`
   - **Payload**:

```
<parameters>
<parameter name="script" value="'Hello, world! ' + (1 + 2 + 3);"/>
</parameters>
```

2. Navigate to **ECC** > **Queue**, sort by **Created**, and watch for the reply that has a Topic of JavascriptProbe:

The response in the XML should be

```
<output>Hello, world! 6</output>
```

Writing a complex payload is fiddly, especially with the quotes. Instead, leverage a script include called `JavascriptProbe` on the instance. This wraps up the creation of the **ECC Queue** record in a few function calls.

Try it out in with a few steps:

1. To generate the same **ECC Queue** record as before, navigate to **System Maintenance > Scripts – Background**, and run this code in global:

```
var jsp = new JavascriptProbe('midserver');
jsp.setJavascript("'Hello, world! ' + (1 + 2 + 3)");
jsp.create();
```

It is a good idea to use the `setName` function to label your scripts, so you know where these **ECC Queue** records are coming from. It populates the **Name** field.

2. Navigate to **ECC > Queue**, and watch for the reply.

In this example, a new `JavascriptProbe` object, `jsp`, is created, passing through the name of the MID server. The **Payload** field is set by using the `setJavascript` function, and the record is written to the database by calling `create`.

To react to the results of the command, you can write a Business Rule for the ECC queue that parses the XML and does what is necessary. Use the `XMLDocument2` and `XMLHelper` Script Includes previously mentioned.

It is not good form to include code as strings like this. If nothing else, the quotes quickly get very confusing! Instead, use the MID server Script Includes to contain the majority of your code, letting you write the code in a much saner environment. MID server Script Includes work in much the same way as a typical Script Include; they can be functions or, more commonly, classes, that pack up code in a reusable fashion.

Creating a MID server Script Include

Let's create a new record that mirrors the first Script Include in Chapter 3, *Server-Side Control*.

1. Navigate to **MID Server > Script Includes**. Click New, fill out the fields below, and Save.
   - **Name:** `SimpleAdd`
   - **Script:**

```
var SimpleAdd = Class.create();
SimpleAdd.prototype = {
```

```
initialize: function (n) {
ms.log('Creating new object');
this.number = (n - 0) || 0;
},
increment: function () {
this.number++;
ms.log(this.number);
return this;
},
type: 'SimpleAdd'
}
```

This code is almost identical to a typical Script Include. The only difference is that the logging is done with the ms global variable instead of gs.

The script has two functions. One is run when the object is created and sets the number variable. The second function, increment, adds 1 to number when it is called.

2. Run the following code on the MID server by navigating to **System Definition > Scripts – Background**, and running the code.

```
var script = "var sa = new SimpleAdd(1); sa.increment(); sa.number;"
var jsp = new JavascriptProbe('midserver');
jsp.setJavascript(script);
jsp.create();
```

3. If you go to **ECC > Queue** and look for the response, you should see the result is 2.0.

Notice how the result has been represented as a decimal. The data will be translated into string anyway, so it is a good idea to convert it yourself to stop odd conversions. This could be done with the last line being sa.number + ''; instead.

Using Java on the MID server

One exciting capability of the MID server is that it lets you run Java commands. Just like the instance, the MID server uses Rhino, a JavaScript interpreter written in Java, to execute your scripts. We've just been using this via JavascriptProbe.

However, you may want to do things that JavaScript just can't provide. So Rhino also gives you access to the Java API and other libraries. Included with Java is a huge collection of programming tools, such as encryption algorithms, file and web access, math functions, and database control. It is easy to call these from the MID server, as follows:

```
var out = new Packages.java.io.FileWriter("file.txt");
out.write("Hello, world!");
out.close();
```

Java classes are organized into packages. To use a class, you must identify which package it belongs to, which is often easily achieved by searching the Java API documentation. These are hosted online at http://docs.oracle.com/javase. When referring to a Java class, use the package name, prefixed by Packages.

In this example, the FileWriter class is used. It opens up a file with the given name, and will output data using the write method. The close method writes it to disk. A file called file.txt will end up in the agent directory on the MID server.

Adding additional libraries

Many hundreds of classes are included in the MID server. In addition to the Java API, other libraries are included in the lib directory. Many are focused around communication: org.apache.commons.httpclient is helpful for downloading files, while org.ftp4che gives access to FTP servers.

You may want to add more. Rather than adding files into the lib directory, the platform provides a simpler way of distributing additional Java packages across all the connected MID servers. Navigate to **MID Server** > **JAR Files**, create a record, and fill in the appropriate fields. Once the file is added to the record, any restarting MID servers will pick up the file and have it available for use.

Exporting data via the MID server

While the REST APIs make it very easy for systems to directly select data they are interested in, many applications still require files. An Export Set asks the MID server to write a CSV file containing the data you want.

Let's try this out:

1. Navigate to **System Export Sets** > **Create Export Set** to use the simple record producer. Fill in these fields, and click **Submit**:
    - **Name**: Maintenance export
    - **Select a table**: x_hotel_maintenance
    - **Select a MID server**: midserver (or your MID server name)
    - **File path**: /

2. Once in the Export Set record, click on **Test Export 20 Records**. After a few seconds, you should have an export of all the Maintenance records in the export directory in your MID server installation.

3. Click on **View Export History** to see the logs. If you find that the file is created, but it contains empty lines, ensure that the **Fields** field in System Export Sets > Administration > Export Definitions is populated appropriately.

Another way to create an Export Set record is by choosing **Export** > **Export Set** from the list headings, just like you would select **Export** > **Excel**.

Improving exporting

Export sets are quick to set up, but spending a little longer to optimize is worthwhile:

- Use the **Append timestamp** option on the Export Set record. This means the resulting files don't get overwritten on each run.
- Review the **Export Definition** record. It lets you filter the records you want (for example, just high priority) and which fields should be included.
- Having the export run automatically is easy: just create a **Scheduled Data Export** record. It even lets you create a delta, so only records updated or created since the last run can be included. Scripts can also be run for cleanup or preparation.

Authenticating and securing web services

Communication with a ServiceNow instance has two basic starting points:

- It happens over **HTTPS**. This provides encryption for all the communication and helps prevent man-in-the-middle attacks.
- **Authentication** is almost always required, usually in the form of a username and password. This ensures that the instance knows who you are.

- **Authorization** is then applied. Using Security Rules and other mechanisms, the instance can decide if you are entitled to carry out a particular action.

This section focuses on machine-to-machine authentication. The next chapter, explores authorization in much more detail.

Inbound authentication

When systems want to connect to ServiceNow, the most obvious and common way of authenticating is through a username and password. HTTP Basic Authentication asks that a client send these encoded details in the headers of an HTTP request.

The header for basic authentication is `Authorization: Basic username:password`,with the username and password Base64 encoded. For example, with a username and password both of `admin`, the full string is this:

```
Authorization: Basic YWRtaW46YWRtaW4=
```

Since Basic Authentication is part of the HTTP standard, virtually every application supports it. It does not encrypt or otherwise protect the username and password. Instead, the safety of the credentials relies entirely upon HTTPS. The secure connection is always established before the headers are sent, meaning that the details cannot easily be captured via a network traffic capture. Note that by default, ServiceNow does not validate certificates at almost any point.

The username and password may be that of a system account or a real end user. The latter is often used for custom interfaces.

In addition, the REST API supports OAuth. This allows you to send the username and password of a user once and receive a token in return. Then, the token can be used for subsequent interactions with the REST API.

To get a token, first create an entry in **System OAuth** > **Application Registry**, creating an API endpoint. Then, send a POST request to `https://<instance>.service-now.com/oauth_token.do`, and send the following in the HTTP Body:

- `grant_type`: `password`
- `client_id`: `<client_id>` as specified in the application registry
- `client_secret`: `<client_secret>` as specified in the application registry
- `username`: `<username>`
- `* password`: `<password>`

In return, you will be given a time-limited token that can be sent in the header of other REST requests. The cURL command below will work, if you replace the values appropriately:

```
curl --data
"grant_type=password&client_id=<client_id>&client_secret=<client_secret>&us
ername=<username>&password=<password>"
https://<instance>.service-now.com/oauth_token.do
```

The formatted (and truncated) response from my instance looks like this:

```
{
    "access_token": "UVY80...CA",
    "refresh_token": "wcGJJ...Bw",
    "scope": "useraccount",
    "token_type": "Bearer",
    "expires_in": 1799
}
```

Then, instead of using Basic Authentication, send an authorization header with the access_token prefixed with Bearer like this:

```
curl -H "Authorization:Bearer UVY80...CA ...
```

The product documentation has much more information here:
`https://docs.servicenow.com/bundle/helsinki-servicenow-platfor`
`m/page/integrate/inbound-rest/task/t_EnableOAuthWithREST.html`

Outbound authentication

When creating an outbound REST message, you can specify how the system authenticates itself:

- Basic Authentication simply sends a username and password, as just described.
- OAuth asks for a token and then sends it for every request. To set this up, grab the information from the third-party system (such as Facebook or Twitter), and populate a new record in **System OAuth** > **Application Registry**.

> The product documentation outlines all the details:
> ```
> https://docs.servicenow.com/bundle/helsinki-servicenow-platfor
> m/page/administer/security/task/t_UseAThirdPartyOAuthProvider.
> html
> ```

- Mutual authentication uses the exchange of SSL certificates to prove identity. In a standard HTTPS transaction, the client connects to the server and validates its certificate. In contrast, mutual authentication sends a client certificate as well. To set it up, navigate to **System Security** > **Protocol Profiles**, and select Java Key Store. ServiceNow only supports outbound mutual authentication – when connections are initiated from ServiceNow.

> The product documentation outlines how you can create a keystore using Java:
> ```
> https://docs.servicenow.com/bundle/helsinki-servicenow-platfor
> m/page/administer/security/concept/c_MutualAuthentication.html
> ```

Designing integrations

How you connect other systems to ServiceNow requires considerable thought. Most of the time, the plumbing is fairly easy, but you need to know where to route the pipes. You don't want to get fresh and waste water mixed up!

At a very high level, there are two points to consider when importing data or creating an integration:

- What data points am I transferring? For example, which fields should I match it with?
- When do I want to transfer it? Is it on a nightly basis, whenever a ticket is created, or even when the Work notes field is updated?

This information should feed into whatever mechanism you eventually use.

Transferring bulk data

In general, if you are exchanging data that represents more than one record at a time, ServiceNow uses a pull mechanism. This generally happens on a scheduled basis, usually nightly, to keep the two systems in loose synchronization.

Importing an XML or CSV file is easy with ServiceNow. Place the file on an FTP server and have ServiceNow check it periodically. Often, the only trick is finding a suitable FTP/FTPS/SFTP server and scheduling the generation to always place it with the same filename.

Similarly, if you want to get multiple records out of ServiceNow, it expects the remote system to initiate the connection and ask for what it wants. Use the CSV and XML web services to retrieve what you need, or use SOAP direct web services to pull multiple records at once.

The image below represents a pull, initiated and controlled by System A, getting content from System B.

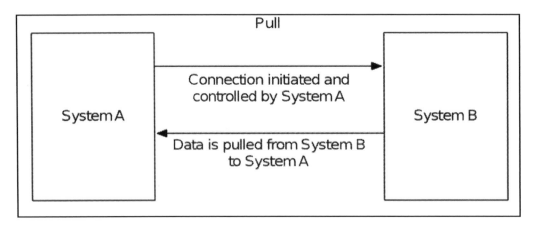

Real-time communication

In contrast, transferring single records often involves a push. This is most common if you want to transfer ticket data, so an outsourced team can be told within a few seconds that they've been assigned a task. This mechanism is far more efficient than polling for updates every few seconds.

REST is the favored mechanism for sending real-time data within ServiceNow. Functionality such as the REST Rxplorer makes it very easy to understand and work with the REST APIs, and the simpler syntax and data methods mean it is preferred over SOAP.

> ServiceNow is focusing on improving the capabilities of REST, and while SOAP is not likely to be depreciated soon, the level of attention is reduced.

eBonding is an extension of this real-time communication, to allow tickets to be updated on either side at any point. Both sides will push data to the other upon any change. Serious logical challenges are raised through this, including race conditions, data synchronization, and reliability. For example, if a particular category is set on one side, it follows that it should be updated on the other. But what if the categorization structures don't match? Should user data be transferred alongside each ticket? What if both systems update the ticket within seconds of each other?

> Think carefully about the impact that eBonding will have on your processand how you work with the resulting system. Often, compromises have to be made, such as aligning the systems so they are very similar (such as the fields and potential contents of those fields) or to have a looser bond and to transfer less information.

One mechanism that isn't recommended is integration via e-mail. This is often seen in legacy systems, since e-mail is so ubiquitous. However, the delivery and security of an e-mail can never be guaranteed, and the data exchange format is often a free text field. Nonetheless, as explored in previous chapters, inbound email scripts can process incoming e-mails just as easily from a machine as a person.

This diagram shows a push. The connection is initiated and the data is sent from System A to System B.

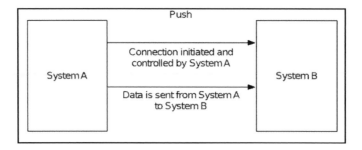

Communicating through the firewall

Perhaps the most important capability of the MID server is that it can communicate with other systems from inside the firewall. This may be in a DMZ or perimeter network, but often, a MID server has better access to systems than the instance does.

This is useful in several situations but isn't a cure-all. Due to the polling design of the MID server, there will be a latency of a second or two at least. Nonetheless, a MID server is very useful for grabbing data from sensitive systems, such as LDAP servers or databases.

This diagram shows how the MID server can connect to many different systems – but that the ServiceNow instance can deal with most systems without it.

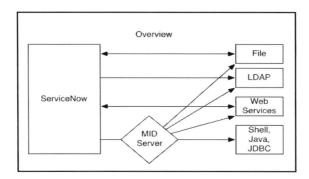

An alternative option is using a VPN tunnel. A secured, encrypted IPSEC link can be set up between the ServiceNow datacenter and a customer's infrastructure. ServiceNow recommends, however, that whenever possible, secure protocols be used instead. For example, instead of using LDAP through a VPN tunnel, use LDAPS over the Internet. This allows greater flexibility and is often more efficient.

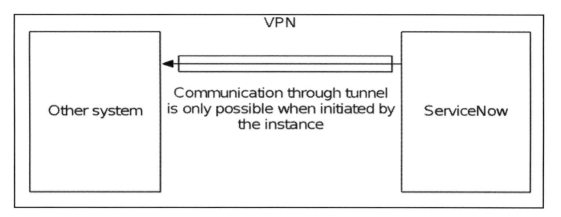

 See the product documentation for more details on how to set this up: `htt` `ps://docs.servicenow.com/bundle/helsinki-servicenow-platform/p` `age/administer/encryption/reference/r_VPNSetup.html`

Summary

ServiceNow provides many different integration options. In this chapter, the majority of the mechanisms to get data in and out of the platform were discussed.

CSV and XML are universal file formats. Almost any system that can import or export data can use CSV and XML to store data, and ServiceNow is no different. It's easy to export data from the list, or from a URL.

Import Sets are a very powerful way of pulling data into your instance. They again support a variety of data formats and provide transform maps to translate the incoming information into the appropriate schema.

LDAP is probably the most common integration. It pulls in users and groups, most often from Active Directory. This is typically the source of user information – and the next chapter shows that it can also be used for authentication.

The REST Table API provides easy access to read, create, modify, and delete any record in ServiceNow. However, using web service import sets gives much more flexibility and control.

When web service import sets are not enough, build scripted web services. These allow you to create any sort of web service, or indeed support almost any data format whatsoever.

The ECC queue is a mechanism for storing jobs. The MID server uses it heavily; commands are placed in the ECC queue, which the MID server (placed within a customer's datacenter) will pick up and process. This gives secure access to internal systems when you don't want to open up the firewall.

The next chapter provides much more detail about authentication and securing ServiceNow.

8
Securing Applications and Data

Data is often one of the most important assets of a business, and your ServiceNow instance is likely to contain a lot of it. Companies are often concerned about the mechanisms that protect data in ServiceNow in order to control against various types of loss:

- Stolen **financial information**, which can create loss of revenue, customers, and partners as well as leading to fines or legal action
- **Personally identifiable information** (**PII**), which must be secured to ensure that data privacy laws and the privacy of your employees are respected
- Information regarding the **separation of duties** and authority checking, such as during approvals and when updating other sensitive information
- **Knowledge-based information**, such as trade secrets and other intellectual property

Security should be included from the beginning. The ServiceNow platform provides a wide variety of functions and capabilities to protect against data loss and unauthorized manipulation. In this chapter, we will explore the main considerations to take into account when you build or configure an application:

- Understanding **roles** and how they get assigned to individuals
- Controlling data with **contextual security** (ACLs)
- Reviewing various **encryption** options
- Using **domain separation** to isolate fulfillers in a single instance
- Controlling the login process by choosing the right **authentication** process

Understanding roles

Some systems work very well as cooperative endeavors. For example, anyone can go and edit Wikipedia. This gives it a very low barrier for entry, letting anyone provide their knowledge and wisdom to others, by assuming that everyone is well intentioned.

However, open access does have its issues, especially with its pseudo- anonymity. Wikipedia often suffers from data "vandalism", and some editors have even introduced malware and malicious links. To combat this situation, some Wikipedia editors are tagged as administrators, which allows them to protect pages or block users that are dubious or behave inappropriately. Standard users cannot do this.

In a similar fashion, ServiceNow has different levels of access, which gives some people more privileges than others. For example, some users may be able to approve orders for a new tablet or mobile phone while others may be able to edit or update financial information. Controlling who can do what is incredibly important for an information security department.

The level of access is also typically tied in to the licensing model. The essence of this closely tied structure is that someone who uses ServiceNow intensively is a licensable user.

The licensing model of ServiceNow is constantly under revision, and as such, different customers often have different terms. If there is any confusion as to how ServiceNow is licensed, you should contact your ServiceNow representative.

Defining a role

The starting point of controlling who can carry out a particular function is a role. A **role** is essentially a tag or category that grants access to a particular function. Roles are associated with a user account, so someone using a particular account will have access to a particular function.

Roles always grant additional privileges. They don't subtract or take away access.

There are two broad categories of roles:

- Job roles, such as `team_leader`, `maintenance`, or `admin`
- Functional, such as `filter_global`, `soap`, or `view_changer`

To explore the roles provided in the ServiceNow platform, navigate to **System Security** > **Users and Groups** > **Roles**. They are stored in the database as a record with a text name. In scoped applications, they will always be prefixed with your scope.

In contrast to other areas of the system, roles are often referred to by name, especially in scripts. Therefore, it is the convention to keep the name short without spaces and in lowercase. The snake case form (where words are separated with underscore characters `like_this`) is encouraged.

Assigning roles to users

Roles can be associated either with users directly or a group. In the case of the latter, members of the group will automatically be associated with a role. This even works with hierarchical groups: assign the role at the top and everyone underneath it will be granted the role.

It is a good idea to use groups to assign roles to users whenever possible, since this makes administration easier. Giving the `maintenance` role to the Maintenance group means that if you get added to an assignment group with the expectation you can deal with tasks, you also get the appropriate access rights. You don't need to get in the situation of manually assigning privileges, with all the error that comes with.

Don't assigned roles via groups if you are using Scoped Administration, discussed later. It can let an administrative user assigned protected roles when they should not.

Nirvana is achieved when another system, such as an Active Directory LDAP server, notifies ServiceNow about changes to a group's membership. This makes the process of assigning roles completely painless: associate the right roles with the right groups, and let import automation do the rest!

This does assume that you have groups that are well thought out and are organizing people effectively. If you start finding that you need to add roles to individuals, instead consider if you have the right group structure in place.

Finding a user's role

Roles are associated with users via a many-to-many table called **User Role** [sys_user_has_role]. The platform provides access to this via a virtual field called Roles in the User table, making it possible to create simple filters. For server-side scripting, the hasRole function of GlideSystem and GlideUser will return true if the user has the desired role.

Differentiating between requesters and fulfillers

In Chapter 5, *Getting Things Done with Tasks*, the concept of a requester and fulfiller was introduced. A **requester** is someone who asks for the work to be done, while a **fulfiller** is someone who does it. The ability to carry out these actions ties in closely with roles and therefore impacts ServiceNow licenses. Whilst these two types of users are the most common, there are others who use the instance too.

When someone uses the instance, such as loading a form or a list, the platform will either use an existing session or create a new one. The session records information about the user, such as their name, whether they are using the HTML web interface or accessing the Web through web services, and their roles. And it is the information in this session, primarily the roles they have, that helps to controls what the users can see and do:

- Someone who has not logged in has public access. This session is unauthenticated and the user has not entered a username or password. By default, in ServiceNow, access is extremely limited. In the majority of cases, the user will be redirected to the login page to enter their credentials.

For example, some reports can be made public, but they will often be empty. The data itself is protected by security rules, which are discussed later. Entries in the **Public Pages** [sys_public] table define exactly which pages you can see while you are unauthenticated.

- A requester is typically someone who has logged in but does not have any roles. The user cannot see or interact with anything that is not directly associated with them. A requester typically creates tasks.

An extremely common request is for a requester to have access to their team's Incident tasks. This data is restricted by a query business rule. Since requesters should only have access to their own tickets, changing this may affect your licensing agreement.

- Someone who is logged in and has any role is typically a **fulfiller**. The most common role that is granted is the `itil` role, which gives a fulfiller access to the ITSM applications and is key to many contextual security rules. This provides the capability to see and potentially work with any task on the system.
- The **admin** role is a special one. It grants almost unrestricted access to the instance. If a user has the admin role, then they have all the other roles too. In addition, most contextual security rules apply to anyone other than admins.

Think very carefully before assigning the admin role because an admin user has the power to do almost anything in the system. Delegated Development, explored in `Chapter 2`, *Developing Custom Applications,* lets you control that power a little more finely, and will only allow alterations to the scoped app.

Previously, having a role was the only way used to differentiate between requesters and fulfillers. This resulted in many workarounds to minimize the use of roles.

ServiceNow is moving towards a more sophisticated understanding based on usage. Rather than having the simple statement of "has role, is fulfiller", the licensing position will be interpreted based on what the users actually do. For example, if user A updates a record created by user B, user A could be considered a fulfiller, regardless of the roles user A has.

Licensing is a complicated subject. It is dependent upon the agreement made upon purchase as well as the applications in use. Contact your ServiceNow representative to confirm your exact situation.

Roles and Delegated Development

Chapter 2, *Developing Custom Applications*, showed how you can give administrative capabilities to a standard user. Delegated Development lets you be more selective about who can make changes to an application, including writing code, without giving the admin role.

This functionality uses, in part, roles to identity and control this functionality. You can see these by navigating to **User Administration** > **Role**, and looking for role names that start with sn_dd.

> It's a good idea to leave the management of these roles to the Delegated Development UI in Studio.

Activating Subscription Management

To better understand exactly which users are consuming licenses, use the Subscription Management application. Your ServiceNow instance will automatically pull down the licensed applications, referred to as subscriptions. You can then associate users with these subscriptions, and monitor your usage. For example, you may have a subscription for 100 users of the HR application, or for 500 of the ITSM application. By creating a user set for HR, you can see how many users are actually using up those licenses, and see if you are consuming more or less than what was purchased.

A user set is essentially criteria that defines who is consuming a license. To keep it simple, it will likely be who has the appropriate role. As before, if you have the itil role, you have access to the ITSM applications, so it is appropriate to have the user criteria specifying that those users are consuming ITSM licenses.

> Configuring the Subscription Management application is straightforward: create a subscription set at **Subscription Management** > **Subscription User Sets**, and then monitor usage at **Subscription Management** > **Subscription Overview**. More information is available on the product documentation here: https://docs.servicenow.com/bundle/helsinki-servicenow-platform/page/administer/subscription-management/concept/c_SubscriptionUsage.html

Using impersonation

To verify what a particular user can see, use impersonation. A user with the `impersonator` role (which includes admins) can select the **Impersonate User** option on the user menu, available by clicking the profile name in the top right of the screen. This launches a list where another user can be selected, and choosing an account will alter the session to enable you to do and see everything that the user can. The following screenshot shows the Impersonate User list:

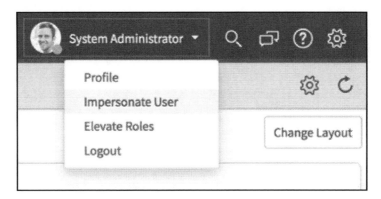

Impersonation is very useful when dealing with security and for testing in general. After you have created a security rule, consider using impersonation to validate that your rules work properly. To do this, keep some representative testing accounts ready for your use.

 There are several demo user accounts that you can use; `ITIL User` and `Joe Employee` are the most common, but the `Beth Anglin` account has several other roles, such as `catalog_manager` and `asset`. Having representative accounts that reflect real use cases provides a better test.

Impersonation in a production system is incredibly useful to validate and reproduce defects. However, it can also be a security concern, because any updates or actions will appear to have been made by the impersonated user. Therefore, grant the privilege carefully.

 When someone uses impersonation, an entry is written in the logs. In addition, you may want to configure a Business Rule that sends an e-mail when impersonation starts. You could use the `impersonation.start` event to trigger the notification.

High-security settings

All new instances have the High Security plugin enabled by default. This provides many of the functions, including contextual security, that are discussed in this chapter. Many of the capabilities are embedded into the platform but can be switched on or off, as desired, by navigating to **System Security** > **High Security Settings**. The options include:

- Enabling strict session cookie validation
- Rotating HTTP session identifiers
- Enabling escaping by default
- Checking security rules on inbound and outbound requests
- Requiring authorization for WSDLs, SOAP, and other requests

In general, the most secure settings are selected by default.

 A great resource to check the available settings against is the Instance Hardening guide, available on the Hi Customer Service system here: `http s://hi.service-now.com/kb_view.do?sysparm_article=KB55654`

Elevating your role

In order to change many security settings, including the creation of contextual security rules, you need the `security_admin` role. Unlike most other roles, admins do not automatically inherit it, and you also need to activate it when you want to use it. This is designed to reduce mistakes. By performing these actions, you confirm your responsibility each time.

To activate the role, open the user menu, and choose **Elevate Roles**. Tick the `security_admin` role, and click **OK.**

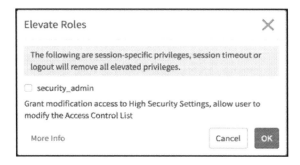

However, elevated privileges won't easily *stop* malicious admins from making security-related changes, since an admin can easily give themselves the `security_admin` role, just like any other role. It just reduces the risk of accidental changes. So, instead of the elevated privileges, you may want to create a report that looks at the system logs or configure e-mail notifications to alert you for suspicious activity.

Controlling access to applications and modules

The most immediate use of roles is to control the menus and modules in the Application Navigator. As discussed in `Chapter 1`, *ServiceNow Foundations*, the menu on the left-hand side of the window contains links, typically to forms and lists. The definition for an application menu or module contains a list field that lets you select a role. If the user has the role (and remember that an admin has all roles), then the user will see the option. If they do not, then it will not be visible to them.

It is very important to understand that this does not control access to the data itself, only the link. A knowledgeable user can still navigate to the table list by entering `<table>_list.do` in the address bar of their browser, as we saw in `Chapter 1`, *ServiceNow Foundations*.

Most of the time, controlling visibility via roles is good enough. However, what if you want to create an application menu and show it only to a subset of requesters? Perhaps you want to let only some users see the option to create a new Maintenance request?

Controlling access to modules with groups

`Chapter 2`, *Developing Custom Applications* discussed the concept of query Business Rules. These scripts are executed by the instance when a user attempts to access a table. This means they are very useful for controlling access to records. Let's create a new query Business Rule that checks what groups a user is in and use that information to control access to modules.

This work will not be captured in the Hotel scope application, since we will be working on core system tables. This means that the protections of scoping will not apply. Additionally, if you wanted to move this customization to another instance, it would need to be captured in an Update Set, as discussed in `Chapter 10`, *Packaging with Applications, Update Sets, and Upgrades*.

If you would like to see how to control modules with groups, follow these steps.

1. First, switch out of the Hotel scope, and into global. Use the application picker at the top of the standard interface, or click the Settings button top right and choose **Developer**, then **Global** in the Application selection.

2. Let's add a new field to the Module table. To do so, navigate to **System Definition** > **Tables**, and choose the **Module** [sys_app_module] entry in the list. Using the Table Columns related list, add the field with the given corresponding values, and **Save.**

   - **Column label**: Group
   - **Type**: Reference
   - **Reference**: Group [sys_user_group]

3. Click the Design Form button. The new field should have been added to the form already, but drag it into the Visibility group. Save once done.

4. Navigate to **System Definition** > **Business Rules**, and click **New**. Use the following values, and **Save:**

   - **Name**: Control visibility via group
   - **Table**: Module [sys_app_module]
   - **Advanced**: <ticked>
   - **When**: before
   - **Query**: <ticked>
   - **Condition**: !gs.hasRole('admin')

This business rule will only run if the user does not have the admin role. Otherwise, the administrator will not be able to see the record, even to edit it!

- **Script**: (insert inside the provided function, as normal)

```
current.addQuery('u_group', '').addOrCondition('u_group', 'IN',
getMyGroups());
```

This script is run when the Module table is queried. It adds a condition to return only the records where the Group field is empty or where the field contains one of the groups that the user belongs to.

5. Jump back into the Hotel scope using the application picker.
6. Navigate to **System Definition** > **Modules**, and edit the **Maintenances** module record, setting the following values. Save once done.
   - **Title**: Maintenance list
   - **Group**: Maintenance

To control the visibility of modules, you can now use either a group or a role. To test this, grant the x_hotel_maintenance_user role to two user accounts: one that is a member of the Maintenance group and one that isn't. Use impersonation to validate that only the former can see the Maintenances module.

Another way to achieve the same result is with a read contextual security rule. The next section gives you the background to do something similar.

This example is not only a useful customization in itself, but it also affirms that roles are just one way to control visibility. Since virtually everything in ServiceNow is a record, the use of Business Rules and contextual security gives us many ways to achieve the same goal.

Protecting data with contextual security rules

The first few chapters showed how data could be protected using business rules and Data Policies and that forms can be manipulated with Client Scripts and UI Policies. For example, a script can be used to ensure that you can write to a field only when the task is open. For a better experience, it'd be best to do it both on the server (to ensure that the browser didn't cheat) and the interface (to give feedback to the user). Wonderfully, Contextual Security helps with both!

ServiceNow has two different security managers. These protect data as it leaves and enters the instance. The simple security manager controls who can update a field through roles. The Dictionary entry for each field has several list fields where roles are selected: one each for `create`, `read`, `write`, and `delete`. However, this doesn't give you any flexibility over when these actions can occur. If you have the role, you can perform the action at any time.

> CRUD, or create, read, update (often substituted with write), and delete, are the four actions that can happen to a data item. They map directly onto SQL commands (`INSERT`, `SELECT`, `UPDATE`, and `DELETE`).

In contrast, the contextual security manager uses the *context* of the record. You have far more control over whether an action can occur through the use of conditions and scripts.

Understanding contextual security

The security managers are designed to allow or stop CRUD actions. They cannot force an action to happen, so security rules have no mechanism to make fields mandatory. Think of them as a guard on a building site. They check people as they come in or out, but they can't force people to enter the site-they can only stop them.

Contextual security runs in two main places:

- As forms and lists are generated
- When data is submitted from a form

This diagram shows how the security manager checks data, both on the way out to the browser, and also the data that has been submitted through it.

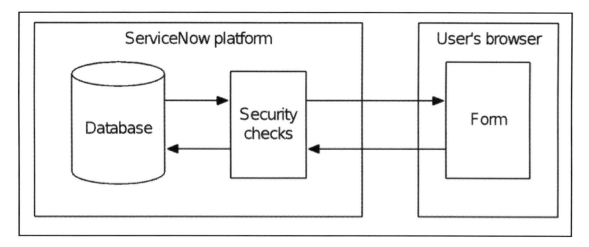

If a field cannot be read, it will not be shown. In fact, the data won't be included on the page at all. If a field cannot be written to, it is rendered as text. Any attempts to manually alter a field by altering the browser's DOM, as shown in `Chapter 2`, *Developing Custom Applications*, will fail. If a record cannot be created or deleted, the **New** or **Delete** buttons will not be shown.

All this means that contextual security should be your starting point when you think about access control.

 The Security Rule form has a checkbox on it called **Admin overrides**. If this is ticked, then the rule will always allow the action for someone with the admin role.

Specifying rows and fields to secure

One of the most powerful features of contextual security is that it can apply either to a particular field or an entire row. This also causes much confusion, since there is a delicate way to specify what you are trying to achieve.

Elevate to the `security_admin` role (selecting **Elevate Roles** in the user menu) and navigate to **System Security** > **Access Control (ACL)**. Then, click on **New** to see the access control form and, in particular, the **Name** field.

The **Name** field specifies what you are securing. There are two ways of looking at it: a text-only version and the one with drop-down menus. Use the blue arrow toggle to change between them. For the sake of clarity, I'll use the text-based form:

- To control a field, use the **<table>.<field>** structure.
- To control a whole row in a table, use the **<table>** structure, without choosing a field. (Note that this is rendered as **<table> –None —** in the drop-down menu.)

For example, if the **Priority** field in the **Maintenance** table needed to be secured, it would be specified as `x_hotel_maintenance.priority`.

Securing rows

When a user attempts to make a change to a record, the platform first checks the security rules that are listed against the table. If a write-row rule prevents access, the record will be completely read-only. The fields cannot be written to or changed, and there is no **Update** or **Save** button on the form.

Similarly, if a create-row rule prevents access, the **New** button will not show in a list; a delete row rule will control the **Delete** button.

The UI actions are not shown since they have conditions that check the `current` object of `GlideRecord`. The `canWrite` and `canRead` functions of `GlideRecord` are far more preferable to use than building complex code using `gs.hasRole()` and other logic in the **Condition** field. It is a great idea to include `current.canWrite()` as part of the condition in a UI action.

A read-row rule will prevent access to the row entirely. This renders in ServiceNow in a frustrating manner, with a message at the bottom of a list that says **Number of rows removed from the list by Security constraints: <number>**.

This screenshot shows what the **Reservations** list would look like if there were two records in the table, and you were denied to read them both:

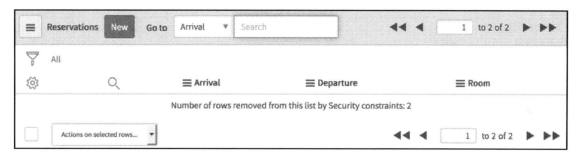

This happens because security rules are evaluated after the data has been retrieved from the database. Each record in turn is analyzed by the security rules, and if necessary, the platform will not render it. Instead, it presents this message in the list.

This has a big usability impact. Consider a scenario where there are 100 records in a table, and a user has set their page's size as 20. If the row-read rules allowed access to all records, the user could happily page through five pages and see 20 at a time.

If the row-read rule restricts access to, say, 80 of these records, then there will still be five pages. Depending on the sorting settings, the user may see 10 rows on the first page and a message saying that 10 rows are restricted. On the next page, they may see nothing aside from a message that says that all 20 rows are restricted, and so on.

This is intensely frustrating for a user. In my experience, they will not understand this message, and they will not appreciate that you can page through to find the records they want.

I strongly recommend that a row-read rule be saved for situations when all rows need to be inaccessible, or as a backup. Instead, you can use before query Business Rules, as shown previously. Its benefit is that it controls what the database actually returns, is more intuitive to use, and is just as secure.

To try this out for yourself, create a table with no automatically created security rules. Make several test records. For your read rule, ensure that it is specified for the table, and enter a script such as `answer = (Math.floor(Math.random() * 2) == 1);`. This will mean that on average, half of the rows will be readable and the others won't.

Controlling fields

Most people intuitively understand the controls for a field, especially read and write. If a field is restricted for the create rule, it is read-only only when the record has not yet been saved. In the absence of a `create` field rule, the platform will use `write` rules for the field. This means that `create` field rules are often not used.

Even less relevant are `delete` field rules. They have no effect at all.

Just like `GlideRecord` has `canWrite` and `canRead` functions, so does `GlideElement`. So, you can call `current.<field>.canWrite()` in server-side scripts to see whether the rules let the user edit a field.

When creating field rules, especially if there are many fields on the table, consider whether you will be generally permissive or restrictive. If more fields are going to be disallowed than allowed, it is a good idea to create a default `<table>.*` rule and make it always evaluate as `false`. Then, open up the fields that you want by using more specific rules, as explored shortly. Creating this rule will also give you 'deny by default': to be able to write to a field, you explicitly need to create the appropriate security rule.

The order of execution

Contextual security rules are applied in a specific sequence. It can often be confusing to work out which rules are being applied if you aren't familiar with how they execute. However, once you are comfortable with the logic, contextual security rules let you control any CRUD situation!

To help you understand what will happen, use the **ACL Execution Plan** UI Action, available at the bottom of the security rule. The output is explained later.

The following logic is used by the contextual security manager to determine whether access is granted.

Executing the row and then the field

For every record that is pulled from the database, row-based rules are determined first. They have priority over field rules. For instance, if the write-row rules return `false`, then all the fields will be read-only. If the row rule returns `true`, then the field rules are considered.

Rules are searched until one is found

The platform will work through the rule list in a specific order until it finds the best match. Once a relevant rule is found, it is taken into consideration. This level is then considered definitive. If the rule returns `true`, the action is allowed. If it returns `false`, the action is not allowed.

Defaults are possible

In addition to specifying field or table names, such as `priority`, `short_description`, or `x_hotel_maintenance`, an asterisk (*) can be used in either the table or field part of the Name field. This provides a default rule. If there are no other more specific rules, this default will be used instead.

The table hierarchy is understood

In our Hotel application, the Maintenance table is extended from the Task table. When looking for row rules, the platform first checks for any with the name x_hotel_maintenance. If one is not found, it looks at task. If one is not found, it looks for *.

If no rules are found, the action is allowed. However, the contextual security baseline rule set includes a * row rule. By default, this rejects the action.

Multiple rules with the same name are both considered

It is perfectly possible (and encouraged) to have two rules with the same name and action. For instance, there could be two read-row rules that have the name x_hotel_maintenance. In this situation, both will be executed. If *either* returns true, then the action will be allowed.

Field rules check the table hierarchy twice

When looking for a field rule on an extended table, the platform checks each part of the rule in a term. First, the table gets less specific, and then, the field.

For instance, if the Priority field on the Maintenance table is being secured, then the platform will first look for rules with the name x_hotel_maintenance.priority, then task.priority, and then *.priority. Then, it looks for x_hotel_maintenance.*, then task.*, and finally *.*.

If a rule is found at any point, its decision is taken and the platform will stop searching. Two or more rules with the same name will result in being true if any are true. If all are false, the result will be false.

The following diagram graphically shows the logic the contextual security manager goes through:

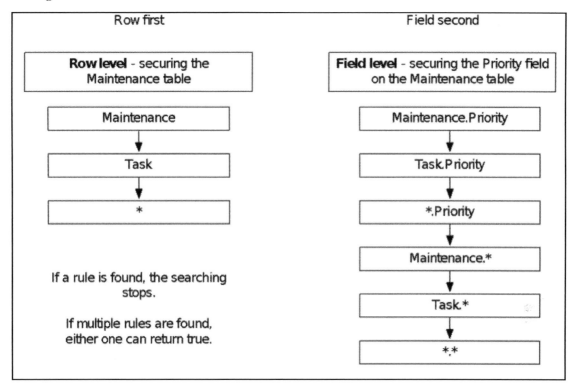

Summarizing the execution

Contextual security analyses a great combination of rules. When a record is shown in a form, the row security rule is found first. If this returns `true`, then every single field on the form will trigger a rule check. Due to the great number of combinations, it is easy to lose track of what the platform is doing at each point.

To help, the ACL Execution plan shows what rules will be executed. This can be accessed at the bottom of every security rule, and it will also be shown on any security rule alteration. The example later shows this in action.

In the next chapter, we will look further at how to debug security rules and watch the decisions that the platform takes.

Scripting and access controls

The majority of JavaScript code that runs on the server, such as in Business Rules and workflows, is unaffected by contextual security. When `GlideRecord` accesses the database, it does so without regard for any security rules. The majority of the time, this is what you want-a UI Action script can change the state of a read-only field. This means that it is the scriptwriter's responsibility to ensure that a user cannot do something that they shouldn't. Use the `canRead` and `canWrite` functions of `GlideRecord` to check whether the logged-in user has the correct privileges to access the data.

 Whilst security rules aren't usually considered in scripts, scope is. As `Chapter 2`, *Developing Custom Applications* explains, scope is like a bubble around an application, and Application Access controls what CRUD actions are allowed from outside the scope. If you need more finely grained control, create a Script Include as an API.

Checking every record and field for access can be a bit frustrating and inefficient. Instead, consider using `GlideRecordSecure`. This extends the `GlideRecord` class, so it inherits all of its functions, but it will only perform actions that the user is allowed to do. For example, rows that are made read-only by access controls won't be available in `GlideRecordSecure`.

 One of the reasons ServiceNow is so flexible and powerful is that you can accomplish almost anything with server-side scripting. You can add a role to a user, delete almost any record, and read all data. Treat scripting the same way as someone with the admin role-they have the keys to the instance!

The client can sometimes ask the server to execute JavaScript. For example, in a filter, you can specify `User - is - javascript:gs.getUserID()`. This JavaScript command will be run on the server. Although it is very useful, it also opens up a large security hole: it is not a good idea to allow arbitrary JavaScript specified by the client to run!

 Consider the consequences if a user specified this filter as `User – is – javascript:(var g = new GlideRecord('sys_user'); g.query(); g.deleteMultiple())`. Don't try this at home!

To protect the database from a malicious user, the majority of code that is passed through from the browser is run in a sandbox. This takes it one step further than `GlideRecordSecure`, since it totally prevents any records from being written onto or deleted. So, the example code given in the preceding box will actually have no effect.

One notable exception to this policy is a Script Include that is marked as **Client callable**. By checking this box, which allows code to be called from the client, the scriptwriter confirms that they will handle any security checks themselves.

Securing other operations

In addition to the CRUD operations, ServiceNow lets you create access control rules to control access to several other parts of the system:

- To control the visibility of UI pages, set the Type field to `ui_page` and select `read` from Operation. Then, set Name to be that of the UI page.
- Script Includes used by `GlideAJAX` can be prevented from running by setting `Type` to be `client_callable_script_include`. Operation is automatically set to `execute`. Processors can similarly be restricted.
- The `report_on` operation very usefully restricts the table list that is available in the reporting interface. Since ServiceNow is very open and lets you report on almost any table, the list is by default quite cumbersome to sort through!
- To control the fields that can be set in a template, use `save_as_template`. Then, set Name to be the field you want to control. This prevents users from overwriting, for example, the Approval or Number fields from a template.

Building security rules

As we work through the rest of the chapter, we'll use the following scenarios to implement different security rules. They outline particular use cases. I find this very helpful to organize exactly what is necessary to implement.

- Only authorized users are allowed to create or edit Maintenance tasks. The records become read-only when the tasks are closed.
- Only a team leader is allowed to edit the Priority field when any task is not closed.
- A user can only add to Work notes for a Maintenance task if they are on the Work notes list or in the Assigned to field.

Conditioning contextual security

A contextual security rule is made up of three elements. These are evaluated together to determine if the user can carry out a particular action:

- A **condition** (if it applies to the record)
- A **script** (that returns `true`). This is available when the Advanced checkbox is ticked.
- One or more required **roles**, where a user must have at least one

A rule can have any combination of these elements. A rule could consist of a condition and a few required role, or it could just consist of a script. However, all must be satisfied for the rule to return `true`. A blank element will not be considered.

> More than one role can be listed against a security rule. In this situation, the user must have one of the roles. If the situation is such that the user must have multiple roles to carry out the action, then you must script it. Or better yet, create a new role!

By analyzing these statements, we can implement them using conditions, scripts, and roles. Conditions can cater to the majority of scenarios, but occasionally, a script is necessary.

The following table summarizes what we want to achieve:

Item	Action	Condition	Role required	Script
1. Maintenance tasks	Write	State is not closed	Maintenance	–
2. Maintenance Priority field	Write	–	Maintenance team leader	–
3. Maintenance Work notes field	Write	–	–	The logged-in user is in Assigned to *or* The logged in user is in Work notes list

When you create a new table, the platform automatically builds a basic set of security rules. By default, the platform will create a read-, write-, create-, and delete-row rule, each with a new role based on the table you've created. That means there should 5 new roles created automatically, all in the style of x_hotel_<table>_user. You can see these roles by navigating to **User Administration** > **Roles**. We will need to edit these rules to make things work as we want.

We are only going to work with the **Maintenance** table. The other tables (like Reservation, Check-in and Room) will likely also need to be dealt with.

Editing the automatic security rules

For the first requirement, which is to only allow Maintenance tasks to be edited if they are not closed, we must edit an automatically created row rule:

1. First, ensure you are in the Hotel scope, using the application picker.
2. Then use **Elevate Roles** from the user menu to get the security_admin role.
3. Navigate to **System Security** > **Access Control (ACL)** and find the rule with the name x_hotel_maintenance and the operation write.
4. Add the following values, and Save.
    - **Admin overrides**: <unticked>

If the Admin overrides field is ticked, the security rule will be disabled for admins, regardless of the other conditions. This lets the admins override normal procedures to "fix" records or deal with unforeseen circumstances. Uncheck it to facilitate easier (though less realistic) testing.

- **Condition**: State – is not – Closed Complete

5. To test, navigate to **Hotel** > **Maintenancelist**, and find or create a Maintenance record with the state **Closed Complete**. Once you've saved the setting, you'll notice that the form is entirely read-only, and the **Update** and **Save** buttons have been removed, just like the screenshot below:

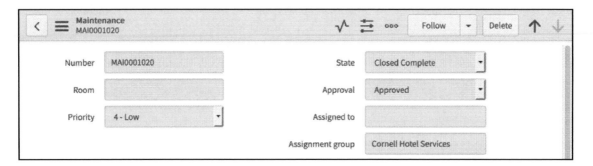

Testing using impersonation

Testing best practice involves using a more realistic user account. The interplay of security rules can be complex. Follow these steps to do so:

1. Firstly, add the role to a group. Navigate to **Hotel** > **Maintenance groups**. Select Maintenance, click on Edit under Roles, select all five roles that begin with x_hotel from the slush bucket, and hit **Save**. We want these team members to have full access to the Hotel tables.

A better way to do this would be create a job role (maybe called x_hotel.housekeeping) and then include each of these functional roles in it. Then you only need to associate the job role with the group, making maintenance easier. We'll do just this with a team leader role in a moment.

2. Then, ensure there are users in this group. If needed, click on Edit under Group Members, select a user and save. I've used an account I've created called Polly Sherman. Since Polly is in the Maintenance group, her account has therefore inherited the x_hotel_maintenance_user role.

3. Once done, use the user menu to select **Impersonate User**, and select your test account.

It is often helpful to use a second browser when using impersonation so that you can keep your admin user account open in one window and your test account in another. An alternative is to start a Private Browsing session/Incognito mode, or use the multiple user account feature in Chrome.

4. As Polly, navigate to **Hotel** > **Maintenance list** and select a record that *isn't* in **Closed Complete** state. Take a look at the available fields. Room and Assignment group are writeable, and the Work notes field is not visible. The Update button is available. This is quite restricted, as the screenshot shows. Why is this?

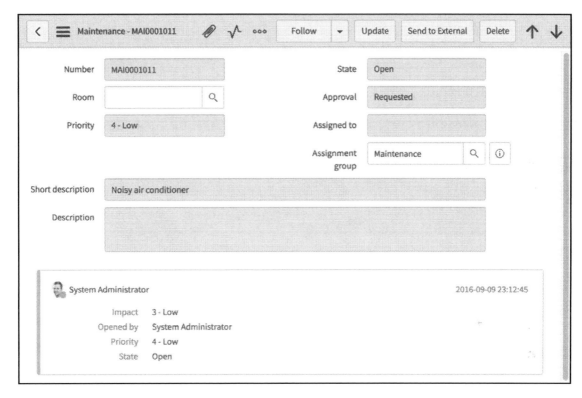

Since the Maintenance table is inherited from Task, some default field rules have been included. Specifically, there are rules named task.short_description, task.assigned_to, and task.description. As an admin, you can navigate to **System Security** > **Access Control (ACL)** and create a filter to look for all security rules with names beginning with task. to see them all.

The majority of these security rules require the user to have the `task_editor` or `itil` roles. While you could create more specific rules, such as `x_hotel_maintenance.short_description`, to override these default rules, it is easier and more maintainable to include `task_editor` as part of the `x_hotel_maintenance_user` role. Use built-in functionality whenever you can!

1. Use the Impersonate User option to return to your admin user.
2. Let's fix it up. Navigate to **User Administration** > **Roles**, find `x_hotel_maintenance_user`, click **Edit** in the **Contains Role** Related List, and select `task_editor`. Save once done.

> Unfortunately, in the default configuration of ServiceNow, some security rules are entirely dependent on the `itil` role. However, using the `itil` role instead of `task_editor` would give you access to many more applications than would probably be appropriate. We'll fix the particular issue with `read` access to the **Work notes** field for our third scenario.

3. Finally, in order to test, impersonate your test user again. Roles are only read after a user logs in, so log out or switch to System Administrator then back to the test user using the impersonate feature. You should now also be able to edit the Priority, State, Assigned to, Short Description, and Description fields.

Setting security rules quickly

An often-overlooked interface feature of ServiceNow is how you can create a security rule without using the access controls form. We'll use this method for our second security rule: only team leaders can edit the **Priority** field.

Follow these steps to do this:

1. Ensure you are an admin, and have used **Elevate Roles** to get the `security_admin` role.
2. Then create a new role by navigating to **User Administration** > **Roles**. Then, click on **New**, fill the following and **Save**.
   - **Suffix**: `team_leader`

3. Click **Edit** on the **Contains Role** Related List. Select all the roles beginning with **x_hotel**, and Save.

4. Navigate to **Hotel** > **Maintenance list** and select a record. Right-click on the **Priority** field label, and choose **Configure Security** from the menu. (If it isn't there, ensure you have used **Elevate Roles** from the User Menu to get `security_admin`!)

5. Set the **Operation to Secure** field as `write` and set the `x_hotel.team_leader` role. Finally, click on **OK** to save. The **Security Mechanic** dialog will look as follows:

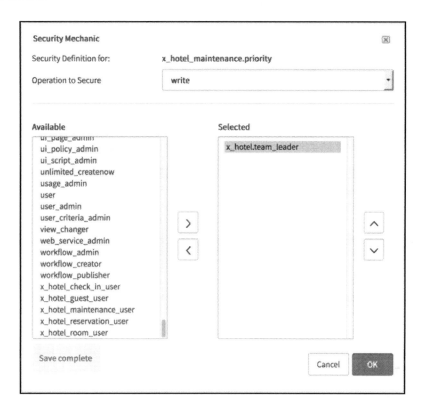

6. Click on **Cancel** to close the window. Don't worry! The rule would have been saved if a message displaying **Save complete** appeared. You can confirm this by navigating to **System Security** > **Access Control (ACL)**. There, you should find a new entry with the name `x_hotel_maintenance.priority`.

Scripting a security rule

Our final scenario is to control how work notes are used. There is an existing read-security rule named `task.work_notes` that only lets users with the `itil` role see the field or its output. This even extends to the activity log. This ensures that requesters will not see anything entered in the Work notes field. However, to ensure that our Maintenance team users get access, that should be extended to the `task_editor` role.

Follow these steps to do that.

1. Navigate to **System Security** > **Access Control (ACL)**. Click **New**, fill out in the following values, and **Save**.
   - **Operation**: `read`
   - **Name**: `Maintenance [x_hotel_maintenance] - Work notes` (using the drop-down version of the name field)
   - **Requires role**: `task_editor`

     When you save, you will get a pop-up message that explains that more specific name of x_hotel_maintenance.work_notes will be prioritized above the original task.work_notes rule. The original rule will be **masked**. Click **Continue**.

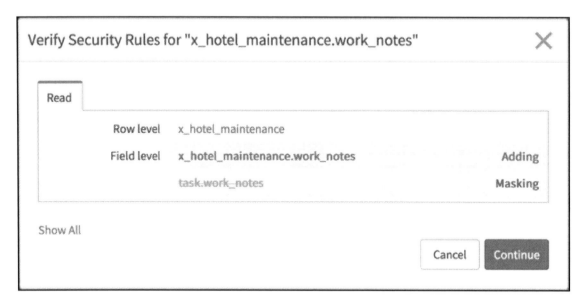

The `write` security rule needs a little more work. A script in a security rule needs to provide a binary answer-`true` or `false`-to the global `answer` variable. As we will discuss in the next section, you must ensure that the security rules are executed very quickly. They are called frequently, so avoid the temptation to perform complex lookups or even write to the system log.

2. Navigate again to **System Security** > **Access Control (ACL)** and click **New**. Set the following.

   - **Operation**: `write`
   - **Name**: `Maintenance [x_hotel_maintenance] - Work notes`
   - **Advanced**: `<ticked>`
   - **Admin overrides**: `<unticked>` (for testing purposes)
   - **Script**:

```
answer = (current.assigned_to == gs.getUserID()) ||
((current.work_notes_list + "").indexOf(gs.getUserID()) > -1)
```

This one-line script has two separate conditions. The answer variable will be set to `true` if either of the conditions are `true`. Firstly, the Assigned to field is checked. It succeeds if the contents of the reference field match the `sys_id` of the currently logged-in user. Secondly, the Work Notes List field is checked. This is a comma-separated string of `sys_id` values. This is searched to see if the `sys_id` of the current user is in it.

Save the record, and click Continue to confirm that `x_hotel_maintenance.work_notes` will override `task.work_notes`.

3. Try this out. Navigate to **Hotel** > **Maintenance list**, and find or create a **Maintenance** record where the Assigned to and Work Notes fields are empty, and note that the Work notes textbox is not displayed. Then, add the System Administrator to the Work notes list field (or whichever user you are logged in as), save it, and you'll now be able to see that it is visible.

The rendering of a read-only journal field, such as **Work notes**, is different than a multiline text field, such as **Description**. With the former, the text area is completely removed, while for the latter, it is disabled.

Using security rules effectively

Contextual security rules can be confusing at first. To get used to how they work, it is critical to understand the order of execution. Even after this is understood, it is easy for you to slow the system down with inefficient security rules. While the platform does cache results and attempt to optimize, where possible, follow these key points to use security rules effectively:

- Read-row rules are not user friendly. Query business rules are almost always more effective. They may also be quicker since they ask the database to filter out the records and prevent their processing.
- Read-field rules can be very intensive for the system to process. Consider a `<table>.*` security rule that returns `false` for every field. This will mean that in a list of 10 columns and 20 records, the security rule will be executed 200 times.
- Scripts in general should be avoided wherever possible. It is very easy to write inefficient code. Always try to avoid querying the database using `GlideRecord`. Instead, consider calculating it once, storing it in the session with `gs.getSession().putClientData(<key>, <value>);` and retrieving it with `getClientData(<key>);`. An even better option is to avoid it entirely!
- Use the Requires role related list wherever possible. The platform caches which roles a user has and can perform some smart optimization; for example, if a read-field rule requires a role that the user doesn't have, then the whole column is disabled in a list. Don't use a script for this as `gs.hasRole()` won't be so clever!
- Try to keep Admin overrides ticked. A system administrator is responsible for the whole platform. It is inevitable that sometimes things will go wrong, and the admin may need to fix data and change records in a way that was not initially envisaged.
- Security rules are designed for securing data. Always use them over UI policy and the Read only checkbox in the dictionary. Since these only work on the client side, a malicious end user could easily override them.
- If a UI Policy or Client Script makes a field read only, its value can still be changed through a client-side script, as you saw in `Chapter 4`, *Client-Side Interaction*. If this happens, `onChange` client scripts associated with that field will fire. However, this will not happen for fields that are made read only via access rules.

- Security rules can do more than protect records. They can also control the access of processors, UI Pages, and Script Includes.

Using Scoped Administration

The System Administrator is generally responsible for a ServiceNow instance. With the addition of the `security_admin` role, an admin user can change security settings, alter logic in Business Rules and see all data elements. Because all admins have all roles, adding a security rule that says that only users who have the **x_hotel.team_leader** won't restrict an admin.

 You may try to script an access control rule to stop admins from carrying out certain functions, or perhaps using the nobody role to disallow everyone. But just as an admin can create these rules, they can delete or change them!

Sometimes however, this is not desirable. Scoped Administration changes this premise by stopping admin users from inheriting a particular role, and disabling their access to edit the scope. Only those users who have been specifically allowed to work with a particular application can get access (either administratively, via Delegated Development, or as a fullfiler or requester).

A typical use case for this functionality is for a HR application. HR organizations are very protective of their data, since it may include disciplinary information, sensitive salary data, or even personal information like social security numbers. A System Administrator may not be authorized to see this information.

In order to control who can get access to a Scoped Administration enabled app, each role must have the Assignable by field set. This specifies who can allocate those roles out. Once done, the option to enable Scoped Administration is set in the Application Settings.

Controlling the Hotel application

As an example, let's lock down access to the Maintenance table in our Hotel app. Access to read the records is granted via the `x_hotel_maintenance_user` role, but we haven't need to give this directly to our admin users because admins have all roles. Instead, let's say that a user with the `x_hotel.team_leader` role must allocate this privilege.

To see how this works, follow these steps:

1. Navigate to **User Administration** > **Roles**. Using the Personalize List Columns option available via the cog, add the **Assignable by** field, and click **OK.**

2. Then, double click the **Assignable by** field of the `x_hotel_maintenance_user` record. Set it to `x_hotel.team_leader` as the screenshot below shows, and click the green tick.

It is necessary to edit via the list because a UI Policy is enforcing that all scoped roles need a suffix, even though this role was auto-created by the platform without it! This little trick is useful for getting round rogue client side checks like this.

3. Then, navigate to **User Administration** > **Users**, and select the admin user you are logged in with. Since I'm logged in with the provided admin account, I chose the user record with the User ID of `admin`.

4. In the **Roles** Related List, click **Edit**. Select the `x_hotel.team_leader` role, and click Save. This grants our user the role used to assign access to others, so we don't lock ourselves out!

5. To apply the roles to your user account, logout from the user menu, then back in again.

6. Finally, open up Studio by navigating to **System Applications** > **Studio,** and clicking Go next to Open Studio. Select the Hotel application.

7. From the File menu in Studio, click **Settings.** Tick the Scoped administration field, then click **Update.** Close the window when done.

Time to test. When you are logged in with your standard admin account (System Administrator in my case) everything you should behave as normal. This is because that user has the `x_hotel.team_leader` role. Now try impersonating another admin. In the standard demo data, the Fred Luddy user has the admin role, or you can create your own.

1. As per the instructions in the beginning of the chapter, using the User Admin menu, click **Impersonate User**, and select `Fred Luddy`.

2. The page should refresh, and you should notice there is no entry for the Hotel application, as per the following screenshot.

3. Indeed, even if you try to navigate to the **Maintenance** table directly (or any other of the **Hotel** tables), you will find that you get an error message. Try going to `<instance>.service-now.com/x_hotel_check_in_list.do` in a new browser to see this.

4. Finally, open up Studio by navigating to **System Applications** > **Studio**, and clicking Go next to Open Studio. Select the Hotel application, and notice how you have no access to edit anything. You may also want to see that as Fred you cannot assign yourself any Hotel roles.

5. End impersonation and return your main admin account. If you wanted to grant Fred access, you would need to grant him the appropriate roles from the System Administrator account.

It is important not to use roles group membership to assign roles if you are using Scoped Administration. Otherwise, a user who can add and remove users from a group would also be able to assign them the protected roles. In this example, Fred would be able to make himself a member of the Maintenance group, and inherit the Hotel roles.

Encrypting data

ServiceNow provides support for three types of encryption. Two occur within the server, and the data is decrypted before it leaves the instance, whereas **Edge Encryption** ensures data is always protected outside of the customer's network. The three types of encryption are as follows:

- **Full disc encryption** protects a disk if it is physically stolen from the ServiceNow data center. The instance itself is unaware of any differences to a normal operating environment.
- **Field and attachment encryption** stores encrypted data in the database. This provides a level of protection against a malicious database administrator. It is decrypted using an encryption key stored on and controlled by the instance.

 These two methods are different forms of protecting data at rest. All communication with the instance occurs over HTTPS. This means that all the data is also secured in transit, but in both cases, the instance can work with the unencrypted data.

- Edge Encryption uses a gateway sitting in the customer network. The gateway, which functions like a proxy server, has all traffic routed through it, and it selectively encrypts data elements. Unencrypted data never leaves the customer network. If a user does not access the instance through the gateway, encrypted text is seen in the relevant fields.

Disadvantages of field encryption

Many customers see field encryption as a highly desirable feature. Most security policies need personal or other protected data to be properly secured, and field-level encryption is a feature that may help in some circumstances. For example, an HR team may want to ensure that unauthorized people cannot see certain private information. However, field-level encryption does suffer from some significant disadvantages:

- The only field type is a large multiline text field.
- Encrypted fields cannot be used in a list to filter or sort records.
- The data in an encrypted field is not exportable from a list.

Encrypted fields are accessible through web services; this gives us an alternative data-extraction technique.

- When impersonating a user, encryption contexts are not inherited. Impersonation is used by the platform when it runs a transform map; this means that encrypted fields cannot be used when importing.
- It does not protect from malicious administrators. It is simple to associate the security context with another role and let the administrator see the data.

There are some enterprising workarounds to minimize some of these drawbacks. Since encrypted data is still accessible via web services, it is possible to write a business rule that moves the submitted data out of a field and saves it into another by connecting to the same instance via a SOAP or REST call.

There are very few use cases where encrypted fields are truly useful. It is often far more useful to implement a well-designed and tested set of access controls. They are more flexible and provide a similar level of protection since both rely on the system to control the data and only show it to the appropriate users.

Evaluating encryption gateways

Many companies, including ServiceNow, offer encryption gateways. They all attempt to solve the same concern: that sensitive data is stored outside of the company. With both disk and field-level encryption, the encryption keys are stored within ServiceNow-the instance has access to unencrypted data. Law enforcement or government agencies could compel ServiceNow to decrypt the data. With edge-encryption gateways, the key is stored on the gateway; ServiceNow is never in possession of and never sees the clear text. It cannot therefore decrypt the data.

There are several competing solutions, but all work using a reverse proxy-based technology that sits within the customer's infrastructure. Instead of connecting directly to ServiceNow, users connect to the gateway. The gateway proxies all interaction to the instance, encrypting and decrypting specified fields as it passes through. This ensures that the encryption of data is fully under the customer's control. The general workflow is as follows:

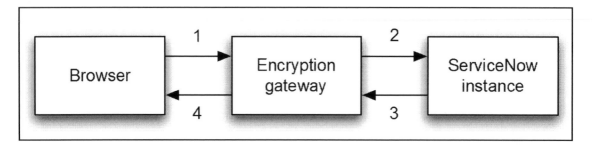

Now, let's walk through the process gradually:

1. The user's browser sends data to the encryption gateway. The encryption gateway encrypts any sensitive data.
2. The instance receives encrypted text and saves it in the database.
3. When the instance is requested to get data for a list or a form, the encrypted information is sent to the gateway.
4. The encryption gateway decrypts the data for the user.

Typically, the encryption gateway has an interface to choose which data elements to work with. The gateway inspects the data submitted by the browser and only encrypts the items that it has been configured to touch. This means that the gateway must understand the traffic it is presented with; often, it scans the instance to allow you to select which fields it should encrypt.

 A great feature of Edge Encryption is the ability to use a regular expression to encrypt any data that matches a particular pattern. This means that it does not need to fit into a particular field, and means capturing things like credit card or social security numbers is straightforward.

Evaluating encryption gateways

While these gateways effectively encrypt the data and provide extra security, careful evaluation is necessary. Since the instance no longer has access to the actual data, many seemingly basic functions may be impacted. For example, fields may not be sortable, and server-side processing logic that is dependent upon the contents is not possible.

The benefits of third-party encryption solutions involve having a single gateway for many products. For example, it may protect Salesforce, SharePoint, and Dropbox as well as ServiceNow. The instance may even be oblivious to the existence of the gateway. This can cause some functionality loss:

- Importing and exporting data is usually difficult or not possible
- Access to the web service APIs may be restricted
- Manipulation of the encrypted text with server-side scripts may be difficult
- Searching and sorting will be impaired
- Certain user interface elements may be impacted if they need to use encrypted text
- It is important that all use cases (including administrative functions, such as importing) be fully evaluated when you select an encryption gateway

The ServiceNow edge encryption solution does mitigate against some of these issues (such as being able to import and export data successfully, including using REST and SOAP APIs) since it is integrated into the platform. However, the architecture of the solution still presents fundamental challenges. The Product Documentation provides an overview here:

https://docs.servicenow.com/bundle/helsinki-servicenow-platform/page/administer/edge-encryption/concept/c_EdgeEncryptionLimitations.html

Introducing Domain Separation

Domain Separation is designed to control what fulfillers can see and do. ServiceNow applications have been typically designed so that a fulfiller has access to all the tasks in a particular application and the application works consistently for each person. Domain separation tags configuration and data so that the platform can choose what is relevant for a particular user at the appropriate time.

The design for domain separation is focused on the needs of **Managed Service Providers** (**MSPs**). These use ServiceNow for helpdesk and other services and sell their capabilities to their customers. This means that an MSP can provide a large call center, enjoying economies of scale, providing fulfillers who input incidents for multiple companies – all in a single instance.

While the instance should be configured with the MSP's standard processes as a baseline, each customer of the MSP may have specific configuration requirements. Additionally, the MSP's customers may want to have their own users to log in to the instance and work on tasks. Of course, the MSP would only want the users to see the data that they should. Therefore, Domain Separation helps achieve three specific goals:

- **Process separation**: In process separation, configuration such as Business Rules or Client Scripts are selectively applied. A customer of an MSP may have different assignment rules to another.
- **UI separation**: In UI separation, different domains may have different forms and related lists, as well as different options in choice lists. The latter ability is very handy to have different categorization options per MSP customer.

 Process and UI separation are both considered as configuration. When I refer to configuration separation, I'm referring to both process and UI separation.

- **Data separation**: In data separation, records such as other users, tasks, or locations are only available to the right people. This means that a user that works for an MSP's customer, perhaps even one with fulfiller rights such as the `itil` role, would only see records for their company.

 The difference between configuration and data is discussed in much more detail in `Chapter 10`, *Packaging with Applications, Update Sets, and Upgrades*.

Defining a domain

A **domain** is simply a logical grouping of configuration and data. If a certain set of people need to have a configuration that applies just to them or they want to be restricted from seeing certain records, then they may need a domain.

As we discover though, Domain Separation is not a cure-all. Do not assume that this functionality will solve easy use-case regarding to separation.

When you use the Domain Separation plugin, you need a table that provides the domains. This table must have a reference field that refers to itself-the parent field. Most of the time, a dedicated table called **Domain** [domain] is used, but others, such as the Group table, are occasionally used.

The Domain table is created with the Domain Extensions Installer plugin. It also provides typical configurations and best practices.

In turn, every data or configuration record is associated with a domain. When the domain support plugin is turned on, it creates a reference field called **Domain** [sys_domain] on many hundreds of tables. Some tables already have the field available, and once the plugin is installed, it is 'activated'. This allows items, such as an assignment rule, to be associated with a particular domain. Users are also associated with a domain.

Applying Domain Separation

At the most simple level, Domain Separation compares the domain of the user or the record with that of the data or configuration.

If the domain of the logged-in user is the same as the domain of the data, it can be seen, as shown in the following figure:

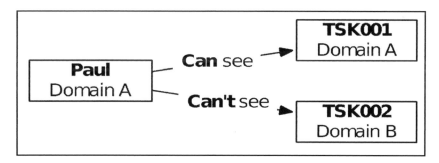

If the domain of the record is the same as the domain of the configuration, it is applied, as shown in the following figure:

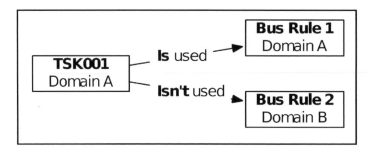

At its most raw level, domain separation adds a WHERE clause to a database query. A highly simplified example is when a query for user records is modified to look like this:

```
SELECT * FROM sys_user WHERE sys_domain = <domain of logged in user>
```

Organizing domains

A domain is typically related to another domain in a parent-child relationship. The domain hierarchy is the backbone of domain separation since it can have a great impact on how configuration is applied or what data can be seen. How the hierarchy is applied depends upon which item is being considered:

- The user's domain is used when viewing **data**. Any records that are associated with that domain or *lower* are visible.
- The record's domain is used when applying **configuration**. Any configuration that is associated with that domain or *higher* is applied.

Introducing global

Not all records in the instance will be tagged with a domain. Some tables, such as those that store properties and Script Includes, do not have a Domain field. These items will be processed regardless of what domain is in use. For tables that are separated by domain, such as Business Rules, it is possible for the Domain field to be empty. In both these situations, the item is considered to be global.

Global is technically not a domain. Instead, it is the *absence* of a domain. If a record is global (ie, the Domain field is empty), then it is outside of domain processing. This means that if a Business Rule has no domain, it is always run. If a group has no domain, everyone can see it, regardless of what domain the user is in.

> Be careful to differentiate between global when working with domains as opposed to applications. They are certainly not the same thing!

If a user is not associated with a domain, they will again be outside of domain processing-they will see everything. If a record is global, then only global configuration will be applied to it.

Understanding domain inheritance

The following diagram shows a simple domain hierarchy. **Domain A** is the parent of both **Domain B** and **Domain C**. We'll use this structure to discover how inheritance works:

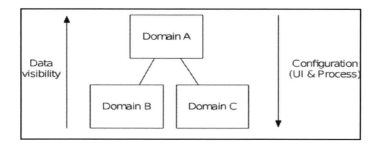

The table lists how the platform uses the domain structure to apply configuration and control data visibility:

Domain being considered	Configuration applied	Data visibility
None (so global)	Global	Global, Domains A, B, and C
A	Global, Domain A	Global, Domains A, B, and C
B	Global, Domains A and B	Global, Domain B
C	Global, Domains A and C	Global, Domain C

The rules have the following results:

- Since domains B and C are siblings, they have no impact on each other
- Global data is always visible, and global configuration is always applied
- A user in domain A will be able to see data associated with global and domains A, B, and C
- A record in domain A will only be affected by configurations that are associated with domain A (and global)
- Users in domain B will only see data that is associated with domain B (and global)
- Records in domain B will use configuration from both domains A and B (and global)

Turning on Domain Separation

In order to use Domain Separation, you must install the domain support plugin. I recommend starting with the **Domain Extensions Installer** process pack, which bundles the plugin together with helpful scripts, demo data, and a sensible default configuration.

 Once installed, Domain Separation cannot be removed from an instance. The functionality can be disabled, but the additional fields and options will still be available. Therefore, install this on a noncritical test instance only.

The Domain Separation plugins cannot be installed by an admin on an instance, due to the substantial impact it has on an instance. (Only activate it on a disposable, sandbox-style instance that you are happy to clone over!) It may also affect licensing costs. How you activate it depends on the instance type:

- If you wish to activate it on a standard ServiceNow instance, log into the Hi Customer Support system, and using the Manage Instance dashboard, request the `Domain Extensions Installer` plugin. Customer Support will then evaluate your request.
- For a developer instance, log into the Developer portal, and select to manage your instance. Using the Action menu, choose to activate a plugin, and then select the `Domain Support – Domain Extensions Installer` plugin.

Looking at Domain Separation

Once the plugin is installed, follow these steps to review the standard functionality and examples:

1. Firstly, lets make selecting a domain much easier. As your normal admin user, click the Settings menu top right, and in the **General** options, activate **Show domain picker in header**. This will give you a drop-down selection that sits next to your application picker.

2. The **Domain Extensions** plugin contains a few example domains that are useful to understand how the system works. To see a list of these domains, navigate to **Domain Admin > Domains**. You can see that the eight example domains are related to one-another via the Parent field.

3. To see a graphical representation of this, navigate to **Domain Admin > Domain Map**, as per the screenshot below. Unfortunately, this has been rotated to how it is typically visualized, meaning the top parent domain is on the left, but it still provides a good idea of how the domains are related to one another.

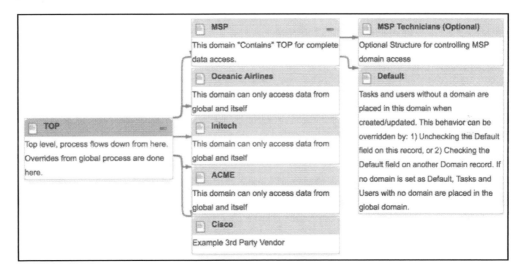

Most often, domains are related to companies. In the example data, ACME, Oceanic Airlines, and Initech all buy services from the MSP. Cisco supports the MSP as a vendor. There are records in the both Domain table and the Company table to represent this.

The `Domain Extensions Installer` plugin contains scripts that automatically set the domain when the **Company** field is populated on a task or a user record. If a domain cannot be found, a business rule will move the tasks into a domain called **Default**. This ensures that the tasks don't get put into the global domain by accident and are thus visible to everyone.

Exploring domain visibility

The best way to understand how Domain Separation works is see it in action:

1. Navigate to **User Administration** > **Users** to show all the users in the system. Click the Personalize List icon, and add Domain field into the Selected list. Click OK once done. The list should look like the screenshot below:

2. Use the **Domain Picker** to select different domains. As you do so, the records that are shown in the list will change. It is easiest to see the differences if you sort or group by the **Domain** field.

3. If you pick the Initech domain, you will be subject to Initech's data visibility rules. This means that you will see the data tagged with no domain (that is, global), TOP, and Initech. In contrast, if you switch to the Cisco domain, you will see Cisco's users and not Initech's.

Domains are usually represented with their hierarchical name in the interface. Since Initech is a child of TOP, it will be titled TOP/Initech. Note that once you have switched domains, there is no indication that you are not seeing the full dataset, beyond the domain picker. All queries, filters, and actions will be applied only to the limited list.

Understanding Delegated Administration

When discussing domain separation, the product documentation talks about delegated administration. Many think that this allows a user to have a "sub-admin" capability: the ability of a user to change a part of the configuration in a certain domain. However, this is not the case.

Delegated Development uses scoped applications to give a similar effect. This capability is discussed in `Chapter 2`, Developing Custom Applications.

Delegated Administration simply means that a configuration can be applied to a particular domain. In the example dataset, the configuration could be applied to the Initech domain, thus ensuring that it is only applied to Initech (and any subsequent children).

A user with the admin role has control over the whole instance. The truth of this statement does not change with Domain Separation. An admin can choose which domain they are currently associated with and control the domain configuration and data it is associated with.

Overriding configuration

Configuration from a higher domain may be considered as a template. It will be applied to domains that are lower in the hierarchy unless it is overridden. In a domain-separated instance, all configuration will have a field called **Overrides** [`sys_overrides`] in addition to **Domain** [`sys_domain`]. The Overrides field is a reference field to the table on which it is created. For example, the Overrides field on the Business Rule table will point to the Business Rule table.

The definition of a configuration in a domain-separated instance may be considered as a table that has both the Domain and Overrides fields.

When altering configuration that is inherited from a higher domain, the platform will automatically use this field to create copies. This ensures the right domain receives the right version.

Displaying different messages for different domains

To show how a configuration can be overridden at a particular domain, let's create a simple Business Rule and then override it at a lower domain level:

1. Firstly, use the Domain Picker to switch to the TOP domain. It is good practice to put all your configuration into a domain rather than use global.

2. Then, navigate to **System Definition** > **Business Rules**, click **New**, and fill out the form using the following values. Save the record once done.
   - **Name:** Display message (TOP)
   - **Table:** User [sys_user]
   - **Advanced:** <ticked>
   - **When:** display
   - **Add message:** <ticked> (In the Actions tab)
   - **Message:** TOP domain

3. Change into the TOP/Initech domain using the Domain Picker. Then, in the same Business Rule that you just created, and change the values in the following items:
   - **Name:** Display message (Initech)
   - **Message:** Initech domain

4. Ensure that you click on the **Update** (or **Save**) button to *update* the current record (do not use **Insert and Stay**).

   A message will appear letting you know that the platform hasn't actually overwritten the Business Rule, but it has created a copy and set the Overrides field:

A new 'Business Rule' has been inserted to override 'Display message (TOP)' for domain 'TOP/Initech'

5. To see what has happened, switch to global in the Domain Picker and navigate to **System Definition** > **Business Rules** table. Then, scroll to the bottom of the list and click **Expand Domain Scope** under Related Links. Also add the **Domain** and **Overrides** fields using Personalize List to be to see what has happened.

The Domain field specifies which domain will run the script. Any domain underneath TOP will run the `Display message (TOP)` business rule, except for records associated with the Initech domain. It has its own Business Rule that will run instead and specifies this with the **Overrides** field.

6. To try this out, navigate to the **User** table and open up a variety of users. The message that will appear will depend on the domain of the user:

    When you view user records in the Global domain (such as `Joe Employee` in the following screenshot) you will not receive a message:

    User records in the Initech domain (such as `Initech Employee` in the following screenshot) will show **Initech Domain** due to the specific business rule associated with this domain:

User records in the ACME domain (such as ACME Employee in the following screenshot) will show **TOP Domain** since they inherit the configuration from the TOP domain:

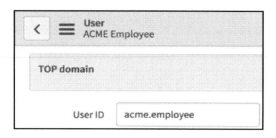

Creating more domain relationships

In addition to hierarchical relationships, a domain can **contain** other domains. This can be accomplished by using a related list on the Domains form and populating the **Contained Domains** [domain_contains] table.

When containing a domain, you indicate that you want to see all the data that the domain can. Since data flows up, you effectively specify another parent.

In the example data, the MSP domain contains TOP. This means that a user in the MSP domain can see all of the data that TOP can see, and since TOP is at the top of the hierarchy, this means that the user can see everything. Even though MSP is a sibling of Initech, because MSP contains Initech's parent, which is TOP, MSP can see all of Initech's data. Unfortunately, the instance doesn't represent this on the domain map, but if it did, it might look like this:

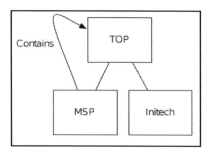

One reason to do this is to allow tasks associated with the MSP domain to have special domain-specific processing rules, but have the users see other domains. They can work on Initech tasks, while Initech users cannot see them.

> Another way to access more data is through a **visibility** group: a specific group can be given the privilege to see another domain's data.

To try this out, switch to the MSP domain, where you can see every user-even those in a sibling domain.

Using Domain Separation appropriately

Domain Separation is sometimes seen as a magic fix for separation needs. Although it is a powerful feature, it isn't always the right choice. It is a complex technology, and there are simpler alternatives to each of its features:

- For UI separation, you can use views with view rules and dependent fields to drive choice lists
- For process separation, you can use conditions on business rules and other functionality, such as assignment rules, and add conditions into client scripts
- For data separation, you can use access controls and before query Business Rules

> It may also be more appropriate to create a custom app for a particular situation, perhaps by using table inheritance. For instance, consider creating a dedicated app for the grounds keeping team instead of trying to break up a hotel room maintenance system. Two tables are much easier to deal with than one that is domain separated.

However, for MSPs, it provides a great way to provide a global template that allows processes to be overridden at appropriate levels.

Take the following items into consideration when implementing Domain Separation:

- Ensure that the hierarchy is well thought out. Are some domains similar? Should they share a common parent?
- There should be a good common ground to consider process separation, since it cannot overcome very diverse ways of working.

- Domain Separation provides more options, which leads to complexity. When changing form layouts, you must consider each domain in addition to each view.
- Tables and fields are global. If you create a field, it will be available to all domains (it may not be on the form, but it can still be selected in a report or on a list). Access control rules can stop visibility, if necessary.
- System properties are global. Domain separation will likely lead to further configuration and customization to control this.
- Someone with the admin role has control over all domains. For example, update sets (which will be discussed in `Chapter 10`, *Packaging with Applications, Update Sets, and Upgrades*) are global.

Authenticating users

The vast majority of the content in a ServiceNow instance is private and not available to just anyone browsing around the Internet. To control what users can see and do, you firstly need to know who they are. There are many different authentication mechanisms in ServiceNow, ranging from a simple username and password to complex industry-standard protocols such as **Security Assertion Markup Language** (**SAML**) and OpenID.

Using internal authentication

The standard way to prove your identity to your instance is with a username and password. The User table contains user ID and password fields. When an unauthenticated user accesses the instance, a login form is provided. The values that the user provides are compared with those in the User table, and if a set matches, a session is created, the roles associated with that user are recognized, and the user can begin their work. If the optional Remember me checkbox is checked, a longer-life cookie is stored in the browser during the login process. This cookie means a username and password is not prompted for; instead, the cookie identifies which user to use for the session.

Controlling authentication

Installation Exits contain the logic to deal with authentication requests. To see them, navigate to **System Definition > Installation Exits**. They consist of a block of code that is called whenever a user wants to log in or out, or when a password change is necessary during login. The platform looks for installation exits that override `Login`, `Logout`, or `ValidatePassword`. If one is found, it is executed. Otherwise, the default behavior is used.

Installation Exits are actually designed to work as scriptable 'installation settings' which work on every transaction, but their functional use is for authentication. There are some exceptions to this, such as the `SetDomain` Installation Exit.

Installation Exits also provide you with the opportunity to add controls. You can edit the `ValidatePasswordStronger` script to force longer and more complex passwords. Or do you only want admins to log into ServiceNow when they are on your internal network? Perhaps you want to restrict what time of the day ServiceNow can be logged into? All these are achievable with an Installation Exit. Indeed, custom authentication methods can be written to receive a token and check it for validity. SAML and other single sign-on mechanisms all use Installation Exits as their hook into the ServiceNow login process.

Once a user is logged in, an event named `session established` is fired, letting you log the usage or perform further session processing using a Script Action.

Using an LDAP server for authentication

In – Import Sets, Web Services, and other Integrations">Chapter 7, *Exchanging Data – Import Sets, Web Services, and other Integrations*, we explored how an LDAP server can be used as the source for user data. ServiceNow connects to it on a regular basis and synchronizes the data with the User table.

LDAP servers can also perform authentication, with Microsoft Active Directory being almost ubiquitous in enterprise environments. Therefore, it is common to use it and offload the decision of whether a user should have access to the instance. This can be accomplished by connecting to the LDAP server with the username and password that the user gave. If the credentials are accepted, a session is created.

A User record contains two fields that are not visible on the form but are populated during the import of user records. **LDAP Server** is a reference field to the record specifying a particular server, as set up in – Import Sets, Web Services, and other Integrations">Chapter 7, *Exchanging Data – Import Sets, Web Services, and other Integrations*, and **Source** contains an identifier that uniquely specifies a particular object: the **Distinguished Name (DN)**. Along with some details supplied by the user, these elements give the platform everything that it needs.

ServiceNow follows these steps when you use LDAP authentication:

1. A user seeks authentication by entering a username and password.
2. The username is matched against a User record.
3. If the User record contains an LDAP server, a connection is opened.
4. The instance uses the DN in the Source field and the password supplied by the user.
5. The LDAP server signals whether the credentials are valid.
6. If they are, the platform creates a session, and the user can start their work.

A graphical representation of the preceding process is shown in the following figure:

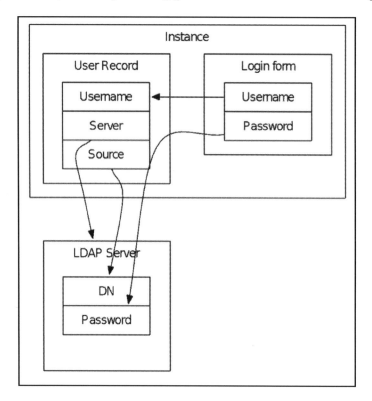

Typically, this process happens in only a few seconds. Using an LDAP server is an easy way to improve the authentication experience, for the following reasons:

- Users do not need to remember another username and password. Familiar credentials can be reused, reducing the risk of "password fatigue."
- The passwords are never stored within ServiceNow, meaning password changes don't need to synchronize and are kept securely in the LDAP server.
- Password policies are unnecessary in ServiceNow as the LDAP server controls the authentication.
- If the LDAP user account is disabled, then the authentication will fail. This means that lockout policies and inactive accounts will automatically apply to ServiceNow.

The mechanism that ServiceNow uses relies on the continuous availability of the LDAP server. Any downtime of it will mean that ServiceNow will be inaccessible. Additionally, many companies prefer not to expose their LDAP server over the Internet even with the use of a secure protocol such as LDAPS or via a VPN tunnel. In this instance, other external authentication protocols such as SAML can be used, which provide further security advantages. Note that while a MID server can be used to pull data from an LDAP server, you cannot perform authentication through it.

LDAP authentication has many of the advantages of Single Sign-On, such as a single reusable username and password, but it also means that a user must type their private authentication details into a website not hosted internally. The security policies of many companies do not like this!

Enabling Single Sign-on through SAML

The use of **Single Sign-On (SSO)** has exploded in the past few years. **Active Directory Federation Services (ADFS)** and, more recently, **Azure AD** have contributed to this growth by providing a mechanism to which many companies can easily hook in. ADFS provides a SAML 2 endpoint with which cloud-based solutions such as ServiceNow can authenticate.

SAML is by far the most common SSO solution (mainly because of ADFS), so it is discussed in this section. Other technologies such as OpenID get very similar results.

SAML is a relatively complex XML-based protocol that provides many different ways to exchange authentication data securely. ServiceNow supports the **browser post profile**. This means that the instance will redirect the user's web browser along with a packet of information to the **identity provider**-the system that does the actual authentication. That system can use many different mechanisms, such as a simple username and password or a more complex multifactor authentication involving smart cards or physical dongles.

> SSO integrations are referred to as external authentication since ServiceNow offloads the decision to another system.

Once authenticated, the identity provider generates a token-an XML document that is Base64 encoded. It returns this to the user's web browser, which in turn sends it to the instance. This happens through a series of form submissions. The identity provider never directly communicates with the instance, which means that it is possible (and common) for it to reside on an internal network. Only the user's web browser needs to communicate with both sides.

The token contains a reference, such as a username, that the instance can use to match with a **User** record. Once this has been found, a session is made, in just the same way as any other method. A graphical representation of the process is shown in the following figure:

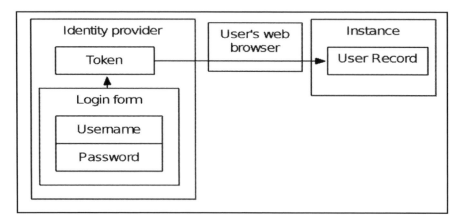

The instance must be able to trust the token. In order to know that the right identity provider created the token (and therefore it isn't a fake), the token must be signed using a certificate. ServiceNow needs the public key of the certificate, and it uses this to ensure that the identity provider has the private key. The certificate can be self signed or from a certificate authority.

Automatically creating users

ServiceNow also supports populating new users based on the information in the token. It can dynamically call a Transform Map (discussed in – Import Sets, Web Services, and other Integrations">Chapter 7, *Exchanging Data – Import Sets, Web Services, and other Integrations*) to create or update the appropriate record in User table, keeping ServiceNow in sync with your SAML system. We'll see how this is done with a comprehensive example in just a moment.

As discussed in – Import Sets, Web Services, and other Integrations">Chapter 7, *Exchanging Data – Import Sets, Web Services, and other Integrations*, try to find the best source of user information to ensure ServiceNow has the right information. You may want to augment the data from your SAML source with information from your HR or other systems.

Logging out

Once the user is finished with their work, they may decide to log out of ServiceNow. Doing so will end the session for ServiceNow, and if it is configured to, ServiceNow will ask the identity provider to end its session too. Some identity providers, such as ADFS, require that this request be signed. To achieve this, ServiceNow must have the private key of a certificate. This must be stored in a Java key store in order to protect it.

Java key stores need a password for access. Private keys need more protection than public keys.

Using Multiple Provider Single Sign-on

The **Multiple Provider Single Sign-On** plugin allows any combination of the local and external authentication mechanisms already discussed. In other words, it allows you to use, in a single instance, any of the following:

- SAML 2.0
- LDAP
- Local authentication (that is, managing the usernames and passwords in the ServiceNow instance)
- Digest authentication (a simple token-based system not commonly used)

Despite the name, it is recommended to enable this plugin even if you currently only plan to use one source of authentication, since it provides flexibility for the future.

If you do use multiple authentication mechanisms, then the instance needs to know which one to offer to a user. It does this by asking for the user's username (by default) in order to lookup the mechanism listed against their user record; it can then redirect to the right identity provider for them or ask for a password. This is only needed once-a cookie is set so the instance will, in the future, immediately offer the user the correct authentication mechanism.

There are ways to immediately direct a user using a special URL: `https://<instance>.service-now.com/login_with_sso.do?glide_sso_id=<sys_id of the sso configuration>`
You could mask this URL or embed it in a company intranet page. Refer to the product documentation for more details: `https://docs.servicenow.com/bundle/helsinki-servicenow-platform/page/integrate/single-sign-on/task/t_LoggingIn.html`

Configuring Single Sign-On

Enabling SAML is a multistep process. The product documentation has a long article that describes in detail how to achieve this here: `https://docs.servicenow.com/integrate/single_sign_on/task/t_SettingUpMultiProviderSSO.html`. In the majority of cases, enabling SAML is not hard: you just need to know the appropriate configuration settings and upload the right certificate. Be sure that you turn on SAML debugging and inspect the logs.

If you wish to experiment, **SSOCircle** (`https://www.ssocircle.com/`) provides a free identity provider. Indeed, the example configuration in ServiceNow is aimed at this service. In `Chapter 9`, *Diagnosing ServiceNow – Knowing What Is Going On*, we will discuss debugging in more detail.

> SSOCircle provides a wide variety of external authentication methods. Aside from username and password, you can see how a client certificate, hardware token, or even mobile provider could be used.

Consuming metadata from SSOCircle

The easiest way to integrate with an SSO system is using metadata generated by the identity provider. For example, the metadata provided by Azure is available at `https://login.microsoftonline.com/<tenant domain name>/FederationMetadata/2007-06/FederationMetadata.xml`, as described in the Azure documentation at `https://msdn.microsoft.com/en-gb/library/azure/dn195592.aspx`.

SSOCircle also produces metadata, so we can use that as our starting point.

> As before, this work will not be captured in the Hotel scope application, since we will be working on core system configuration. If you wanted to move this customization to another instance, it would need to be captured in an Update Set, as discussed in `Chapter 10`, *Packaging with Applications, Update Sets, and Upgrades*.

Follow these steps to configure Sign-Sign On with SSOCircle.

1. In your ServiceNow instance, switch to the global scope and the global domain using the respective pickers. This is global configuration, so be sure not to do this if your instance is not a sandbox.
2. Navigate to **System Definition** > **Plugins**, and select the `Integration – Multiple Provider Single Sign-On Installer` entry. In the form, click **Activate/Upgrade**, then **Activate**. Wait for it to complete, then click **Close & Reload Form**.
3. Navigate to **Multi-Provider SSO** > **Identity Providers**, and click on **New**. Choose **SAML2 Update1**. (Don't select the existing demo record, but create a new record.)

4. In the pop-up window, enter the following URL and click on **Import**.

URL: http://idp.ssocircle.com/

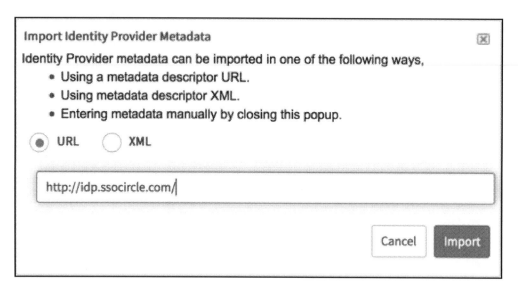

You should see all the fields on the form filled out with information from SSOCircle. A certificate is also created. You can view it at **System Definition > Certificates**.

5. By default, the new configuration is turned off. Change that by modifying the following fields, and Save.
    - **Name**: SSOCircle
    - **Active**: <checked>
    - **Default**: <checked>
    - **Auto Provisioning User**: <checked>

6. Click on **Generate Metadata** button. A new window should open: copy the text it gives into your clipboard.

7. Navigate to **Multi-Provider SSO** > **Administration** > **Properties**, enable these properties, and save:
     - **Enable multi provider SSO**: <checked>
     - **Enable Auto Importing of users from all identity providers into the user table**: <checked>

8. Visit `http://www.ssocircle.com/en/register/` and create a new account. Make sure you confirm your e-mail address.

9. When you are signed in to SSOCircle, choose **Manage Metadata** in the left menu. Then click **Add new Service Provider**.

10. Fill out the form. The FQDN should be your instance, in the form of `<instance>.service-now.com`. Do not add `https://`. Tick the **EmailAddress** attribute, paste the metadata into the large text field, and click **Submit**.

11. To trigger the creation of the import, we need to try signing in – even though it will fail. To do so, open up a new web browser (or enter Private Browsing) and navigate to your instance. On the username and password screen, you should now see a link to **Use external login**, as per the screenshot below.

12. Click on **Use external login**, and enter the email address you registered with SSOCircle. That will become the User ID in ServiceNow. You should then be redirected to SSOCircle and asked for your SSOCircle username and password.

13. Type in your SSOCircle username and password. You will likely be presented with a **SAML.**
    - **Consent Page**. Follow the instructions, and you should eventually see a notice saying:**Logout successful. You have successfully logged out.**

        This is not a bad thing! The login failed because the Transform Map didn't work properly.

14. To fix this, in your primary window, navigate to **System Import Sets** > **Administration** > **Transform Maps**. You should see the most recent entry of an automatically generated Transform Map. Mine is called `u_imp_saml_user_yyp6c5mdiw`; yours will have the same syntax. Select it.

15. At the bottom of the Transform Map, you will see four Field Maps. These need to be edited to reflect the data coming from SSOCircle. The most important ones are the `user_name` and `email`. For both of those Field Maps, set the Source field to be `emailaddress`, as per the screenshot below. List editing is likely easiest.

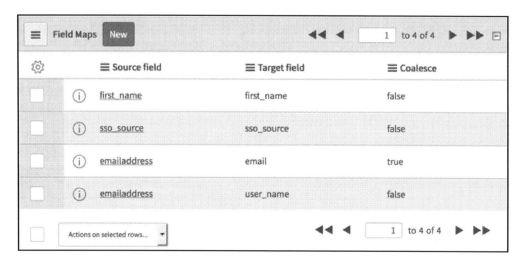

16. Finally, in your other browser, navigate to the instance again (ie, `<instance>.service-now.com`). This time you will be taken directly to SSOCircle. Once you pass their SAML Consent Page, you will be logged into ServiceNow with a brand new user account. Anyone else with an SSOCircle account can now also log into your instance. Cool!

To make SSO the default mechanism to for every login, and remove the ServiceNow username and password prompts, navigate to **Multi-Provider SSO** > **Administration** > **Installation Exits**, and set the active field to true for all three records. These are set to override the default Installation Exits.

Navigating to the side door

What happens if your identity provider isn't available or refuses to log anyone in? The instance will keep attempting to redirect your browser to it, without knowing that it is not working. In order to always have access to internal authentication, a special URL is made available at `https://<instance>.service-now.com/side_door.do`. If you navigate to this URL while logged out, the instance will ignore all installation exits and present the standard username and password login form. You may want to keep an additional admin account with a strong password to ensure that you can login to debug any problems.

Preventing access to the instance

Sometimes you may want to go one step further than authentication and make it impossible for users outside your company's network to access the instance at all. With IP address access control, the administrator can specify a range of IP addresses and specify whether or not they can access the instance.

Navigate to **System Security** > **IP Address Access Control** to add a range. Typically, the configuration involves adding the IP ranges that should access the platform with a Type value of Allow and then specifying a blanket `0.0.0.0` to `255.255.255.255` range with a Type value of Deny. The IP addresses will need to be the public IP addresses that servers on the Internet will see. There are many websites that will tell you what your external IP address is.

The platform will try to stop you from locking yourself out! You must have an Allow range that includes your current IP address before setting a blank Deny.

If the IP address is not in one of the allowed ranges, an **HTTP 403** error will be generated, with a minimalistic error message that will say **Access restricted**. This control is checked at a very early point when connecting to the instance, so it is effective for either the standard web interface or any web services.

IP address authentication works well for companies that have well-defined exits from their networks to the Internet. This may involve a proxy server or a NAT solution. These tend to provide a single IP address for many users. This means only a few IP ranges need to be configured; therefore, it is easily managed.

For a more distributed workforce, IP address authentication is not so useful due to the following reasons:

- Any partners or suppliers that access the instance must have their networks added as IP ranges
- Remote working (such as from a coffee shop) is not possible directly, though stopping this may be desirable
- Accessing the instance through a mobile network (such as through a 3G or 4G phone or tablet) is not feasible since IP addresses are often dynamic and shared through a large NAT range not under the control of the company
- Disaster-recovery locations must be considered, or else your instance will be unavailable when you need it most!

To help with these scenarios, many companies ask their employees to use a VPN tunnel, which gives them access to the internal network. However, it does introduce another step into the connection process and may affect response times. ServiceNow is a web platform, and making it inaccessible to the majority of the Web must be considered carefully.

Securing web services

As explored in `Chapter 7`, *Exchanging Data – Import Sets, Web Services, and Other Integrations*, the web services hosted by ServiceNow use basic authentication as the primary means for proving identity. A username and password should be used by the remote system when it connects to the instance. This is commonly referred to as a system account.

 Basic authentication is HTTP-level authentication. The calling system must provide a Base64-encoded value of `username:password` to the authorization header. The connection is refused if this is not present, making it fast and efficient. In addition, since headers are protected by HTTPS, malicious users cannot intercept this in transit.

When creating a user account for use in web services, it is a good idea to consider the following points:

- Create a new user account for each integration target, especially for those used by external suppliers. Don't use the same one each time, in case you need to disable it!

> Note that integrations cannot use external authentication accounts (such as LDAP or SSO).

- Tick the **Web Service Access Only** checkbox. This means that someone with the user account cannot enter the web interface.
- Grant the right roles, since access control rules will still be applied. You may want to create a role specifically for integration to your application; perhaps `x_hotel.integration`, with write access to only certain fields, might be useful in our application.

If you are creating a REST integration, that's all you need. Since the REST APIs are used heavily in the user interface, all users can interact with the REST APIs automatically (which reinforces the point that ACLs are critically important to control – don't rely on UI Policy or client side controls). SOAP is a little different and requires the user to have the "do-everything" `soap` role or a more specific `soap_query`, `soap_update`, or `soap_delete` role.

> In `Chapter 7`, *Exchanging Data – Import Sets, Web Services, and Other Integrations*, we used an admin account to access web services. Since the admin role has access to all the roles, we did not have to grant these specifically. However, it would be a bad idea to give a third-party system an admin account!

In the rest of this section, we will discuss some advanced options to authenticate web services. The majority of integrations do not need mutual authentication or WS-Security.

Using WS-Security

In addition to basic authentication, the instance can also insist that all SOAP messages be signed. The **WS-Security** standard provides a mechanism to ensure that SOAP messages are trustworthy and not tampered with.

ServiceNow can verify the identity of a remote system in two ways: through a certificate or with a username and password. In both cases, it is usually an addition to basic authentication; however, by navigating to **System Web Services** > **Properties**, you can choose what to use.

Improving security with signatures

If the message is signed, then the platform will validate that the data within the message hasn't been changed or tampered with. In order to do this, the public certificate must be uploaded. The instance will also compare it to the certificate embedded in the message and ensure that it matches. Store the certificate at **System Definition** > **Certificates**, and reference it at **System Web Services** > **WS Security Profiles**.

SOAP messages that conform to the WS-Security standard contain a timestamp. If the timestamp varies too much from the current time on the server, the message is rejected. This can help reduce replay attacks.

The instance can also impersonate a user once the message has been deemed valid. The user can either be chosen upfront be contained as part of the message.

WS-Security can be used for both incoming and outgoing messages:

- For outbound messages from ServiceNow, you must upload a Java keystore. It should contain the private key that ServiceNow will use to sign it. Specify that you want to use it in the outbound SOAP message function. Check out the product documentation here: `https://docs.servicenow.com/bundle/helsinki -servicenow-platform/page/integrate/outbound-soap/task/t_WebServiceS ecurity.html`.
- Inbound SOAP messages can be validated with a WS-Security profile. It will be applied to all messages in the **User** table except for those marked as **Internal Integration Users**. Specify the certificate you want to validate with. More information is in the product Documentation here: `https://docs.servicenow.c om/bundle/helsinki-servicenow-platform/page/integrate/inbound-soap/t ask/t_EnableWS-SecurityVerification.html`.

While inbound WS-Security and the security features it brings sounds alluring, it can quickly become inflexible, and difficult to work with. Because of the all-or-nothing nature of the properties and policies, you may find that all the products you need to integrate with will need to use it.

Mutual authentication

The vast majority of HTTPS sessions rely only on one certificate, which is provided by the server when the client connects. This provides two fundamental benefits:

- The identity of the server is correct, which means that the client is not connecting to a man in the middle
- The communications are secure and encrypted

However, the server has no idea who the client is. By accepting all connections, the server needs another way to find out who the client is; as this chapter has shown, this is often done by the application layer (by creating a session) or through basic authentication.

However, ServiceNow also supports mutual authentication for outbound messages. When an SSL connection is set up, the instance provides proof of its identity to the systems that it is connecting to. Both sides then swap certificates, letting the remote system verify the ServiceNow instance.

> Mutual authentication is outbound only. ServiceNow will not validate or check any certificates that are presented to it in a HTTPS connection. In fact, ServiceNow does not validate any certificates anywhere by default. You can force the instance to check the CA by setting the `com.glide.communications.trustmanager_trust_all` property to `false`.

Setting up outbound mutual authentication

Enabling mutual authentication involves uploading a Java Keystore. The keystore should contain the client certificate with the private keys and any root certificates that provide trust. These should be uploaded in the list available at **System Definition** > **Certificates**, and then referenced from **System Security** > **Protocol Profiles**. Here, you define a new protocol name, such as `mauth`. You have two options to use this profile:

- Every time you want the instance to use mutual authentication, alter the URL to read `mauth://<target>` instead of `https://<target>`. This URL could be used anywhere-not just for web service requests but also in an Import Set data source.
- Alternatively, and probably more simply, you can choose to use mutual authentication in an outbound REST or SOAP message by selecting the protocol profile in the configuration record.

Using OAuth

Most modern web apps use OAuth to reduce the necessity of usernames and passwords. It works like basic authentication in that you send authentication information in the header of the message, but it differs by being time bound and token based. Typically, you send a web service your username and password once, and the system generates a token that lasts for several hours. Then, on subsequent requests, you only provide the token and not the username and password.

> The *Inbound authentication* section of `Chapter 7`, *Exchanging Data – Import Sets, Web Services, and other Integrations* shows how you can get an OAuth token from ServiceNow.

Summary

The security aspects of a cloud solution are always under great scrutiny. Many companies consider data to be their greatest asset, so they demand that it be well protected. The ServiceNow platform has a range of functionality to address this concern. Of course, this must be coupled with assurances that the ServiceNow security team can deliver on physical security, penetration tests, and code reviews of the platform itself.

The chapter started with a discussion of roles. Roles are an immediate way to classify users, and ServiceNow slices the population into requesters, fulfillers, and admins. As such, the use of roles is closely tied to the licensing module. It is important that an administrator understand the impact of adding a role to a user; this may mean a financial commitment for their company. A ServiceNow representative should be consulted if there is any uncertainty.

Contextual security uses access control rules to control access to records. Create, read, update, and delete actions are either allowed or rejected by the evaluation of roles, scripts, or conditions. Since almost all configuration and data items are stored in records, access controls provide a powerful way to determine what a user can do and see. The ways in which rules are evaluated seem complicated when you see them for the first time!

Domain Separation is a method to partition data and configuration, again to ensure that the right person can see and do the right thing. By associating users and configuration into a domain, the platform will use hierarchical rules as the basis of control. Data flows up, meaning a user in a domain at the top of tree can see data associated with its descendants. Configuration flows down, with domains at the bottom of the tree being affected by those further up. Configuration, such as a Business Rule, can be overridden at a particular level. Other relationships, such as contains, can also be used.

A key part of security is authentication. To ensure the right people are logging at the system, internal or LDAP passwords can be typed into the instance and checked in the appropriate place, or SSO can be used to hand off the decision entirely. Installation Exits contain scripts that are called to log in users, sign them out, and change passwords.

Finally, the web services provided by the platform can utilize advanced methods to control access. WS-Security is an industry standard that allows ServiceNow to check timestamps and signed messages on incoming messages. Mutual authentication uses certificates from both sides when it sets up an HTTPS session, allowing systems to check that a client who connects is valid.

In the next chapter, we will look in detail at how to debug and determine what is happening when things don't work as you expect-and that includes security!

9
Diagnosing ServiceNow – Knowing What Is Going On

Have you ever written code that is longer than a few lines and had it work the very first time? Has a script always worked perfectly? The answer probably is no. Things don't always go according to plan during a complex implementation. Functionality doesn't quite work as you-or someone else-expects. Therefore, the tools and techniques needed to investigate the issue, come up with a diagnosis, and hopefully find a solution are a critical part of any administrator's toolkit.

ServiceNow provides a wide variety of ways to understand what is happening in the system. This chapter covers many of the ways through which the instance can tell you what's going on:

- **Session logs** give you insight into what decisions are being made by the instance
- The typical **system log** is where the system records messages while it processes
- The database records its activity in the **SQL log**, giving you insight into slow queries
- Every request is stored in the **Transaction log**, indicating where performance problems may lie
- **Versions** track how configuration has changed
- The **Audit log** keeps detailed information on who did what and when

Building a methodology

ServiceNow can support itself. As you build your ServiceNow instance, consider using the software development applications to track features and functionality requests. Then, as people start using the instance, you can track their success (and failure) within the platform. This makes it easy to identify areas that need improvement and track progress effectively. Use the reporting functionality within ServiceNow to track your efforts so that you can avoid going back to using spreadsheets!

ServiceNow provides quite a few applications to manage your work. The Agile Development plugin lets users to submit feature requests, stakeholders to prioritize functionality, and developers to track progress. Alternatively, the Demand Management plugin lets anyone submit ideas, and then portfolio administrators can visualize demands according to cost and other metrics. Find out both products in the Product Documentation: `https://docs.servicenow.com/bundle/helsinki-it-business-manage ment/page/product/sdlc-scrum/concept/c_SDLCScrumProcess.html` and `https://docs.servicenow.com/bundle/helsinki-it-business-ma nagement/page/product/planning-and-policy/concept/c_DemandMana gement.html`

Identifying the issue

When an issue is reported, you must get a good bug report before any investigation can begin. Understanding what happened is fundamental since this will help you determine what steps should be taken next. This typically requires at least the following information:

- **What was done?** What buttons were clicked and which fields were filled out? Who was the user, what was the time, and what was the record number on which the action was carried out?
- **What happened?** Were any error messages shown? What fields were changed (or not changed)? A full browser screenshot is often very useful.
- **What was expected?** The system didn't work as the user thought it would. What should have happened? Did they expect it to produce a different output? Sometimes the systems is working as it was designed – but the design was wrong!

Once this information has been collected, it is much more straightforward to replicate the issue. The system administrator can then use impersonation to verify the issue, check the logging functions, and subsequently simply ensure that any fix works.

Looking at the system log

The majority of the diagnosis starts with the system log. This is the place where most of the applications in the platform display their warnings and errors, generating entries that can fall under these three levels: **Information**, **Warning**, or **Error**. You can view them all at **System Logs** > **System Log** > All. There are also modules for individual levels. Add the **Created by** field to the list to show which user generated the entry.

The system log can become pretty huge. Each of the modules contains a filter that only shows items that are `Created - on - Today`. If you build your own filter, keep a date filter in place, even if it is modified.

The platform and applications will record any scripting or internal errors in the system log. If things aren't working quite right, the system log will give you an indication. For example, if the instance can't connect to an FTP server that is used while importing data, this will be registered in the system log. If the platform itself fails, then often a Java stack trace will be recorded. Additionally, some normal usage is also included, such as when records are deleted. This is useful when you want to understand why a table that once contained data is empty now!

The level of the log message gives an indication of its seriousness:

- **Information**: Normal system functionality is working as expected, but a log message is added so you know what is happening.
- **Warning**: Something isn't quite right, but the functionality typically still works, or the error was recovered from.
- **Error**: Something has occurred that means the functionality has aborted. The instance will continue to work in other areas, but the reason behind the error should be investigated and dealt with.
- **Debug**: This is low-level information that provides details about how processing is going. This may be how a SAML token or REST message is dealt with.

Keep an eye on the system log. Aim for zero errors; to achieve this, you may need a scheduled report or a homepage that helps you understand what is happening in the instance. Try looking at how many messages are logged over time. A sudden spike might indicate trouble. Try making a trend chart, for instance, to spot the increase.

Writing to the system log

Use the `info`, `warn`, `error` and `debug` functions of `GlideSystem` to add your own messages when you are writing scripts. If you'd like to see an example, try running the following script in **Background Scripts** and check the output by navigating to **System Logs > System Log > All**:

```
gs.info('Hello, world!');
```

> `gs.log` is the older, non-scoped version of logging a message. Although it does not work in scoped apps, it does have the advantage of a second, optional parameter that you can see in the log table. This lets you filter the messages in the list very easily.

The `JSUtil` class has an incredibly useful function to investigate the contents of a JavaScript object. `JSUtil.describeObject` returns a string while `JSUtil.logObject` adds it to the system log.

The following line gives an example of how `logObject` could be used:

```
JSUtil.logObject({'str': 'value', 'num': 1});
```

It is logged like this:

```
*** Script: Log Object
  Object
    str: string = value
    num: number = 1
```

> Unfortunately, JSUtil is not available from scoped applications. You may want to make a copy of those two functions and make your own!

Using the file log

The system log is stored in the database in the `syslog` table. Therefore, it is accessible from any node and could be manipulated like any other record. There is also a slight overhead when you write to the database, so writing many entries in a tight loop will slow down the instance.

Instead, consider using the node file log. This is a simple text file that is stored in the instance and contains more detailed debugging information. It is around 10 times faster to use `gs.print`, which writes to the file log, than `gs.log`.

Note that `gs.print` only works for global applications.

Anything that is written to the system log will also be written to the file log. However, the file log only records things that happen on that particular node. Keep in mind that you might not be on the same node as the user you are trying to help!

The file log can be accessed through several different interfaces, as follows:

- The `logtail` interface presents the log file in a continually updating text window. It is great to keep this open in another browser tab, enabling you to easily monitor the system. Access it by navigating to `https://<instance>.service-now.com/channel.do?sysparm_channel=logtail`.

- The file log is saved on the server with a name like `localhost_log.yyyy-mm-dd.txt`. Every day, a new file log is generated, and the instance keeps log files for about a month. You can download the one you want by navigating to **System Logs > Utilities > Node Log File Download**.

Note that a busy instance might have a multi-gigabyte log file, and even though it is delivered zipped, it can still be rather big. Therefore, try to use cURL to download it.

- To **search** through the log file, use the **Node Log File Browser**, available by navigating to **System Logs > Utilities > Node Log File Browser**. This lets you specify a date and time, along with some other parameters to filter. The session ID is very useful to only look at the entries for a particular user.

The file log is timestamped with US Pacific time, reflecting ServiceNow's San Diego roots. This can become immensely confusing, but the log file browser filter does convert the time for you when you are searching.

The file log and system log are intrinsically linked together. There is a related link on the system log form that creates a filter for the file log. It often shows a little bit more information about a request.

Logging appropriately

The `log` and `print` functions of `GlideSystem` are incredibly useful. They provide a permanent and central store of runtime information. However, there is a performance impact from logging, and especially for the system log, since the database must be engaged. Having lots of logs can also be overwhelming when it is difficult to identify what is important and what is not.

It is good practice to not record superfluous information. Logging is very helpful for difficult-to-replicate or rare errors, so reserve it for when it is necessary. Another strategy is to only log information if a property is set, meaning you can easily enable more detailed information if necessary. Consider the following example:

```
if (gs.getProperty('debug.hello', false))
  gs.log('Hello, world!', 'Test');
```

This only writes the message to the log when the `debug.hello` property is set to `true`.

For scoped application, you more options. The `isDebugging` method of `GlideSystem` tells you whether session debugging (**Session Diagnostics** > **Session Debug** > **Enable All** and discussed next) is activated, or if the property `<scope>.logging.verbosity` is set to debug. The following code example could then be used:

```
if (gs.isDebugging())
  gs.debug('Hello, world!');
```

In the rest of this chapter, we will look at many additional ways to find out what is going on instead of just filling logs.

Using the debugging tools

If the reason for an error is not immediately obvious, then it is time to use the session debuggers. Each provides an insight into what the platform is processing and the decisions it takes. This can even include watching all the database activity with the SQL debugger. There are many others too!

The session debuggers can be found by navigating to **System Diagnostics** > **Session Debug**. Once activated, they will continue while you are logged in and provide you with feedback until you choose to stop (by navigating to **System Diagnostics** > **Session Debug** > **Disable all**), log out, or your session times out. This means that you can enable debugging and then impersonate a user; the debugging will continue. This is critically helpful when you debug security or any other permission issues since an admin account is often treated very differently to a standard user.

You can also active debugging for a particular application scope with the following function call: `gs.enableSessionScopeDebugging()`

Debugging Business Rules

Let's turn on debugging to investigate some of the server-side scripts written earlier:

1. Navigate to **System Diagnostics** > **Session Debug** > **Debug Business Rules (Details)**, and extra output will appear at the bottom of the screen. It shows the scripts that have been evaluated while processing that page. The detailed version of the Business Rules session debugger also shows the fields that were changed by the script.

Business Rules are evaluated is several places. Display rules will fire whenever you pull up a record, and query Business Rules are fired when you issue a database query. This means that you will often see lots of output with this turned on.

Earlier, we made a simple Business Rule called `Maintenance assignment events` on the Maintenance table. It logs an event when the Assignment group field changes. Let's fire this Business Rule.

2. Navigate to **Hotel** > **Maintenance list**, and click **New**. Fill out the form as you wish, making sure to populate the Assignment group field. Once done, save the record. The platform will show an output that is similar to following somewhere at the bottom of the screen:

```
14:46:00.690: App:Hotel ==> 'Maintenance assignment events' on
x_hotel_maintenance:MAI0001010
14:46:00.691: App:Hotel <== 'Maintenance assignment events' on
x_hotel_maintenance:MAI0001010
```

Let's analyze the preceding output:

The first elements (14:46:00.690 and 14:46:00.691) are the exact times when the business rule started and finished. The arrow pointing to the right means the start of Business Rule execution, and the arrow to the left means that it finished. In total, this Business Rule took 1 millisecond to run.

In this case, nothing happened inside the Business Rule beyond the logging of a message on the screen. If the rule had changed a field, a message noting which field changed and how would have been included between these two lines. The output from any logging would also have be shown here.

If the Business Rule affects another record, such as performing an update of a GlideRecord object, this itself would cause a series of Business Rules to run. The output of those scripts would be indented and included inline.

The application scope is recorded, and the name of the business rule is given and rendered as a link. To see the code, click on the link. The table and the display name of the business rule is also given.

3. Change only the **Short description** field, then save the record again. Some different output will be given:

```
14:51:28.608: App:Hotel === Skipping 'Maintenance assignment events' on
x_hotel_maintenance:assign; condition not satisfied: Filter Condition:
assignment_groupVALCHANGES^assignment_groupISNOTEMPTY^assigned_toISEMPTY^EQ
```

Much of the output here is similar, except that the condition is shown. Since the condition did not return true, the script in the Business Rule was not executed.

Debugging contextual security rules

Besides **Debug Business Rules**, **Debug Security Rules** is probably the most frequently used option. Without it, it can be rather difficult to understand what the contextual security manager is doing. Let's start by performing the following steps:

1. Firstly, end the Business Rule debugging by navigating to **System Diagnostics** > **Session Debug** > **Disable All**.

2. Then activate the security debug by navigating to **System Diagnostics** > **Session Debug** > **Debug Security**. This will cause the platform place little bug icons on all the fields and again add lots of logs at the end of every page.

3. Once enabled, impersonate a user that has the Hotel roles; I'll use Polly Sherman again, like I did in `Chapter 8`, *Securing Applications and Data*. Click the User menu, choose **Impersonate User**, and select `Polly Sherman`.

4. Navigate to **Hotel** > **Maintenance list**, and select any record. Click on the little bug icon on the **Priority** label. This gives the result of the security rules, which are color coded appropriately:

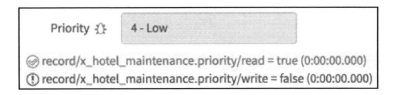

The message comes in two parts: the first message, (here in green) is the result for read access and the second is for write access.

The colors and icons indicate success or failure. The read access was successfully granted, but the permission to write to the field was denied. But why?

The text at the bottom of a form contains the details of every rule that has been run. There are three icons for each of the elements that make up a security rule: roles, conditions, and scripts:

- A green tick represents a successfully evaluated element. It means that the security rule element either returns `true`, or it is blank.
- A red cross represents an element that was returned `false`. This will prevent access.
- A blue tick or cross is a cached result. This is often seen on default rules – those with an asterisk in the name – because they are evaluabled very often.

The following screenshot shows the details of the rules run against the Priority field:

14:57:45.848: TIME = 0:00:00.000 PATH = record/x_hotel_maintenance.priority/read CONTEXT = MAI0001001 RC = true RULE =
record/x_hotel_maintenance/read App:Hotel   record/x_hotel_maintenance.*/read App:Hotel
14:57:45.849: TIME = 0:00:00.000 PATH = record/x_hotel_maintenance.priority/write CONTEXT = MAI0001001 RC = false RULE =
record/x_hotel_maintenance/write App:Hotel   record/x_hotel_maintenance.priority/write App:Hotel

This output shows that the user has read access to the priority due to the
`x_hotel_maintenance.*` rule, and that write access is denied because a role was missing.

If you hover over the icon, a little window gives even more detail: exactly which role is
missing, as the screenshot shows:

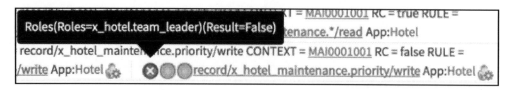

This shows you need the `x_hotel.team_leader` role to write to this field.

 Permission issues are very quickly evident. If an administrator can carry
out an action but another user cannot, it is very likely that a security rule is
preventing the user. Use impersonation to replicate and confirm.

Scrolling through the output will show you how much work the contextual security
manager performs. All the related lists and their fields along with the tables pointed to in
reference fields are also checked. This reinforces how important it is to have security rules
that execute quickly.

 Each rule shows how long the security rule took to execute. Be cautious of
any rule that takes more than a few milliseconds.

Enabling the JavaScript client side log

The debug log that shows the output of Business Rules is very useful to display which
Business Rules are running and when. To help with the client-side, there is a basic
JavaScript watcher lets you see output from Client Scripts.

The JavaScript debugger that was in previous versions of ServiceNow allowed you to edit Business Rules, set breakpoints, and inspect JavaScript variables during execution. This functionality has been removed in the Helsinki version, and will be revamped for the Istanbul release.

Seeing client-side messages

The alert box is probably the most often used way to display information. It's probably also the worst! It interrupts and distracts the user, and the message isn't stored or logged. In addition, for a user, it can be difficult to cancel multiple invasive popups.

 Try not to use alert boxes when you are diagnosing an issue or providing error messages. It can really affect the experience, and users typically don't know what to do with the information if they see it. If you must log on the client, use `jslog`, which is discussed next.

All modern browsers provide client-side debugging tools. These allow you to see client-side JavaScript errors in a client-side log, and the majority of these tools give you the same variable exploration, call stack, and breakpoints that exceeds the functionality that ServiceNow provides.

 Access the tools in Chrome by clicking on the menu icon and navigating to **Tools** > **JavaScript Console** or **Developer Tools**. In Firefox, go to the menu icon, select **Developer**, and then select **Debugger** or **Web Console**.

The **JavaScript Log** tab is a simpler alternative to these. It will display some debugging information that is otherwise displayed in the browser's console, such as which client scripts that have run.

Logging to the JavaScript log

A global client-side function is used to populate the JavaScript log: `jslog`. This will output to both the JavaScript log and the browser's console. Perform the following steps:

Firstly, ensure you are an admin, ending impersonation if necessary.

Activate the JavaScript debugger by opening the system settings menu in the top right, choosing the **Developer** options, and toggling on **JavaScript Log** and **Field Watcher**. Close the settings dialog to see the new section added to the page, as per the following screenshot:

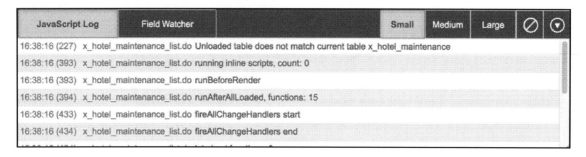

1. Select the **JavaScript Log** tab.
2. Then, in the main interface, navigate to a form or list and invoke the JavaScript executor that we first explored in `Chapter 4`, *Client-Side Interaction*.
3. Press *Ctrl + Shift + J* to bring up the dialog box.

The **JavaScriptExecutor** also allows you to explore variables. Change the drop-down selection to **Browse vars**, type in `g_form` and click **Show list** to look through the GlideForm-based object.

4. In the dialog window, enter the following example and click on **Run my code**:

```
jslog('Hello, world!');
```

5. At the bottom of the **JavaScript Log** window, you'll notice an entry like the following one:

```
16:26:15 (519) x_hotel_check_in.do      Hello, world!
```

> This shows the time of execution with the milliseconds in brackets. The page from which the message came is also listed.

6. Close the **JavaScript Executor** option and navigate around lists and pages. The debug output will be displayed, showing which client-side JavaScript is executed and how. The square brackets contain the information about how long the script took to execute. For example, the `Remove External Repair state` Client Script on the Maintenance form that created in `Chapter 4`, *Client-Side Interaction,* was executed nice and quickly!

```
16:32:43 (725) x_hotel_maintenance.do  [00:00:00.003] Remove External
Repair state
```

In the next section, we'll discuss the **response time indicator**-an alternative and more graphical way of knowing how quickly every element was rendered on the page.

The items in the JavaScript Log will also be put in the console of your browser. It is likely that you will prefer using those developer tools which provide much more functionality.

Tracking each page request

Each time that a user attempts to access something in ServiceNow-a list, a form, or anything else-the request is logged along with several useful data points in the **Transaction Log**:

- The exact date and time at which the request was managed
- The type of item, which includes **Form**, **REST**, **List**, **Scheduler**, **Report**, and **SOAP**.

You may notice just how many REST requests UI16 runs for Connect. Sometimes they become overwhelming, so you may want to filter them out. Note that AJAX requests are not recorded.

- The URL that often includes the query or record that was being accessed, for example, `/x_hotel_maintenance_list.do?sysparm_query=active=true`.

If the request is an update to a record, this will most likely occur through a UI action that contains the whole form as parameters. The action name of the UI action is recorded in a URL parameter called `sys_action`. The value of the parameter is the `sys_id` of the UI action.

- The username that made the request
- The IP address from which the user is connecting
- The node that served the request

This information is incredibly useful in narrowing down exactly when a user performed a particular action, and what they did just before. It may even help to verify and replicate their experience, just by copying the URL in the transaction log and pasting it into your browser.

The Transaction Log is accessible by navigating to **System Logs** > **Transactions**. The **All user** and **Background modules** provide extra filters for users to focus on interactive and non-interactive transactions, respectively.

 You can access several very useful reports by navigating to **Reports** > **View / Run** and then looking for reports in the **Transaction Log Entry** and the **Client Transaction Detailed Log Entry** tables.

Recording the time taken

Performance is important. So, the platform records many statistics to help you understand why things might be slowing down.

Every request into the instance follows the same pattern and involves three key groups of systems:

- The **instance** must work with the database to get the data and turn it into something useful for the user.
- The **network** must deliver this data to the user. The instance administrator typically has the least control over this step.
- The **browser** must understand the information and display it on the screen.

The instance records lots of time-based statistics for every request. This includes for how long the database was busy, the time taken by the network to send and receive data, and how long the browser took to understand the form. Each of these statistics is broken down to a granularity of milliseconds, letting you identify areas where things are working well or not so well.

The following diagram breaks down a page request transaction into these groups:

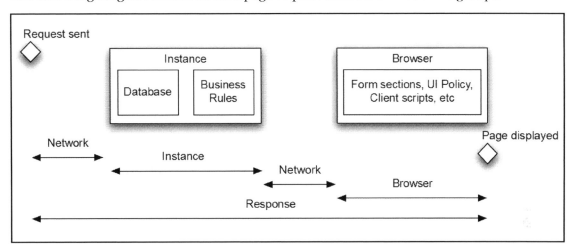

Monitoring the instance's performance

Once a request for some data is received by the instance, the platform will start timing how long it takes to produce the page. The transaction log contains the results of the following timings, listed here:

- The **server or instance time** is saved in the transaction log in the **Response time** field. This is a summation of the many activities that the instance carried out, indicating how long it took to process the whole transaction. This will be more than the addition of SQL time and Business Rule time since it also includes the time taken for form generation and other processing.
- **SQL time** and **SQL count** record how long the database took to deal with a request and how many SQL queries were executed. The SQL time is usually less than one second, though for complex home pages, reports, and global searches in particular, it may be more.
- **Business Rule time** and **Business Rule count** show the time that any associated scripts take to process the record. If these are particularly high, then it means there might be an opportunity for optimization, such as moving scripts to asynchronous operation.

Recording the browser's perspective

On the majority of webpages delivered by the instance, some JavaScript is included that asks the browser to run some timings of its own. Once the page has finished loading, the statistics are returned and stored in the database in the transaction log. This provides a holistic view of the user experience.

The **transaction time** is stored in the **Client response time** field. It's a simple summation of the factors that contribute to the loading of the web page. This number is obtained when the following three points are added together:

- **The network time**: This is the time it takes to deliver the response from the server to the browser.
- **The server time (from the perspective of a client)**: This is how long it takes for the server to respond, from the moment the request was sent to the first response back (this will very closely match the response time discussed in the preceding point, but it will not match it exactly due to timing inaccuracies). This is not saved in the transaction log.
- **The browser time**: A web browser needs to interpret the HTML that the instance provides. This will include building the DOM and displaying the page. A faster browser, such as Chrome, will accomplish this much more quickly than an old version of Internet Explorer.

This information can be viewed on the delivered web page. At the bottom-right corner, a small clock icon called the **Response Time** indicator can be clicked on to show the details on demand:

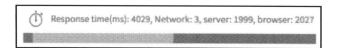

In this example, the user had to wait **4029** milliseconds (or 4 seconds) for the page to be displayed. This is made up of **3** milliseconds of network transmission time, and the server spent **1999** milliseconds to generate the page. The browser also spent **2027** milliseconds to render the page.

Breaking down the browser's time

You may wonder what the browser was doing for almost two and a half seconds: that was the biggest part of the transaction. Although it is not obvious, the **browser: 2027** text in the preceding screenshot is a clickable link. This expands to show where the browser is spending the time:

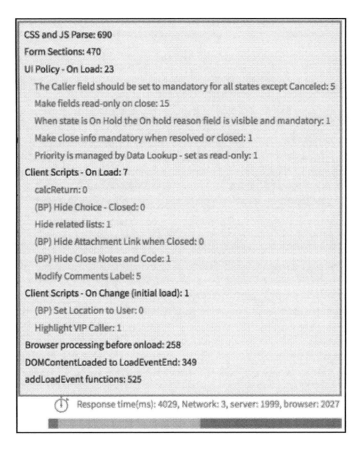

Some of the sections are expandable, providing further detail on how long the page took to load:

- The **Form sections** section times how long the browser took to render the form. In this example, the majority of the time was spent manipulating the DOM and laying out the page. The number of fields that are placed on the form has a dramatic impact on how long the form takes to load.

- The client side configuration sections break down each item. In particular, the on-load **UI Policies** and **Client Scripts** should be examined closely and kept as minimal as possible. **Display Business Rules** is often a very close replacement for these sorts of activities.

These items can be easily reported on to find problem areas. Try the **Browser Timings by Table** (form) report as an example.

Visualising the data

Another way to investigate the data is through the page-timing bar at the bottom of the page. Again, the bar is clickable, though it is not obvious:

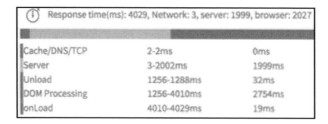

This reveals more details. Each section provides several timings: the first is the time in milliseconds from the start of the transaction to the start and end of the item, and the second is the time it took. For example, in the previous screenshot, the numbers can be explained as so:

- The **Cache/DNS/TCP** took no recorded time. The browser was table to immediately connect to the instance.
- The **Server** started processing at **3** milliseconds after the transaction started and completed its work in **1999** milliseconds. Adding these together shows that the server was finished processing **2002** milliseconds from the beginning of the transaction.
- The **Unload** time is when the browser receives the data from the instance. Again, the timing information records how long this took. This plus the next two sections added together to make most of the browser time.
- The **DOM Processing** section often takes up significant time as the browser deals with the information. Use the browser breakdown to see what this comprises.
- Finally, **onLoad** is the JavaScript that is called once everything is complete.

Going through other logs

In our journey through ServiceNow, we've already used several tables that are useful for finding out what is happening. Of course, you can use the techniques shown in other chapters to better get at this data: create scheduled reports and receive information via e-mail or put filters of the tables on a home page so that you are aware of issues quickly.

ServiceNow provides an overview homepage that collects some of these items together already. Select one of the **ServiceNow Slow Performance** homepages.

Some of the logs you may want to use are as follows:

- **The event log** (which can be found by navigating to **System Policy** > **Events** > **Event Log**), which was first discussed in Chapter 6, *Events, Notifications, and Reporting,* stores data about deferred or asynchronous transactions. Events often send e-mails or trigger script actions to run arbitrary code. The time taken to run these actions is recorded in the **Processing duration** field. If this is very short (under a few tens of milliseconds), then it is likely that the system did nothing and something has gone wrong.

Try not to fire too many events that do nothing. The platform will diligently check to see what is listening each time, which is a waste of time if nothing is!

- The transaction log also lists the runtime of scheduled jobs. If they take a long time (more than 10,000 milliseconds) you may want to optimize. A filter can be found by navigating to **System Scheduler** > **Scheduled Jobs** > **Slow Job Log**.
- **E-mail** communication, both inbound and outbound, is stored in the **Email** [sys_email] table. This is accessible by using filters in the **System Mailbox** application. Different form views are used for each situation, with outbound e-mails showing the events that caused them and inbound e-mails recording the details of the user it was from. If you need to track exactly when an e-mail was processed, the relevant timestamps allow you to match it up with other mail servers.

If you aren't receiving e-mails, step through the steps listed in Chapter 6, *Events, Notifications, and Reporting*. There are many steps that the instance needs to go through, and almost all of them can gone wrong!

- A few integrations, including the ones involving the MID server, utilize the ECC queue. It can be found by navigating to **ECC** > **Queue**, as discussed in detail in Chapter 7, *Exchanging Data – Import Sets, Web Services, and other Integrations*. It again stores outbound and inbound messages and lets you understand exactly what was sent and received. By sending SOAP messages via the ECC queue, you can keep a detailed record of the messages that were sent.

- The instance summarizes details about the REST and SOAP messages that the instance dealt with in the **API Transaction Stats** [sys_api_stats] table. It records how often each API has been called against each version, allowing you to see what the popular APIs are. Navigate to **System Web Services** > **REST & SOAP API Analytics** > **Usage Overview** or **Usage by API**.

- To log all the REST messages that are received by the platform, create a new property called glide.rest.debug and set its value to true. This will put a bunch of output in the session log. To access it, navigate to **System Diagnostics** > **Session Debug** > **Debug Log**. When you navigate through pages, you'll see output like the following – which shows the multiplication service being used:

```
02:17:23.718: #46096 [REST API] RESTAPIProcessor : Processing REST Request
/api/x_hotel/math/multiply/3/4
02:17:23.718: #46096 [REST API] RESTAPIProcessor : Request Method:GET
```

Finding slow database transactions

The transaction log shows an aggregated performance metric for how long the database is involved. So, how will you know whether the database is struggling for a particular query or whether your reports and lists have inappropriate filters? The **Slow Query** log gives you valuable insight into how the platform is used. You can access it by navigating to **System Diagnostics** > **Stats** > **Slow Queries**.

The instance uses a concept of total execution time. This is calculated by adding together all the execution times of similar individual transactions. Two transactions are considered similar if their SQL queries are the same, except for the values of the WHERE clause.

As a very simple example, these queries are considered similar since only the value of the WHERE clause changes:

```
SELECT * FROM task WHERE state = 5;
SELECT * FROM task WHERE state = 3;
```

In contrast, the following queries are not similar since they select different information and have dissimilar conditions:

```
SELECT number FROM task WHERE state = 5;
SELECT * FROM task WHERE state = 3 AND active = TRUE;
```

Classifying slow queries

By determining the total execution time, you can see where the database spends its time. Any query with a total execution time of more than 5 seconds is recorded. In order to provide a representation of what queries are doing, example SQL queries, URLs, and stack traces are provided.

A stack trace indicates what the Java platform is doing at that moment. Each line from the bottom up lists which classes and methods are being stepped through. As one method calls another, another line is added.

You can break down the entries in the slow query log into several categories listed here:

- **Very frequent and very fast queries**: These will have a high execution count but a low average execution time. These tend to be internal platform queries or from other scripts, such as those in calculated fields. I've seen instances where a "simultaneous update" AJAX script is run after the record is saved. This attempts to avoid one user "overwriting another". Although this check may only take 5-10 milliseconds to complete, it will have been done hundreds of millions of times. This means that, in total, the database will have spent a long time on this!

This particular script is often a hangover from older systems that performed record locking, which only allowed one user to work on a ticket at one time. In a more modern system such as ServiceNow, this becomes a process question: anyone can add Work notes, but only the Assigned to user is in charge of changing the ticket. Connect and the live form updates makes identifying which users are changing each field very easy.

- **Very slow queries that only happen occasionally**: These will have a low execution count. Often, these will be scheduled jobs or reports. If an example stack trace begins with `glide.scheduler.work`, then this is probably happening on a worker node. Stack traces that begin with `http` or have an example URL that starts with a forward slash (/) have been initiated by a user. If these slow queries happen when the instance is not busy, then they may not impact many users.
- **Slow queries that happen often**: These should be avoided and are often great candidates for optimization. Check the scripts associated with **Scheduled Imports** and look at the queries provided in URLs. You will often see `/home.do` as the example URL; this indicates a slow report on a home page. You can make it better!

Examining the Slow Query log

A development instance is unlikely to contain the same sort of results as a heavily utilized production system. My development instance spends the vast majority of its time on scheduled jobs. In fact, there are no user-initiated transactions that have taken a total execution time of more than 5 seconds.

Lets find some queries that fall into this last category and are candidates for optimization:

1. Navigate to **System Diagnostics > Slow Queries** and create the following filter:

   Average execution time (ms) – greater than – 1000

   Example URL – starts with – /

2. Order by **Total execution time (ms)**, with the **z to a** condition, so the largest is at the top:

> This should return a list of database queries that should have been initiated by the user. On average, the database takes over a second to return this data to the user, suggesting that the query is inefficient. On a busy instance you are likely to receive several examples of either lists or a home page.

3. Choose a record and investigate the **Example URL** field. For a list, you'll see the query that was given to the instance. One example I found gives the Example URL simply as `/task_list.do, sysparm_query=GROUPBYassigned_to`. In this scenario, the instance was asked to group by the Assigned to field for every task in the instance, which is a big job. This task took the database over 10 seconds to return the data, which is still not bad considering there are half a million records, but this is still something to be avoided. Here, the database is spending a long time returning data that is not necessary. No one will page through 500,000 records, so add a filter!

4. At the bottom of the form, you will see some graphs that have been placed into the form to show how often queries of this type are run. This can provide extra insight into when-and perhaps why-these queries are run.

Understanding behaviour

Most users use the modules in the application navigator as the starting point for queries. To perform the aforementioned inefficient query example, there may be a module called **All tasks** in the application navigator that returns all the 500,000 task records, and then users simply perform the grouping.

 Understanding what users are doing is often very instructive. For example, why did they perform this query? What are they trying to achieve? You may want to review the transaction log to get the answers, but simply asking them can be more useful.

Providing efficient modules that show relevant, filtered data is a good way to nudge the user into making more efficient queries. An optimization would be to add a time-based filter to the module and just show active tasks. This means that when the user does the grouping, it'll do it on a smaller set of records, hopefully making it faster.

Of course, education is critical too. Helping the users use the platform efficiently will speed up their interactions and make it easier for the instance!

Seeing the plan

The Slow Query log also includes a field labeled **Example** that contains a SQL statement. This will show you exactly what the database was asked to do and gives an insight into how more efficient queries can be made. This includes what data has been asked for and what joins have been made.

To get more information, the **Explain Plan UI** action asks the database how this query would be carried out. Then, a related list containing the data appears, showing which database indexes would be used (if any) and how the data would be selected. If the Key field is empty and the transactions are taking a long time, the queries may benefit from an index.

You can create an index via the Database Indexes Related List on the **Tables** record. Note that adding indexes may not always be beneficial; whilst it will typically speed up queries, the impact of record locking may actually slow down updates. Use the Explain Plan to find good candidates for indexes, but consult with ServiceNow Technical Support or a database expert if you are unsure.

More information is available in the Product Documentation: `https://doc s.servicenow.com/bundle/helsinki-servicenow-platform/page/admi nister/table-administration/task/t_CreateCustomIndex.html`

Dealing with other performance issues

The hints and tips in this book try to give the best possible experience of a ServiceNow instance to its users: administrators, fulfillers, and requesters alike. Tricks such as using client-side code to check a form before submission can really help the system *feel* faster.

However, performance issues can occur. An out-of-date browser running on a slow terminal server whose virus-checking tools are checking Client Scripts can quickly frustrate a user. Most of the time, there is no single issue that causes performance problems, but there will be a combination of factors, perhaps including some of these:

- The transaction log has a **GZipped** column. Research the circumstances of any user where this is `false`-this is a red flag! The instance compresses the HTML that is generated before sending it out, but it only does so for browsers that support it. All modern browsers do, but inefficient proxy servers or older browsers don't. These users will typically receive a poor experience.

- If there is a time period that is consistently slow-perhaps Monday morning between 09:00 and 09:30-where all transactions are slow, this may indicate there is **a scheduled job** that is sucking up resources. This is often an import, but it can potentially be an extract initiated from another tool.

- Every **field on the form** will increase the amount of data that the instance needs to prepare, how long it will take to send this data across the network, and the amount of effort the browser needs to render it. This is applicable for related lists or anything else on the form.

> Having large sections of the form hidden by UI Policy is a common configuration. However, this means the browser and instance do work that won't be used!

- **On-load client scripts** are usually unnecessary, and the ones that use AJAX should never be used. They require the browser to change the form just as the page is loading. Instead, try ensuring that the form renders the right way to begin with. Display Business Rules are very useful for this.

- **Reference fields** search through the **Display** values of records. Normally, this uses a `startswith` operator, but it can be configured to use a `contains search` instead. This query is much more complex for the database to perform. For 5,000 records, this will probably be okay. However, for 5,00,000 records, it will likely be much slower.

    Instead, use a feature that searches multiple fields during autotype. For example, you could search for both a user's name, their user ID and their employee number when filling out a reference field. This extra flexibility also improves the user experience!

Check out the product documentation for more information on this: `https://docs.servicenow.com/bundle/helsinki-servicenow-platform/page/administer/field-administration/task/t_ConfigAutoCompleteForRefFields.html`

Use **Client Scripts** effectively. If it does not need to be done immediately, do it on the server. For example, routing a ticket is probably best done by the server, especially if there are lots of rules to consider. It is best to do this in a business rule, but unless it is absolutely necessary, `GlideAJAX` may be an alternative.

In general, excessive configuration can cause problems. If there are large numbers of fields, client scripts, business rules, sections, workflows, SLAs, and so on, these can combine to create issues. There are very few hard limits in ServiceNow, so the platform won't stop you from creating and adding 200 fields to a form. However, it will be slower to use than one with 20 fields. Use the logging capabilities and test them thoroughly to find out what is acceptable for you.

Managing large tables

Large tables, such as Task or the system log, can become slow to query and work with. You need to balance the benefits of keeping data to give an audit and historical trail, against the disadvantages of clutter and simply wastefulness. Correspondingly, there are several functions in the platform that are employed for large tables.

Archiving data

It is best to never delete a task. ServiceNow acts as the store of all requests, and it is very useful to have a full audit trail of information. However, closed tasks that are more than a few months old are likely less important, and you certainly don't need them in a shift handover report. Removing them from the primary table will let the database work quicker, because it doesn't need to consider them during queries.

The **System Archiving** functionality lets you set a condition for a particular table. Most of the time this is based on the active flag and a date range. If the record is inactive and hasn't been edited for a year, it could be a candidate for archiving.

Create entries by navigating to **System Archiving** > **Archive Rules**, and when your condition is met, matching records will be moved into a separate table. This data is flattened and denormalized. This means that the archived record will only consist of strings; all references will be replaced with their display values at that time.

For example, consider an archived Maintenance record. Instead of having a reference to a Room or an Assignment group, the archived record just stores the room number and the group name.

The following diagram shows how the archival system splits records that were in a single table into two, along the lines of a condition. Typically this is whether the record is active or not.

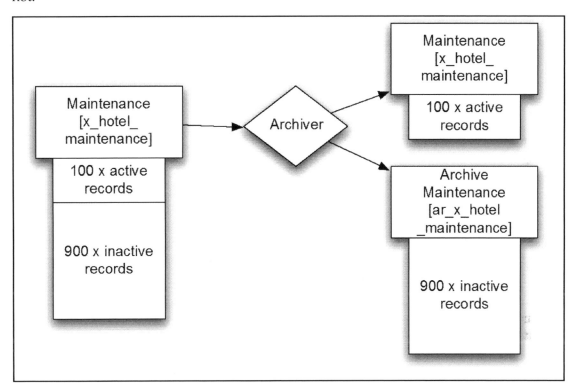

There are some considerations that should be kept in mind when you set up the data archiving plugin:

- The archival and primary tables are not connected. Searching or filtering in one will not show the matching records in the other.

- The exception to this unconnected behavior is reference fields. If you archive a record, such as an old maintenance task, any reference fields pointing towards it will continue to work. But instead of showing you data from the primary table, the instance will work with the archived record. (If you view the referenced record, you will very likely see a different form, with all the fields read-only.)
- You can change this behavior. When defining archive rules, there is an option to archive related records. For example, child tasks may need to be archived along with their parents. This is similar to the situation when you delete a record but the archiving functionality lets you choose different actions for different fields. You can choose from **Archive** (to archive the related record), **Clear** (to clear the reference field), or **Delete** (to entirely remove the record). Most of the time, **Archive** is the best, though it can result in a cascade effect.
- An archived record can be restored, which will recreate it in the primary table. The instance keeps a separate store of the original data in XML format (discussed further in the next chapter) in the **Archive Log** table. But be careful when you use the clear or delete option in **Archive Related Records**; then the association is gone permanently.
- If you wish to remove data permanently, you can. Use **System Archiving** > **Archive Destroy Rules** to achieve this. You can delete data from an archive after a while (thus making something similar to rotating a table) or directly from the table.

Rotating and extending through sharding

Some other large tables, such as the system log, are not archived. Rather than moving records into a single other table based on a condition, sharding moves data into one of several tables based upon the date. The table that records get moved in to changes every 1 to 30 days or so, depending upon the configuration:

- **Table rotation** has a preset number of tables over which the data is spread. If the last is exhausted, it starts at the beginning again, overwriting the contents of the first table.
- **Table extension** has an ever-growing number of tables. When a new table is needed, the platform simply creates another table.

Either method will break up a very large set of data into more manageable chunks that will be easier for the database to deal with. These chunks are known as shards. The use of a rotated or extended table is transparent to the user since the platform will decide which shards need to be queried in order to find the relevant data.

When a user looks at a rotated table, the platform joins (actually unions) all the underlying shard tables together, as necessary. If a date is specified, it makes the queries quicker since the database has to look at a much smaller dataset. Inserting new records is also quick. However, general search must involve many shards, slowing things down considerably. For this reason, always use a **Created on** date filter on large log tables. The following screenshot shows that a query for two months' data involves searching two database tables. If there were no date filter, it could search many more.

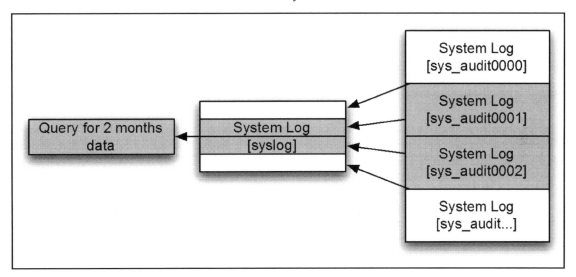

Choosing table extension

Tables that need to keep large amounts of data indefinitely but which will not be subject to searching are great candidates for extension. The baseline configuration has the Email table set up to use archiving, but you could potentially use table extension if you want to keep more e-mails accessible.

Selecting table rotation

Information that doesn't need to be kept, such as logs, is best suited to table rotation. This means that data can be written to it quickly, and the most recent information can be accessed easily, but it is self limiting. For example, after 8 weeks, the oldest system log shard will be removed. This keeps the table smaller and more manageable.

 It is worth checking with ServiceNow customer support if you wish to make any changes or additions to the baseline configuration. The tables involved are very large and choices made can significantly impact performance.

Auditing and versioning

Some tables, such as the Task table, are audited. Every time a record is updated, the platform records what was changed, when it was changed, and who changed it by recording an entry in the **Audit** [sys_audit] table. Every entry in the Audit table represents a change to a field. This is tremendously helpful when you diagnose issues since you can clearly see how a record was manipulated over time.

Turning on auditing

To make the platform audit a table, go into the Dictionary entry of the table and check the Audit flag. I almost always enable it on the User table since it is very useful to see how the records are changing over time. Note that you need to enable it for every extension, so turn it on for the Guest table too!

Let's see how it is done for the Guest table.

1. Navigate to **System Definition** > **Tables** and choose the Guest entry.
2. Use the Additional actions menu and select **Show Dictionary Record**.
3. Tick the **Audit** field and save.

You can turn on Text Indexing in the same place. This enables the for text option in the **Go to** search bar. You don't need to do this for the **Maintenance** table and the Guest table because they inherit the option from Task and User respectively. But you would need to do it for the new tables like **Reservation.**

Viewing audit

You've already seen the output of the Audit table. The activity log presents the data that is captured by the auditing process and presents it in a filterable, a more attractive way. However, it is possible to see all the data using the History Calendar view. If you've turned it on for the **Guest** table, navigate to **History** > **Calendar** from the context menu. This gives you a breakdown per change and can highlight them on a calendar-style interface. The following screenshot shows what this looks like for a Guest record:

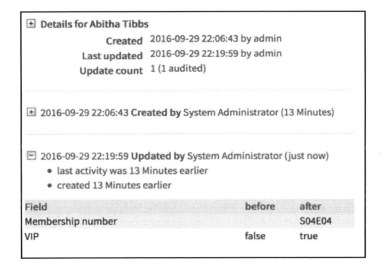

Using auditing responsibly

There is some impact from turning auditing on, but its advantages often outweigh the negatives. Consider the following points to get the maximum benefit:

- To prevent some very frequent updates from swamping the system, you can add the `no_audit` attribute to the dictionary entry of a field. A good candidate for this is the **Last Login time** element on the User table, which is very frequently updated.

- Never directly report on or even query the Audit table. Its size likely to be in several gigabytes. I have seen some instances getting overwhelmed with scripts that scan the Audit table, so don't do it! Use the History link instead.

- Don't try to change the contents of the Audit table. This is designed to be a permanent storage of the changes. To improve performance, the Audit table works in conjunction with the **History Set** [`sys_history_set`] table. The platform works to keep them synchronized, and it is difficult and quite risky to alter this behavior.

Versioning configuration

While the audit log is available for every table, **versioning** provides richer functionality for configuration such as Business Rules and Client Scripts. It takes advantage of the way in which applications capture changes in order to provide an easy way to compare differences and restore unwelcome alterations.

> Applications are discussed in the next chapter, where more detail is given about how this data is stored and which records are considered a configuration.

You may have already spotted the Versions related list at the bottom of many forms. Whenever you save a record that is considered to be a configuration, the platform automatically creates an entry in the **Update Versions** [`sys_update_version`] table. This stores details such as who made the change and when they were made. In contrast to the Audit table, the entire contents of the record are stored here and not just the changes.

Reviewing the changes

Since every attribute about the record is stored, the platform can easily show the differences between any previous versions and the current one.

In order to see this at work, use these steps:

1. Navigate to **System Definition** > **Business Rules**, and choose one that's had multiple changes.
2. In the **Versions** related list, right-click on on an earlier version, and click on **Compare to Current**.

   This will produce a page that will lists out every field, enabling you to see what has changed over time.

   What makes versioning particularly useful for scripts is that by clicking the pop-up dialog button on a script field, you can also see a line-by-line difference comparison. Any lines that have been added or removed are clear to see, and as you scroll, the two scripts are kept aligned, line by line. This makes it very easy to identify the changes that have occurred over time.

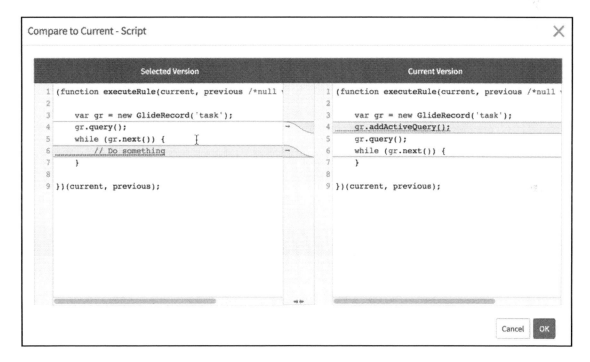

In addition to the changes that the System Administrators have made, the platform will also record the changes that are made by system upgrades. The **Source** field of the Version record will list in which version of ServiceNow the configuration was included.

If you wish to go back in time, you can revert to an older version. This also helps if you want to restore an out-of-the-box version of a script or if you determine that things were better the way they used to be.

> There are also list actions to compare two records so you don't have to use the current version. The list context menu also contains the commands to revert.

Optimizing hardware resources

ServiceNow allocates a pre-determined set of resources for each instance. As discussed in Chapter 1, *ServiceNow Foundations*, an instance is independent, and a high load in one should not impact another instance.

Nonetheless, users do share resources with all those who use the same instance. To ensure that the platform can serve their request, the following strategies are employed by the ServiceNow cloud operations team:

- **Horizontal scaling,** which gives busier instances more application nodes. The load balancer distributes users over the nodes. Read replicas are used to help fully loaded databases.
- **Vertical scaling,** which includes providing the right level of memory and database connections.

> These parameters are controlled by the ServiceNow cloud infrastructure team. You can work with your ServiceNow representatives if you feel these are inadequate.

- **Preventing long running transactions** and terminating those that exceed a preset time. By default, UI transactions that last more than 298 seconds will be automatically canceled. This is slightly less than the 5-minute timeout that the load balancer enforces.

Transactions that last more than 15 seconds will prompt a message and give the user the option to cancel them. You can also visit `/cancel_my_transaction.do` to attempt to cancel any in-progress transactions for your session.

- Other transactions are subject to different **quotas**. For example, the `typeahead` functionality on a reference field won't run for more than 15 seconds. A transaction started in the background can run 100,000 business rules, while one run via the UI has a maximum of 5,000. These are defined in the **Transaction Quota Rule** [`sysrule_quota`] table.

If you are manipulating a considerable amount of data, such as large imports and the like, you may start running into these limits. While you can adjust them, they are there for a reason!

- **Limiting session concurrency**, which means that one session cannot run more than one transaction at one time. This can be experienced by opening up multiple browser tabs at once; note that each will be served in turn.

To start a new session, start your browser in **Private Browsing** or **Incognito mode** or open another browser.
Some transactions may be marked as cancelable (using the `sysparm_cancelable=true` URL parameter). These will be automatically canceled if another such transaction comes through.

Gating access with semaphores to ensure that a running transaction has reasonable access to shared resources.

Controlling resources with semaphores

The ServiceNow platform uses a semaphore gating system to control access to system resources. The aim is to prevent one user from monopolizing resources and to even out access in times of heavy contention.

Whenever a node receives a request, it is classified into a set: it may be a REST message, the use of Connect, someone using the UI, or a debug transaction. Then, the platform sees whether there are any available semaphores in that set. If there are none, the transaction is forced to wait until one is free. This will, paradoxically, help the overall responsiveness of the platform since the platform does not need to switch between threads frequently. The transactions in progress have resources they can rely on.

> Sometimes you just need to concentrate on something to get it done. Semaphores work just like this, as would-be distractions are queued up in a to-do list!

On a smaller instance, you may have eight semaphores in the default set, which is the classification for UI transactions. This means that a maximum of eight transactions can be carried out simultaneously on a single node. The consequence of this is that if 10 users tried to access the instance at precisely the same time, 2 would need to wait. In reality, it is very unlikely that 10 users would need server time at the same instant since there would be some natural variations. In addition, the load balancer will spread out transactions across nodes, providing a natural scaling system.

Accessing the system internals

The system logs tend to focus on what is happening inside the application layer. ServiceNow also lets you dig deeper into the nuts and bolts of the server. Lots of statistics are available, including summaries of performance indicators, thread statistics, and more database information.

Understanding the ServiceNow Performance homepage

System Administrators can access the **Performance** homepage by following these steps:

1. Navigating to **Self-Service** > **Homepage**.
2. Selecting **ServiceNow Performance** in the homepage selection box from the top left.

The top controls specify the time range and the size of the graph (I always select **Extra Large**!).

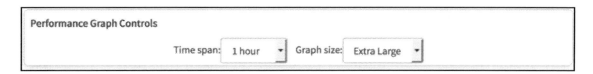

Performance Graph Controls

Time span: 1 hour ▾   Graph size: Extra Large ▾

The other controls let you drill into a particular node, focusing on particular attributes. Choose the node that you want to view by selecting it in the CI selection list.

 The typical naming convention is `<hostname>.<datacenter>.service-now.com`. You can review the technical details (such as uptime, memory, and database connections) of your nodes through the **System Diagnostics** homepage.

As noted in `Chapter 1`, *ServiceNow Foundations*, an instance is made up of several nodes. Every instance typically has at least two nodes, but an instance that is sized for a large number of users will have many more. In particular, a production system will have redundant nodes across two data centers, so the CI selection list of a busy instance may contain eight or more choices.

 Since the nodes are redundant, the nodes from one data center are likely to be very quiet, and with very little work being done.

The full set of data is very comprehensive and often not relevant to a typical System Administrator. However, the ServiceNow servlet set provides several interesting graphs that give you an indication of performance.

The **system overview** graph indicates how busy the instance is and what it spends its time on. Every second, it looks to see what each thread is doing and categorizes it appropriately:

- The `business_rule_mean` category indicates that a thread is executing business rules. This shouldn't be a significant part of the platform's work. If it becomes overwhelming, investigate the causes of this.
- The `concurrency_mean` category should be low, unless the server is very busy. If a thread is in this state, it is waiting for a semaphore or some other access.
- The `cpu_mean` category represents other processing that cannot be categorized as a business rule. Typically, this is the Java platform that is processing transactions. This is the bedrock of a standard graph.
- The `db_mean` category shows that the platform is waiting for the database. If a business rule is currently causing database work, it will be recorded in this state.

- The `network_mean` category is usually very low. This is when the platform is writing data to the network.

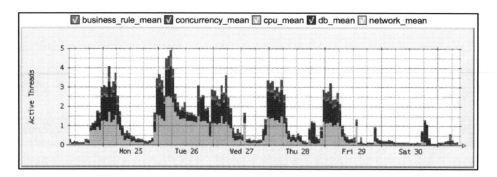

The number of **sessions** gives an indication of how many users are logged in. There are often more sessions than users, with a simple explanation being a single user might have opened multiple browsers. If an integration user doesn't reuse sessions and logs in afresh for each transaction, this will climb very high. This can potentially be an issue since the platform uses resources to maintain information that will never be used again. Instead, you should have the integration present the session ID authentication cookie to make things much faster.

To see which users are logged in on your node, navigate to **User Administration** > **Logged in Users**. The session can be ended if desired. Eventually, if there is no activity, each session will time out. The default is 30 minutes. Look here for more information:
`https://docs.servicenow.com/bundle/helsinki-servicenow-platform/`
`page/administer/user-sessions/task/t_ModifySessionTimeout.html`

The **session wait queue** is how many of the sessions are unable to progress with their transactions because the platform is gating their requests. Typically, this is due to a thread waiting for a semaphore or mutex. If this is a high number, it means that these sessions are waiting for a scarce resource or perhaps the database is very busy, slowing things down.

A **mutex** is a way to stop two threads from changing the same thing. For example, some code may attempt to query the database to determine the next record to work on. If two threads ask at exactly the same time, they will both end up working on the same item and causing conflicts.

The **transactions count** is a simple graph showing the number of transactions per minute. This is a great way to understand when your peak times are-most likely during working hours.

Response time graphs the maximum, median, and minimum time that a transaction takes. The median often hovers around 1 second.

The next few graphs focus on how Java handles **memory**. These are generally less relevant to the system administrator. However, if you are creating lots of custom Jelly pages, you may wish to keep an eye on the PermGen levels. Writing inefficient Jelly depletes PermGen memory and leads to performance issues and even outages.

Specifically, this happens when you use a JEXL (the `${<JavaScript}` syntax) in a Jelly tag, like this: `<g:evaluate> ${jvar_bad_things} </g:evaluate>` We touch on Jelly in `Chapter 11`, *Making ServiceNow Beautiful with Service Portal and Custom Interfaces*, but Service Portal now means working with it is less necessary.

The **CPU usage** graph is reported by the operating system. It shows how much processing is happening. The platform is not often CPU bound, so the graph should show user and system usage at a low level.

Finally, the **scheduler** shows how many jobs are being processed. If the instance is busy, jobs will begin to queue. For example, this will cause e-mail delays and slower asynchronous processing of web service calls. If lots of jobs are scheduled at the same time, try to spread them out.

The product documentation has a useful page that dives into these items in more detail:
`https://docs.servicenow.com/bundle/helsinki-servicenow-platform/page/administer/platform-performance/concept/c_PerformanceMetrics.html`

Flushing the system cache

In order to improve performance, the platform employs caching. Instead of continuously loading the same data from the database, the platform just grabs it once, stores it in memory, and then reloads it from the cache when it is needed the next time. Some of the items that the cache stores are as follows:

- The business rules and UI Policies that are associated with each table
- Contextual security rules
- The layout of a form

- Choice lists
- System properties
- `GlideUser` objects, such as the one retrieved with `gs.getUser()`

When the underlying records change, the platform should clear the cache appropriately in order to allow the use of the new configurations. For example, there is a Business Rule that flushes part of the cache when a UI Policy is updated. The next time that information is asked for, the platform gets it directly from the database and stores it in the cache again.

Sometimes, this does not work effectively and the values are not removed when they should be. This causes the use of old ("stale") configuration to continue. When doing development work, you may find that you need to empty the cache completely to force the platform to reread the configuration.

To perform a cache flash, navigate to `<instance>.service-now.com/cache.do`. You will see that the platform gives you some before and after figures for memory usage.

 Avoid performing cache flushes on your production instance unless it is strictly necessary. This has a big impact on performance!

The performance impact is considerable. Some example timings suggest that a cached form can be displayed in 150 milliseconds of server time, while just after a cache flush, it could take over 1500 milliseconds. This tenfold difference underlines how important caching is and why any clearing of the cache should be done with caution.

Reviewing the system stats

In the worst circumstances, an instance could be unresponsive and it isn't possible to view the system log, performance graphs, or even any standard page in the interface. This may occur when the database is totally overwhelmed. Since every standard page requires records from a database, severe contention may mean you can't see or do anything.

To enable you to see what is happening to the instance at a glance, even in times of stress, a page is available at `<instance>.service-now.com/stats.do`. You will always see the information of the node that you are currently allocated to. Therefore, this may not reflect everyone's experience.

There is no deterministic way to choose which node you are on. The ServiceNow load balancers make the decision. In order to continue your session on the same node, a cookie is set by the load balancers. Therefore, clearing your cookies and connecting again will force the load balancer to route you anew. If you try it several times, you may get lucky!

The Stats page provides a great deal of useful data:

- The **build information** displays exactly what version of ServiceNow is running. The build tag contains which release (Fuji, Geneva, Helsinki, and so on) and which hotfixes and patches are included (patch1, hotfix2, and so on). The node that you are using is listed at the top.
- The same **Servlet Memory** that is displayed when you clear the cache is also shown.
- **Servlet Statistics** provide counter-based information about uptime, the number of transactions, errors, sessions, and handled requests. This gives a little insight into the demands on the system.
- The **Semaphore Sets** section shows the current groupings in which the transactions are bundled. The number of semaphores is a big factor in the number of users that a node, and consequently an instance, can support. If users are awaiting session synchronizers, they are listed here too.

Most transactions get bundled into the Default set. If the instance is busy and you must absolutely see a result without queuing, try adding sysparm_debug_transaction=true as a parameter. For example, try /x_hotel_maintenance_list.do?sysparm_debug_transaction=true. This will cause the transaction to use the debug semaphore set (reserved for the JavaScript debugger), which will be much less congested.

- The perhaps familiar **server**, **network**, and **client** times are averaged over several time periods, from 1 minute to 1 day. This provides a better idea as to how the system is performing over time. To reduce outliers, a 90-percent statistic is produced too. This prevents very slow transactions, such as a difficult report, from overly influencing the numbers.

- In a similar way to semaphores, the **Database Connection Pool** controls access to the database. Some transactions may be held until the others are completed. Any slave databases are also listed here, letting you see whether the redundant systems are up to date.

 Full text searching is very intensive for the database. While the platform has an optimized search engine called Zing, it requires many queries to find the relevant information. A separate database pool is sometimes used to prevent these from swamping other requests.

- Finally, the **Background Scheduler** that was discussed in Chapter 5, *Getting Things Done with Tasks*, has some statistics. E-mails, events, SLA updates, and so on, all use scheduled jobs to perform work at the most appropriate time. The queue length is listed as well as how long, on average, jobs are waiting and how long each is taking.

Some customers want to feed their own monitoring systems with information that is provided by the instance. To grab all this data and a whole load more, use the XML data available at `<instance>.service-now.com/xmlstats.do`.

Summary

In a complex system such as ServiceNow, there are many elements that work together to provide the functionality that you need. Consequently, there are many ways to find out what really is going on.

The system log is the primary source for platform and application messages. It is especially useful for working out what just happened when you weren't able to see it in person. Use it to diagnose issues on the production system. Everything in the system log and much more is also stored in the file log. It is a more detailed read-only store of information. You can download it for forensic analysis. Additionally, the Transaction Log records all access to the platform and stores who did what and when. Timings are also saved, breaking down how long things took on both the server and the client.

Performance is critical for enterprise applications. If the speed of database access isn't quite what it might be, the slow query log will help you to identify what is happening. In addition, you can take into consideration whether archiving and rotating large tables will help, though this does impact on how the tables can be queried.

The auditing and versioning capabilities of ServiceNow let you record the changes on a record-by-record basis. If a business rule doesn't work out, then you can revert to an earlier version or find out who edited the user record.

ServiceNow provides a great deal of information about how the server and the platform are running. Semaphores are used by the platform to controls resources such as CPU time and the database. They stop one user from monopolizing the platform. They can also be monitored, along with many other elements, on the System Performance homepages and statistics pages.

In the next chapter, we will look at how to make the most effective use of your instances, how to share configuration, and what moving to production means.

10

Packaging with Applications, Update Sets, and Upgrades

A ServiceNow instance is independent. Making changes to one instance will not affect another. But since every customer has multiple instances, how should you move your carefully developed and tested scripts between them? Obviously, you wouldn't want to repeat the configuration over and over again, and copying and pasting is time consuming and fraught with mistakes.

This chapter explores the mechanisms that will help you to implement an effective development methodology, letting you release good-quality configurations in a consistent manner. It will review the following topics:

- **Update Sets** record configuration into groupings, bundling code and other items together.
- **Source control** lets you link your instance to a Git repository, letting you store your configuration in an external system.
- **Applications** provide another way to bundle work together, with Studio letting you publish them to other instances.
- All data and configuration can be exported and imported to **XML files** to make portable, self-contained stores of data.
- **Cloning** copies an instance, replacing the destination with a perfect replica of the source. This is the best way to ensure that two systems are almost exactly alike.
- ServiceNow releases regular platform **upgrades**, which can range from minor fixes and improvements to new applications and user interfaces. The upgrades are carefully designed to be as safe as possible.

Using your instances

ServiceNow provides at least two instances to every Enterprise customer. One is the production system that is used for live data and is used by requesters and fulfillers to do useful work. In the case of Gardiner Hotels, the production instance would manage guest reservations and maintenance issues. The other instances are sub-production. The software is identical to a production instance; it differs only with the resources that are allocated to it. Sub-production systems tend to be used only by system administrators and testers. Many more people use the production instance, so it needs extra hardware.

It is common for a customer to have three or more instances. The instance names are often the name of the company, and the sub-production instances are suffixed with their intended functions, which are typically a development environment and a testing environment. In the case of Gardiner Hotels, the instances may be called as follows:

- `gardinerhotels.service-now.com` is the production system. It is used by all the requesters and fulfillers.
- `gardinerhotelstest.service-now.com` is the testing system. It is used to validate new or updated functionality before it is released into production.
- `gardinerhotelsdev.service-now.com` is the development system. It is used by system administrators and other developers to create new functionality.

 These options do vary, so contact your ServiceNow representative for more information.

This chapter explores several ways to move information from one instance into another instance, combining these instances to produce an effective implementation cycle. Towards the end, we will discuss a common methodology for managing the instances.

Serializing records to XML

As we saw in `Chapter 1`, *ServiceNow Foundations*, virtually everything in ServiceNow is a record. The database stores all configurations, such as business rules, UI policies, and contextual security rules in addition to all the data, such as users, groups, and tasks. And while – Import SetsImport Sets, Web Services, and Other Integrations">Chapter 7, *Exchanging Data – Import SetsImport Sets, Web Services, and Other Integrations*, showed how data can be exported to CSV and Excel, those formats don't typically contain all the information of every field.

In order to get an exact representation of a database record, the platform can store data in an augmented XML schema called the **unload** format. This stores the entire contents of a record in a serialized manner, but with a few added instructions. Each field in the record is represented as an element, and the `action` attribute specifies what should happen when the data is read. As a truncated example, a business rule may be serialized as follows:

```
<unload unload_date="2016-06-09 07:46:52">
  <sys_script action="INSERT_OR_UPDATE">
    <name>My Business Rule</name>
    <when>before</when>
    <insert>true</insert>
    <update>true</update>
    <script>
      var gr = new GlideRecord('task');
      ...
    </script>
    <sys_id>62b8d8abebf21100be5be08a5206fe1a</sys_id>
    <sys_updated_on>2016-06-04 19:43:33</sys_updated_on>
  </sys_script>
</unload>
```

This data provides the platform with enough information to completely and exactly restore the record. Once loaded, a record will be created or updated, and all the fields will be identical to the XML document, including the `sys_id` value and the date and time on which the record was last updated.

If the `action` parameter in the second line were replaced with `DELETE`, the platform would not update the record; it would be completely removed without a trace.

Exporting and importing serialized XML

All records can be exported to an XML file. Simply navigate to a list, right-click on on the column headings, and choose**Export** > **XML**, or add the parameter of **UNL** to a list URL.

A maximum of 10,000 records are exportable via XML at one time. Think it over carefully before you raise the limit, because this can cause performance issues and may even encourage security breaches. Instead, you can use filters to get them in chunks.

Importing an XML file is powerful. The platform blindly follows the instructions given to it, and there is little trace of what's happened. To show what you can do, follow these steps:

1. Navigate to **Hotel > Maintenance List**. Right click on the column headings, and choose **Export** > **XML**. Click **Download** when prompted.
2. Save the file to disk, then open it in a text editor, such as Notepad or TextEdit.
3. Replace any field values, such as the **Short description** field, or change the **action** attribute to DELETE.
4. Navigate to a list, right-click on the column headings, and choose**Import XML**. The platform will ensure that the database reflects the data in the XML file.

This import will not trigger any Business Rules, apply any validation, or even leave much logging. This makes the import very powerful but also rather dangerous. Since the audit log is not updated, you cannot see who altered the data. Additionally, invalid information can be entered; you can change the sys_id field to anything you wish and break references. You must be extremely careful with this functionality.

Using the **Import XML** functionality on a list is very different from importing XML via an Import Set. The latter, as described in – Import SetsImport Sets, Web Services, and Other Integrations">Chapter 7, *Exchanging Data – Import SetsImport Sets, Web Services, and Other Integrations*, uses Transform Maps to validate and check data before it is put into the target table.

Transporting data via XML

Since the **Import XML** menu uses a precise extract of data from any table, this is a useful mechanism for copying information from one instance to another instance. For example, to move groups configured in the production instance to development, it is easy to export the production data to XML, save the file to disk, then import it into your development environment. This ensures that the development instance has all the same groups as production, including the sys_id value.

 Some configuration, such as Assignment Rules, relies upon data, such as groups, and needs their sys_id values to remain constant. As discussed in the next section, Assignment Rules are captured in Update Sets, but groups are not.

For more complicated situations, this process quickly becomes more difficult. Since the XML extraction commands discussed so far only contain the data from a single table, you may need to repeat the process several times. For instance, a useful UI Policy is made up of at least two records, one in the **UI Policy** [sys_ui_policy] table and at least one in the **UI Policy Actions** [sys_ui_policy_action] table. Each of the records would need to be exported individually and uploaded.

The file can be uploaded using the Import XML menu choice from any table. This is because the XML element contains the name of the table into which the data should go. This does mean that multiple XML files can be merged together, but be careful of making mistakes!

Recording configuration in Update Sets

Moving data via XML is useful, but what if the platform automated the process for you? In fact, what if the platform watched what you were doing and recorded the changes that you made to the records that matter? This is essentially a description of Update Sets.

An Update Set is a container for configuration. By navigating to **System Update Sets** > **Local Update Sets**, you can create a new **Update Set** or choose an existing one. The **Make Current** button on the form sets a user property to tell the platform which Update Set you want to use.

Alternatively, you can put an Update Set picker in the header bar, just like the Application picker and the Domain picker. It's a good idea to turn this option on (available in the **Developer** section of the **System** menu) so you can easily switch between them.

Now, whenever you make a configuration change in ServiceNow, the platform will create or update an entry in the **Customer Update** [sys_update_xml] table. This includes information such as the table you worked with, who made the change, and the Update Set with which the change is associated. However, the most important field in the **Customer Update** table is the **Payload** field. This contains the serialized XML data that represents the entire altered record.

 Whenever you do some configuration (which we define properly in just a moment), its current state is recorded in its entirety-it does not just record the delta. Update Sets also capture whether records (such as Business Rules) are deleted, if a field is created, or a form is reorganized.

In this way, the **Customer Update** table keeps a list of the configuration that is made on an instance.

Capturing configuration

Update Sets only record changes to **configuration** and not **data**:

- **Configuration** is something that affects how the system and application or process works. For example, scripts, workflows, field changes, and so on. Configuration is generally performed in the **development** instance.
- **Data** is typically what the configuration acts upon, for example, users, groups, and tasks. Data is maintained in the **production** instance.

This distinction is made for a good reason. Imagine that you built some new functionality, perhaps a Hotel application, in the development instance. At some point, after it is tested, it should be moved into production where everyone can use it, including the workflows, fields, and forms that you designed. However, you don't want your test user accounts and sample Maintenance tasks to be copied too.

So, if a Business Rule is created or a Client Script is updated, the system will record the event. However, if a user is edited or a group is updated, the platform will not create an entry in the Update Set for it. So, how does the platform know what to do?

The dictionary entries of both the business rule and client script tables contain an attribute called `update_synch`. This defines the table as one that contains configuration and is used by the Update Set handler to know what to record.

> Do not add the `update_synch` attribute yourself. The platform attempts to stop you, since adding it on a very busy table, such as the Task table, will cause significant performance problems. Update Sets are not designed to transfer data. Instead, consider using the **Add to Update Set** utility available on Share:
> https://share.servicenow.com/app.do#/detailV2/e7779b38138ea600f6 09d6076144b0a5/overview

Some configurations are handled more intelligently than just recording a single change at a time. The records that make up lists and forms are shared across several tables, and they interact with each other. This means that when you alter a form section, the position of every element is recorded.

To see exactly which tables are recorded in Update Sets, run the following query against the **System Definition** > **Dictionary** list:

```
Attributes - contains - update_synch
```

Many hundreds of tables are listed, which shows the vast array of configuration options in ServiceNow!

Transferring an Update Set

Once the State value of an Update Set is set to `Complete`, no further configuration will be recorded against it. Anyone who is using that Update Set will be warned that any further configuration that they perform will be placed into the default Update Set.

Even though there is a warning, get into the habit of regularly checking your Update Set to ensure you haven't been moved into the default Update Set. This should never be transferred between instances. Mistakes happen, but try to minimize them!

A complete Update Set is then ready to be moved. This can be done in a couple of ways:

- Using the **Export to XML UI Action**. This will give a single XML file that captures all the changes recorded against that Update Set. Update Sets can be uploaded through your browser by using the **Import Update Set from XML** UI Action on the **Retrieved Update Set** table. (But don't confuse this with unloading a record via **Export** > **XML** discussed earlier!)

Moving an Update Set via XML is a great way to share code. The ServiceNow Share platform, which is discussed later, lets you submit Update Sets to the community.

- One instance can retrieve Update Sets directly from another. Create a new **Remote Instance** record at **System Update Sets** > **Update Sources**. Provide a username and password to an account with the admin role on the remote instance. Then, use the **Retrieve Completed Update Sets** UI action, and the platform will pull in all the complete Update Sets.

Once an Update Set is set to **Complete**, don't reopen it and add any more entries. The **Retrieve Completed Update Set** functionality won't detect additional entries in an Update Set that it has already seen.

The ability to pull Update Sets directly from your development instance is a useful feature, since you will be sure to get all of the completed Update Sets and you won't miss any. It is helpful to have all the Update Sets the same on both instances so the previewing functionality will be able to detect if you are applying out of order.

Applying an Update Set

Once an Update Set has been moved into an instance, the configuration stored within it can be replayed. This will alter the instance as you require by deleting records, adding fields, and altering forms, depending on what the Update Set contains. The instance to which the Update Set is applied to is known as the **target** system, while the instance from which the Update Set comes is the **source**.

 Applying an Update Set may cause huge changes to your system. It will replay the instructions inside it, which may include deleting tables, changing field types, and changing core configuration

The process is depicted in the following figure:

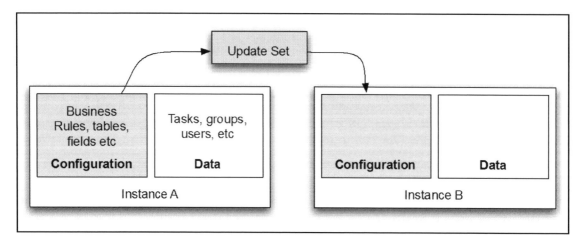

Before the changes occur, the Update Set is **previewed** first. This attempts to minimize issues by checking for what are referred to as **Preview Problems**. If any are discovered, the administrator must make a decision about what should be done before the commit happens.

Some of the Preview Problems that might occur are as follows:

- **Collisions happen** when the record on the target instance is updated after the one recorded in the Update Set. For example, imagine that a Business Rule is edited and captured in an Update Set in the source instance. Five minutes later, the business rule with the same sys_id value is edited in the target instance. The item in the Update Set is now out of date, and the instance will not apply it without further instruction.
  - The error shown is **Found a local update that is newer than this one**
  - In general, changing configuration in the production and test instances is very poor form.

 If you use Update Sets, you must always use them. Collisions often happen when manual changes are made to the target system. Don't change the same record twice in two different instances. Instead, use Update Sets or another controlled method to synchronize the changes.

- **Missing object** problems occur when two changes depend on each other. If, for whatever reason, a UI Policy Action is included in an Update Set but the UI Policy itself is not, then the platform will notice this and produce a problem. A mechanism to fix this is discussed later.
- **Uncommitted** or **reference** problems occur when Update Sets are applied out of order. Perhaps a field that has been created in an Update Set is included on a form. This is discussed further in the upcoming sections.

Understanding multiple Update Sets

Virtually every development instance has multiple system administrators changing and building configuration. While one user can only use one Update Set at a time, another administrator may be using a different one. This can cause some challenges.

Consider two administrators working on a client script, at roughly the same time. Each time they save their changes, the entire contents of the Client Script are saved into the Update Set. The platform will not add two versions of the same record in a single Update Set.

However, now consider our two administrators are using two separate Update Sets. Now the changes they make are saved in their respective Update Sets. This means that there are now two versions of the same record that are stored in two Update Sets.

The follow diagram attempts to show the situation:

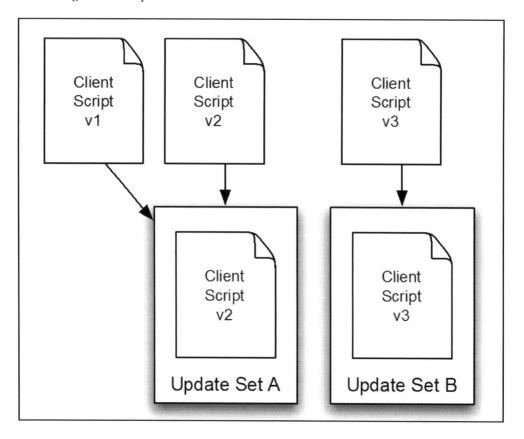

If the Update Sets are applied out of order (for example, based on the preceding figure, **Update Set A** is applied after **Update Set B**), then a collision problem will occur during the Update Set preview. The System Administrator who applies the Update Set will need to decide which version to keep. This may not be so obvious!

Relying upon other updates

Some dependencies can be detected. If a UI Policy Action is missing the UI Policy or if an onChange client script is registered against a field that does not exist, then the platform will produce a record of the problem. However, this is not always successful, especially when the dependency is in a script. The following diagram shows this situation:

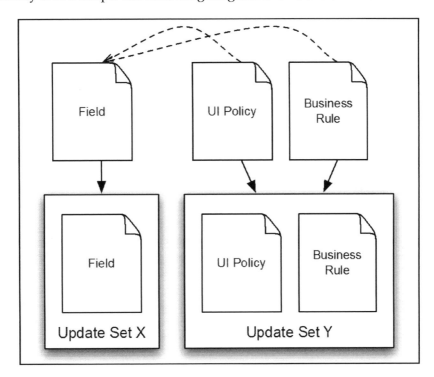

In this example, both the UI Policy and the Business Rule rely on the new field. Perhaps the UI Policy makes the field mandatory in some circumstances, while the Business Rule script will validate the data.

If only Update Set Y is applied to the target instance and Update Set X is forgotten, then the configuration will not be valid. UI Policies and Business Rules cannot affect a field that does not exist.

In this circumstance, an Update Set problem will be raised against the UI Policy. The missing field can be detected in the structured data, and the administrator will need to resolve the error.

However, the platform will not be able to detect that the script in the Business Rule is referring to a missing field. The Update Set could still be applied, but the script simply would not work.

Managing Update Sets

In order to reduce potential problems, Update Sets must be managed very carefully. When multiple administrators have several Update Sets open, it is critical that they use and apply the right ones. There are several strategies to manage this situation.

- Using a **single Update Set** for all administrators: This is the simplest solution where all the configurations for a particular development period are made in a single Update Set. However, if a staggered development cycle is in progress, some partially finished functionality is likely to be captured in the Update Set and promoted through the environment. This can cause unexpected behavior.
- Applying the Update Sets in the **correct order** and fixing problems as they are presented in the Update Set preview: This provides the most flexibility but is time consuming and error prone. This procedure may miss out on some dependencies.
- **Merging all Update Sets** before moving on: The Update Set merge tool will take multiple Update Sets and pick the latest version of each record from each. The resulting new Update Set can then be transferred to the next environment. The correct Update Sets must be picked for this strategy to be successful, and this is not always obvious.

Using the wrong Update Set

The success of Update Sets relies upon the administrator using the correct Update Set. Do you want that configuration to be moved now or later to another instance?

It is common to see a configuration recorded in the wrong Update Set. Perhaps the administrator didn't notice that their Update Set was closed, or he or she was doing two tasks at once and forgot to switch to the correct Update Set. If this happens, how can you move the configuration to another Update Set?

While it is possible to edit the Customer Update record and change the Update Set field manually, this is not recommended. It will cause issues, for example, if there is an entry already recorded against that record. In addition, never attempt to commit the default Update Set.

The safest way is to switch to the correct Update Set and make a non-destructive change to the record. For example, you could add a comment to a script or alter the Updated date using List Editing. Any change to the record will force a new version of the entire record into the Update Set – or use the previously mentioned **Add to Update Set** utility.

This concept is similar to the `touch` command-line program on Unix-derived systems.

However, this procedure is fraught with difficulties because all the records must be touched, including any related records. For example, all the UI Policy Actions must be recorded as well as the UI Policy record itself. Fixing these mistakes can be a very often a long and error-prone process.

Working with workflows

Update Sets and Graphical Workflow don't work well together. A workflow uses many records to store all the relevant information. Therefore, workflows only touch Update Sets when they are published.

There are several situations where the workflows won't be properly transferred to the target instance:

- When the main workflow is published, subflows are not recorded. Each workflow must be published separately to ensure that it is recorded in the Update Set.
- Update Sets will capture all the versions of the current workflow, but in some circumstances, it is possible to have the wrong version active.
- Variables are written to an Update Set upon their creation rather than when the workflow is published.

The best practice is to merge and transfer all Update Sets when you are dealing with workflows. There is more detail on these scenarios in the product documentation:
`https://docs.servicenow.com/bundle/helsinki-servicenow-platform/page/administer/workflow-administration/concept/c_WorkflowMovementWithUpdateSets.html`

Having the wrong IDs

Chapter 1 introduced the use of the `sys_id` value as the unique identifier of a record. Much of the configuration uses reference fields to record links between records. If the `sys_id` values change, the relationship breaks. This can happen when the `sys_id` value of the same record changes between production and development.

A good example is when the configuration relies upon data. For example, assignment rules are tracked in an Update Set as configuration, but the **Group** reference field contains the `sys_id` value of a group record, which is not included.

Consider a scenario where a new group is created and a rule is made to assign tasks when specific criteria are met. Both the Assignment Rule and group are made in the development system, but only the Assignment Rule is tracked in the Update Set since only that is considered configuration.

If the Update Set is committed to the production instance, the Group reference field of the Assignment Rule will contain the `sys_id` value of a group record that does not exist on the target instance. Creating a group with the same name will not fix the issue since creating a new record will generate a new `sys_id` value.

One way to resolve this is to export data such as groups from the source instance as XML. This can then be imported on the target system, which will help maintain the same `sys_id` values.

Alternatively, you can force the platform to add dependent data like this to the Update Set. Use a utility such as **Add to Update Set**, and use it to include the group in the Update Set. Applications have this problem too, but have a built-in way to include the records in the application, as we'll see.

The more proactive way to deal with this is through clones, and a complete enforcement of data always being created in the appropriate place (configuration in development, data in production). The way to deal with this is through a clone, which is discussed next.

Backing out Update Sets

It is unusual for things to work well the first time in all situations even if thorough testing has taken place. A completed Update Set has a **Back Out** UI action, which reverses the configuration that it contains. It will delete any tables that have been created, add deleted fields, and restore changed records.

Backing out an Update Set will restore a record to how it was before the Update Set was applied. If any records affected by the Update Set were altered subsequent to the application of the Update Set, the procedure will be aborted. This means that Update Sets almost always need to be backed out in the order they were committed.

The ability to back out Update Sets is sometimes used as a fallback to allow the administrator to "restore from backup." However, unless the Update Sets process is rigorously enforced, backing out a series of Update Sets while not be feasible. Instead, it is often more appropriate to "fix forward" and make the changes that are needed to make it work or even just deactivate broken business rules and other configuration.

Backing out an Update Set is fraught with issues, and while the functionality has become more robust, it will not always work. Instead, you can directly restore functionality using versions, mentioned in the previous chapter, and explored further later. This is much more targeted since you only roll back the single record rather than many items. Reserve the back out process for the worst-case scenario.

Using Update Sets effectively

Since Update Sets are sometimes difficult to work with, ServiceNow has layered on further functionality to make the process more robust. Team development uses a Git-inspired overlay over Update Sets, while Studio uses alternative mechanisms to collect and export data. It can export the configuration to an Update Set, to the ServiceNow application repository, or in an external Git source control system:

- The Application Repository is useful for storing applications and to deploy the latest version to the production instance.
- Team Development is useful for synchronizing changes across multiple development systems. However, it is often more appropriate to use Studio and applications.

- Update Sets are useful for storing the delta of an application or a specific version of that application, but should generally reserved for functionality built in the global scope.

The publishing capabilities of ServiceNow Studio and applications are discussed in more detail in later sections-use that whenever possible.

Cloning instances

Update Sets are designed to move some configuration from one instance to another. They allow administrators to push new functionality-or bug fixes-to another instance, thereby migrating only the configuration that has changed.

In contrast, a clone is much more complete. It shifts almost the entire database from one instance to another instance. Since ServiceNow stores pretty much everything in the database, this results in everything being copied from the source to the target. This includes all the configuration and the data. It could even include the System Log and Audit tables. The following figure is a diagrammatic representation of the cloning process:

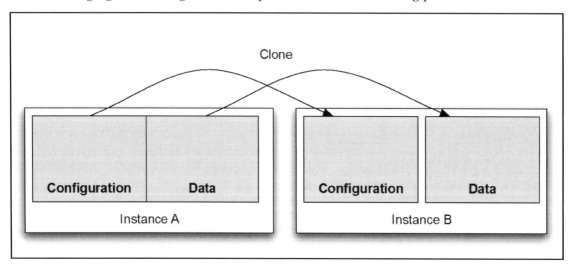

 A clone results in an almost identical copy of an instance. The target system will be wiped, including any in-progress work. All the tasks will also be overwritten. A clone cannot be undone.

Cloning is performed through the **System Clone** menu in the Application Navigator. Since it is so absolute, it works in conjunction with the ServiceNow customer support system, which records and schedules the work. This provides an opportunity to stop the cloning before it happens. It also ensures that the two instances run the same version of ServiceNow and perform any adjustments appropriately.

Cloning is accomplished by copying the database using a JDBC connection between the instances. This means that the instances must be able to communicate, so ensure that IP address restrictions do not block traffic.

Preserving and excluding data

Copying every record without exception between two instances is probably not desirable. Some items, such as e-mail accounts or some properties, are necessarily specific to an instance. In addition, copying e-mail logs to the target instance won't be helpful. So, ServiceNow provides some flexibility regarding which items are copied and which are preserved, as follows:

- The **System Clone** > **Clone Definition** > **Exclude Tables** list provides a short list of records that won't be copied from the source to the target. This normally tends to be logging information, but if a table is identified as holding sensitive information, it can be added to this list.
- The **Clone Data Preservers** work on the target system. Typically, all tables on the target instance are dropped and emptied before cloning, but if some items should be retained, a data preserver will keep them. Items that match a conditional criterion will be kept. For example, CSS colors are often used to identify an instance, and this is a way to keep them.

 Unfortunately, hierarchical tables cannot be preserved. This means that Task tables cannot be protected against a clone. For this reason, a clone cannot be used as a release technique.

- **Cleanup scripts** are the final items that run on the target system. These prepare the newly cloned instance for use. This is a great place for any obfuscation to take place, if you are copying from production. For instance, **personally-identifiable information (PII)** could be removed or changed from the Location or User tables.

A script always disables e-mails after cloning. Otherwise, scheduled jobs may send out notifications, resulting in mass confusion! Always check the e-mail outbox before enabling e-mails again.

Using clones effectively

Cloning ensures that two environments are identical, so it is a good idea to make a clone before any configuration work to existing applications. This ensures that the development instance uses fresh, realistic data for testing and development purposes.

The process to do so is as follows:

1. Clone from production to development.
2. Perform the configuration work.
3. Use Update Sets to migrate the configuration to production.

Using this technique provides us with several great benefits, as follows:

- Data used by configuration will be properly synchronized. This ensures that items such as Assignment Rules will reference the data using a `sys_id` value that is the same in development and production.
- Testing is more complete and accurate. Using dummy data often doesn't provide realistic scenarios as it is often shorter and simpler than real life. For instance, have you tested your new client script against a 30-character description or a more realistic 30-KB error log that has been pasted in?
- Development work is focused on real use cases and includes outliers and edge cases. If we consider certain real-world examples, is it right to assume that all users have a first name followed by a last name? What about Asian cultures, which may be the other way round?
- Optimization strategies can be found through in-depth analysis. Rather than focusing on every scenario, focus on the most used scenario. For example, which catalog items are ordered most often? How can they be improved?

Sometimes, it may not be appropriate to use all production data in development. ServiceNow does not typically hold consumer information, but if so, privacy laws may only allow data to be used for the purpose it was supplied. Testing may be excluded from this. In this scenario, consider obfuscating the data to remove sensitive information.

Packaging with applications

Studio provides a faster, simpler way to build applications quickly, easily, and with useful defaults. But it also provides a mechanism to package up your work, send it to another instance, and export it in an Update Set or in a Git repository.

> When an application is created, a new entry is made in the Application Picker in the System menu. This mechanism of selecting the app you are currently working on is similar to an Update Set; when you perform a configuration, it gets recorded against that application.

Application use cases

We first started seeing the benefits of applications in Chapter 2, *Developing Custom Applications*. The ability of scope to control how users and other applications interact protect the instance's ability to secure data and get stuff down. Additionally, as we'll see in the next few sections, scoped applications provide a great way to package configuration work together in a controlled fashion-and then share it between instances.

Applications are used in several different ways:

- To build a brand new platform application, without building on an existing ServiceNow application. The Hotel application built in this book is an example of a platform application: it is unconnected to other ServiceNow applications.
- To build an extension application, which extends and significantly alters a ServiceNow application. Typically, this involves extending ServiceNow application tables, such as Incident.
- To contain configuration of a ServiceNow application, without materially changing that application's purpose. Typically, this would involve not extending ServiceNow tables. Instead, you would use Studio to create Business Rules, Script Includes, and fields and associate them with an existing ServiceNow application, such as Incident Management. Studio and the application system would then be used to package and move this configuration.

> As of the Helsinki release of ServiceNow, a Platform Runtime license is necessary to build new Platform and Extension applications, but not to contain the configuration of other ServiceNow applications. Licensing is complex; ask your ServiceNow account representative.

Regardless of the type, applications are registered in the **Custom Applications** [sys_app] table. The metadata stored here describes your app and how it works. When you create a new app through the Studio (as in Chapter 2, *Developing Custom Applications*), you create an entry in that table. Select which application you are working on using the application picker in the System menu, just like an Update Set, or use Studio.

> The **Custom Applications** table is an extension of sys_scope. It is this table that all the artifacts (like Business Rules) point to.

The philosophy of scoped applications

Chapter 2, *Developing Custom Applications*, discussed that the scoping protection capabilities in applications is a break from the past, moving away from the old idea that the functionality running on the ServiceNow platform is not bounded by many rules.

Instead, the design philosophy of scoped applications gives clear instructions about applications will work, and how the platform will enforce it:

- **Applications shouldn't break the system**. The improved scoped API and the quotas applied to scoped applications means you can have more confidence that scoped applications run within limits. If things go wrong, the platform will intervene.

> There are standard limits defined in **System Definition** > **Transaction Quota Rules**, but you can also make your own in **System Definition** > **Application Quota Rules**.

- **Applications shouldn't break other applications**. As we saw in Chapter 2, *Developing Custom Applications*, Application Access lets you control how multiple applications work together. You can define how much co-operation there should be.
- **Applications should be self-contained**. It is easy to understand if something belongs to an app. Every Business Rule and Client Scripts (and every other bit of configuration) has a reference field that points to the relevant entry in sys_scope. There is no doubt as to where the functionality sits, which makes things like installation much easier

- **Applications should have clearly defined dependencies**. As we've been developing the Hotel application, we've been leveraging a variety of platform functionality. But as mentioned above, you can also make application extensions, which build upon other applications. You can clearly see the dependencies in the Custom Application record, accessed via the Application Settings link in Studio.
- **Applications should only access what they need**. In a similar vein, you can set controls about what system functionality the platform uses. The Hotel app currently uses many elements such as Workflow, the REST APIs and of course GlideRecord and its friends.
- **Applications can be uninstalled**. Being able to easily remove applications is a good thing. It gives confidence to install and improve applications, knowing that you can easily change your mind. There is not a point of no-return. The source control functionality, discussed in a moment, uses this to great effect when switching branches.

Identifying configuration

Update Sets use the `update_synch` attribute on a table to know whether it is considered a configuration. If the attribute exists, the Update Set handler adds a copy of the record to the current Update Set.

Applications have a similar concept of separating data and configuration, but the mechanism of identifying it is different. Simply, every table that holds configuration is extended from the **Application File** [`sys_metadata`] table. This means that each time you perform some configuration, you are making an entry in this table.

 To see what is considered configuration to an application, navigate to **System Definition** > **Tables**, and create a filter that shows everything extended from Application File. In my version of Helsinki, over 450 entries are returned, from the common Business Rules and Client Scripts, to more specialized entries like Interceptors and Guided Setup.

The fields common to all configuration includes a reference to the application itself, whether it should be updated on an upgrade, and whether the configuration is protected (read-only, non-readable, or available to all).

This means that a particular item of configuration, such as a Business Rule, can only be tied to a single application. It cannot be shared. When you create new configuration, the application you've currently selected populates the application field. If you try to edit configuration that is not in your application, you will get the surely familiar error message.

> This record is in the Global application, but Hotel is the current application. To edit this record click here.

In contrast to Update Sets, this makes ownership very clear, reduces mistakes and is an immediate benefit of applications: you know exactly what you are working on.

Moving applications

Once an application is built, it is likely that you will want to move it to another instance. To do this, the platform can publish the application into the ServiceNow store or to the private application repository or export it to an Update Set. Additionally, Studio can also store applications in a Git repository to allow distributed teams to work on the same application.

 Don't use a Git repository as the way to publish an application on your production instance. Instead, publish it through the ServiceNow application repository, as we will now see.

Publishing applications

Publishing an application uploads it to the ServiceNow Application Repository. Once there, it is available for download from any other instance that has the same scope prefix. This central location makes it very easy to install or update applications: reduced to only a few clicks.

You must be running an instance using a customer or partner vendor scope prefix to have these options. The free instances provided as part of the developer instances are restricted and cannot publish applications. If you do have the appropriate instance, follow these steps. This would typically be done on your development instances.

1. Navigate to **System Applications** > **Applications**, and select **Edit** next to Hotel.
2. From the File menu, choose **Publish**. The options that are available are determined by several factors:

- If you are running on a customer instance, with a vendor prefix, a dialog will open, letting you choose only to publish to your own instances. This will then be available to download in instances that share the same vendor prefix.
- If the instance belongs to the ServiceNow Technology Partner Program, you will have the option to submit it to the ServiceNow Store for review. You can choose whether to monetize it, allowing others to download it to their instance. Your app will be available at `https://store.servicenow.com`.

 There is more information about the Technology Partner Program on the ServiceNow website:
`http://www.servicenow.com/partners.html`

To download an application from your private application repository, follow these steps. This would typically be done on your test and production instances.

1. Navigate to **System Applications** > **Applications**, and select the **Downloads** tab.
2. The application that was published using the **My Instances** option should be listed. Click on **Install**.

Publishing applications has the advantage that updates to applications are quick and easy. There is no need to deal with uploading and downloading Update Sets, and because of the benefits of the scoped application model, there are no conflicts!

Exporting applications

All instances can export an application to an Update Set. This gives you a single file that contains all the configuration contained within an application. This can be useful as a backup or if the Application Repository cannot be used:

1. Navigate to the **Custom Application** [sys_app] table. Perhaps the easiest way to do this is to type sys_app.list in the Application Navigator filter and press Enter.

 You may want to add a new Module to the System Applications menu to give you easier access.

2. Choose the Hotel application, and click on **Publish to Update Set...**
3. Fill in the **Version** and **Description** if desired, and choose **Publish**.

It is better to add data to the application by making application files rather than relying on the Include demo data option. This is covered in the next section.

4. An Update Set with the status set to **Completed** will be created, and you will be redirected to the record. This can then saved to disk by clicking on the **Export to XML** UI Action.

Using a Git repository

Source control is a necessity when building more complex applications, whether using ServiceNow or not. They bring great advantages, including a mechanism of sharing code between many developers, having multiple versions that can quickly be switched between, and tracking the history of changes.

ServiceNow introduced the concept of **Team Development** in the Dublin release of ServiceNow. This brought some Git-style concepts to ServiceNow, including comparing instances and pushing and pulling record versions between instances. However, the Helsinki version of ServiceNow supports Git repositories directly, letting you store applications in either your own repository or a public service such as GitHub.

Whilst team development is still available, and is perhaps useful if you are not using scoped applications, using Git provides many advantages, including clearer usage, more functions, and off-instance storage of the code.

Many of the useful functions of a Git client are available in ServiceNow. Let's explore some of the options. Do not carry out these out if the Hotel application is already linked to a Git repository, which you may have done in Chapter 1, *ServiceNow Foundations*.

If you imported the Hotel application from the Update Set, follow these steps:

1. Create a new repository. GitHub provides them for free, though only paid-for plans include making repositories private. Sign up at `https://www.github.com/` and create a new repository. You should end up with a repository URL like `https://github.com/<username>/<repository>`.

There are many other services, including Bitbucket and GitLab. GitHub required a paid account to have a private repository, while those are free.

2. Open up Studio via **System Applications** > **Applications**. Choose **Edit** next to **Hotel**.

3. In the **Source Control** menu, click on **Link to Source Control**, set the following values, and then click **Link to Source Control**:
   - **URL:** `<the repository URL from GitHub or otherwise>`
   - **User name:** `<your GitHub username>`
   - **Password:** `<your GitHub password>`

The account will need read-write access. Note that all users of the instance will use these credentials. Your GitHub account is linked to the instance, not your ServiceNow user account. This means you won't know from GitHub which ServiceNow user checked things in and out.

Once the Hotel application has been pushed, open up the GitHub website, and see what has been created in the repository. See how the configuration has been serialized into XML to be stored.

More options are now available in the **Source Control** menu in Studio. These perform Git commands:

- **Apply Remote Changes** performs a pull. This ensures the local application matches the one on the Git server. If you have locally changed files on your instance, you get the option to stash them. This saves them locally so that you can apply them to the newly refreshed application.

For example, you may have modified the Reservations form of the Hotel application but know that someone else working on another instance has created some Business Rules and saved their progress to the Git repository. You can use **Apply Remote Changes** to get the updated application, including the other user's Business Rules, while temporarily stashing your form updates. Once the application has been updated, you could then see whether your edits still make sense and apply or discard them.

Using **Apply Remote Changes** frequently helps ensure everyone is working on the same code. If there are conflicts, with the Git server storing changed configuration that you are also working on, then you will be prompted to resolve the conflicts, just like in an Update Set.

- **Commit Changes** is a push. It updates the Git repository with the application. It's a good idea to do this regularly to help keep others up to date, monitor progress, and see how the application changes over time. Provide a commit message as documentation.
- **Stash Local Changes** grabs the latest changes from the Git server, while saving your current progress. It essentially does the same thing as Apply Remote Changes, but doesn't provide the choice of stashing or discarding local changes-it always stashes.
- **Create Branch** lets you start working in a different direction. It lets you create a new feature or fix a bug without jeopardising the main code base. For example, you may wish to add a few new fields to the form and write some business logic, but you aren't ready to have everyone else receive these changes. Or perhaps you need to fix a bug in the production version of an application without introducing all the new features. If you are not using a branch, you are using master-the central code base. All branches are stored on the Git server.
- **Switch Branch** lets you switch between the branches. It does so by uninstalling the current application and recreating it from the source on Git. The branch you are currently using is in the top right of the Studio.
- **Create tag** is often used to specify a release by providing a version number. It highlights this point as important, and effectively serves as a release. GitHub lets you download the zipped code for a particular tag very easily, for example.

Unfortunately, Studio does not support the Git `merge` command. This is very important for bringing two branches together again. Consider that you created some experimental feature in a new branch and decided that you wanted to keep it and include it as part of the main code base. The `merge` command enables you to bring both parts together. Instead, use the stash to apply the same configuration to two branches, by following this procedure:

- Switch to the experimental branch, and then make the changes you need to.
- Use **Stash Local Changes**, which will save your edits, pull the latest code, and then choose to apply them to the application.
- Commit your changes to the repository, and then switch back to the other branch.
- Finally, using **Manage Stashes**, apply the local stashed changes to the second branch.

You may want to use Git tools directly (such as the GitHub interface) and merge two branches manually, but it is very likely to fail. Don't do it! The mechanisms that Git uses to deal with conflicts are not sensitive to the format that ServiceNow uses, and unless you fully understand how to edit the unload format, it will result in the application not matching the checksum. If this happens, the instance will not import the repository, and you will need to manually revert the changes.

Using source control effectively

Source control is a great way to manage multiple versions of the application. You can have different branches of the same application, say, one for your production code and another for a version in development. While it is not as elegant as a proper merge, you can work around it.

Source control is however much more effective than Team Development-and especially Update Sets-for developing in multiple instances. With source control, each instance stays more independent, but the applications are shared. Each administrator should commit their changes frequently so conflicts can be caught early.

Including data in applications

Applications typically include only configuration: things such as business rules, tables, fields and form layouts. As discussed previously in the Having the wrong IDs section, sometimes, configuration can depend on data, such as a group or a user. Alternatively, you may want to provide sample data in an application to demonstrate usage or options.

Applications use Application Files to record what database record is associated with an application. All records associated with that application are included when an application is published or exported. While data does not have Application Files automatically created, you can make them manually. Let's ensure that the Maintenance group is part of the application so that the `sys_id` stays the same and the Assignment Rules work.

 Don't move anything you haven't created into an application. If you move a ServiceNow Business Rule or Script Include into an application it will almost certainly break. Only move data in.

To do so, follow these steps:

1. Navigate to **Hotel** > **Maintenance groups**.
2. Using the checkboxes, tick the records you want to include. Select all three group checkboxes for this example.

 Alternatively, you can use the menu option of **Create Application Files** to include all records that meet the current list filter.

3. Using the **Actions on selected rows...** selection box, choose **Create Application File**. A dialog box will appear.
4. The dialog lets you choose what sort of data this is using the **Load When** selection:
   - **New Install and Upgrades** will be included each time this application is installed. Use this for data that is absolutely necessary for proper application functioning. It will overwrite any changes on the target instance.
   - **New Install** will only be included the first time the application is installed. This is useful for providing data that may be modified on the target instance.
   - **New Install with Demo Data** provides the option to include it when it is being installed.

5. Ensure **New Install and Upgrades** is selected, so we can be sure the group is always present.

6. When you click on **OK**, the instance creates a **Metadata Snapshot** [sys_metadata_link] record, which include the table name, the sys_id value of the originating record, and the record in serialized XML form. This table is an extension of the **Application File** table, and so will be included in any application export.

 The capture of data is a one-time snapshot, taken at the time of the creation of the **Application File**. If the original record changes, the updates are not copied into the metadata snapshot.

7. Finally, you may wish to copy across the group membership too. This ensures that your admin user will be included as a member of the Maintenance group. To do this, navigate into the Maintenance group record, and under Group Members, tick System Administrator (or as appropriate), then choose **Create Application File** again, clicking OK when done.

Sharing with Share

ServiceNow customers are rather creative. The platform has been used to build some amazing developer functions, useful tweaks, and powerful utilities. To help everyone benefit from ideas from the platform, the ServiceNow **Share** portal is designed to bring them all together in a very accessible manner. You can visit the ServiceNow Share portal at https://share.servicenow.com/.

Any customer can submit an Update Set to be stored on Share. This is then available for other customers to download and use as they wish. Some of the more popular items on Share are as follows:

- **Dynamic Knowledge Search** provides a means to automatically search the knowledge base
- **Xplore: Developer Toolkit** adds extra features to understand server- and client-side JavaScript objects, visualise the table structure, and test regular expressions
- **Client-Side PDF Document Generator**allows you to create custom PDF documents from a record
- **File Builder FTP** exports data from the instance and uses a MID server to save it on an FTP server
- **UAT Application** manages the users and their tasks when it tests your ServiceNow application

Content that is shared this way is not supported or vetted by ServiceNow. Some basic scans of the content do take place to encourage good practice, but any applications that are installed should be understood, especially if they are to be relied on.

Selling on ServiceNow Store

While Share focuses on utilities and tweaks, ServiceNow Store is designed to offer more fully featured applications and integrations. This results in the following differences:

- ServiceNow only accepts applications that have been checked and verified to ensure they meet guidelines to protect the security and performance of the instance.
- While many applications are free, a significant proportion are paid for. They can typically be trialed before purchase. ServiceNow handles the billing.
- The application creators are responsible for supporting the application.

You can visit ServiceNow Store at https://store.servicenow.com/. Once purchased, applications appear in the list at **System Applications** > **Applications**, under the **Downloads** tab.

Only partners registered for the Technology Partner Program can list applications on the store.

Adding more with plugins

Every ServiceNow instance includes many hundreds of plugins. Each contains a different part of the ServiceNow system: some provide licensable functionality, some provide integrations or additional add-ons, and some provide core platform capabilities. Together, they provide all of the native functionality of ServiceNow.

There is a wide variety of capabilities contained within plugins. This short selection gives an indication of what is available:

- **Approvals with e-Signature**asks for your username and password whenever you perform an approval
- **Coaching Loops** lets your staff review how a task has been completed by using an automated framework

- **Email Filters** helps you delete spam automatically and sort the rest into separate mailboxes
- **Restore Deleted Records** stores deleted records as serialized XML, letting you undo some mistakes
- **Self Service Password Reset** allows users to reset their ServiceNow password if they forget it

To see the available plugins, navigate to **System Definition** > **Plugins**.

The Product Documentation also has a full list of plugins at `https://docs.servicenow.com/bundle/helsinki-it-service-management/page/administer/plugins/reference/r_ListOfPlugins.html`.

Activating plugins

Some plugins are activated by default when the platform is started up for the first time. These include the ITSM applications or those that contain the core capabilities of the platform. Others require activation. Of these, a system administrator can activate some plugins, while others must be turned on using an account with the `maint` role-a privilege that is generally reserved for ServiceNow personnel. It could be possible that one of these plugins will enable functionality that is licensable separately, or may cause functionality changes that need to be controlled. To enable those plugins, use the Hi Customer Support system and submit a plugin activation request.

The activation of a plugin is not recorded within an Update Set. If a plugin is necessary for some configuration, ensure that it is manually enabled before any Update Sets are applied.

Plugins can be considered very similar to Update Sets. They consist of a package of serialized XML data files that are stored on the filesystem of the instance. Once a plugin is activated, the data is copied into the appropriate records of the instance database. A plugin may contain additional tables and fields, Business Rules, Application Menus, or any other record, just like the applications a system administrator can make.

Activating a plugin creates database records. They do not alter what the core Java platform can do. However, a plugin may activate latent functionality that is not otherwise exposed.

Choosing the right plugin

Since there are so many plugins, it can be difficult to know which are useful. It is tempting to turn them all on, just like that, but there are some disadvantages with this:

- Once a plugin is enabled, it cannot be turned off. It is a decision that cannot be reversed.
- Some plugins affect existing functionality. This may be an upgrade to an existing app, but you cannot roll back if you don't like the changes. Domain Separation is a good example here.

 Often, you can set a property to deactivate functionality, but you won't be able to remove it entirely.

- Plugins often have demo data. This is very helpful to understand what the plugin does, but it may create data you weren't expecting.
- Enabling lots of plugins may make areas cluttered, such as the Application Navigator. It is difficult to navigate through lots of options that you don't actually need.

The only way to reverse the effects of a plugin activation is to arrange a clone or ask customer support to restore the instance from the previous night's backup. Be cautious about which plugins you activate.

Instead, try out new plugins in a sandpit environment or be prepared to clone over your instance if it doesn't work out.

Configuration and customization

ServiceNow provides a great deal of functionality. However, the platform is also designed to be adaptable to specific requirements that are not available out of the box. The platform and any ServiceNow apps can be configured or customized to make them work as desired.

But there is always a tension when building new functionality: can I make it it secure? Will it be fast? Can I maintain it easily? Will platform upgrades be straightforward? As discussed in the previous section, ServiceNow has designed scoped applications to help as much as possible, and if you build in an application, the risk of your app doing something 'bad' is low.

But what happens when you build in the global scope? Unlike some other software, it is difficult to define the difference between configuration and customization. It is generally accepted that the former is less at risk of you regretting it later, and the latter is something you should only do if you have to.

- **Configuration** is generally defined as the addition of new records. It's a new business rule that updates a new field, which in turn triggers a new graphical workflow. Anything you create in a scoped application has got the highest protection.
- **Customization** is accepted to be the alteration of existing, out-of-the-box records or those provided through an upgrade. For example, if the way in which SLAs are calculated is not the same as your business, then the Script Include can be edited-even though this may not be a good idea!

 Both configuration and customization happen in the same way through the standard interface. The only difference is if you are creating something new or editing something provided by ServiceNow.

During an upgrade, the platform will avoid changing any configuration or customization. This is by design. Simply overwriting all the changes may undo your hard work and mean that the platform no longer meets your needs.

Knowing areas of risk

ServiceNow provides enormous flexibility. Almost everything about the platform can be edited and changed. However, it is recommended that you avoid customizations whenever possible. An upgrade will avoid overwriting them, but you may miss out on improvements and bug fixes. The customization of a particular record is, therefore, referred to as the system administrator **owning** the record. This refers to how the system administrator, rather than ServiceNow, is responsible for the maintenance of this item.

 Some configuration and customization will result in disadvantages, such as maintenance or performance, as mentioned throughout this book. There is no single rule to follow, other than understanding how the platform works so that decisions can be taken with all the available facts.

Owning some areas are very low risk. It is expected that the system administrator would want to control these items by performing the following steps:

- **Data, such as users and groups**: It would not be appropriate to keep the demo user data, such as Fred Luddy, in your instance.
- **Adding fields, forms, lists, and UI actions**: Within reasonable limits, you can add as many fields to a form as you wish and name them as you like. Adding many hundreds though will result in slower rendering times, both on the server and on the client browser.
- **Adding scripts, such as business rules and client scripts**: This is a very common activity. However, inefficient scripting, such as performing synchronous calls from the client to the instance, will result in performance issues.

Other areas involve more risk. Many of these have been restricted in the scoped API. Even if you are building in the global scope, consider these actions carefully:

- **Editing existing scripts**: Any scripts edited by the system administrator will be kept after an upgrade; however, other areas of the platform may assume that a script works in a particular way or a function returns a particular range of values. After any upgrade, be sure to test it carefully.
- **Performing DOM manipulation in client scripts**: This assumes that the DOM will remain the same after an upgrade. Ensure that code is written in such a way that a script will "fail safe" if it does not.
- **Editing existing UI macros and UI pages**: This is not recommended since it changes how the platform renders the interface. UI Macros and UI Pages are discussed further in Chapter 11, *Making ServiceNow Beautiful with Service Portal and Custom Interfaces*.
- **Using package calls on the instance**: – Import Sets, Web Services, and other Integrations">Chapter 7, *Exchanging Data – Import Sets, Web Services*, and other Integrations discussed how MID server scripts could use Java packages. It is possible to access Java classes on the instance, depending on the version, but this is strongly discouraged.

Protecting your scripts

If you are building an application, especially one for the Store, you may not want people to alter or even see your code. To help, you can change the Protection Policy for a Script Include. This will hide and encrypt the script fields when it is installed on another instance.

To see how it is done, follow these steps:

1. Navigate to **System UI > Script Includes**.
2. Select the `square` Script Include to show the form.
3. At the bottom should be the Protection Policy field. By default it is `Read-only`, but change it to `Protected` and Save.

You can also find the field by using the Additional actions menu, and choosing Show File Properties. You could set other records to Read-only to prevent them being changed.

This setting will only take affect when the application is downloaded from the Application Repository. It will not affect records that are exported or saved into a Git repository through Source Control.

Upgrading ServiceNow

ServiceNow has a quite unique upgrade capability due to its cloud-based, single-tenant architecture. Releases happen more frequently in ServiceNow than boxed software, with new functionality being released twice a year. However, unlike multi-tenancy architectures, the customer is more in control of when and how often each upgrade occurs.

The release roadmap and methodology that ServiceNow follows is constantly being refined, but as of 2016, the following strategy applies:

Category	Example name	Contains	Frequency
Feature release	Calgary, Dublin, Eureka, Fuji, Geneva, Helsinki, Istanbul, Jakarta	New functionality and many fixes	Twice a year
Patch release	Patch 1	Includes all previous patches and hotfixes as a bundle. It should not contain new functionality.	As needed
Hotfixes	Hotfix 1	Fixes for a specific bug or issue	As needed

The product documentation contains release notes for each version. The Helsinki release notes are at
`https://docs.servicenow.com/bundle/helsinki-release-notes/page/r elease-notes/helsinki-release-notes.html`.

Customers can schedule an upgrade by using the self-service functionality in the HI customer service system, or customer support can recommend a particular patch or hotfix to solve an issue. Some releases need to be authorized by ServiceNow to ensure that they are appropriate, but otherwise a customer has the choice about when to select an upgrade, if they have the appropriate entitlement.

Each feature release moves through three phases of distribution:

- **Phase 1**: Early access by invitation only
- **Phase 2**: Opt-in or auto-upgrade schedule based on available dates
- **Phase 3**: Opt-in, on-demand, or auto-upgrade

Use the HI customer service system to manage your entitlements to upgrades.

ServiceNow does reserve the right to force instances to upgrade, primarily if there is a security issue. This typically happens on a quarterly basis.

Starting up an instance for the first time will enable many default plugins, and these plugins may change between instances. Upgrading an instance does not typically enable any feature plugins. This means that an instance upgraded from Fuji to Geneva to Helsinki will have a different set of enabled plugins to one that starts on Helsinki.

Understanding upgrades

ServiceNow is a Java application and is compiled in a WAR file. This is essentially a large compressed file that contains all of the resources that are necessary to run the ServiceNow platform. Upgrading or patching involves applying a new WAR file to the instance in question. This updates the two core areas that make up a ServiceNow instance:

- The Java class files that are the bedrock of the platform
- The XML files that make up the plugins

Once the WAR file has been expanded, the XML files are parsed. Each of these XML files represents at least one database record. So, the platform copies the information into the database. For example, if a ServiceNow developer has created a Business Rule, the XML file will contain the new code, and upon upgrade, the platform will add the record in the `sys_scripts` Business Rule table.

> For updated records, the logic is a little more complicated, as discussed below. The aim is to not affect anything that has been configured or customized.

Finally, the instance will run fix scripts. These perform any necessary conversions to ensure that new functionality dovetails appropriately with the old. For example, an application may change its data structure and create all-new tables. A fix script can move the records from the old table into the new and manipulate the data to fit.

> The upgrade process, and how it affects configuration, is discussed in much more detail over the next few sections.

ServiceNow has automated the upgrade process, embedding it into the instance itself. Every hour, a scheduled job contacts an upgrade controller and asks it whether there is a new version of the software for the instance. If there is, the WAR file is identified, downloaded, unzipped, and applied. These items are monitored in **System Diagnostics > Upgrade Monitor** and also under the **Upgrade History** and **Upgrade Log** modules.

Applying upgrades

When an instance receives a new WAR file, it starts to upgrade. It looks in each XML file to find what record it represents and checks it against the **Customer Updates** [`sys_update_xml`] table.

If there is no entry in the Customer Updates table, then the action in the upgrade is applied. This could be `insert`, `update`, or `delete`. No entry means ServiceNow owns the record, and it will be kept "out of the box" even if the upgrade means "out of the box" is changing.

If an entry does exist, the upgrade process will do a little more work. First, it looks to see whether the Replace on upgrade field in the Customer Updates record is ticked. If it is ticked, then the action will be applied, as before.

Checking the Replace on upgrade checkbox in the Application File will create an entry in the **Customer Updates** table if one did not already exist and will set the Replace on upgrade field there.

If the Replace on upgrade field is *not* ticked, then it is likely the platform will *skip* the update: no changes will be made to the record, and things will carry on as they were.

If the upgrade skips the record, it will still create an entry in the **Versions** [sys_update_version] table as mentioned in – `Knowing What Is Going On">Chapter 9`, *Diagnosing ServiceNow – Knowing What Is Going On*, but isn't set to the current version. This allows you to compare and apply the changes manually, if you'd like to.

However, there is one final check to consider. The platform will determine exactly *what* has been changed. If only excluded fields have changed, then the upgrade process will still change the record. The Active field is an excluded field.

For example, consider a system administrator editing an out-of-the-box business rule:

- If the Script field is changed, the platform will keep it as the system administrator configured it.
- If the Active field is unchecked on the Business Rule (and that is the only field that is changed), then the Business Rule will be updated in the upgrade. The Active flag will remain unchecked, but the Script field (and the other fields) will be changed to represent the upgrade.

For more information about this, check out the product documentation: `https://docs.servicenow.com/bundle/helsinki-application-developm ent/page/build/system-update- sets/task/t_ExcludingFieldsFromUpdates.html`

Most of the time, this is exactly what you want. Consider that you have edited a form's layout to make it look the way you want. You'd be rather annoyed if the upgrade undid your hard work! However, if you didn't use a certain Business Rule, you could deactivate it and still be certain that the code is of the latest version; you could always reactivate it later.

Reverting customizations and restoring out of the box

To get the latest out-of-the-box updates for a record, the following methods are available:

- Set the **Replace on Upgrade** checkbox on the Application File record. Navigate to it using the **Show Application File** option in the menu of the record. This will ensure that on the next and subsequent upgrades, the record will be upgraded.

- If the upgrade has already happened, navigate to **System Diagnostics** > **Upgrade Monitor**, and review the changes that the upgrade has made. Click on **Review Skipped Updates**, and in the **Upgrade Details** related list, find the record that you dealing with. The **Revert to Base System** UI action will be available if the **Disposition** value is **Skipped**. The **Resolve Conflicts** button lets you inspect what has changed in the record field by field and line by line-very useful for scripts.

The **Reapply Changes** button will let you toggle between the customized and out-of-the-boxes versions.

Managing instances

Making the most effective use of your allocated instances means understanding and implementing an effective plan. Following a simple set of rules will ensure that the configuration and data is in the right place at the right time. The following diagram shows the typical actions to a customer's instances:

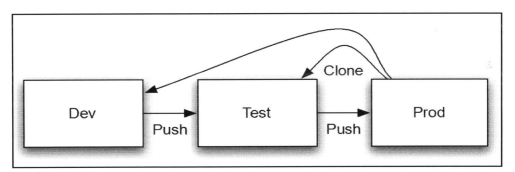

Managing a complex system with multiple stakeholders and business-critical applications is challenging. However, by leveraging the platform in the right way, it can be made easier to deal with ServiceNow. These tips will help:

- Use a three-tier hierarchy. Ensure that you know what activities will be carried out on each instance and who will be carrying them out.
    - **Prod** is the production system. The requesters submit work while fulfillers carry out the process to get it done. There's no tester access and very limited system administrator access in order to ensure stability.
    - **Test** tries out new functionality before it is put into production. The instance is used by a testing team. They carry out regression and new functional testing. There's limited system administrator access.
    - **Dev** is where new functionality is configured. This is used by the system administrators.
- Limit customizations, and test thoroughly if any are needed.
- Use ServiceNow to manage ServiceNow. Software release applications such as **Agile Development** let you document requirements and manage their implementation within the platform.
- Be nimble. Release new functionality frequently rather than storing it up for months.
- Clone as frequently as possible from **Prod** to **Dev** and **Test**. This should follow any development cycle. This ensures that you have great testing and development data.
- Use applications to capture configuration and move functionality between instances.
- Upgrade frequently and take advantage of the fixes and new features in the product.

Summary

Configuration is independent. It only affects a single instance, unless you decide to copy it elsewhere. ServiceNow provides many tools to let a system administrator share configuration (and customization) and data with other instances.

Data can be exported and imported from a list into an XML container. This is often very useful when moving small, discrete data chunks from one instance to another. No validation or automation occurs when you import XML.

Update Sets take the same thought and automate it. An Update Set collects the configuration that you perform and stores it in a named collection. This can be exported or transferred to another system, where the configuration will be replayed, applying the same changes automatically. But Update Sets come with many challenges, including collisions and conflicts.

Applications provide a better way to package functionality. After publishing an application to the Application Repository, you can install and update applications on other instances with only a few clicks. During the build phase, you can use the source control integration with Git to allow many developers to work on the application.

In addition to the work that you do in your instance, ServiceNow provides regular platform upgrades. These can range from minor fixes and improvements to new applications and a brand new user interface. In many ways, upgrading an instance is straightforward, but it still needs thought and consideration to be successful.

In addition to these targeted changes to an instance, ServiceNow can arrange a complete overwrite of the database with a copy from another instance. Cloning is an effective technique to ensure that two systems are exactly alike.

The next chapter describes how the interface can be altered to make it work the way you want. Service Portal makes it easy to create a beautiful self-service interface, but you can also dive into the depths of UI Pages and UI Macros. These represent the way the platform displays records throughout the platform. Configure away!

11
Making ServiceNow Beautiful with Service Portal and Custom Interfaces

ServiceNow is a great platform for managing data. Tools such as Graphical Workflow, Business Rules, and Client Scripts make it easy for you to create an application geared toward Service Management that processes information quickly and efficiently. However, function without form makes for an unappealing experience! Many companies have design patterns that their users understand; their web properties look familiar and consistent. Taking advantage of this will make your applications much more trustworthy, accessible, and easy to use.

In this chapter, we will examine some of the capabilities in ServiceNow for changing its look and feel and make it work the way you want it to. These include the following:

- Service Portal, which wraps a much more user-friendly skin over the logic and data already in the instance, making what you already have much more beautiful
- Using standard web design technologies, such as CSS, to change colors, control text size, and add images to create the Self-Service interface.
- Adding custom design elements to the ServiceNow interface, such as GlideDialog boxes, decorations, and contribution reference icons
- Creating completely custom interfaces with UI Pages and UI Macros, giving you complete creative freedom

Making it self – service

Service Portal lets you create a custom interface that builds over existing data and logic. All of the chapters so far have concentrated on building, configuring, or customizing application logic-Service Portal allows you to change how it looks so that you move away from plain forms and lists.

This means that Service Portal should not generally bring any new functionality to your application. Instead, the creation of a portal is intended to provide a new way for requesters to access capability that has already been built. The Hotel application for Gardiner Hotels includes a way to raise maintenance tasks and create reservations. Wouldn't it be great if the hotel guests could do this themselves, if they wanted to?

Providing self-service access

Service Portal is ServiceNow's response to the consumerization of technology. ATMs let you withdraw cash whenever you want, and telephone calls no longer need to go through an operator. Similarly, we want to let our hotel guests communicate with us anytime, day or night. Of course, Gardiner Hotels has some of the best reception staff in the business, but we want to make it easy to reserve a room while being in the middle of a conference call.

Layering on a better look and feel

As discussed in Chapter 5, *Getting Things Done with Tasks* and Chapter 8, *Securing Applications and Data*, a requester is someone without a role that asks for some work to be done on their behalf. Having a self-service interface typically lets those requesters browse the Service Catalog, see the status of existing tasks, or create new requests in their own time.

There are two interfaces built into the platform to allow a requester to submit new tasks:

- The first is the standard user interface, with the application navigator, lists, and forms. To submit a request, open up your instance (or use a demo system), and log in or impersonate a user with no roles. Joe Employee is the out-of-the-box example. You should get an interface like the following screenshot:

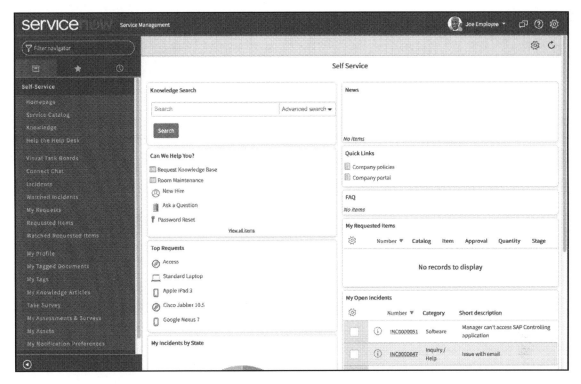

- The second is Service Portal. It uses a more graphical, user-friendly interface. To take advantage of Service Portal, you must activate the plugin. Follow these steps to do so:
    1. Navigate to **System Definition** > **Plugins**, and find **Service Portal for Enterprise Service Management**.
    2. Open up the plugin record, and click on **Activate/Upgrade**.
    3. Tick **Load demo data** and then **Activate**.
    4. Once the plugin has finished loading, click **Close & Reload Form**, then navigate to **Service Portal** > **Service Portal Home**.

The following screenshot shows the Service Portal interface:

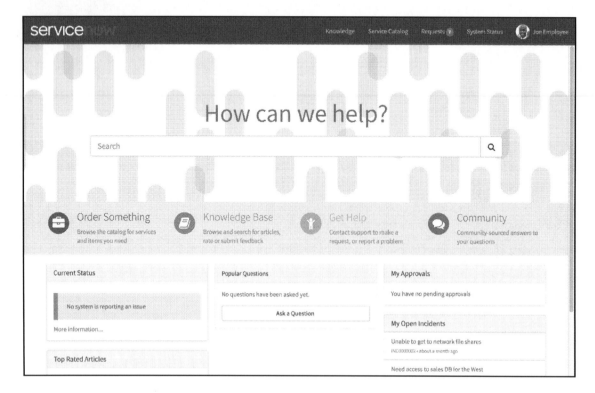

Although the two look quite different, they have several common threads:

- The Service Catalog can be accessed by navigating to **Self Service** > **Service Catalog** in the standard interface or through **Order Something** in Service Portal. When you navigate to the Catalog, the same categories and items are used, though the way they are displayed is different.
- Open Incidents can be viewed either by navigating to **Self Service** > **Incidents** or **My Open Incidents** at the bottom left of the page.
- Knowledge Base articles can be accessed by navigating to **Self Service** > **Knowledge** or using the **Knowledge Base** link in the middle of the Service Portal page.
- Items such as the user menu (and the ServiceNow logo!) is present in both interfaces.

The point is that while Service Portal looks and feels different, it simply takes the data already present in the instance and transforms it, making for a more *delightful* experience for your users. Most application logic keeps on working, but Service Portal ensures that your users get a better visual experience.

Starting with Service Portal

A Service Portal page is a collection of widgets. Each widget performs a function, such as listing active Maintenance requests or details about a single task, providing a way to add or remove attachments, or even displaying your location on a map.

In many cases, there is already a widget that does what you want. There are around 100 widgets provided by the base configuration, most of which have ways to make them work for you. And the Service Portal designer provides a very easy-to-use interface to let you add, remove and configure these widgets to whatever page you choose. Of course, you can build your own, too!

Getting the assets

Creating a visually attractive portal usually means that logos and graphics will be required. We asked the design team at Gardiner Hotels for the company logo as well as some icons for the menus. They provided us with a ZIP file that contained these items and also informed us that their corporate font is Lucida Grande. Orange and blue are the company colors.

Download the example asset pack: `http://www.gardiner-hotels.com/a ssets.zip`

Branding the existing portal

In many cases, the example interface that the Service Portal provides is the best starting point. Using a point-and-click interface, you can change colors, upload images, and alter text.

The example portal is built for the global scope, and you will be making changes that affect the OOTB functionality. It will be easy to undo these changes, but be aware that you are altering functionality that is not stored in the Hotel application (and thus you can't uninstall it). Skip this section if you wish, and especially if you are not using a sandbox instance.

To start making the portal on your own, follow these steps:

1. Ensure the **Service Portal for Enterprise Service Management** plugin is activated, as per the aforementioned instructions.

2. Then switch out of the Hotel scope, and into global. Use the application picker at the top of the standard interface, or click the Settings button top right and choose **Developer**, then **Global** in the Application selection.

3. Navigate to **Service Portal** > **Service Portal Configuration**. A new window should open up.

4. Click on **Branding Editor**. Ensure Service Portal is selected in the dropdown in the top left.

5. Let's make the portal reflect Gardiner Hotel's needs and make the following changes:
    - **Portal Title**: Guest Portal
    - **Logo**: <upload the logo.png image from the asset pack>
    - **Logo Padding Left**: 10px
    - **Tag Line**: Welcome!
    - **Tag Line color**: white
    - **Background Image**: <upload the hello.jpg image>
    - **Navbar background**: #e6e8ea (In the Theme Colors tab)
    - **Navbar link hover**: #455464

6. Immediately, we have altered the look and feel. In the standard interface, navigate to **Service Portal** > **Service Portal Home** to see the changes.

If you wanted to continue editing the provided site, the next step would be to add, move, or alter the widgets on the page. This can be done through the **Designer**, which we'll meet in the next section. Whilst the current design is attractive and better than many portals, Gardiner Hotels wants something more.

Reviewing Service Portal fundamentals

A **Service Portal** site is made up of several elements that work together. Each element builds on every other to contain the configuration for your site.

This chapter assumes that you have a working knowledge of AngularJS, CSS, and HTML. There are many resources on the Internet that will teach you the basics. You may want to refer to these resources as we progress. The **Mozilla Developer Network** (**MDN**), which can be found at `https:/ /developer.mozilla.org/`, is full of great reference material.

Code School have a free AngularJS tutorial at `https://www.codeschool. com/courses/shaping-up-with-angular-js`

The **AngularJS API Docs** is also useful. Find it here: `https://docs.angul arjs.org/`. There is another tutorial there too.

- A **Portal** [`sp_portal`] record lets you specify elements common to many pages, including the theme. It also specifies what the index, or landing page, is as well as the URL suffix. The example portal URL suffix is `sp`, giving access to Service Portal at `https://<instance>.service-now.com/sp`.
- The **Theme** [`sp_theme`] contains header, footer, and CSS information that is applied to all the pages, providing greater consistency.
- The **Page** [`sp_page`] is what you design. Containers are placed on a page, and then widgets placed inside each one. The layout is built off Bootstrap, which gives up to 12 columns, and a widget can take up as many of these as necessary. A page has an ID, which is used in the URL. For example, to open the index page on the default Service Portal instance, navigate to `https://<instance>.service-now.com/sp?id=index`.

Each page is independent and isn't directly related to a portal-so a single page may be used across many portals. Try it by changing the portal prefix but keeping the page ID the same.

- **Widgets** [sp_widget] contains all the elements that the user interacts with. Each time a widget is placed onto a page, a Widget Instance record is created. Each widget is made up of an HTML structure augmented by AngularJS and CSS extended with SCSS (a subset of SaSS) as well as client- and server-side scripting.

Widgets can pull information from the URL to know what to display, which is typically built around a record. The table and sys_id parameters are used to identify the record in question.

- The **Widget Instance** [sp_instance] record represents the configuration for the widget. This consists of its size, color, where it is placed on the page, and any advanced options.

The diagram below shows show each element is related to another. Headers are related to a Theme, which is related to a Portal and so on. Pages are independent, but contain Widget Instances, that refer to Widgets, etc:

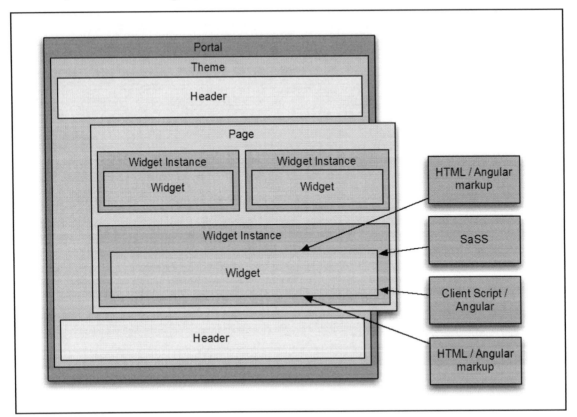

Service Portal makes use of many common Internet technologies, providing front end developers with tools they are likely already used to:

- **Bootstrap** provides the basic page template, giving you a flexible interface that makes creating and styling interface components easy.
- **AngularJS** is used to provide a dynamic framework, binding parts of the page to data, providing a very dynamic and fluid interface. Note that AngularJS v1 is used, not the rewritten v2.
- **SCSS** is used alongside Bootstrap to allow custom CSS styling of widgets. SCSS is a subset of SaSS, which allows the use of variables, nesting, operators, and mixins.
- **Server-side** scripts let you leverage the power of `GlideRecord` and other APIs to get data to the browser easily and efficiently.

Service Portal and the Service Catalog

Service Portal and the Service Catalog are heavily entwined. As described in `Chapter 5`, *Getting Things Done with Tasks*, the Service Catalog provides an easy way for end users to submit requests. Service Portal makes using it much more beautiful.

The baseline Service Portal uses several Catalog Request Items and Record Producers to provide the right form to the requesters. This may range from a password reset Record Producer that creates an Incident record to a computer loaner Catalog Request Item that uses the Request Fulfillment tables (Request, Requested Item, and Catalog). The provided widgets and pages make it easy to use these items.

Again, this underlines how Service Portal presents the existing capability in the instance rather than building new logic and functionality.

Selecting the widgets

A Service Portal implementation is approached slightly differently than other configurations. Building a portal involves more graphic design than a ServiceNow development. So, the first step often involves building wireframe diagrams that provide a mockup of what the site might look like. This generally includes at least two items:

- Deciding which pages are needed and ensuring you have the right catalog items
- Deciding which widgets should be on the pages and how they should be laid out

> The adage "Paper is cheap" is helpful when building a Service Portal site. Spending time up front to determine what should be built is a good investment.

After a few late nights and several cups of coffee, the Gardiner Hotel team have decided on the following functionality for the Hotel service portal. There should be three pages:

- The main home page, providing links and status updates
- A page that shows the appropriate Service Catalog Item and allows the user to submit new requests for Maintenance, or add a new Reservation.
- A details page that lets the user see more details about their request, and track what is happening

The structure of the page is shown in the following diagram. The details page and the catalog items page will be dynamic, showing the right content depending on the navigation:

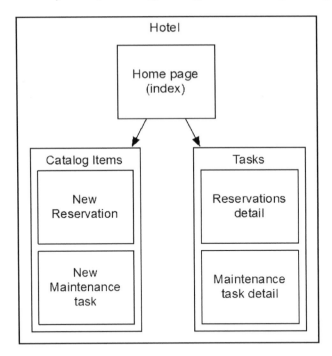

When creating a Service Portal, pictures may be worth more than a thousand words. Create a quick sketch to get a better understanding of what the pages will look like. Gardiner Hotel have decided upon the design for a few pages, taking heavy inspiration from the example portal.

For consistency, all the pages should have a header with Gardiner Hotel's logo on it as well as some quick navigation links. The footer caps it off. The main page provides a large, friendly welcome image, a simple menu block, and quick navigation to the open-reservation and maintenance records. The menu block provides quick access to the main functions by using some large icons. The following figure shows what the home page should look like.

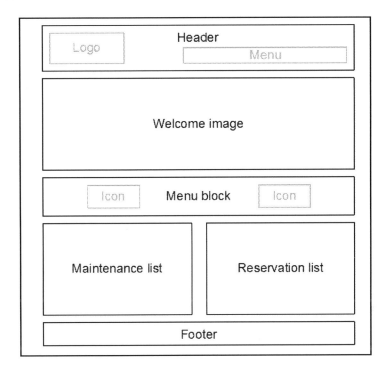

The other pages are simpler. They contain the header and the footer, but the majority of the page is either the catalog item or the Maintenance or Reservation record details. They would look like this:

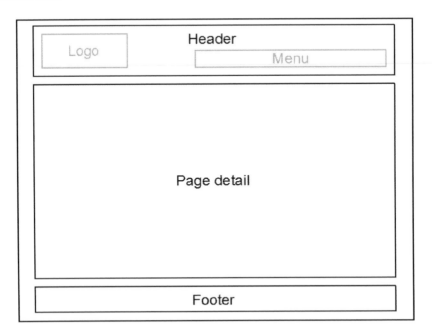

Creating the reservation

In Chapter 5, *Getting Things Done with Tasks*, we create a record producer so an end-user could easily submit a maintenance request. It does need a little editing to work with the Service Portal. Similarly, we also need a way to create a new Reservation record. We created this table way back in Chapter 2, *Developing Custom Applications*, it represents that a guest wants to stay a night or two at Gardiner Hotels. Have a look at **Hotel > Reservations** if you want a refresher.

 Make sure you are caught up with the examples before continuing (perhaps using the instructions at www.gardiner-hotels.com to apply updates through source control).

Follow these steps to create another Record Producer to create a new Reservation:

1. In the standard interface, switch back to the **Hotel** scope. Use the application picker at the top and select Hotel, or use the Settings menu top right.
2. Navigate to **System Definition** > **Tables** and select the Reservation table.
3. Click on the **Add to Service Catalog** link at the bottom of the table definition. Enter these values into the form:
   - **Name**: New Reservation
   - **Short Description**: Stay again at Gardiner Hotels
   - **Category**: Can We Help You?
   - Pick **Arrival** and **Departure** from the slush bucket.

4. Click on **Save and Open**.
5. Edit the **Script** field to include the following code, and Save.

```
var m2m = new GlideRecord('x_hotel_m2m_guests_reservations');
m2m.newRecord();
m2m.reservation = current.sys_id;
m2m.guest = gs.getUserID();
m2m.lead = true;
m2m.insert();

current.arrival = producer.arrival;
current.departure = producer.departure;
```

> In this script, a record is added to the many-to-many table that lies between the Guest and Reservation tables. The currently logged-in user will be added as the lead guest. This button automates the potentially fiddly and error-prone mechanism of adding guests with the Related List.
>
> The script also copies the two variables into fields. In the standard interface, if you have a variable named the same as a field, it'll get automatically copied over. An alternative would be to navigate into the variable definition and tick the **Map to field** option.

6. We need to do the same thing on the Maintenance Record Producer. Navigate to **Service Catalog** > **Catalog Definitions** > **Record Producers** and select Room Maintenance.

7. Append the **Script** field with the following. Again, it simply copies over the variables into the new record. Save once done:

```
current.short_description = producer.short_description;
current.room = producer.room;
current.description = producer.description;
```

All of the other items have already been built in previous chapters, so we can now assemble our self-service portal.

Creating the portal

Now that we know what the pages should look like, let's start creating them. One of the great advantages of the Service Portal system is that it's super easy to use existing pages. Because of this, we already have a page that is done: we can reuse the `form` page to display the details of a Reservation or Maintenance task.

Additionally, there is a page that displays Service Catalog items-though it comes with extra elements we don't want. And we should create our own to understand the process! The fastest way to create pages is through the **Designer**:

1. Navigate to **Service Portal > Service Portal Configuration**, and click on **Designer**.
2. Click on **Add a new Page**, fill out the two fields, and click on **Submit**.
   - **Page Title**: `Hotel Catalog`
   - **Page Id**: `hotel_catalog`

Note that all pages can be used in any portal. If you wish to keep them more separate, having a consistent prefix to the page ID can help. We will use `hotel` as a simple identifier.

3. Pages use the **Bootstrap** strap layout that provides you up to 12 columns that scale as the browser window changes. You decide whether you wish to divide up the page into quarters, thirds, or uneven sections.
4. For now, drag in the large **12** layout from the pane on the left onto the preview.

5. Then, find **SC Catalog Item** and drag it onto your layout. Although it may not look like much now, that's it for this page!

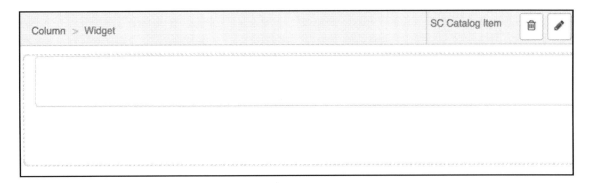

Building a home

Next is the index or home page. This involves a few more steps, since the design is more demanding:

1. Let's create another new page. Click on **Hotel Catalog** at the top of Service Portal Designer.
2. Click on **Add a new Page**, fill out the two fields, and click on **Submit**.
   - **Page Title**: Hotel Home
   - **Page Id**: hotel_home

3. The first element on the home page is the background image. We can use the default container on the page for this.
4. Click on the box in the main window (not the plus button) so the pencil icon appears on the right. Click the pencil icon, and the container form dialog should appear. Fill out the form as follows and click on **Save**:
   - **Name**: Welcome image
   - **Background image**: <upload hello.jpg>
   - **Background style**: Cover

5. You should see the image appear in the preview. To add some text, drag in the large **12** layout onto the container from the layout pane on the left.

6. Then, in the widget list, scroll to find the **HTML** widget. Drag that onto the layout.

7. Use the pencil icon you see while hovering over it on the far right to configure the widget, as per the screenshot below:

8. You should see a dialog with a **Title** and **HTML** field. While you could use the WYSIWYG editor to add some text, click on the source code (<>) icon on the right.

9. Enter the following HTML (which uses Bootstrap styles), and click on **OK** and then on **Save**.

```
<div class="wrapper-xl">
<div class="wrapper-xl">
<h1 class="text-center text-4x text-success">Hello there!</h1>
<h2 class="text-center text-2x text-success">How can we help?</h2>
</div>
</div>
```

 It is a little inappropriate to misuse styles, such as text-success here. This is meant for messages when an action has succeeded. We are taking a few shortcuts for speed, since by reusing a style like this, we can use the Branding Editor to change the colors.

10. The preview should show the text over the top of the image. So far, the screen should look like the following screenshot:

11. To add the next element, the menu block, drag a container underneath the image. Use the pencil icon top right to set the following field, and then click on **Save**:
    - **Background color**: #EB9D02

12. Once the container is a nice orange, drag the **6 – 6** block on top.

13. Find the **Icon Link** widget and drag that on to the leftmost block. Select it, and click on the pencil icon, fill out the following information, and then click on **Save**:
    - **Title:** Call for help!
    - **Short description:** Need your room cleaned? Or got a leaky tap? Come this way!
    - **Glyph:** <home icon>
    - **Type:** Catalog Item
    - **Catalog Item:** Room Maintenance

14. Repeat the previous step by dragging the **Icon Link** widget on to the rightmost block. Click on the pencil icon, fill out the following information, and then click on **Save**:
    - **Title:** Stay again!
    - **Short description:** Come and stay at Gardiner Hotels! Just tell use when you'd like to visit.
    - **Glyph:** <plane icon>
    - **Type:** Catalog Item
    - **Catalog Item:** New Reservation

15. The final set of elements is the lists. Drag a container underneath the icon menus, and then drag the **6 – 6** block in.

16. On the left-hand side, add the **Simple List** widget. Use the pencil icon and set the following fields:Table: Maintenance [x_hotel_maintenance]
    - **Display field:** Short description
    - **Glyph:** <home icon>
    - **Link to this page:** form
    - **Secondary fields:** number, opened_at (shown as Opened when you are typing)
    - **View:** Self Service

17. On the right-hand side, add another **Simple List** widget. Use the pencil icon and set the following fields:
    - **Table:** `Reservation [x_hotel_reservation]`
    - **Display field:** `Arrival`
    - **Glyph:** `<plane icon>`
    - **Link to this page:** `form`
    - **View:** `Self Service`

The preview should now look very similar to the mockup design. Only the header and footer need to be added and the rest of the styles configured.

Creating a theme

What's nice about the configuration for Service Portal is that you can edit everything you need without needing the standard interface. Let's use Service Portal Configuration (which itself is built using Service Portal!):

1. Find the **Service Portal Configuration** page (navigate to **Service Portal > Service Portal Configuration** to reopen it), click on **Portal Tables** in the menu at the top and then on **Themes**.

2. This list shows you the records in the **Themes** [sp_theme] table, as if you went to **Service Portal > Themes** in the main interface. Click on **New**, fill in the following fields, and click on **Save**:
   - **Name:** Hotel Theme
   - **Header:** Stock Header
   - **Footer:** Sample Footer
   - **Fixed header:** <unticked>
   - **Fixed footer:** <unticked>

3. Then, go to **Portal Tables, Service Portal,** and click on **New**. Fill in the following fields, and click on **Save**:
   - **Title:** Hotel Portal
   - **URL suffix:** hotel
   - **Homepage:** hotel_home
   - **404 page:** 404
   - **Login page:** login
   - **Theme:** Hotel Theme

4. Let's see what our configuration has given us. Open a new tab in your browser and navigate to https://<instance>.service-now.com/ /hotel?id=hotel_home.

In only a few steps, we've got a portal. The front page looks relatively built-out, with some nice graphics and bold links, and all the pages work fine. But the default colors aren't right, the header doesn't have the menu options in it, and the management team have decided the footer needs to be, well, funnier. So a few more steps to go!

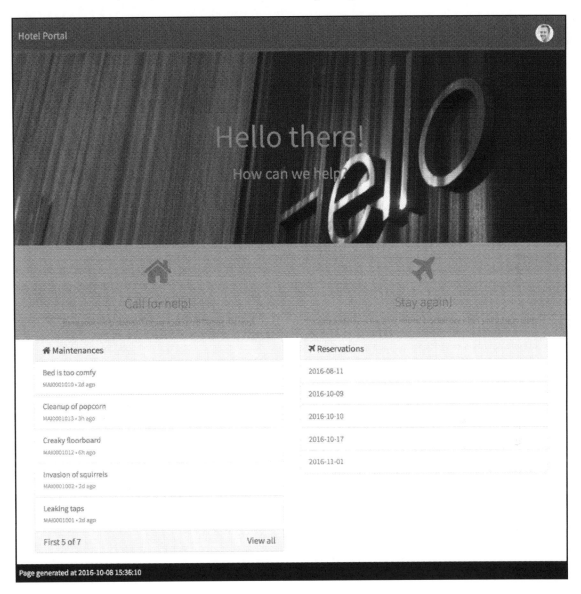

Creating some style

While the standard portal is nice enough, it doesn't fit with Gardiner Hotel's style guidelines. Let's fix that first:

1. Navigate to **Service Portal > Service Portal Configuration**, and click on **Branding Editor**.

2. Select **Hotel Portal** from the selection box in the top left, and fill out these options:
   - **Logo**: `<upload logo.png from the asset pack>`
   - **Logo padding Left**: `10px`

3. Switch to the **Theme Colors** tab, and fill out these options:
   - **Navbar background**: `#EBC302`
   - **Navbar divider**: `#021828`
   - **Navbar link color**: `#000000`
   - **Navbar link hover**: `#000000`
   - **Page background**: `#FFB019`
   - **Primary**: `#000000`
   - **Text color**: `#000000`
   - **Text success**: `#FFFFFF`
   - **Text muted**: `#000000`
   - **Text link color**: `#0E052B`

If you view to the portal now (`<instance>.service-now.com/hotel?id=hotel_home`), things will look much better! It's amazing what a bit of color can do!

Adding a menu

While there are navigation elements on the front page, we need them in the header too. To create the menu items, a widget instance needs to be created. The widget instance contains the options that a widget will use to know what to display. There are some specialist types of widget instance, including for menus:

1. In the standard interface, navigate to **Service Portal > Menus**, and click on **New**. Set the following field, and then choose **Save** to stay on the same page:
   - **Title**: `Hotel header menu`

2. In the **Menu Items** related list, click on **New**, fill out the form, and then click on **Submit**:
   - **Label**: Help!
   - **Type**: Catalog Item
   - **Page**: hotel_catalog
   - **Catalog item**: Room Maintenance

3. Repeat the step by clicking on **New**, filling out the form as follows, and then click on **Submit**:
   - **Label**: Stay again
   - **Order**: 200
   - **Type**: Catalog Item
   - **Page**: hotel_catalog
   - **Catalog item**: New Reservation

4. Before the menu can be displayed on the page, the widget instance needs to be associated with the menu widget. The easiest way to do this is through list editing, since the form does not show the field.

5. Navigate to **Service Portal** > **Menus**, find the record where **Title** is Hotel header menu, and list-edit the **Widget** field:
   - **Widget**: Header menu

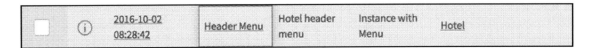

6. Finally, navigate to **Service Portal** > **Portals**, select **Hotel Portal**, populate the Main menu field, and save:
   - **Main menu**: Hotel header menu

7. If you visit your portal and refresh, you should now see your menus in the top right. Great! The main thing missing is that the footer is showing the time, and we need something more humorous.

Adding a client-side widget

Unfortunately, the ServiceNow developers did not see fit to include a widget that displays jokes. However, it is simple to remedy this by creating a new one. Normally, we'd use the widget editor, but we need to use the standard interface to create one in the right table.

For this example, we will leverage a web service that the ever-funny guys at Cornell Hotel Services created. When you call it, you get a random joke returned to you. Here's how to do it:

1. Navigate to **Service Portal** > **Headers & Footers** and click on **New**. Fill out the following fields, and click on **Save**:
    - **Name:** Funny Footer
    - **Body HTML template:**

```
<div class="joke-footer">
  {{c.result.joke}}
</div>
```

This is mostly standard HTML but uses some Angular syntax to bind the contents of the div element to a variable. This means that whenever that variable changes, so do the contents of this div.

- **CSS:**

```
.joke-footer {background-color: #EBC302;
  color: black;
  padding: 5px;
}
```

CSS is used to provide some styling for the HTML.

- **Server script:** <blank>

In this example, all the work is done on the client. This is not good practice, but it does demonstrate how you are able to drop in Angular code and make it work for you.

- **Client controller:**

```
function ($http) {
  var c = this;
  $http.get('https://www.gardiner-hotels.com/chs/joke/').
  success(function(data) {
  c.result = data;
```

```
    });
}
```

This code is almost pure Angular. The **Client controller** script is where you define the variables and functions for the template binding. In this case, the controller uses the built-in $http service to perform a GET call to the CHS web server. Note that it is injected (or passed as a parameter) into the function, so it is available to be called. When the call succeeds, the result variable is updated, and since it's bound to the div element, the page updates.

2. Once you've saved the code, navigate to **Service Portal** > **Themes**, and choose **Hotel Theme**. Set the following field and Save:
   - **Footer**: Funny Footer

Exploring dynamic widgets

Just as you finish up, a last-minute request comes in. Wouldn't it be a great idea to recognize guests who have stayed with us several times? We can do that with a custom widget.

A widget can be considered an AngularJS directive. The **Controller as** notation is used to get away from the need to use the Angular $scope service for many actions. Unless changed, the controller is instantiated as the c variable and so acts as the main mechanism to manipulate and control data. Most scripts start with declaring var c = this; to easily bind the output of the client script to the DOM.

If you use Angular scripts from elsewhere (which typically use $scope), keep this in mind. You can use $scope, but you need to inject it as a parameter into the client script function. A great article is at this blog post: https://toddmotto.com/digging-into-angulars-controller-as-syntax/

It is very easy to transport data to and from the server. There is a global variable called **data** available to both the server and client scripts. Simply set a value on the server, and it is available on the client. No need to create complex `GlideAJAX` calls or perform slow `GlideRecord` lookups! The platform moves the data quickly and easily, according to this pattern:

1. When the page is generated, the server script is run, which can populate the data object with whatever information is necessary. It has access to several other variables:
   - `options`, which are set in the widget instance
   - `input`, which contains extra parameters passed by the client script `get` call
   - `$sp`, which contains many convenient methods, such as `getParameter`

There is unofficial documentation written by the developers that lists all of these functions:
https://github.com/service-portal/documentation/blob/master/do cumentation/widget_server_script_apis.md#getForm

2. The client script is run and has immediate access to the `c.data` variable.
3. The HTML of the widget may be bound to the data variable, and so the page will display the information as appropriate.
4. The user may interact with the widget, which could cause client script functions to be run. The client script may need to get more data from the server, and it could call several methods:
   - `server.get(obj)` passes a variable to the server. Use this if you want to send some custom data.
   - `server.update()` sends the `data` object to the server, which updates it and returns it to the client. Think of it as similar to `server.get(data)`.

Both of these functions return a promise, which work like callbacks to deal with the result asynchronously. This allows chaining, in a form like this:
`c.server.update().then(function() { ... })`.

- Finally, server.refresh() builds on server.update() and automatically updates the data object on the client. This is similar to `c.server.update().then(function (r) { c.data = r.data });`

5. One particularly cool trick is that a client script can subscribe to the asynchronous message bus through the record watcher. This allows a widget to show live data-when the records in a table change, a function is called within the client script. This provides the most up-to-date information possible.

Building the dynamic widget

Let's use several of these features to create a new custom widget that displays whether a guest has had reservations in the past and thanks them for their loyalty:

1. Before we do anything, we need to open up the security rules a little. The many-to-many table that we made in `Chapter 2`, *Developing Custom Applications*, doesn't have any security rules around it which means the default *deny policy* kicks in. In the main interface, click **Elevate Roles** from the user menu.

2. Navigate to **System Security** > **Access Control (ACL)**, and click **New**. Fill out the form as follows, and Save.
    - **Operation**: read
    - **Name**: x_hotel_m2m_guests_reservations (looks like Guest Reservation [x_hotel_m2m_guests_reservations] – --None--)

3. Now, navigate to **Service Portal** > **Service Portal Configuration**. Click on **Widget Editor**.

4. Click on **Create a new Widget**, fill out the form as follows, and click on **Submit Query**:
    - **Widget name**: Guest Loyalty
    - **Widget ID**: hotel_guest_loyalty
    - **Create test page**: <ticked>
    - **Page ID**: hotel_guest_loyalty

5. Select **Guest Loyalty** from the dropdown list to edit it. Click the **CSS-SCSS** checkbox at the top to have 4 panes, then fill them out:

- **HTML Template**: (replace the contents of the pane)

```
<div ng-if="c.data.count > c.data.min">
  <div class="wrapper loyalty text-center">
    <i class="fa fa-{{::options.glyph}} fa-5x"></i>
    <h1 class="text-3x">Thank you!</h1>
    <h2 class="text-2x">For being one of our best customers!</h2>
    <h3>You've stayed with us {{c.data.count}} times.</h3>
  </div>
</div>
```

> This Bootstrap- and Angular-infused HTML adds some text onto the screen. The first line includes ng-if, which, if the condition doesn't evaluate to true, removes the element from the page. Additionally, the page includes an icon (the glyph), which we'll set in the options in a moment.

- **CSS – SCSS**:

```
.loyalty h1 {
  margin-top: -10px;
  margin-bottom: -20px;
}
.loyalty h2 {
  margin-bottom: -16px;
}
```

> This standard CSS changes the margins of the text to compress things a little.

- **Client Script**: (replace everything in the Client Script pane)

```
function($scope, spUtil) {
  var c = this;
  c.data.min = c.options.minimum || 2;
  spUtil.recordWatch($scope, "x_hotel_m2m_guests_reservations", "",
    function() {
      c.server.update()
    });
}
```

While this script is very short, it does some cool things. The `c.data.min` variable is set either from the options if it is set or set to 2 if not. JavaScript makes it easy to provide a default.

`spUtil` and `$scope` have both been injected into the function as parameters. `spUtil` is a utility class for Service Portal. It only provides a few functions at the moment, but they are rather useful. One of them, `recordWatch`, subscribes to the **asynchronous message bus (AMB)**. This lets you specify a table and a filter (blank here) and effectively watches for changes to records that meet the criteria. In this case, if anything is altered in the many-to-many table (field changes or records are added or deleted), then `RecordWatcher` will run `c.server.update();`. This causes the Server script to run again, repopulating the data variable. This could be made more efficient through a filter, which would be better practice.

Check out more of the `spUtil` functions on the unofficial documentation here:
`https://github.com/service-portal/documentation/blob/master/do cumentation/widget_client_script_apis.md`

- **Server script**:

```
(function() {
  data.count = 0;
    var m2m = new GlideAggregate('x_hotel_m2m_guests_reservations');
    m2m.addAggregate("COUNT");
    m2m.addQuery('reservation.arrival', '<', new
GlideDate().getDisplayValue());
    m2m.addQuery('guest', gs.getUserID());
    m2m.query();
    if (m2m.next())
    data.count = m2m.getAggregate('COUNT');
})();
```

You should be relatively comfortable with this script: it is standard ServiceNow `GlideRecord` (okay, `GlideAggregate`) code. It counts how many records have reservations in the past, where the currently logged-in user is the guest. It populates the result into the `data.count` variable, which automatically gets transported to the client.

6. Use the menu button on the right and click on **Edit option schema**. This allows you to specify one of the two options being used. Add the following option using the `plus` button:
   - **Option label**: `Minimum stays required`
   - **Name**: `minimum`
   - **Type**: `integer`

7. Click **Save** when done.

   Because we made a demo page, it's easy to test. To prove the power of `RecordWatcher`, open up a new browser, log in as your admin user then impersonate a guest using the option in the User menu. I used Roger Tarry. Navigate to `<instance>.service-now.com/hotel?id=hotel_guest_loyalty`

8. It's likely you'll get an orange screen, like this screen shot. That's because the records in the Guest Reservations table don't meet the GlideAggregate criteria (arrival before today, guest is the test user).

9. To ensure you see the text, as your admin user, navigate to **Hotel** > **Reservations,** and create at least three entries with the arrival date in the past. Associate your test user with them using the Guests related list.

10. In your other browser, you should see the widget show up, without refreshing. Cool, eh?

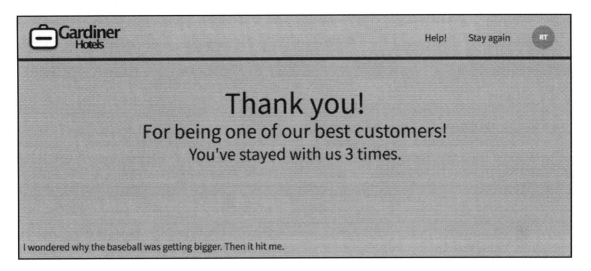

The next step is to add a little graphical flair to the page. You may have noticed that the HTML of the widget referred to a glyph. Lets make it easy to add that to the page, and then finally add it to the home page.

11. In the standard interface, navigate to **Service Portal** > **Widgets.** Select the Guest Loyalty record, fill out the following, and **Save.**
    - **Fields**: Glyph

    By selecting the **Glyph** field like this, we make it easy to configure in the Designer view, as we'll see.

12. Now, navigate to **Service Portal** > **Service Portal Configuration.** Click on Designer, then select Hotel Home.

13. Drag a container between the hello text and the menu icons, like the screenshot below.

14. Click on the newly added container, then use the pencil icon top right, set the following option, and click on **Save**:
    - **Background color**: #EBC302

15. Drag a 12 layout on top of your container.

16. Finally, add **Guest Loyalty** on top of the layout. Use the pencil icon to set the option of the widget. Note how both the **Glyph** field and the **Minimum stays** option are shown. Populate them as follows, and click on **Save**:
    - **Glyph**: <smile glyph>
    - **Minimum stays required**: 2

17. Finally, lets remove the annoying gap just above the hello image. In the Designer, click on Edit Page Properties top right. Fill out the following fields, and click Save.

   • **Page Specific CSS**:

```
section.page {
  padding-top: 0px !important;
}
```

18. The design is done! Visit `<instance>.service-now.com/hotel/` and admire your homepage!

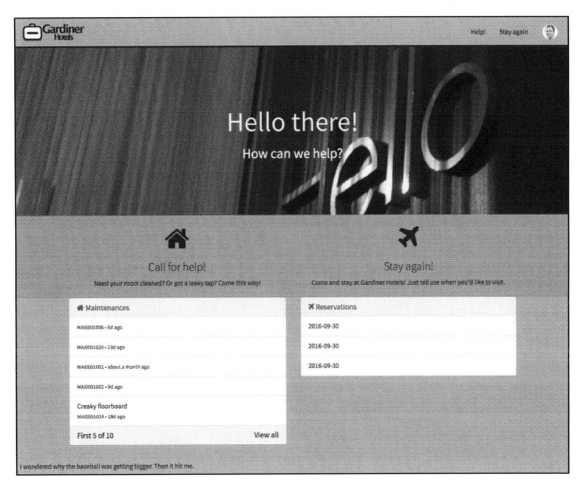

This widget was relatively simple, but they can be far more complex and include custom CSS and JavaScript. Create a new widget dependency, and add the files as UI Scripts or CSS Includes. The Angular module name must match exactly.

You can also create Angular directives, factories, or services. Once defined, they can be injected into the controller. Before using them, associate them with the widget using the related list.

Locking down the data

With the design in place, the portal is looking good. But the data being returned is not what is expected. The **Reservation** and **Maintenance** widgets show a list of all records and not just the ones that are relevant to the current user. In order to have a great self-service portal, we need it to not only look nice but be secure, too.

Filtering maintenance tasks

The easiest way to control visibility is by creating a filter. Follow these steps to generate an encoded query that we can configure the widget with:

1. In the standard interface, navigate to **Hotel** > **Maintenance list** and create a filter with the following conditions:

   ```
   Active - is - true

   Opened by - is (dynamic) - Me
   ```

2. Click on **Run** to perform the query.
3. Right-click on the rightmost breadcrumb and choose **Copy Query**. You will get an encoded query string in your clipboard, such as
   `active=true^opened_byDYNAMIC90d1921e5f510100a9ad2572f2b477fe`.

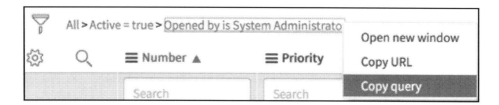

4. Navigate to the Hotel Service Portal homepage in another tab (`<instance>.service-now.com/hotel/`) and Ctrl + right click click on the **Maintenances** list. Choose **Instance Options**.

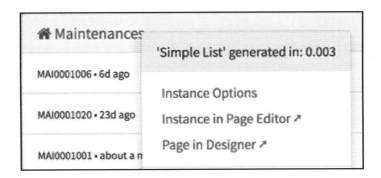

These options provide a really great shortcut to jump to the page design, and even jump to the widget editor.

5. Paste the contents of the query string into the **Filter** field, and click on **Save** at the bottom.

Finding the reservations

Controlling the **Reservations** list is more complex. There isn't a filter we can use directly on the **Reservations** table, because the information we want to filter it by is in a Related List. There are still several ways to achieve it, but one is through a query Business Rule, discussed in `Chapter 8`, *Securing Applications and Data*:

1. In the standard interface, navigate to **System Definition** > **Script Includes**, create a new record, populate the following fields, and click on **Save**:
   - **Name:** `findReservations`
   - **Script:**

```
function findReservations() {
  var m2m = new GlideRecord('x_hotel_m2m_guests_reservations');
    m2m.addQuery('guest', gs.getUserID());
    m2m.query();
  var res_arr = [];
  while (m2m.next()) {
    res_arr.push(m2m.reservation + '');
  }
```

```
    return (new global.ArrayUtil()).unique(res_arr).join();
}
```

The aim of this function is to find the logged-in user's reservations.

First, the script queries the many-to-many tables that store the relationship between the guests and reservations. Only entries where the user is in the Guest field are returned. All of the matching records are looped through, and the results are put into an array, being sure to convert the `GlideElement` objects into a string. The array is then processed using an out-of-the-box Script Include called `ArrayUtil`, which removes any duplicate entries. The result is converted into a comma-separated string and returned.

2. To use this function, navigate to **System Definition > Business Rules**, click on **New**, use the following values, and **Save**:
   - **Name:** `Filter reservations`
   - **Table:** `Reservation [x_hotel_reservation]`
   - **Advanced:** <checked>
   - **Query:** <checked>
   - **Condition:** `!gs.hasRole('x_hotel_reservation_user')`
   - **Script:** (Paste this line inside the provided function)

```
current.addQuery('sys_id', 'IN',
findReservations());
```

This simple Business Rule alters the query that will be sent to the database whenever the **Reservations** table is looked at. This runs when the user does not have the `x_hotel_reservation_user` role and asks the database to return records only when the `sys_id` value matches the array returned by `findReservations`.

This is potentially inefficient. Whenever a self-service user queries the **Reservations** table, another query is run against the many-to-many table, doubling the database access. This could be mitigated by caching, but that would mean it is not live-a key feature for Service Portal.

Altering access controls

In addition to query Business Rules, access controls need to be altered. Currently, only users with the right roles will be able to read, write, create, or delete records, and requesters should be able to read them at least. If you impersonated a user with no roles right now, they couldn't see any data.

The Record Producer takes care of creating records without access rules (but you need them for the script). We'd only want to open up the access controls more if we wanted to let users create records through the standard interface. Also, we'd need to add write access controls to allow users to add comments and the like. You can add this functionality if you'd like.

There are several tables that need to be controlled: Rooms, Maintenance and Reservations. All need read rules at the field and row levels. This means that six access controls need to be made in total. Since the aim of the rules is to allow access, simply creating the rule with the right name and operation will suffice. No conditions, scripts or roles are needed:

1. First, elevate to the `security_admin` role by clicking on the user menu, choose **Elevate Roles**, tick the checkbox, and then click on **OK**.
2. Navigate to **System Security** > **Access Control (ACL)**, and click on **New**. Populate the following fields, and click on **Save**, clicking Continue on each popup window. Repeat this step six times, until each rule has been created.

Name	Operation	Description
`x_hotel_maintenance`	read	**Allows everyone to read every Maintenance record**
`x_hotel_maintenance.*`	read	By default, allows everyone to read every field on the Maintenance table
`x_hotel_reservation`	read	Allows everyone to read every Reservation record (subject to query Business Rules)
`x_hotel_reservation.*`	read	By default, allows everyone to read every field on the Reservation table

Name	Operation	Description
`x_hotel_room`	`read`	Allows everyone to read every room record, so they can be picked from reference fields
`x_hotel_m2m_guests_reservations`	`create`	Used in the Record Producer when creating reservations

We are relying on the filters and query Business Rules to control what the user sees. A user could see Maintenance tasks for other users if they knew how to manipulate the interface. In a more fully featured implementation, these rules would be more specific.

This could be controlled by reusing the `findReservations()` function—but that would be very inefficient, and I don't recommend it!

Testing the site

Let's try out all this new functionality. Perform the following steps:

1. Impersonate a guest with no roles by clicking on the user menu and choosing **Impersonate User**. I'm using **Roger Tarry** again.
2. Navigate to `https://<instance>.service-now.com/hotel/`.
3. Verify that you can create a new Reservation.
4. Check that you can only see your own records in Reservations.
5. Check whether you can create new **Maintenance** tasks.

6. Validate whether you can only see the Maintenance tasks that you created.

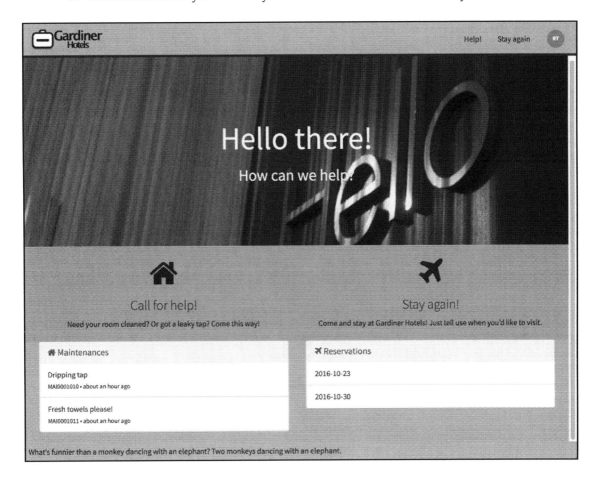

Digging into Jelly

The web's language is HTML. Every page rendered by a web browser has some HTML content. Therefore, the ultimate job of any website is to generate the HTML that contains data formatted in the desired manner. The browser then renders it and hopefully displays something beautiful, informative, and useful.

ServiceNow uses Jelly to generate HTML. The Jelly processor in ServiceNow takes in an XML template and produces HTML. There are a variety of Jelly elements, including variables, loops, and conditions, which means that the produced HTML depends on the data that the processor is fed. In addition, ServiceNow has extended beyond the standard Jelly tags, allowing JavaScript to be used inside a Jelly XML document while also incorporating caching. This makes it powerful and fast!

 The name Jelly was originally short for Java Elements. You can find more information about it at `http://commons.apache.org/jelly`. It is not something to eat!

While Jelly is very powerful, it is slowly being replaced in ServiceNow. It is difficult to work with, and there are very few resources to deal with its foibles. Although Angular is not a direct replacement, it can perform many of the same tasks. Often, the basics are written in Jelly, and Angular is used to top up.

Creating a UI Page

As is customary, we need to create a *Hello, World* page to demonstrate the basics of a UI Page:

1. Navigate to **System UI** > **UI Pages** and click on **New**. Then, fill in the following fields with the given values, and save your changes:
    *   **Name:** `hello_world`
    *   **HTML:** (replace the contents of the field)

```
<?xml version="1.0" encoding="utf-8" ?>
  <j:jelly trim="false" xmlns:j="jelly:core" xmlns:g="glide"
xmlns:j2="null"  xmlns:g2="null">
  <b>Hello</b>, <i>world</i>!
</j:jelly>
```

2. When you create a new **UI Page** [`sys_ui_page`] record, a template provided. For the third line, some standard HTML has been used. Click on the **Try It** button to display your first Jelly page.

3. To test it, open up a browser window and navigate to `https://<instance>.service-now.com/x_hotel_hello_world.do`. The new page will be displayed. The UI Page is accessed by using its name in the URL, prefixed with the scope.

Adding interactivity to UI pages

You've probably noticed the **Client Script** and **Processing Script** fields. Let's update our test record with some more code:

1. Navigate to **System UI > UI Pages**, find and edit `hello_world` by populating these fields. Save once done:
   - **HTML:**

```
<?xml version="1.0" encoding="utf-8" ?>
  <j:jelly trim="false" xmlns:j="jelly:core" xmlns:g="glide"
xmlns:j2="null"  xmlns:g2="null">
  <form action="ui_page_process.do" onsubmit="return check();">
    <input type="hidden" name="name" value="hello_world"/>
    Name: <input name="user_name" id="user_field"/>
    <input type="submit" value="Submit"/>
  </form>
</j:jelly>
```

The **HTML** field is not HTML, but Jelly! However, HTML can also be used. Tables, forms, images-any tag can be used. The data is passed to your browser to render, like a normal web page. In this case, a form is used that provides a simple input field and submit button. When the form is submitted, the browser runs the `check()` function. Everything is standard HTML.

- **Client script**:

```
function check() {
  if ($('user_field').value == '') {
    alert('Please enter your name');
    return false;
  }
}
```

The Client script field is JavaScript. Any code that is placed here is placed in a `script` tag, directly after the HTML.

Note the use of the Protoype library, which checks to see whether the input field is empty. While it isn't perfectly safe to use these core libraries due to the changes that may happen during upgrades (as discussed in `Chapter 4`, *Client-Side Interaction*), since you are in control of the DOM that you are making, the risk is reduced.

- **Processing script**:

```
gs.addInfoMessage('Hello ' + user_name);
```

The Processing script field is server-side JavaScript. It is run when `ui_page_process` is called and handles forms that have been sent via `POST` or `GET`. As shown in this example, parameters are automatically copied into JavaScript variables, allowing easy access to data that is sent from the client.

2. Click on **Try It** to see your new interactive page. With a few lines, we have produced a little interactive form that shows off quite a few features of UI pages!

Including UI macros

Jelly is a template system. It allows you to create an HTML structure and control its output through loops and conditions. However, you can also create reusable components using UI macros. These are little blocks of Jelly that you can call from other Jelly elements to build more complex structures. Let's begin by creating a simple UI Macro:

1. Navigate to **System UI > UI Macros**, click on **New**, and fill in the following values in the fields. Save once done.
    - **Name**: `instructions`
    - **XML**:

```
<?xml version="1.0" encoding="utf-8" ?>
  <j:jelly trim="false" xmlns:j="jelly:core" xmlns:g="glide"
xmlns:j2="null" xmlns:g2="null">
  Please type in your name below.
</j:jelly>
```

2. Then, navigate to System UI > UI Pages, and edit the `hello_world`. Insert the following tag on a new line, right above the `<form ...>` tag:

```
<g:x_hotel_instructions />
```

The first four lines of the UI page will look like this:

```
<?xml version="1.0" encoding="utf-8" ?>
  <j:jelly trim="false" xmlns:j="jelly:core" xmlns:g="glide"
xmlns:j2="null" xmlns:g2="null">
  <g:x_hotel_instructions />
<form action="ui_page_process.do" onsubmit="return check();">
```

3. In another browser tab, navigate to `https://<instance>.service-now.com/cache.do` to clear the cache. Jelly is very aggressive at caching. Note that clearing the cache, as discussed in – Knowing What Is Going On" target="_blank">Chapter 9, *Diagnosing ServiceNow – Knowing What Is Going On*, will impact performance until the cache reloads.

4. Click on the **Try It** button on the `hello_world` UI page to view the results.

Now, when you look at the output, you'll see that the contents of the UI Macro has been inserted onto the page.

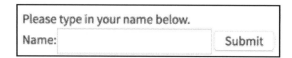

It's pretty cool that UI Macros can call other UI Macros. This means that you can quickly build a library of Jelly snippets. It is a good idea to create lots of smaller blocks of code that can be easily debugged.

 Setting attributes in the tag will pass variables to the UI macro; the `<g:instruct jvar_test="hello" />` will set the `test` variable to `hello`. In addition, content that is entered between opening and closing tags (such as `<g:instruct>hello</g:instruct>`) can be accessed with the `<g:insert/>` tag in the UI Macro.

There are lots of UI Macros that you can leverage when you build Jelly. The ones prefixed with `ui_` are rather useful; in addition to other uses, they also help create references, date/time fields, forms, and tables.

Looping with Jelly

Even on its own, Jelly can do some clever things. When the processor runs, it'll find the custom tags and evaluate them. The content of the tag could contain other tags, either Jelly or HTML. Consider them as functions or commands.

 Since Jelly tags are XML, they'll have attributes that work as parameters for the command. The contents of a tag are typically the body of a command.

1. To see an example, create a new UI Page (**System UI > UI Page**, click **New**), fill out the form, and click on **Try It**.
   - **Name:** LoopWorld
   - **HTML:** Insert this inside the template, on line 3.

```
<j:forEach indexVar="i" begin="1" end="3">
  <p>Hello, world!</p>
</j:forEach>
```

2. This simple example shows the `forEach` tag. This is supplied with three parameters: `indexVar`, `begin`, and `end`. When it is executed, it'll take these parameters to execute something very similar to a JavaScript for loop. In this example, it will repeat Hello, world! three times.

To set a variable in Jelly, use the `set` tag. To write out a variable, use the curly braces syntax. The following couple of lines contain a JEXL expression, which works in a way similar to a macro-the contents are evaluated and replaced.

```
<j:set var="jvar_message" value="Hello, world!"/>
<p>${jvar_message}</p>
```

JEXL is **Java EXpression Language**, which is another Apache project that is hosted at `http://commons.apache.org/proper/commons-jexl/index.html`. For our purposes, we can consider that it just runs JavaScript.

In essence, Jelly does two things: it makes decisions on what HTML should be rendered using conditions and loops, and it programmatically generates the HTML with JEXL expressions. There are several more core tags, including a very common `if` tag. Often, the `evaluate` attribute has a JEXL expression in it to determine whether the contents of the tag should be output.

There is a full listing on the Apache Commons site at `https://commons.apache.org/proper/commons-jelly/tags.html`.
The ServiceNow product document at `https://docs.servicenow.com/bundle/helsinki-servicenow-platform/page/script/general-scripting/reference/r_JellyTags.html` shows a more limited set, but it has more realistic examples.

Extending Jelly

ServiceNow has taken Jelly and extended to integrate better into the platform. One of the most important tags that ServiceNow has added is the `evaluate` tag. It runs server-side JavaScript. If you create a JavaScript variable, it can be accessed using JEXL.

Let's create a simple dice roll UI Page:

1. Navigate to **System UI > UI Page**, click New, fill out the form, and click on **Try It**.
   - **Name**: dice
   - **HTML**: Insert this inside the template, on line 3.

```
<g:evaluate>
  var roll = Math.round(Math.random()*5) + 1 + "";
</g:evaluate>
${roll}
```

Each time you go to `<instance>.service-now.com/x_hotel_dice.do` in your browser, you should get a random number.

This code creates a variable called `roll`; using some standard JavaScript, it generates a random number between and 5, rounds it down, adds 1 (so that it can be between 1 and 6), and finally turns it into a string. The JEXL expression then simply outputs it.

Using Angular and Jelly

We could spend far more time on Jelly. It has huge capability, including a comprehensive mechanism for controlling caching, but the mechanism for ensuring that data and variables are in the right place can quickly become very complicated. Instead, Jelly is often used as the launch point for launching an Angular page. Using a UI Page means you have complete control over how it all works.

Using Angular to say hello

While Angular is used throughout ServiceNow-and especially in Service Portal-you should use your own copy of the library in UI Pages to avoid any compatibility problems. This is the first step to using custom Angular in action.

1. **Download** Angular from `https://angularjs.org/`. You need version 1 rather than 2; and I'm using version 1.4.12-use that if you have any problems. A direct link is `https://ajax.googleapis.com/ajax/libs/angularjs/1.4.12/angular.min.js`.

2. In ServiceNow, navigate to **System UI > UI Scripts**. This is the place (as mentioned in `Chapter 3,` *Server-Side Control*) where external libraries can be stored. Click on the **New** button, set the following fields, and click on **Submit**. Click **OK** on the warning.

- **Script Name:** `angular.min.1.4.12`
- **Script:** `<the contents of the Angular script>`

3. Then, it's time to create the UI Page. Navigate to **System UI > UI Page**, click on **New**, fill out the following fields, and click on **Try It**:

- **Name:** `helloAngular`
- **HTML:** (Insert into the template, on line 3)

```
<g:requires name="x_hotel.angular.min.1.4.12.jsdbx" />
  <div ng-app="helloWorld">
    <div ng-controller="helloController as h">
      <h3>Hello {{h.name}}!</h3>
      <input type="text" ng-model="h.name" />
    </div>
  </div>
```

This HTML has a sprinkling of Angular in it. Firstly, it includes the Angular library in the page, suffixing the UI Script's name with `.jsdbx`. It does this with a Jelly tag, though a standard `script` tag could be used to the same effect. Then, it sets up the Angular app in a `div` tag and uses the *controller as* syntax to instantiate it on the page. Then there are two bindings, in the `H3` tag and the input text box, to the `h.name` variable. If you alter the value of the text box, the contents of the `H3` tag will alter too.

- **Client script:**

```
var helloWorldApp = angular.module('helloWorld', []);
  helloWorldApp.controller('helloController', function () {
  this.name = 'World';
});
```

This First, the `helloWorldApp` is created. Then, `helloController` is created and associated with the app. This is pretty standard Angular syntax. In the function, the name variable has been initially set.

It's not really necessary to create a controller for a simple example like this, but it is good form to have it so you can extend it later.

Interacting with the database

Jelly can get data out of the database using `GlideRecord` in an evaluate `tag`. If you wanted to iterate over a record set, then you could combine that with the `forEach` tag. But you can also do that with Angular and ServiceNow REST web services. Let's see how:

1. Create a new UI Page at **System UI > UI Page**, click on **New**, fill out the following fields, and click on **Try It**:
   - **Name**: showMaintenanceTasks
   - **HTML**: (Insert into the template, on line 3)

```
<g:requires name="x_hotel.angular.min.1.4.12.jsdbx" />
  <div ng-app="maintenance">
    <div ng-controller="maintenanceController as m">
      <h3>Active maintenance tasks</h3>
    <ul>
      <li ng-repeat="d in m.data">
        {{d.number}}
      </li>
    </ul>
    </div>
  </div>
```

2. Much of this is similar to the previous example. The introduction of the `ng-repeat` directive though is what makes it special. Angular will repeat the `li` tag as many times as there are elements in the `m.data` array. In each `li` tag, it'll place the number variable.
   - **Client script**:

```
var maintenanceApp = angular.module('maintenance', []);
  maintenanceApp.controller('maintenanceController', function($http) {
    var m = this;
    var fields = 'number';
    var query = 'active=true';
    var table = 'x_hotel_maintenance';
    var url = "/api/now/table/" + table + "?sysparm_query=" + query +
```

```
"&sysparm_fields=" + fields;
    $http({
      method: 'GET',
      url: url,
      headers: {
      'X-UserToken': window.g_ck,
      'Accept': "application/json"
      }
    }).
  success(function(data) {
    m.data = data.result;
    console.log(m.data);
  });
});
```

3. This client script is much more fully featured. The majority of the script is about working with the `$http` service that lets Angular call REST APIs. A series of variables are set to use the ServiceNow table API. The query is for all Maintenance records where the Active field is `true`. This builds a URL that is passed to the `$http` service. Two headers are set: one to allow ServiceNow to perform the query without reauthentication (and to prevent cross-site request forgeries), and the other to ask for JSON-formatted data. On success, the data object is updated with the results-and also put in the console for logging purposes.

Updating records

The ServiceNow REST API has more capability than just getting data. Let's see how Angular can make changes to records and, while we are there, filter data too:

1. Navigate to **System UI > UI Page**, choose **New**, fill out the following fields, and Save:
   - **Name**: updateMaintenanceTasks
   - **HTML**: (Insert into the provided template, on line 3)

```
<style>
  table, th , td {
  border: 1px solid grey;
  border-collapse: collapse;
  padding: 5px;
}
  table td:nth-child(2), td input {
  width: 300px;
```

```
}
</style>
  <g:requires name="x_hotel.angular.min.1.4.12.jsdbx" />
    <div ng-app="maintenance">
    <div ng-controller="maintenanceController as m">
      <h3>Maintenance tasks</h3>
      <table>
        <tr>
          <th>Number</th>
          <th>Short Description: $[nbsp] <input type="text" ng-
model="search" /></th>
        </tr>
        <tr ng-repeat="d in m.data | filter: search">
          <td>{{d.number}}</td>
          <td><input type="text" ng-model="d.short_description" ng-
blur="m.update(d)" /></td>
        </tr>
      </table>
    </div>
    </div>
```

The HTML is built up again. This time, things are made slightly more attractive using a table and some CSS to style it. Some further Angular magic is used to create a filter. Note how this needs no custom JavaScript: by using the | filter: <term> syntax, you can easily create dynamic lists.

A custom function is used to update the Short Description field. A text box is rendered and bound to the d.short_description variable. If you edit it and then click outside the text box, the blur event is used to run the update function.

Having inline CSS like this isn't that maintainable, so you could store it in the **Style Sheets** [content_css] table. Find that at **Content Management** > **Design** > **Style Sheets**. Refer to it in scripts as <sys_id>.cssdbx, where <sys_id> is the sys_id value of the style sheet record.

- **Client script**:

```
var maintenanceApp = angular.module('maintenance', []);
  maintenanceApp.controller('maintenanceController', function($http) {
    var m = this;
    var fields = 'number,short_description,sys_id';
    var query = 'active=true';
    var table = 'x_hotel_maintenance';
    m.get = function() {
```

```
        var url = "/api/now/table/" + table + "?sysparm_query=" + query +
"&sysparm_fields=" + fields;
    $http({
      method: 'GET',
      url: url,
      headers: {
        'X-UserToken': window.g_ck,
        'Accept': "application/json"
      }
    }).
    success(function(data) {
      m.data = data.result;
      console.log(m.data);
    });
  };
  m.get();
    m.update = function(data) {
    var url = "/api/now/table/" + table + "/" + data.sys_id;
    $http({
      method: 'PUT',
      url: url,
      headers: {
        'X-UserToken': window.g_ck,
        'Content-Type': "application/json"
      },
      data: data
    });
  };
});
```

While the client script is longer, it's not that much more complicated. The main change is putting the code to retrieve the data in a function called get. This could then easily be linked to a refresh button and run on demand. The update function uses the PUT method with the REST APIs to send the data to the instance. A header specifies that the contents are JSON and simply passes the object to the server.

2. Click **Try It** and use the interface to find the Maintenance task you want with the filter, and edit the short description as you'd like. Although there is no logging or even any user feedback, it shows how Angular combined with ServiceNow can make really useful custom interfaces very quickly.

Including Jelly in the standard interface

Jelly is not reserved for building custom pages. Since the ServiceNow platform is built using the language, there are several places you can inject your own code to further control your instance.

Adding formatters

One of the simplest things to do with Jelly is to create a formatter. This provides a mechanism to include a UI Macro in a form. Navigate to **System UI** > **Formatters** to see the out-of-the-box items. There are several examples, including the process flow formatter, the activity log, and the variable editor placed on the ITSM tables, that show what is possible.

Let's cover a simple but useful example. This will run on the **Maintenance** form, making it more obvious when an SLA has been breached:

1. Navigate to **System UI** > **UI Macros**, click on **New**, fill out the form as follows, and Save:
    - **Name**: check_breached_sla
    - **XML**: (Insert inside the provided template, on line 3)

```
<j2:if test="$[!current.isNewRecord()]">
  <g2:evaluate>
    var gr = new GlideAggregate("task_sla");
    gr.addQuery('active', true);
    gr.addQuery('has_breached', true);
    gr.addQuery('task', current.sys_id);
    gr.addAggregate('count');
    gr.query();
    gr.next();
  </g2:evaluate>

  <j2:if test="$[gr.getAggregate('COUNT') > 0]">
    <h3 style="color:red; margin: 5px; margin-top: -5px">
    There are breached SLAs</h3>
    </j2:if>
  </j2:if>
```

This Jelly code mostly consists of a `GlideAggregate` object to count records. It uses the `current` global variable to know which Maintenance task is being viewed and accesses the Task SLA table. If any records meet the criteria of being breached, being active, and matching the current record, then a red warning message is displayed. All the logic only runs if the `current` object has been saved and, thus, `isNewRecord` is `false`.

You may be wondering why a bunch of the tags have 2 in them. This indicates that it should be run in the second phase of Jelly processing and should not be cached. To understand more about phases, read this useful blog post:
`https://community.servicenow.com/people/SlightlyLoony/blog/2011/12/09/2119`

2. To include the UI Macro in the form, create a new formatter by navigating to **System UI > Formatters**, click **New**, filling out the form as follows, and clicking on **Save**:
   - **Name:** Check breached SLA
   - **Formatter:** x_hotel_check_breached_sla.xml
   - **Table:** Maintenance [x_hotel_maintenance]

The Formatter value is made up of the UI Macro name, which is suffixed with .xml. This shows how some formatters are actually stored on the instance server as XML files. It also gives you a hint about how you can override them-by creating a UI Page or UI Macro with the same name. Not a good idea though!

3. Finally, navigate to **Hotel** > **Maintenance**, and select a record. Using the Additional actions menu, click **Configure**, **Form Layout**. The available list will contain an extra entry called **Check breached SLAs**. Include this in your form, probably at the top, to provide a very obvious warning to your maintenance team!

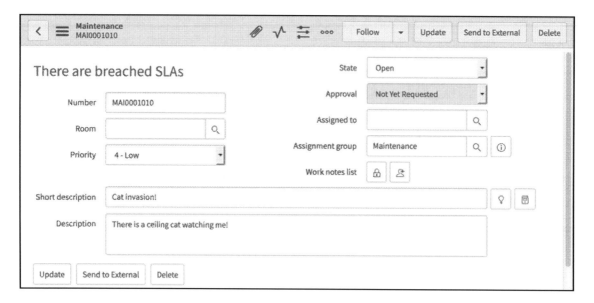

UI macros can also be included in the service catalog. There is a variable type that lets you select the one that you want.

Decorating and contributing to fields

Reference fields often have icons to the right of the input field. For example, on the Task table, the Configuration Item field has a little icon that is shown when the field is populated. Clicking on it will show the business service map. In addition, the Planned Task table has several fields that are calculated from the child fields. These "rollup" fields then have a little icon next to them to indicate this situation.

The mechanism to create a decoration and contribution is straightforward:

1. Create a UI Macro with the desired functionality. Often, this involves a little Jelly and some client script.
2. In the Jelly code, you can refer to the `ref` JavaScript variable that stores the name of the field, while `__ref__` is a JavaScript `GlideRecord` object to whatever the reference field is pointing to.
3. Edit the Dictionary entry for the field you want the icon for. There, set an attribute called `field_decorations` or `ref_contributions`-Either will work. Then, provide the name of the UI macro as the attribute value.

For example, the Configuration Item field on the Task table has two contributions. When the field is populated, an icon is provided that launches a dialog box that lists other active tasks that are related to the same CI. The other icon opens the dependency map. The Dictionary entry for this field contains the `ref_contributions=task_show_ci_map;show_related_records` attribute, which has the names of the two UI macros.

The `show_related_records` UI Macro itself is relatively complicated. It creates an icon that is positioned on the page next to the reference field. It performs a `GlideAggregate` query, similar to the aforementioned one, and shows the icon whether there are other active tasks.

It then includes client-side JavaScript that uses the ServiceNow event handlers to register a function for the `onchange` event of the Configuration Item field. When the field is changed, a function is run to determine whether or not to show the icon. This logic uses a GlideAJAX call to a Script Include to make the determination. Finally, if the icon is shown, it launches the dialog box when clicked.

The `GlideEventHandler` class will call a function if an `onchange` event occurs to a field. The parameters for a `GlideEventHandler` object are a unique identifier, the function, and what field should be watched. This object should be put into the `g_event_handlers` array. Note that this function is undocumented, so it is unsupported.

Quite a few admins try to duplicate this UI Macro to provide similar functionality to other fields. While this is achievable, care must be taken to make unique JavaScript function names so that there aren't any namespace collisions.

Launching a dialog box

Modal dialog boxes are quite common in user interfaces. They provide a very direct and visual way to prompt the user, usually to provide input. ServiceNow provides several ways to do this. Often, these dialog boxes are presented after a client-side UI action click.

All these techniques are undocumented, so although some baseline apps use the functionality, they are not supported.

Launching UI pages with GlideDialogWindow

If you've built a cool UI page, you can easily display it using `GlideDialogWindow`. To start things off, let's just launch the dialog box using the JavaScript executor:

1. Navigate to a form or a list, like **Hotel** > **Maintenance list**.
2. Press *Ctrl + Shift + J* to launch the JavaScript Executor, and use this code to create a dialog window:

```
var dialog = new GlideDialogWindow('x_hotel_hello_world');
dialog.setTitle('Hello, world!');
dialog.render();
```

The script initializes a new `GlideDialogWindow` object, passing to it the name of the UI Page made earlier. The `setTitle` function specifies the title of the dialog box. Once created, the UI Page is contained in a floating `div` (so be careful with including libraries such as Angular-they may conflict with what's on the page already). If you submit the form, the whole page will reload.

Use the `setWidth()` function of `GlideDialogWindow` to adjust the size and pass parameters with the `setPreference('sysparm_name', 'value')` function. The `destroy` function closes the `window`. This is useful if you have a Cancel button on the UI Page.

Fitting in a form

The UI Page is the ultimate in flexibility. However, you don't always want to write Jelly just to make a dialog box when all you may want is to create a new record or show an existing one. With `GlideDialogForm`, which is an extension of `GlideDialogWindow`, you can do just that. You pass in the name of a table, and `GlideDialogForm` opens up a floating window.

To see how it works, let's create a new UI Action on the Room table to easily create a Reservation record for that room:

1. To do this, navigate to **System Definition** > **UI Actions** and click on **New**. Fill out the fields as follows and Save:
    * **Name**: `Create Reservation`
    * **Table**: `Room [x_hotel_room]`
    * **Client**: `<checked>`
    * **Form link**: `<checked>`
    * **Onclick**: `launchReservationDialogForm();`
    * **Script**:

```
function launchReservationDialogForm() {
  var dialog = new GlideDialogForm('Create Reservation',
'x_hotel_reservation',
  function() {
  alert('Reservation created!');
});
  dialog.addParm('sysparm_view', 'ess');
  dialog.render();
}
```

This script isn't very long. The `GlideDialogForm` object requires three parameters: the title, the table, and a callback function, which is called when the form is submitted. In this script, the callback function doesn't accept any parameters, but it supports four: the action, the `sys_id` value of the record, the table, and the display value of the record. This is very useful to populate fields on the original form from the dialog box.

The `addParm` function sets parameters similar to `setPreference`, here setting the form to use the Self Service view.

Note that when this dialog is submitted, only the dialog closes, not the whole page.

2. To test, navigate to **Hotel** > **Rooms**, and choose a room. Click the **Create Reservation** link at the bottom, and the dialog should open, as per this screenshot:

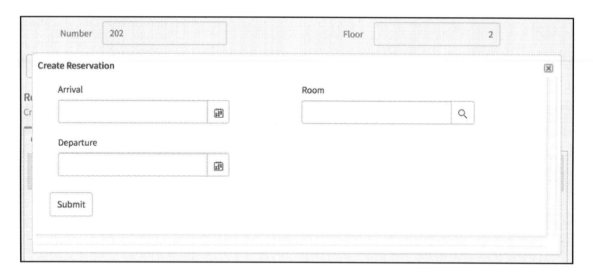

Displaying any page with GlideBox

If a form is not flexible enough, then GlideBox is available. It accepts a URL and displays it in an iframe, letting you show anything you want-perhaps a map, a complex page, or even something on another website.

Let's use GlideBox to show the Service Portal interface of the **Maintenance** record even in the normal interface. To do this, follow these steps:

1. Navigate to **System Definition** > **UI Actions** and click on **New**. Fill out the fields as follows and Save:
   - **Name**: Show Service Portal interface
   - **Table**: Maintenance [x_hotel_maintenance]
   - **Client**: <checked>
   - **Form link**: <checked>
   - **Onclick**: launchSelfServiceMaintenanceView();

- **Script**:

```
function launchSelfServiceMaintenanceView() {
  var box = new GlideBox({
    iframe: '/hotel?id=form&view=ess&table=' + g_form.getTableName() +
'&sys_id=' +   g_form.getUniqueValue(),
    width: '95%',
    height: 500,
    title: "Service Portal interface",
    fadeOutTime: 1000
  });
  box.render();
}
```

1. The style to create a `GlideBox` object differs somewhat from `GlideDialogWindow`. It accepts a single object with `name-value` property pairs. Here, the `iframe` property is set by building up the URL programmatically. The `width`, `height`, and `title` attributes are set along with the time in milliseconds for a gradual fade out.

2. Navigate to **Hotel** > **Maintenance list**, and select a record. Click **Show Service Portal interface**, and you should get something like the screenshot below:

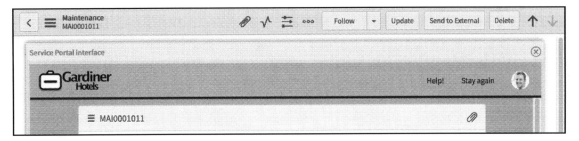

`GlideBox` supports many options. Instead of an `iframe`, HTML could be supplied with the body parameter. Lots of events, such as `onHeightAdjust` and `onBeforeClose`, will notify a callback function if you pass one.

Summary

One of the benefits of a web-based application is that anyone can access it. Web browsers are built in to phones and tablets. This accessibility means that ServiceNow is great for building a self-service interface, something that allows guests of Hotel Gardiner to see and submit information themselves.

The easiest way to provide a self-service portal is to use the standard interface, with requesters logging in and using similar forms and lists to fulfillers. This provides a very quick setup, with mainly security rules to think about.

However, the look and feel of the standard interface is likely to be overwhelming to a non-technical user. List and forms provide lots of functions, with checkboxes, menus, and icons. This is great for power users, but perhaps intimidating to those just wanting to know if the menu includes a Club sandwich.

 As noted in `Chapter 1`, *ServiceNow Foundations*, these plain forms do provide a consistent and clear experience. There is a great deal of benefit to this.

To provide a more attractive interface, usually for requesters, Service Portal should be employed. A range of methods to configure and customize the portal are available, starting with simple point-and-click branding and a drag-and-drop page designer before moving to building new portals and custom widgets.

The many widgets provided with the instance provide lots of different functions, from simple HTML blocks to complex menus and headers. AngularJS, Bootstrap, and SCSS are used to superpower the interface, providing a framework that frontend developers are likely familiar with.

In the core of ServiceNow is Jelly. Jelly is an executable XML format, and while it can be difficult to work with, it provides a powerful way to conditionally output HTML. By combining the basics of Jelly with the power of Angular, you can quickly build your own completely custom interfaces.

Jelly can also be included in the main interface. Custom UI Pages can deliver a new interface, while UI Macros can be embedded in forms using formatters and next to fields using decorations or contributions.

Service Portal helps provide a beautiful, delightful user experience. Alongside the powerful workflow capabilities of ServiceNow, you can build and configure wonderful applications that help work get done every day.

Isn't the view wonderful from the top of the ServiceNow tower? Where will you go next?

Index

D

X